GREAT DESSERTS

GREAT DESSERTS

LORENZA DE' MEDICI STUCCHI

International Culinary Society
New York

This 1989 edition published by International Culinary Society
a division of dilithium Press Ltd
distributed by Crown Publishers, Inc.
225 Park Avenue South
New York, New York 10003

ISBN 0-517-69094-2

hgfedcba

Printed and bound in Italy

Note

Follow the step-by-step photographs which illustrate some recipes by
working from top to bottom, beginning with the left column.
Unless otherwise indicated (as in certain molded desserts, ice cream,
and cakes, where pan or mold capacity is given) all recipes serve six.

CONTENTS

• • •

The preparation of sweet foods, in its simplest form, can be traced back to the dawn of civilization. Bas-reliefs carved into the stone of the tomb of Rameses III at Luxor in Egypt more than thirty centuries ago, for example, show an assortment of cakes, probably made with a mixture of wheat flour, fruit, honey, and spices. The basic ingredients have not changed all that much since then: flour, butter, sugar, eggs, fruit (both fresh and dried), and natural flavorings are still the basic materials which combine to create mouth-watering and visually appealing sweet things for our delight.

In the beginning there was bread, something which bore only a slight resemblance to bread as we know it. Unleavened bread dough was made by mixing very coarse wholemeal flour with water and then cooking the mixture on the hearth or in a primitive oven. Honey, milk, and fruit were sometimes added to the flour and water mixture when appetizing offerings were baked to propitiate the gods.

A QUESTION OF TASTE

The Ancient Egyptians used to shape small pieces of dough to represent animals and make small votive offerings of these baked figures. The Ancient Greeks were the first to produce cakes worthy of the name, made with honey, almonds, raisins, and figs. Recipes from the fourth century B.C. include one for "Basyma," a sweet bun made with flour, honey, cheese, and dried figs, and one for "Gastritis," a sweet flatbread containing eggs, cinnamon, walnuts, almonds, and cheese. Goat's cheese was used where we would now use butter, as well as olive oil. This must have resulted in what would seem a strong, strange taste to our palates, but which remained popular for centuries. The distinction between sweet and savory was no clearer later on, in Roman times: vinegar, honey, fish, vegetables, cheese, and fruit could be used in various combinations for both desserts and main courses. The taste for sweet things as we understand it today evolved much later; it originated in the Far East,

mainly from south China and India, where sugar cane grew wild. When the Arabs colonized Sicily and Spain, they brought with them the knowledge of how to use sugar in cookery and the Crusades subsequently helped open up the trade in sugar to satisfy growing demand for this exotic substance in Europe.

By about the year 1000 A.D. confectioners were already plying their trade, making marzipan, a gastronomic delicacy which cost so much that only the very rich could afford to eat it. Contracts between the doges of Venice and Arab traders have survived, which prove that large quantities of cane sugar were imported.

The Sicilians developed their own art of marzipan confectionery and fruit candy, which survives to this day. Court pastrycooks and the religious orders were largely responsible for developing the pastrycook's and the confectioner's art in Europe, creating countless delights such as *panpepato*, a type of sweet fritter. It is interesting to note that in the days before closed ovens, monastery cooks baked everything in an open hearth, and eventually began to "enclose" certain ingredients with a lid or wrapping of pastry, thus inventing what we now know as the pie.

Pastries containing eggs date from the years 1200–1300. Here is a recipe from an anonymous fourteenth-century cookery manuscript: "take some almonds; peel them and pound them into a paste; moisten with very hot water; heat a little milk together with breadcrumbs or with flour; beat in very fresh egg yolks. Gradually work

INTRODUCTION

· · ·

in the almond mixture before adding saffron, sugar, and a little salt." From the fifteenth century onward an increasing number of recipes for cakes and desserts appear in cookery texts. In his *Book of Culinary Art* Martino of Como includes a chapter on "How to make sundry pies, cakes, and sweetmeats" in which he discourses on cherry cake, a sweet chestnut dessert, fried millet custard, date and almond cake, white rice and almond cake, and marzipan in the same breath as vegetable and meat pies. In the following chapter, "On fritters of various descriptions," he gives recipes for fritters made with almonds, figs, rice, and apples: "Wash and wipe the apples very thoroughly, boil them or bake in the embers; remove the core. Mix the soft cooked apple flesh with a little yeast and flour, and sugar; shape into fritters and fry in good oil." Cristoforo da Messisbugo, cook to the Duke of Ferrara, devoted a whole chapter of his treatise on cooking (dated 1549) to "various types of cakes": German apple cake enriched with butter and sugar; medlar pie; peach, pear, and apple pies. A few years later Bartolomeo Scappi describes utensils for pastrycooks such as sieves, cake pans, and other equipment; he also

mentions "sprinklings of grated sugar" (sugar loaves, shaped like tall, rounded cones, were sold by spice merchants).

Dessert courses served at court banquets soon developed into performances in their own right, planned by architects, cooks, and sugar and spice merchants. The banquet for the Medici christening included a vast choice of wonderful savory dishes followed by iced confections, with lilies (the emblem of the city of Florence) sculpted in low relief; little baskets bearing small fruit jellies; ring-shaped cakes; wickerwork hampers spilling over with fruit; cookies; little waffles; large, transparent molded jellies; a centerpiece of carved sugar paste . . ."
In 1600, when Marie de' Medici married Henry IV of France, the steward of her household kept a record of all the preparations; he tells us of carved sugar statues, and model buildings in *pastillage*. A great number of boxes full of sweetmeats and sugar work were sent to France with the very young queen, containing, among other sugar confections, ". . . multicolored turtles, marzipan animals, dolphins, fishes, shells, and several varieties of lily, all made out of sugar . . ." Such princely magnificence and luxury was imitated by those who did not belong to court circles: the prosperous middle classes served simplified versions of such sweetmeats. Toward the end of the seventeenth century the first recipes for "sugar in pastry cookery,

INTRODUCTION

· · ·

confectionery and candying, . . . how to make sugar cakes" and how to make pies and tarts resembling those we are familiar with were published in German.

The modern love of sweet things started to develop during this period as sugar was imported by Europe in great quantities from Brazil, as well as from Cuba and Peru. The crystallized sap of the sugar cane, raw sugar was refined in Antwerp, Amsterdam, London, Dresden, and Nantes ready for sale to those who could afford it. The price was still very high, out of the reach of the vast mass of the population, but this new taste was now well established. During the seventeenth century another commodity arrived from Spain's South American colonies: chocolate. The new craze for this exotic substance spread from Spain to France, Germany, and Italy (the Kingdom of Naples) while theologians debated as to whether drinking a cup of chocolate constituted breaking a fast. In 1678 the first license for chocolate making was granted in Turin. In the eighteenth century the Austrians became confirmed chocolate addicts, later to be emulated by the newly independent citizens of the United States.

The eighteenth century saw a tremendous improvement in the quality of patisserie; not only were ingredients like sugar and chocolate more widely available but great advances had been made in the design of ovens and stoves: increasingly complex recipes could now be made successfully.

In 1719 the Bishop of Salzburg's head cook published a cookery book which contained 318 illustrations of advanced patisserie and elaborate decorative techniques. In France La Varenne published two books which laid the foundations of the pastrycook's art: *Le pâtissier françois* and *Le parfait confiturier*, these were followed by Carême's *Le pâtissier pittoresque*. In 1766 *Il cuoco Piemontese perfezionato a Parigi* (The Paris-trained Piedmontese cook) appeared in Italy, with a large section devoted to the pastrycook's art. A revolution in sugar manufacture came about in the early nineteenth century. While the British Navy blockaded European ports during the Napoleonic Wars, France was unable to import cane sugar; a French chemist named Achard took up research into alternative methods of sugar production where a chemist from Berlin, Marggraf, had left off and managed to extract commercial quantities of sugar from a type of beet. Mass production of one of the main raw materials in confectionery soon meant that everyone could enjoy sweet things. There had always been a tradition of home baking and candy making using honey but soon the majority of people could enjoy specialties hitherto reserved only for the very rich. Confectionery and other sugary delights of all kinds could now be part of everyday life.

INTRODUCTION

. . .

Perhaps there has always been a suggestion of self-indulgence connected with eating desserts, small cakes and pastries, cakes, ices, bonbons, cookies, and all sorts of candies – frivolous, superfluous food intake without the worthy connotations associated with eating to nourish ourselves and to satisfy good, honest hunger. Such delicacies used once to be reserved for high days and holidays, for special meals and celebrations, a tradition which survives to this day. When an elaborate cake, pudding or other confection is served, it still emphasizes the festive nature of the occasion: we have only to remember wedding, birthday and christening cakes, the log cakes and rich fruit cakes of Christmas, and, of course, chocolate Easter eggs.

The earliest sweetmeats were only variations on the theme of bread, when honey, milk, almonds, raisins, butter, honey or eggs were added to the dough before baking. Later these were joined by other ingredients, sugar and chocolate among them and gradually pastrycooks turned what had been simple, homely preparations into elaborate works of art. In the eighteenth century pastry cooks borrowed, adapted, and combined discoveries made by their predecessors and contemporaries to widen the scope of this relatively new branch of cookery. From the nineteenth century onward, as food production grew ever more sophisticated and more people experienced prosperity, cakes, desserts, and candy became part of the family's daily fare, although still considered something of an indulgence and a treat. Even now, a slice of cake, a doughnut, or a piece of candy can still promise a few unforgettable moments of pleasure.

SERVING AND DECORATION

Appearance is almost as important as taste in patisserie. Anyone who has gazed at the cakes, gateaux, and candy arranged in a tempting display in a shop window will agree that devouring them with our eyes in pleasurable anticipation is a very important preliminary part of our enjoyment. Then there are those unforgettable aromas, guaranteed to lure passersby inside the shop: the fragrance of vanilla or the scent of fresh baking.

Finally, the consistency: creamy fillings, contrasting with crunchy praline or toffee brittle, featherlight sponge cake, crisp pastry.

It is important to choose the correct serving vessel. Glass, porcelain, silver, earthenware, even basketware can all play their part in increasing the appeal of cakes, pastries, and confectionery. Simple cakes, buns, or scones obviously need to be presented in a different way to the more elaborate creations produced by artists in sugarwork. A Sachertorte, for example, looks elegant on a crystal cake stand, a glinting silver cake knife resting alongside it, while a rustic earthenware dish would be ideally suited to a crusty Italian *panettone* yeast cake full of nuts and raisins. Apart from personal preference, which is often the best guide, there are certain conventions: for ice cream, served with or without added fruit, cream and candied decorations, custards, fruit jellies, and all sorts of desserts which are usually presented in individual servings and eaten with a spoon, small, deep glass or crystal dishes or coupes are best. Gateaux should ideally be served on a silver dish, with or without a snowy white napkin underneath or a lace mat. The guest of honor may be given the responsibility of cutting the first slice with a special cake knife; if a trifle or pudding is served, he or she takes the first helping with a large silver spoon. The aim is to help yourself to a suitable portion without destroying the visual appeal of the dish for the other guests. Sometimes it is better just to ask your hostess to help you to a little if you lack the confidence to make the first cut!

Cake plates which match or complement the larger serving plate are usually small. Even the forks and spoons used for eating cakes and other sweet confections are miniaturized and often very ornate, in engraved or *repoussé* silver.

Knives would be out of place. Cake forks seem to have gone out of fashion and have tended to be spurned by those who consider them "over-refined" but they can be both elegant and useful. However, if napkins are provided and the cake or pastry is not too messy, it is just as acceptable to eat a cake with your fingers.

Doilies can also be used, although they are more usual in cafés and cake shops. White embroidered cambric or linen is preferable for home entertaining in that it is more elegant and traditional.

White plastic lacy mats should be avoided, however: the plastic, as well as looking inelegant, seems to impart a disagreeable taste and smell to the delicate creations placed on it.

DECORATION

A good color sense, an eye for proportion and plenty of imagination are all that is needed for this task. It is often a good idea to sketch out a plan for the decoration before starting work. It is equally important to know when to stop as how to start. Cluttered, fussy, overstated decoration will detract from the appeal of the finished product.

The project can be approached in much the same way as a problem of scale and geometry. You have a certain amount of space in which to exercise your imagination and you must suit your ideas to the shape of your "canvas," be it round, square, rectangular, etc. Color plays a vital role in patisserie. White is hardly ever out of place, and shows off decoration in pastel shades such as pink, very pale green or pale blue to perfection. A dark chocolate covering looks wonderfully rich and tempting, as does a lighter chocolate frosting or topping. The harsh tones of the primary colors (red, yellow, and blue) should be avoided at all costs, as should any harsh secondary colors (bright green etc.) Psychedelic shades are guaranteed to make most people suddenly lose their appetite.

INTRODUCTION

· · ·

When embarking on the design for a decoration there are parchment, tin or plastic patterns to help us. The last two can be bought in many shops specializing in kitchen equipment, while a pair of scissors will soon provide us with what we need if we use parchment, wax or greaseproof paper. Decorating the top of a cake or flat pastry needs patience rather than great skill; when it comes to decorating something like a round or domed confection, however, a little more expertise is usually required. There are some basic implements without which it is difficult to achieve the desired effect. First of all, a set of spatulas of various sizes with which to spread frostings, coverings of cream, buttercream, fondant etc. Choose some which are rigid as well as others which have more flexible blades to allow for different consistencies. You will need a selection of pastry bags made out of material, paper or synthetic fiber as well as at least six different pastry tubes, in various sizes and shapes. It is wise to practice piping with these pastry bags and tubes so that you are not a complete beginner when you come to carry out your design. A good way to acquire skill is to pipe out the letters of the alphabet, in capitals and in script. A revolving cake stand will be a great help so that you will not have to move around at awkward moments, but this is not indispensable.

One of the basic materials for decoration and other purposes in patisserie is *couverture* (literally, "covering" chocolate), a blend of cocoa, cocoa butter, and sugar which can be bought in blocks and melted over warm water; it is, however, less easy to work with than baker's chocolate, which also has a high fat content and is usually easily bought in smaller quantities than *couverture*. If you are a novice you will find *couverture* remains easier to handle, and for longer, if you mix a little thick sugar syrup with it.
Among the most rewarding decorations a beginner can make is a chocolate leaf: choose a small leaf with pronounced veining (rose leaves or lime leaves are excellent); rinse in cold water and dry very thoroughly (this is crucial, otherwise the chocolate and water will react with each other). Wipe the leaf very gently all over with a piece of kitchen towel dipped in mineral oil (the oil must have no scent). Place the leaf on the bottom of an upturned plate or on any surface which is barely convex and cover with melted chocolate. Leave for few hours before you remove the real leaf, to make sure the chocolate has set totally.

You can buy very small tin or plastic molds and pour melted chocolate into them to make smooth or ribbed disks and tablets, animals, and all sorts of different shapes. Alternatively, spread a layer of melted chocolate on a sheet of heavy-duty greaseproof paper and, just as it is setting, use very small cutting shapes (like mini

• • •

pastry cutters) to make all sorts of chocolate cutouts. By scraping a knife along the surface of the sheet of chocolate when it is completely set and cold, you can make long thin chocolate curls which look like Russian cigarettes, or shavings. If you are really feeling energetic, you can make your own chocolate sprinkles which are invaluable for decorating almost anything sweet and which keep for some time in an airtight tin: the chocolate is first broken into pieces, then warmed and worked until soft but not liquid, and this paste is then pushed through a sieve with a large wooden spoon (and a good deal of muscle power). Leave to cool and harden.

Marzipan is one of the oldest and most traditional substances used in decoration: for covering the surface of a cake (with or without a second covering of frosting) when the marzipan has to be rolled out as thinly as possible, just as you would roll pastry but in this case a round or oval shaped sheet of paste is easiest to handle (a dusting of confectioners' sugar will stop the rolling pin from sticking) and then cut to the size of the cake which you want to cover. Modeling marzipan (into flowers, fruit, animals, and figures which are then colored to look extremely realistic) is not as easy as you might imagine.

A demanding decoration for the adventurous would be a rose of sweet butter. Dip small balls of butter in iced water, then work them by hand, (your fingers will have to be repeatedly dipped too, so that they remain cold), then press flat between two very thin layers of linen. These little disks will form the petals of the rose. To ensure a successful result, everything has to be kept cold. These butter roses may be used to decorate both sweet and savory items. An entire chapter of this book is devoted to coverings: frostings, buttercreams, and others. Patisserie is "clothed" according to the occasion, depending on whether it is a simple meal or a grand dinner, tending to be lighter in summer time and heavier and richer in winter. Sugar is so important that it needs a special mention, for it is the most crucial material in patisserie and dessert cookery. Refined sugar contains up to 98 percent sucrose and melts at room temperature when mixed with half its weight of water; $\frac{1}{2}$ cup water will hold 1 cup in solution. When sugar is heated on its own, however, it melts at 320° F and changes into a glassy mass, known as barley sugar. If the temperature is allowed to rise to 428° F, the sugar turns brown, becomes bitter, and reaches the dark caramel stage. When sugar is heated with water it gradually alters in density. To measure the temperature of the syrup a candy thermometer is used, marked with Centigrade and Fahrenheit (professionals and manufacturers use a saccharimeter to measure density up to the large or hard ball stage).

The first stage, which occurs when the sugar syrup is just coming to a boil is the *coated* stage; as the sugar cooks it starts to look like a slightly ragged veil, also known as *small thread.*

Next is the *large thread* degree; touch the surface of the boiling sugar momentarily with a dry finger. Join the thumb and the finger together, when pulled apart an elastic thread of sugar will form. This will normally happen when the temperature of the syrup reaches 215–217° F. As the sugar syrup heats up, it passes through the *small pearl* degree, to the *large pearl* or *blow* stage, 224–228° F: when a loop of wire is inserted into the syrup and removed, a thin film will be produced which can be gently blown; at the *feather* stage, (reached at 240° F) this film will form featherlike pieces when blown. Next comes the *pastille* stage: the sugar syrup tends to whiten and crystallize when a drop is pressed between thumb and forefinger which are then pulled apart.

By now the syrup is becoming noticeably thicker and the *small or soft ball* stage is reached at 241–244° F, when a drop of syrup dropped into a little iced water forms a very plastic transparent ball when manipulated with the fingers. By the *large or hard ball* stage (250–255° F); a very much firmer ball is formed when tested. Now the syrup is becoming really thick and from now on the temperature will rise rapidly. Next comes the *soft or small crack* (265–275° F), followed by *hard crack*, 295–300° F (both are marked on your candy thermometer). Finally we reach the *caramel* stage as the sugar colors; if allowed to cook long enough this caramel will become very dark, lose its sweetness and will emit acrid fumes (*brulé* or black jack stage).

Spun sugar is widely used in decoration; professionals use a special implement called a thrower, which looks like a bundle of wires with a handle, but a wire whisk with the end cut off or even a fork will do. The sugar, water, and pinch of cream of tartar are taken to the beginning of the caramel stage (310–311° F) and then left to cool for a minute or so or shock cooled by plunging the pan into cold water for a few seconds. The thrower is dipped into the sugar which is then "spun" across two lightly oiled sticks. It must only be prepared very shortly before it is to be used, as boiled sugar is very prone to absorb moisture, turning into a caramel syrup. Praline or croquant can be cut out into shapes and used for very effective decorations; caramel for this purpose is made with 1¼ cups granulated sugar and 1 tbsp lemon juice. Once the sugar has colored, reduce the heat and add ¾ cup warmed chopped almonds; stir quickly and thoroughly before removing from the heat. Turn out onto a lightly oiled marble slab or work surface. Leave to cool and then reheat in the oven at 300° F before working with it, when it can be rolled out with a rolling pin (do not make it too thin).

Another form of decoration, candied flowers, which some aspiring *pâtissiers* may wish to make themselves, involves dipping fresh flowers or flower petals in a thick sugar syrup four times, leaving them to dry thoroughly after each dipping. Sweet violets can be preserved in this way; traditionally they are used to decorate confections made with *marrons glacés*.

An extremely simple and effective

way to decorate a cake is to cut out your own stencil or use a lace paper doily or mat; place on the top of a cake and dredge with a thin layer of confectioners' sugar. Remove the paper carefully and you will have an attractive design picked out in sugar.

CREATORS OF MODERN PATISSERIE

The word *carême* means Lent in French: an amusingly inappropriate surname for a man who became world famous for his elaborate and sumptuous creations. An ancestor of his, also a chef, had been given the name by Pope Leo X who was delighted with a soup he had prepared for a Lenten meal.

Marie Antoine Carême was born on June 8, 1784, five years before the French Revolution began. He was the seventeenth child of a very poor workman and was effectively abandoned when he was nine years old. A cook in a small eating house took pity on him and soon discovered his protegé was a very gifted and imaginative cook. Carême made his name as a *pâtissier* when working in one of the most famous cake and pastry shops in Paris, the Pâtisserie Bailly, where his triumphal arches, statues and buildings in *pastillage* (confectioners' sugar paste which sets very hard) soon made his reputation: "There are five branches of the fine arts," he used to say:

"painting, poetry, music, sculpture and, lastly, architecture, the main branch of which is patisserie." Carême studied drawings of Greek and Roman buildings in the print room of the Bibliothèque Nationale in Paris before creating detailed replicas made out of *pastillage* or hardened sugar paste in keeping with the prevailing fashion for the Neo-classical style.

Carême was a keen student, not only of the history of art but also of the history of cooking, striving to discover the secrets of long dead master chefs. Before long he was able to set up in business on his own in the Rue de la Paix, supplying all the usual delicacies, as well as creating a number of unusual confections for important banquets and receptions. In court and diplomatic circles all over the world he was the master whom everyone sought to emulate: besides being a culinary artist, Carême also adopted a scholarly approach to gastronomy. He kept a large leather-bound album on a desk within reach as he worked at his ovens in which he noted every tiny detail and observation. "I had the good habit of making a note of all variations on recipes, since not a day went by without my introducing changes and innovations . . . For each thing one prepares, there is a method whereby one will achieve perfection."

In 1818 he published *le pâtissier royal parisien*, in which he propounded a new philosophy: foods should never be camouflaged with ingredients alien to their nature, nor subjected to excessively elaborate decoration. He maintained that fine French cooking, which was by then being accepted as the criterion of excellence all over the world, had first come into its own at the time of the French Revolution, in 1789. More people were able to exercise their right to enjoy the fine things of life and from quantity to quality was but a short step and, indeed by the time the monarchy was restored in France, both the middle classes and the aristocracy could enjoy the pleasures of the table.

Carême was greatly influenced by the political theories of Talleyrand, the bishop turned revolutionary who became Napoleon's Foreign Minister, continuing in this office after the monarchy had been restored in the person of Louis XVIII. Carême worked for Talleyrand, cooking him fabulous banquets, until the time of the First Empire. Then, in his own words: "I became head cook to the Imperial household, with full responsibility for deciding what to buy and for the planning of menus. I was my own master with a degree of unquestioned authority and status that was beyond my wildest dreams." His finest hour, as for Talleyrand, was the Congress of Vienna, during which culinary art and diplomacy bemused the other delegates into revising their view of France as a power laid low and demoralized by defeat in war. Emperors, ministers, plenipotentiaries, and ambassadors were all seduced by the pleasures of the table into an affirmation of belief in French prestige.
One of Carême's most successful creations was his mixed fruit coupe.

Fresh fruit cut into small dice was sprinkled with kirsch, and placed in crystal goblets or coupes; ice cream and sweetened whipped cream were added, together with a little blueberry syrup, the whole topped by a domed covering made out of sugar decorated with small candied cherries.
In spite of extremely tempting offers from the Tsar of Russia and the King of England, Carême preferred to live in Paris, although he did allow himself to be lured abroad for short visits. He died, fittingly, while tasting some quenelles of sole which a friend had cooked for him, in 1833. His last words were: "the seasoning and the sauce are not so well blended; next time you should . . ." Talleyrand declared that future generations would look in vain for a second Carême. And so far he seems to have been proved right.
French influence in patisserie remained in the ascendant during the nineteenth century, as an increasingly wide spectrum of the prosperous middle classes grew accustomed to eating well. Many chefs had had Brillat-Savarin's theories and Carême's practical precepts inculcated into them during their training. From the Belle Epoque onward the number of courses served for family meals was reduced, while *haute cuisine* dishes and peasant cooking were equally at home in a new and happy mood of culinary eclecticism which was well suited to the philosophy of a newly powerful class. The transitional phase was fortunate in having its own zealot, Auguste Escoffier, who brought an original attitude to bear on *haute cuisine*. "We shall simplify methods of cooking and serving food

while striving to enhance taste and nutritional value"; having stated his credo, Escoffier put his beliefs into practice during his travels through Europe and other parts of the world. From 1883 onward his creations featured in such great hotels as the Savoy in London, the Ritz-Carlton in Paris, and the Plaza in New York. He was responsible for many recipes which are now accepted as fundamental in international cooking. One of Escoffier's most famous recipes is Peach Melba, created when he was at the Savoy Hotel in London for the famous Australian soprano Dame Nellie Melba, on the occasion of the premiere of Wagner's opera *Lohengrin*. Here is the original version, to remind us of what it should really be like and all too often is not:

Melt ½ cup sugar in 2¼ cups water and bring to a boil with a piece of vanilla bean. Peel the peaches and cut them in half, adding them to the syrup. Leave to cool. Place 2¼ lb fresh raspberries in a saucepan, sprinkle ½ cup sugar over them; cook without adding any water. Sieve and leave to cool. Take a large coupe [Escoffier used a crystal and silver swan-shaped one], spread 1 lb ice cream in a layer over the bottom, arrange the peaches on top of this with the hollow cavities facing upward: fill these with the raspberry purée and chill in the refrigerator until just before serving.

NATIONAL CAKES, PUDDINGS AND PASTRIES

Each country has its own specialty. Over the centuries many of these pies, puddings, cakes, and candies have become part of traditional celebrations for festivals and important occasions. Some are very rich and filling and are therefore best eaten on their own during the daytime with coffee, tea, or a glass of sweet wine rather than at the end of a large meal. Many involve yeast cookery and others are made with marzipan.

Marzipan

This sweet almond paste, a blend of pounded almonds and sugar, was a favorite with those who could afford it throughout sixteenth-century Europe, each region developing its own version, although it was already known in ancient Roman times. Traditionally, colored marzipan fruit was made for All Saints' Day and All Souls' Day.

Millet bread

Described in the *Tacuinum Sanitatis* (an illustrated domestic vade-mecum produced toward the end of the fourteenth century) as a staple food of woodcutters and charcoal burners which "when eaten hot, straight out of the oven, has a certain sweetness to it."

INTRODUCTION

· · ·

Colomba

Legend has it that the creation of the first dove (*colomba*) cake involved King Alboin of the Lombards. In 572 A.D. he took the city of Pavia after a three-year siege, confiscated all the citizens' worldly goods and declared his intention to carry off the twelve most beautiful girls. One, despairing at the fate which was to befall her, sought solace in the kitchen and baked a cake in the shape of a dove with flour, eggs, and sugar.

Panettone

A dome-shaped Italian sweet yeast bread of ancient origin. Extra ingredients were added to the ordinary, everyday bread dough for the feast of the winter solstice, and gradually a slightly different version of this sweet yeast cake evolved in each region, depending on the local produce available. The recipe most widely used today was one recorded by Pellegrino Artusi, a celebrated nineteenth-century gastronome. To this day *panettone* is eaten by northern Italians in winter, as traditional Christmas fare.

Plum pudding

The very sound conjures up something comforting, substantial, and rich with all the added connotations of hearty Victorian Christmas meals, roaring fires, and seasonal cheer. The plum pudding can be traced back to medieval times; it has admirable keeping qualities due to the amount of dried fruit it contains and actually improves if kept for a year or so after it is made. The pudding is steamed slowly for several hours before being served hot, flamed with brandy or rum. It is traditionally served with hard sauce, or cream and egg vanilla custard.

Crêpes Suzette

Two restaurants lay equally plausible claims to being this dessert's birthplace. Some say that Henry Charpentier, chef at the Café de Paris in Monte Carlo created it in honor of the Prince of Wales, while others maintain that credit is due to the chef of the Mariveaux in Paris and that he named it after Suzette, an actress from the Opéra.

Apple pie

Early settlers in North America had to be largely self-sufficient and it was important for the women to be good cooks: food was often scarce and what there was had to be well cooked with no wastage. They did all their own baking and over the years good, homely apple pies came to typify all that was best about the pioneering spirit. The apple pie still seems to be a symbol of all that lies closest to the hearts of many Americans. Catherine Parson is said to be responsible for the definitive version, in 1898.

Blancmange

The name of this very old recipe is descriptive, literally "eat white." The traditional ingredients give the dessert a wonderful, pure white appearance. Writing in the nineteenth century, Pellegrino Artusi lists the ingredients as almonds, isinglass for setting (nowadays we would use gelatin or agar-agar), sugar, and orange flower water.

INTRODUCTION

• • •

Sachertorte

Franz Sacher (head pastrycook to Prince Metternich) created this celebrated sponge cake in 1832. With a filling of preserve and completely covered with chocolate frosting, it was a tremendous success. Franz passed on all his expertise to his son Eduard who set up on his own, opening the world famous Hotel Sacher in Vienna.

Brioches

Made with sweet, rich, and tender yeast dough, these originated in France, where they were also called *Apostle cakes*, possibly because their shape is reminiscent of the hats which priests once used to wear.

Baba

The first person to enjoy this sweet yeast cake soaked in sugar syrup flavored with rose water was a Polish king in exile, Stanislas Leczinski, in 1740. Stanislas loved the stories of Scheherazade, the Thousand and One Nights, and decided to call his chef's creation Ali Baba, subsequently shortened to baba. The dessert became very popular at the court of his son-in-law, Louis XV of France.

Madeleines

Another delicacy created for the sweet-toothed King Stanislas, this time by an old governess at his country residence at Commercy. He liked the madeleines so much that he sent his daughter Marie Leczinska, Queen of France, a generous consignment of them. The recipe was improved in the nineteenth century by the Julien brothers, Parisian *pâtissiers*, who added butter to the ingredients, resulting in the cake immortalized by Proust.

Saint Honoré

Created by the Julien brothers (see above) who added several delicacies to the repertoire of French patisserie.

Savarin

After an extra ingredient, butter, has been added to baba dough, it is baked in a ring tube mold; this yeast cake is then soaked with a rum flavored syrup and covered with apricot glaze. Named after the famous French gastronome, Jean-Anthelme de Brillat-Savarin.

W hen we preserve fruit with sugar, we store up some of nature's most beautiful colors, scents and tastes, conserving food while it is cheap and plentiful, as well as preventing waste if there is a glut of produce. Fruit can be covered in caramel, canned in sugar syrup, candied, or made into preserves, thus arresting the normal course of decay. Gathering peaches, plums, apricots, pears, and grapes when they are at their finest and proceeding to encapsulate that perfection for many months to come is both satisfying and useful. All you will need is sugar, a number of glass jars, several deep saucepans of varying sizes, scales, a nonmetallic sieve, very sharp stainless steel knives, and wooden spoons, together with a rudimentary understanding of the simple processes which will ensure a successful outcome.

CARAMEL-DIPPED ORANGE SECTIONS

Peel the oranges and carefully remove all the white pith with a very sharp knife. Ideal for decorating chocolate cakes and desserts.

Time: 1 hour
Very easy

3 oranges
½ cup sugar
juice of 1 lemon
1 tbsp almond oil

Try not to puncture the membrane enclosing each section when peeling the oranges. Divide into sections and spread out on kitchen towels to dry thoroughly. Melt the sugar with the lemon juice in a heavy pan over high heat. As soon as the syrup starts to color, reduce the heat and add the orange sections. Stir very gently for the few seconds they are in the pan, using a wooden spoon. Transfer the sections to a large plate lightly brushed with almond oil. Leave to cool separated from one another.

• • •

CARAMELIZED PINEAPPLE

Serve with a little whipped cream piped on top for a refreshing dessert.

Time: 30 minutes
Very easy

1 fresh pineapple
scant ½ cup sugar
2½ tbsp water

☐ *Lemon juice or vinegar or butter can be added to sugar which is being caramelized to prevent it setting too hard. Remove caramelized fruits or orange peel from the caramel before it hardens with the aid of tweezers lightly oiled with sweet almond oil and leave to cool, well spaced out on a lightly oiled baking sheet or plate.*

☐ *Sterilize an empty jar by placing it in water, bringing to a boil and boiling for a few minutes. To sterilize canned fruit, tomatoes (which have a high acid content), or preserves, the hermetically sealed jars should be placed upright in a very large pan; add water to cover. Bring to a boil and continue boiling for 25 minutes, adding more boiling water if necessary. Leave to cool completely before removing the jars. Even low-sugar preserves will keep for a year or more if placed in sterilized jars.*

☐ *When caramelizing sugar, use a deep, stainless steel pan. When the sugar has turned the correct color, remove from the heat immediately and lower into a pan of boiling water (take care none overflows into the caramel pan). This will keep the caramel liquid while you dip the fruit; each fruit is then placed on an oiled plate to set. Hold fruit by the stalk when possible, or use a knitting needle or tweezers. If the sugar starts to set in the pan, return to direct heat for a second or two.*

☐ *Fruit can be preserved in a sugar syrup which has been boiled for two minutes, strained and left to cool. The proportion of sugar used varies according to the fruit: less for pears and peaches, more for raspberries and cherries. See table below for amount of sugar to be used for each 1 quart water:*

Apricots	*1¼ cups*
Pears	*1½ cups*
Skinned peach halves	*2 cups*
Plums	*2¾ cups*
Raspberries	*2¾ cups*
Strawberries	*2¾ cups*
Cherries	*3½ cups*
Red currants	*3½ cups*

Measurements have been rounded up to the nearest convenient cup measure where necessary. Sugar measurements are calculated on the basis that 1 cup is equivalent to 8 oz sugar.

1 tbsp lemon juice
1 tbsp almond oil

Peel the pineapple and remove the hard central core, using a very thin sharp knife or apple corer to keep the pineapple as neat as possible. Slice into rings about ½ in thick. Pat dry with kitchen towels. Cook the sugar, water, and lemon juice over moderate heat until it is a pale golden color. Add the pineapple rings, stir and turn very gently before removing and spreading out to cool thoroughly on a lightly oiled work surface or plate.

• • •

CARAMELIZED STRAWBERRIES

Choose medium to large strawberries which are not very ripe or they will disintegrate. A good finishing touch for lemon-flavored desserts.

Time: 30 minutes
Very easy

2 cups strawberries
½ cup sugar
1 tbsp white wine vinegar
1 tbsp almond oil

Hull the strawberries, wipe gently with a damp cloth, and leave to dry. Place the sugar and vinegar in a wide, heavy saucepan over high heat until it starts to color. Reduce the heat, add the strawberries, stirring very gently with a wooden spoon. As soon as the caramel has turned a little darker, transfer the strawberries to a plate or slab lightly oiled with almond oil. Do not use until they are completely cold.

• • •

MARRONS GLACÉS (CARAMEL-DIPPED SWEET CHESTNUTS)
■ *Chestnuts provide a rich sauce of starch and sugar. They can feature in preserves, cakes and desserts and are also a suitable accompaniment to roast meat, chicken, and game.*

MARRONS GLACÉS

Time: 1 hour
Easy

18 sweet chestnuts, peeled
   and skinned
1 cup sugar
2¼ cups water
1 vanilla bean or a few drops
   vanilla extract
1 bay leaf
1 clove
1 tbsp butter
1 tbsp almond oil

Allow a few extra chestnuts as one or two may break when removing the thin inner skin; this comes off more easily if they are boiled in water for 2 minutes, drained and peeled while still hot. Melt half the sugar in all the water. Remove from the heat, add the chestnuts, bay leaf, vanilla, and clove. Cover, and simmer for 20 minutes over low heat. Remove the chestnuts and spread out on a clean white cloth. Heat the remaining sugar with the butter over very gentle heat until it turns pale golden brown. Remove from the heat and dip the chestnuts in the caramel one by one, leaving them to cool on a lightly oiled plate.

• • •

PRALINE

Invaluable and versatile, praline can be crushed and sprinkled on ice cream, fruit pastries, cakes, etc. Filberts can be used instead of almonds.

Time: 35 minutes
Very easy

1¼ cups whole skinned
   almonds

¾ cup sugar
juice of 1 large lemon
1 tbsp almond oil

Spread the almonds in a single layer on a cookie sheet and roast in the oven at 375° F for about 5 minutes or until golden brown. Melt the sugar with the lemon juice in a saucepan, stirring constantly with a wooden spoon; as soon as the syrup has turned golden brown, add the warm almonds and continue cooking while stirring until the caramel has darkened a little more. Pour the mixture onto a marble slab or work surface lightly smeared with almond oil. Shape into a rectangle about ¾ in thick with an oiled knife. Cut into pieces before it has cooled completely.

• • •

COFFEE CARAMEL CANDIES

These are usually left to harden in little molds but if the mixture is poured into an oiled jelly roll sponge pan, it can be cut into small pieces when set but not cold.

Time: 45 minutes
Very easy

¾ cup sugar
½ cup very strong black
   coffee
½ cup milk
1 tbsp honey
1 tbsp almond oil (for greasing
   the molds or pan)

Heat the sugar in the top of a double boiler until it melts; boil for 2 minutes and then add all the other ingredients. Bring slowly back to a fast boil. Pour

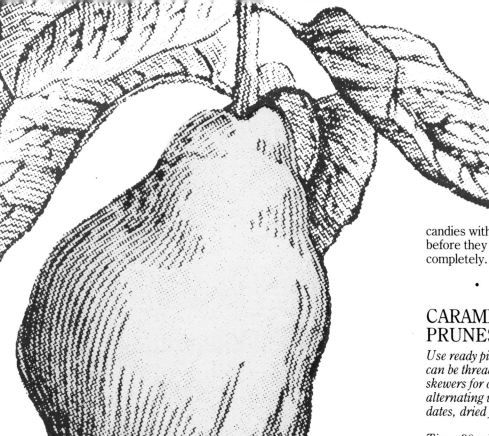

QUINCES
■ *Quinces are never eaten raw. Once cooked, however, their distinctive aroma and flavor can enhance a variety of desserts and preserves.*

MINT- AND LEMON- FLAVORED CANDIES

Wrap these refreshing candies in waxed paper inside colored wrappers or store in airtight glass jars. Their attractive shape makes them suitable for use as decorations. Use a saucepan with a spout or lip if you have one.

Time: 40 minutes
Very easy

⅔ cup sugar
2 tbsp water
10 drops peppermint extract
juice of 1 lemon
1 tbsp almond oil

Melt the sugar in the water in a saucepan and simmer for 2 minutes. Remove from the heat, add the peppermint extract and lemon juice. Return to a higher heat and boil fast until golden brown. Pour a very little at a time onto a lightly oiled marble slab or work surface. Loosen the

into the lightly oiled molds or pan and leave to set. Use an oiled knife to cut into squares or rectangles. Store in airtight containers.

• • •

candies with an oiled spatula before they have cooled completely.

• • •

CARAMELIZED PRUNES

Use ready pitted prunes; they can be threaded onto wooden skewers for caramelizing, alternating with walnuts, dates, dried figs, and apricots.

Time: 30 minutes
Very easy

2 cups pitted prunes
½ cup sugar
juice of 1 lemon
1 tbsp almond oil

If you rinse the prunes before using them, wipe them completely dry or the caramel will not cling to the surface. Cook the sugar with the lemon juice over moderate heat and add the prunes when it starts to turn golden brown. Stir. When the caramel has become a little darker, turn out onto a lightly oiled surface. Make sure the prunes are well spaced out and not touching each other.
All sorts of dried fruits and nuts can be given this treatment.

• • •

CANDIED ORANGE PEEL

Make sure that none of the bitter white pith is attached to the peel for this recipe. Lemon and citron peel is candied in the same way.

Time: 30 minutes + soaking time

Very easy

1 lb orange peel
1¾ cups sugar
2 tbsp almond oil

Cut the orange peel into thin strips; place in a bowl of hot water with a weight on top to keep them all submerged and leave to soak overnight. Drain very thoroughly. Place in a pan with the sugar; stir while heating until the syrup reaches the soft ball stage. Turn out onto a lightly oiled surface; separate the pieces of peel using oiled tweezers. Store in a glass jar when completely cold.

• • •

FIRM QUINCE JELLY

Quinces have a wonderful aroma. In days gone by a quince would be placed in the linen cupboard to impart a sweet, fresh scent to the sheets.

Time: 1 hour
Very easy

2¼ lb quinces
3 cups sugar
1 tbsp almond oil

Choose sound, ripe quinces (they should be firm and deep yellow in color), and wipe clean with a damp cloth. Place in a saucepan with just enough water to cover, and simmer until tender. Drain well before sieving. Put the quince purée and the sugar into a saucepan, bring to a boil, then cook for 20 minutes, stirring with a wooden spoon. Pour into a shallow, rectangular dish (a gratin dish will do) and smooth the surface; the mixture should be about 1¾ in thick. Leave to dry in full sun every day for 10 days (leave in a warm, well ventilated room at night). The mixture should be very firm but not dry. Wrap in waxed paper and store in a cool, dry place. Cut into squares and roll in granulated sugar before you serve.

• • •

CANDIED CHERRIES

Time: 30 minutes
Easy

2 lb cherries
2 cups sugar
2 cups water

Wash and dry the cherries, remove their stalks, and pit. Make a syrup by melting half the sugar in the water, add the cherries and simmer for 10 minutes. Pour into a nonmetallic bowl and leave to stand for 2 days. Add the remaining sugar, return to the saucepan and boil for 2 minutes. Leave to stand in a bowl for another 24 hours. Boil for a third time in the saucepan for two minutes; leave to stand in a bowl for another 2 days. Skim the surface whenever necessary during the boiling stages. Brush a large, flat, drum sieve with almond oil and place the cherries on it to drain and dry, before storing in airtight jars. Roll in sugar before serving.

CARAMEL-DIPPED MIXED DRIED FRUIT AND NUTS

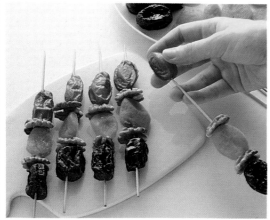

Follow the steps carefully for a surprisingly simple and effective treat for your friends and family. Buy "no soak" dried apricots and prunes, soft enough to eat just as they are.

6 dried apricots
6 prunes
6 dates
12 walnuts
1 cup sugar
2 tbsp water
1 tbsp lemon juice

Thread the fruit securely onto 6 wooden skewers or satay sticks. Have a few extra walnuts if possible to allow for breakages.

Melt the sugar with the water in a wide, heavy stainless steel or copper pan and add the lemon juice.

When the sugar syrup has turned golden brown, lay the skewered fruits flat in it, using tongs or tweezers. Turn immediately to ensure they are well covered with caramel.

Remove the coated fruits from the pan (the whole dipping process should only take a minute or less).

Place on a cold plate, lightly oiled with almond oil.

Push into a grapefruit for easy drying and effective presentation.

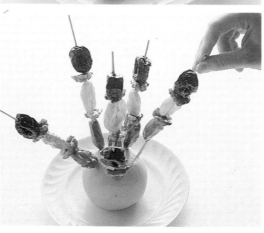

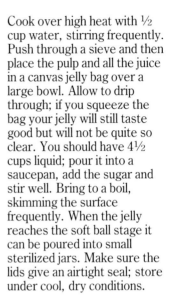

TANGERINE JELLY

A deliciously delicate flavor. Use this recipe for grape, orange, lemon, or grapefruit jellies.

Time: 40 minutes
Very easy

4½ lb juicy tangerines
4½ cups sugar
1 cup water

Squeeze the tangerines; you will need 1 quart of juice. Heat the sugar and water in a saucepan; boil until it reaches the soft ball stage. Remove from the heat, stir in the juice, return to the heat and continue to stir until the liquid has just come back to a full boil. Strain through a very fine sieve. Transfer to jars when warm, not hot.

· · ·

BLACKBERRY JELLY

Besides being excellent uncooked in red fruit salads and when cooked with apples, or served with cream and sugar, blackberries make wonderful jelly and preserves.

Time: 1 hour
Very easy

2½ quarts blackberries
4½ cups sugar
juice of 1 lemon

Choose completely sound, ripe blackberries; rinse thoroughly, drain well, and place in a saucepan with ½ cup water. Bring to a gentle boil and then simmer for 10 minutes. Sieve, reserving the purée and liquid and discarding the seeds. Cook the sugar and

lemon juice over gentle heat, stirring and skimming at frequent intervals, until the syrup reaches the soft ball stage. Add the sieved berries and stir until the mixture returns to a boil. Transfer to hot, sterilized jars, seal very tightly, and store in a cool, dry place.
This method can also be used for pineapple, quince, and kiwi fruit jellies.

· · ·

RED CURRANT JELLY

Time: 30 minutes
Very easy

4½ lb red currants
4½ cups sugar

Make sure you use fully ripened red currants; rinse well and remove from their larger stalks (the rest will remain behind in the sieve).

Cook over high heat with ½ cup water, stirring frequently. Push through a sieve and then place the pulp and all the juice in a canvas jelly bag over a large bowl. Allow to drip through; if you squeeze the bag your jelly will still taste good but will not be quite so clear. You should have 4½ cups liquid; pour it into a saucepan, add the sugar and stir well. Bring to a boil, skimming the surface frequently. When the jelly reaches the soft ball stage it can be poured into small sterilized jars. Make sure the lids give an airtight seal; store under cool, dry conditions.

· · ·

PEACH PRESERVE

Yellow peaches are better for jam making than white peaches as they usually have a more pronounced flavor. Choose ripe, sound fruit: underripe peaches will not ripen once picked.

Time: 30 minutes + standing time
Very easy

2 lb peaches
2 cups sugar
peel of 1 lemon
pinch cinnamon

Immerse the peaches in boiling water for 1 minute then drain and peel. Cut in half, pit, and dice. Place in a bowl with the sugar. Mix well. Cover with a cloth and leave to stand for 12 hours in a cool place. Transfer to a saucepan, add the lemon peel and cinnamon, and cook till the jelling point is reached (217–221° F for this recipe). Remove the peel

before pouring the hot preserve into sterilized jars. Seal very tightly. Store in a cool, dry place.

• • •

QUINCE PRESERVE

This fruit is inedible raw but wonderful when cooked, especially in jams and jellies.

Time: 30 minutes + standing time
Very easy

2 lb quinces
2 lb sugar

Wash, dry, and peel the quinces, discarding the cores and seeds. Cut into thin slices and place in a bowl. Add the sugar, stir well, cover and leave to stand overnight. Transfer to a saucepan; simmer for 30 minutes or until jelling point is reached. Ladle the hot jam into sterilized jars and seal tightly. Store in a cool, dry place.

• • •

GREEN TOMATO PRESERVE

Time: 1 hour 30 minutes + standing time
Very easy

2¼ lb green tomatoes
3½ cups sugar
1 lemon

Select large, sound tomatoes. Wash, dry, remove stalks and cut into thin rounds. Place in a nonmetallic bowl with the sugar. Stir thoroughly, cover and leave to stand for 24 hours. Transfer the contents of the bowl to a nonmetallic saucepan, add the strained lemon juice. Simmer for about 1 hour, stirring at frequent intervals, until the mixture has thickened considerably and the soft ball stage is reached. Ladle the hot preserve into prepared jars, seal, and keep cool and dry.

• • •

CARROT PRESERVE

Being a sweet vegetable, carrot is well suited to preserves and cakes. It contains vitamin E and carotene, good for the skin and general health.

Time: 1 hour + standing time
Very easy

2 lb carrots
1 cup sugar
peel of 1 lemon

Peel and dice the carrots, place in a bowl with the sugar, stir and leave to stand overnight. Transfer the contents of the bowl to a saucepan; bring to a boil, then simmer gently for 1 hour. Sieve. Cook the purée with the lemon peel until very thick indeed. Transfer the hot preserve to prepared jars and seal tightly.

• • •

PECTIN

Many fruits contain pectin, which helps to thicken and set jams, preserves, and jellies. Apples, red currants, and plums are rich in pectin and should set well. Liquid pectin must usually be added to preserves made with other fruits for a good set. If you cannot buy commercially prepared pectin, cook a few quartered apples (do not remove the cores or skin) in a cheesecloth bag with the preserve and remove when jelling point is reached.

PUMPKIN JAM

Pumpkin is extremely versatile, adapting equally well to sweet and savory treatment. It can also be used to add volume to jams made with various fruits, when it takes on their flavor.

Time: 1 hour
Very easy

4½ lb pumpkin
1¾ cups sugar
juice and peel of 1 lemon, grated
1 vanilla bean or a few drops vanilla extract

Peel the pumpkin, remove the seeds and fibrous material containing them, and cut into small dice. Leave to stand overnight in a large bowl, mixed with the sugar, lemon juice, grated lemon peel, and vanilla pod. Transfer to a saucepan and bring to a boil (if you are using extract add it now). Cook, stirring frequently, until the jam is very thick. Discard the vanilla bean, if used, before storing in tightly sealed prepared jars.

• • •

■ *Surprisingly sweet, green
tomatoes are rich in vitamin C
and health-giving mineral
salts. Slice raw for salads or
use to make excellent
preserves and relishes.*

ORANGE AND DATE PRESERVE

Time: 1 hour
Very easy

6 oranges
juice of ½ lemon
1 cup sugar
1½ tbsp rum
1 cup dates

Peel the oranges, cut
crosswise into round slices
and place in a saucepan. Add
the lemon juice, sugar and
rum. Cook for 15 minutes,
stirring now and then, before
adding the dates. Cook fairly
slowly for another 10 minutes
before sieving the mixture.
Return to the saucepan and
boil gently, stirring
continuously, until jelling point
is reached. Ladle into
sterilized jars.

• • •

FIG AND LEMON PRESERVE

*If you can, use organically
grown lemons which have
tender, less bitter peel than
chemically sprayed fruit.*

Time: 2 hours
Very easy

2 lb ripe fresh figs
2 lb lemons
2 cups sugar

Wash the figs, dry, remove
the stalk, and place in a
saucepan. Prepare the lemons
by pricking their skin lightly all
over and boil in three changes
of water, boiling for 5 minutes
each time. Slice thinly and
discard the pips. Add to the
figs, stir and cook for about 1
hour over very low heat. Put

SAUCES

Sweet fruit sauces can be
made very easily by sieving
preserves or processing them
in a blender. Add brandy,
sweet dessert wine or liqueur
if wished but no more sugar.

through a vegetable mill or
process briefly in a blender
(the mixture should not be too
smooth), return to the
saucepan and stir in the sugar.
Cook at a slow boil, stirring
frequently until the preserve
reaches jelling point. Pour into
hot, sterilized, and completely
dry jars; cover the surface
with a circle of greaseproof or
waxed paper (dipped in brandy
if you wish). Seal tightly and
store.

• • •

APRICOT AND
WINE PRESERVE

Time: 30 minutes
Very easy

2¼ lb apricots
1 cup sugar
peel of 1 lemon, grated
1 cup sweet white wine (e.g.
    Vin Santo, Muscat de
    Beaumes de Venise or fine
    California Muscat wine)
1 tsp cinnamon

Wash, dry, and pit the
apricots. Bring to a gentle boil
with the sugar, grated lemon
peel, wine, and cinnamon.
Cook for 10 minutes, stirring
frequently. Drain; sieve the
apricots, return to the pan and
continue cooking and stirring
until setting point is reached.
Pour into hot sterilized jars.
Cover the surface with waxed
paper disks dipped in rum or
brandy (optional), seal tightly,
and keep cool, dark, and dry.

• • •

VIN SANTO

Semidried grapes are turned
into this superb Italian wine
which can be dry, or very
sweet and rich. It is aged in
the wood. Very little is
exported and you may have to
substitute Muscat de Beaumes
de Venise, Muscatel or the
best quality sweet California
Muscat wine.

PRUNES IN GRAPPA

Choose the largest succulent prunes you can find, pitted or not; brandy (good-quality but not the finest), rum or applejack could be used instead of grappa.

Time: 5 minutes + standing time
Very easy

2¼ lb prunes
1 quart good quality grappa or alternative spirit

Wash the prunes, dry well, and pack into jars (do not push down tightly). Add sufficient grappa to cover. Seal and leave to stand in a cool, dark place for 10 days, when the prunes will have absorbed some of the grappa and will need topping up with more. Continue topping up at intervals until the prunes are completely saturated. They will keep almost indefinitely. Dried figs, raisins, peaches, and apricots can be used instead of prunes.

• • •

APRICOTS IN BRANDY

Choose apricots which are just ripe; sweet but not squashy. A pinch of cinnamon can be substituted for the cloves.

Time: 30 minutes
Very easy

2 lb apricots
1 cup sugar
2 cloves
½ cup brandy

Wipe the apricots with a damp cloth, pit, and place in two jars, adding half the sugar and a clove to each. Seal and leave to stand for 10 days, turning the jars upside down several times morning and evening. Leave to stand in a sunny place if possible. When the 10 days have passed, add the brandy, seal tightly, and wait 1 month before using.

• • •

CHERRIES IN BRANDY

Choose firm-fleshed varieties of cherries such as Bing. Morello cherries also work well but you will need to add more sugar.

Time: 30 minutes
Very easy

2¼ lb cherries
2 cups sugar
½ cup water
2¼ cups brandy or alternative spirit

Wash and dry the cherries; snip off the stem to within ½ in of the fruit. Cook the sugar and water over gentle heat for 10 minutes for a clear syrup. Pack the cherries loosely in jars and fill half way up the jars with the sugar syrup. Pour in enough brandy (or other spirit of your choice) to cover; seal tightly and store in a cool dry place for at least 1 month before using.

• • •

33

RAISINS IN BRANDY

Time: 10 minutes + standing time
Very easy

1 lb seedless white raisins
½ cup water
1¼ cups sugar
1 cup brandy

Soak the seedless white raisins in warm water; drain and dry briefly on kitchen paper towels before transfering to jars. Make a clear sugar syrup by boiling the sugar and water together for a few minutes. Fill the jars halfway with this syrup. Top up with sufficient brandy to just cover the seedless white raisins. Seal tightly and store in a cool, dry place. These will be ready to use after 1 month.

•   •   •

CANNED FIGS

Select unblemished, barely ripe, firm figs otherwise they will disintegrate when cooked.

Time: 1 hour
Very easy

2 lb figs
2 cups sugar
2 cups water
2 cloves
1 vanilla bean or a few drops vanilla extract
pinch cinnamon
juice of 1 lemon

Arrange the figs in a single layer, stalks uppermost, in a wide saucepan. Mix the sugar, water, spices, and lemon juice; pour over the figs and cook very gently, without stirring or turning, for 20

□ Choose only the best, freshest fruit for canning when it is just ripe. Rinse the jars and lids with very hot water mixed with a good pinch of soda; dry thoroughly. It is best to use new rubber seals or rubber rimmed lids each time. The fruit should only be washed, peeled and pitted just before it is placed in the jars or it will discolor. Use a very sharp stainless steel fruit knife. Press gently down on the fruit and shake the jar gently once the sugar syrup has been added to release any air bubbles. Seal the jars and then sterilize.

□ Top-quality produce must also be used for candied fruit, to be peeled and pitted just before it has its first soaking in very thick, totally clear sugar syrup. Special dipping pans with a removable basket are available which can also be used for fondants. The fruit is placed in the basket, lowered into the syrup and left to stand undisturbed for at least 12 hours in a warm place, covered by a clean cloth.

□ Many people differentiate between preserves and conserves by stating that in the former the fruit is left whole or cut into fairly large pieces whereas for a conserve it is often sieved. Regardless of what process it undergoes, all fruit must be well rinsed, blackberries and raspberries included, and then gently dried in a clean cloth or kitchen towels. Cooking times before the mixture jells will vary in practice, since the moisture content of the fruit will vary. The boiling mixture should be frequently skimmed to remove foam, and stirred with a long handled wooden spoon; when ready the hot preserve is poured into jars and tightly sealed. A disk of strong cellophane, greaseproof or waxed paper can be placed on the surface before sealing or a thin layer of paraffin.

□ The proportion of sugar to fruit plays a vital part in jelling and keeping qualities of preserves and jellies. Low sugar jams may develop mold growth; too much sugar makes for a sickly jam. The trend toward a lower sugar content often means that sterilization is necessary. Do not use jars with a capacity exceeding 8 oz–1 lb, or they will sit in the refrigerator for weeks once opened.

□ A jelly or candy thermometer is the most reliable method to test for jell, otherwise check by using a cold metal spoon to take up a spoonful; tip the spoon so that the jelly can fall back into the boiling mixture: if it runs off in a stream or series of drips it needs more cooking; if it falls off the spoon in a sheet, it is done. Or place a large drop on a cold plate; tip the plate, and if the jam stays put it is ready. In some cases the fruit can be cooked for a little while in the sugar syrup, then removed with a slotted ladle and the syrup reduced until jelling point; return the fruit to the syrup, bring back to a boil, and transfer to jars. The fruit retains more of its original flavor with this method.

minutes. Leave to cool before carefully transferring the figs with a slotted spoon to sterilized jars. Strain the syrup and juice in the pan and pour over the figs. Seal when completely cold.

• • •

GRAPES IN BRANDY

Time: 20 minutes + standing time
Very easy

2¼ lb white grapes
½ cup sugar
2¼ cups brandy or other spirit (e.g. grappa)
generous pinch cinnamon

few drops vanilla extract
2 cloves

Rinse the grapes carefully in cold water; use sharp pointed scissors to snip off each grape, leaving its tiny stalk attached. Prick each grape in several places with a needle and drop into sterilized jars. Add half the sugar and cinnamon, vanilla, and cloves to the jars and then pour the brandy over the grapes.
Seal very tightly and keep in a cool, dark and dry place for about 2 months. Turn the jars upside down every so often to distribute the flavorings evenly.
Serve in very small quantities at the end of a meal. Use any spare liquid as a liqueur if you wish.

B uttercreams and
custards, simple to
make, yet delicious,
had humble origins as homely
preparations which could be
made in next to no time and were
enjoyed by all the family. The
ingredients are always to hand in
every kitchen and their creation
was probably pure chance, when
a resourceful mother centuries
ago tried another way to make
nourishing foods appeal to her
children. Homemade eggs and
milk or cream custard with
genuine flavoring tastes infinitely
better than commercially
prepared custard and only needs
some careful stirring over gentle
heat for a velvety smoothness.

BUTTERCREAM

Try to use sweet butter for this recipe. It can be flavored with coffee or liqueurs; add the latter a very little at a time or the cream could curdle. Use as a filling for cakes.

Time: 40 minutes
Very easy

1 cup (2 sticks) butter
1 egg white
½ cup sugar

Let the butter reach room temperature before you beat it until very pale and light (use a hand held electric beater or balloon wire whisk). Beat the egg white until stiff but not dry, add the sugar, continue beating for a few minutes and then fold it carefully into the butter, using a metal spoon to avoid pressing air out of the whites.

• • •

CHOCOLATE BUTTERCREAM

A voluptuously rich cream for cake fillings and frostings.

Time: 45 minutes
Very easy

½ cup (1 stick) sweet butter
2 egg yolks
generous ½ cup sugar
4 oz (4 squares) unsweetened or bakers' chocolate

Beat the butter energetically until pale and creamy. Beat in the yolks one at a time and continue beating for 2 or 3 minutes longer. Add the sugar and keep beating the mixture for 10 minutes. Break the chocolate into pieces and melt

□ *There are many different types of custard, far removed from the bright yellow commercially prepared or instant varieties which are useful but inferior substitutes. Classic custard, made with eggs and milk or cream is used hot or cold as a sweet sauce for almost any dessert; left to cool and thicken slightly in small, deep dishes, and served with fruit or biscuit/cookies or on its own. Classic custard (crème anglaise) can be set with gelatin or forms the basis of many ice creams.*

□ *Pastry cream (crème pâtissière) is usually made with flour as the main thickening agent but it can be made with gelatin. The egg yolks also play their part in giving the cream a thick, velvety texture. Both pastry cream and classic custard need careful attention and very gentle heat while cooking or the yolks (when making custard in particular) can curdle; cook over an extremely gentle heat or use a double boiler to prevent this happening. Pastry cream makes a delicious filling for choux pastry buns, fried doughnuts, other yeast dough buns and many other cakes.*
Sabayon sauce and Zabaglione rely solely on egg yolks for thickening, resulting in a very light, airy concoction: always cook over hot water to prevent curdling.

□ *Buttercreams and hard sauces present no problems and other sweet sauces made with butter which have to be cooked just need a little care.*

□ *Sugar syrup forms the basis of many sauces. First a thick syrup is made by boiling 1 lb sugar with 2¼ cups water for exactly 10 minutes. A thinner sauce will result if you vary the proportions to one-third sugar to two-thirds water. This syrup is then added a minute amount at a time to the fruit (such as strawberries, raspberries, apricots) which has been sieved or processed in a blender to make it smooth and creamy. The sweetened fruit sauce is then cooked until it is thick enough, (use a double boiler to prevent the sauce catching and burning) then put through a very fine sieve; it can be used hot or cold for desserts, cakes and pastries.*

□ *Frosting is one of the finishing touches to cakes of all sizes, sponge cakes in particular, when a mixture of sugar, water, flavoring and/or coloring is spread over the cake. Buttercream frosting is not meant to have a very smooth finish and the texture remains creamy and does not harden like sugar frosting as it dries.*

over hot water. Continue stirring the chocolate away from the heat until it has cooled, before beating into the butter mixture.

• • •

COFFEE BUTTER-CREAM

An extra rich version, used for mocha fillings and frostings.

Time: 45 minutes
Very easy

1 egg yolk
⅓ cup sugar
¼ cup all-purpose flour
¼ cup very strong black coffee
1 cup milk
½ cup (1 stick) sweet butter
1 tbsp confectioners' sugar
1 tbsp brandy

Beat the egg yolk with the sugar until it is very pale and the sugar has dissolved. Mix in the flour, followed by the hot coffee. Stir in the milk and cook over very gentle heat (or in a double boiler) until the mixture starts to thicken. Continue stirring until the mixture has completely cooled to avoid a skin forming. Beat the butter and confectioners' sugar until very pale in a separate bowl; beat in the custard mixture a very little at a time and flavor with the brandy.

• • •

GELATIN CUSTARD
■ *this should be chilled for at least six hours in the refrigerator to ensure a firm set in molds; it can also be used for cakes or fruit flans, or poured into individual glass dishes and decorated when set with canned pineapple, candied cherries, and angelica.*

LEMON BUTTER-CREAM

Another filling for cakes and pastries. Use orange juice instead of lemon as an alternative flavor.

Time: 40 minutes
Very easy

½ cup lemon juice
3 egg yolks
1 cup sugar
½ cup (1 stick) sweet butter

Strain the lemon juice. Beat the eggs and sugar until very pale. Beat in the lemon juice a very little at a time. Beat in the butter, cut into very small pieces and softened at room temperature (not melted), a piece at a time. Keep this soft, light cream in a cool place until you are ready to use it.

• • •

GELATIN CUSTARD

Time: 20 minutes
Easy

4 egg yolks
½ cup sugar
2¼ cups milk
peel of 1 lemon, grated
2½ tbsp powdered gelatin

Beat the egg yolks with the sugar in a heatproof bowl for about 5 minutes. Stir in the milk and the grated lemon peel. Dissolve the gelatin following the manufacturer's instructions. Place the bowl containing the lemon custard mixture over gently

simmering water and cook, stirring continuously, until it has started to thicken. Remove from the heat and stir in the gelatin. Stir very thoroughly until the custard starts to cool. Leave to set.

• • •

CHOCOLATE MOUSSE

A very rich yet light mousse made with sweet drinking chocolate powder; serve in a large glass bowl or in individual glass dishes. If chilled in the refrigerator for at

least 6 hours in one or more molds, it can be turned out like a blancmange. You can substitute 3½ tbsp good quality instant coffee or finely grated orange or lemon peel for the chocolate powder.

Time: 30 minutes
Very easy

½ cup (1 stick) butter
8 tbsp drinking chocolate
   powder
4 eggs

Melt the butter in a fairly large bowl over hot water; stir in the chocolate powder. Remove from the heat and allow to cool. Stir in the egg yolks, one at a time. Beat the egg whites until very stiff but not dry; fold them into the chocolate mixture. Transfer to a dish and chill for 2 hours before serving.

• • •

CLASSIC CUSTARD

Time: 20 minutes
Easy

2¼ cups milk
4 egg yolks
½ cup sugar
few drops vanilla extract

Bring the milk to a boil, remove from the heat and set aside. Beat the egg yolks, sugar, and vanilla extract very vigorously for 5–10 minutes, or until the "ribbon" stage is reached (i.e. when the whisk is lifted above the bowl, a continuous ribbon of the pale mixture should fall from it). Combine the milk with the egg mixture; place over hot water and cook, stirring continually, until it starts to thicken. Do not allow to boil or it will scramble. Strain through a fine sieve and serve hot or cold as required.

• • •

CLASSIC CUSTARD
■ A vanilla-flavored pouring custard made with egg yolks and rich milk, equally good hot or cold as an accompaniment to a wide range of desserts. It can also be served in small, deep dishes with cookies or with fresh fruit such as oranges, peaches, strawberries, etc.

CHOCOLATE CUSTARD

A superb but easy and quick dessert can be made by placing slices of sponge cake in a glass bowl, sprinkling with a little liqueur and then pouring this custard all over the top.

Time: 35 minutes
Easy

2¼ cups milk
peel of 1 orange
few drops vanilla extract
4 egg yolks
½ cup sugar
4 oz (4 squares) semisweet
    chocolate

Place the milk in a saucepan with the orange peel (and a piece of vanilla bean if not using extract) and bring to boiling point; remove from the heat. Beat the egg yolks with the sugar and vanilla extract until pale and foamy. Gradually whisk in the warm milk. Place the bowl over a saucepan of gently simmering water; stir continuously with a wooden spoon. Melt the chocolate in another bowl over hot water with 1 tbsp warm water, stirring continuously. Once the custard has started to thicken, stir in the melted chocolate until blended.

• • •

LIQUEUR-FLAVORED PASTRY CREAM

Pastry cream (crème pâtissière) is ideal as a filling for cakes, doughnuts, and pastries; alternatively, serve in small deep dishes, topped with strawberries or orange or kiwi slices. *(See also the step-by-step recipe on page 42.)*

Time: 20 minutes
Very easy

4 egg yolks
½ cup sugar
1 tbsp orange peel, grated
¼ cup all-purpose flour
2¼ cups milk
1 tbsp liqueur of your choice

Beat the egg yolks and sugar with a whisk for 5–10 minutes; add the grated orange peel. Sift in the flour gradually while stirring with a wooden spoon, followed by the hot milk and the liqueur. Heat very slowly until boiling point is reached; simmer for 2 minutes and then allow to cool, stirring frequently to prevent a skin forming.

• • •

TURBAN MOLD
■ *Seventeenth-century French engraving.*

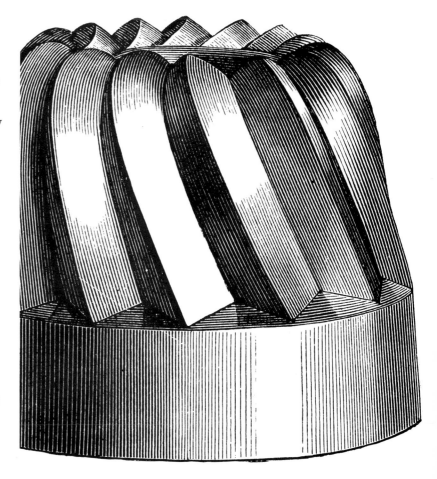

This orange liqueur cream makes a wonderful filling and is also excellent on its own as a dessert. The method is straightforward and preparation will only take about 20 minutes.

4 egg yolks
½ cup sugar
1 tbsp grated orange peel
¼ cup all-purpose flour
2¼ cups hot milk
2 tbsp Grand Marnier

Beat the egg yolks with the sugar until pale and fluffy. (Use a hand-held electric whisk to save time, or a balloon wire whisk.)

Add the grated orange peel and sprinkle in the sifted flour while continuing to beat.

Beat in the milk, adding it in a thin stream. Add the Grand Marnier.

Cook, stirring continuously, over very low heat until the mixture comes to a gentle boil; simmer, stirring, for 2 minutes.

Remove from the heat and stir frequently as the mixture cools to prevent a skin forming.

If serving as a dessert, pour into coupes and decorate.

LEMON CUSTARD
■ *Serve hot in a jug as a pouring custard or pour into small dishes and allow to cool before decorating with orange sections and piped whipped cream.*

SAINT HONORÉ PASTRY CREAM

Half of this cream will be colored and flavored with unsweetened cocoa powder.

Time: 30 minutes
Very easy

1 tbsp powdered gelatin
3 egg yolks
½ cup sugar
½ cup all-purpose flour
generous 1 cup milk
few drops vanilla extract or
   1 tbsp vanilla sugar
1 egg white
1 cup whipping or heavy
   cream
3½ tbsp unsweetend cocoa
   powder

Dissolve the gelatin according to the manufacturer's instructions. Beat the egg yolks and sugar until pale and frothy (5–10 minutes). Stir in the sifted flour a little at a time, followed by the hot milk. Stir continuously while cooking over gentle heat until the mixture begins to thicken. Remove from the heat and add the gelatin. (Continue stirring until the mixture begins to cool. Flavor with the vanilla extract or vanilla sugar. When cold and just beginning to show signs of setting, fold in the stiffly beaten egg white, followed by the stiffly beaten cream. Transfer half the mixture to another bowl and stir in the sifted cocoa powder, a little at a time.

•   •   •

FRANGIPANE PASTRY CREAM

Time: 30 minutes
Very easy

2¼ cups milk
pinch salt
few drops vanilla extract
2 whole eggs and 2 egg yolks
½ cup sugar
¼ cup all-purpose flour
2 tbsp sweet butter
½ cup very finely crushed
   amaretti or crisp macaroons

Bring the milk to a boil with the salt, then strain. Beat the whole eggs and the extra yolks with the sugar in a saucepan. Combine with the flour and then stir in the milk. Cook over gentle heat, stirring all the time, until the mixture thickens; as soon as it reaches boiling point, remove from the heat. Stir in the butter and the finely crushed almond cookies.

•   •   •

LEMON CUSTARD

Time: 30 minutes
Easy

1 cup strained lemon juice
peel of 2 lemons, finely grated
4 egg yolks and 1 egg white
½ cup sugar
generous 1 cup heavy cream

Mix the lemon juice and grated peel. Beat the egg yolks and sugar for 10 minutes in a heatproof bowl; add the lemon juice and peel. Place the bowl over hot water and cook, stirring continuously with a wooden spoon, until the mixture thickens a little (when the coating on the back of the wooden spoon leaves a clear trace if you draw a finger over it, it is ready). Beat the egg white and cream, separately, until very stiff. Fold into the cooled custard first the egg white, and then the cream.

•   •   •

PASTRY CREAM WITH
FRUIT
■ Light and digestible,
cornstarch is a very useful
ingredient for the
storecupboard. When used
for custard, it gives a velvety
and light result. Potato flour
can be substituted for
cornstarch.

PASTRY CREAM WITH FRUIT

Time: 40 minutes
Very easy

EGG WHITES

For egg whites to stay firmer for longer when beaten, add a pinch of cream of tartar after the first few seconds' beating. Add the sugar gradually when the whites are already thick and snowy. The beaten egg white will cling to the bowl and will not move when the bowl is turned upside down. Do not overdo the beating before adding the sugar, or the egg whites will look dry and grainy.

4 egg yolks
¾ cup sugar
few drops vanilla extract
¼ cup cornstarch
2¼ cups milk
2 peaches
juice of 1 lemon

Beat the eggs with ½ cup sugar until very pale and frothy. Beat in the sifted cornstarch, followed by the hot milk. Cook over gentle heat, stirring constantly with a wooden spoon. When the custard has thickened, remove from the heat and stir until it has cooled a little; pour into a bowl and chill, covered with saran wrap to prevent a skin forming. Blanch, peel, pit, and slice the peaches into a bowl; sprinkle with the sugar and lemon juice, stir, and leave to stand for 10 minutes before sieving or blending. Combine the chilled custard from the refrigerator with the peach purée, spoon into a large crystal bowl or individual glass dishes and decorate with fruit.

• • •

PASTRY CREAM (CRÈME PÂTISSIÈRE)

Pastry cream is used as a filling for any number of cakes and also in fruit tarts, as a layer underneath the fruit. The inclusion of flour makes it less likely to scramble than classic custard (crème anglaise).

Time: 20 minutes
Very easy

4 egg yolks
½ cup sugar
¼ cup all-purpose flour
2¼ cups milk

Beat the eggs and sugar with a whisk until very pale and creamy. Add a little of the sifted flour at a time. Gradually pour in a thin stream of very hot milk, beating all the time. Cook over low heat, still beating constantly, and draw aside from the heat as soon as the mixture comes to a boil.

• • •

SABAYON

This quaint old way of measuring the ingredients is very practical: eggs vary so much in size that the "half shell measure" takes care of

proportions. Sabayon, or Zabaglione (as it is known in Italy), is a classic dessert.

Time: 30 minutes
Easy

6 egg yolks
6 half eggshells sugar
6 half eggshells dry Marsala

Beat the egg yolks with the sugar for at least 10 minutes with a whisk. Carry on beating as you add the Marsala a little at a time. Place over barely simmering water and beat until the mixture doubles in volume, becoming light and frothy and rising up in the bowl. The eggs will curdle if they become too hot. Serve hot, with cookies, or continue beating away from the heat until cool. If wished, fold 1 stiffly beaten egg white into the cold Sabayon; a few little wild strawberries could be sprinkled on top.

• • •

SABAYON WITH AMARETTI

If you cannot find amaretti (made with apricot kernels), hard macaroons or ratafias will do. Top with piped whipped cream and a whole amaretto.

Time: 30 minutes
Easy

6 very fresh egg yolks
6 half eggshells sugar
6 half eggshells Madeira or
   port
6 finely crushed amaretti
   cookies
pinch cinnamon

45

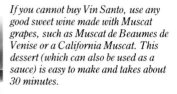

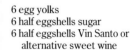

If you cannot buy Vin Santo, use any good sweet wine made with Muscat grapes, such as Muscat de Beaumes de Venise or a California Muscat. This dessert (which can also be used as a sauce) is easy to make and takes about 30 minutes.

6 egg yolks
6 half eggshells sugar
6 half eggshells Vin Santo or
　　alternative sweet wine

Beat the yolks and sugar together for 10 minutes or until very pale, fluffy, and greatly increased in volume.

Beat in the wine a little at a time.

Cook by the bain-marie method (you can use a double boiler or simply sit your small mixing bowl securely on a saucepan of simmering water). Beat constantly until the egg mixture has expanded in volume; it will rise up in the pan or bowl. Do not overheat or it will curdle.

For an exceptionally light (but less traditional) Sabayon, allow to cool a little and fold in stiffly beaten egg whites.

Transfer to small, deep glass dishes or large wine glasses and serve. Add cookies and decoration to taste.

COFFEE SABAYON
■ The basic custard mix may be flavored with liqueurs or sweet, fortified wines such as Marsala. Sweet dessert wine, white wine, champagne, or coffee may also be used.

Beat the egg yolks and sugar vigorously until very pale and greatly increased in volume. Continue beating as you add the Madeira or port a little at a time, followed by the amaretti and cinnamon. Cook over hot water, stirring continuously. Draw aside from the heat as soon as the Sabayon has thickened and risen up in the bowl. Do not overheat or it will curdle.

• • •

COFFEE SABAYON

Time: 30 minutes
Easy

6 egg yolks
6 half eggshells sugar
6 half eggshells very strong
   black coffee
few roasted coffee beans for
   decoration

Beat the egg yolks and sugar until very pale (5–10 minutes) and continue beating as you add the coffee a little at a time. Cook over simmering water, beating all the time until the mixture has almost doubled in volume and become quite thick. Make sure the water continues to simmer and does not boil fast; the Sabayon will curdle if it becomes too hot. When thick, remove from the heat and serve hot or cold (see previous recipe). Spoon into individual glass dishes and decorate with coffee beans.

• • •

CREAM

The least dense part of milk, containing the highest proportion of fat. Do not overbeat heavy cream, and use it as soon as possible. When a pouring cream is needed, use either heavy or light cream. Cream thickens far more quickly when beaten cold, after a few hours in the refrigerator.

CHOCOLATE CREAM

Use to fill and cover all sorts of cakes, especially log cakes. As the mixture sets quickly, use immediately while it is workable before it has time to grow cold and harden.

Time: 10 minutes
Very easy

10 oz (10 squares)
   unsweetened or semisweet
   chocolate
1 cup heavy cream

Grate the chocolate. Bring the milk to a boil. Add the chocolate, and remove from the heat. Stir until the chocolate has melted completely and the mixture has cooled to lukewarm, then use at once.

• • •

CHANTILLY CREAM

Time: 10 minutes
Very easy

2¼ cups very fresh heavy
    cream
½ cup confectioners' sugar
2–3 drops vanilla extract

Chill the cream, the bowl, and
the whisk in the refrigerator
for several hours before
preparing the cream. Beat
until stiff, then fold in the
sifted confectioners' sugar and
the vanilla extract. Chill until
ready to serve.

•   •   •

COFFEE-
FLAVORED
CHANTILLY
CREAM

*This variation is excellent
served just as it is in very small
glass dishes or stem glasses,
topped with a few coffee beans.
Grated orange or lemon peel
make good alternative
flavorings.*

Time: 15 minutes
Very easy

1 quart very fresh heavy
    cream
½ cup confectioners' sugar
2 tbsp coffee extract or good
    instant coffee

Chill the cream, bowl, and
whisk in the freezer for 15
minutes before beating the
cream until stiff. Fold in the
sifted sugar and the coffee.
Chill until required.

•   •   •

CHANTILLY CREAM
■ *The queen of creams, used just as it is or as the basis for many different preparations; it is indispensable for the decoration of desserts. Take the cream out of the refrigerator only just before whipping to speed up the process.*

PRÉSENTOIR
■ A sixteenth-century
German cake slice.

BUTTERCREAMS • CUSTARDS • SAUCES • FROSTINGS

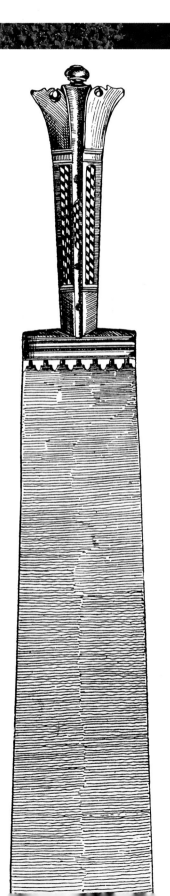

VANILLA SAUCE

Serve this sauce hot with ice cream and puddings, warm or cold with cooked fruit.

Time: 20 minutes
Very easy

1 cup milk or half-and-half
1 cup light cream
few drops vanilla extract
1 egg yolk
¼ cup sugar

Heat the milk and cream over very low heat. Beat the egg yolk with the sugar until very pale and frothy. Add the hot milk and cream in a thin stream to the egg and sugar, beating all the time. If to be served lukewarm or cold, stir until the sauce has cooled to avoid a skin forming.

• • •

COFFEE SAUCE

Hot coffee sauce goes well with vanilla or chocolate ice cream, or with almond or filbert desserts and puddings.

Time: 20 minutes
Very easy

1 cup milk
1 cup light cream or half-and-half
5 tbsp very strong black coffee or 1 tbsp good instant coffee powder
1 egg yolk
¼ cup sugar

Heat the milk, cream (or half-and-half), and coffee very slowly. Beat the egg yolk and sugar vigorously until pale (5–10 minutes). Continue beating as you pour in a trickle of the hot milk and cream. Strain the sauce before serving hot.

• • •

CHOCOLATE SAUCE

A versatile sauce which, served hot, is a good accompaniment to a variety of desserts. It is delicious with mint, orange or raspberry ice cream.

Time: 10 minutes
Very easy

7 oz (7 squares) bitter
  chocolate
1 tbsp sweet butter
generous 1 cup heavy cream
3 tbsp sugar

Grate the chocolate and melt in the top of a double boiler with the butter. Add the cream and sugar and heat, stirring continuously. Serve hot in a sauceboat or bowl.

• • •

FRUIT SAUCE

Time: 10 minutes
Very easy

1 lb raspberries or red
  currants
3 tbsp Beaumes de Venise,
  sweet sherry, or sweet
  Marsala
½ cup sugar

Heat the sugar with 2 tbsp boiling water for 1–2 minutes; place the fruit, wine, and this

FRUIT SAUCES

Very simple to make: peel fresh fruit and then sieve it or put in a blender, and mix with a sugar syrup made by melting sugar in a little water. Fruit sauces go wonderfully well with ice cream and with any dessert or gâteau that would otherwise be a little dry.

sugar syrup in a blender and process until very smooth. (Add one of the following as an extra flavoring if you wish: pinch of cinnamon, ground cloves, nutmeg, grated lemon or orange peel.) Make this sauce with other fruit, such as apricots, kiwi fruit, cherries, etc. to add color and flavor to a variety of desserts.

• • •

FRUIT SAUCE
■ *Many varieties of fruit can be used for these fresh-tasting sweet sauces to enhance ice cream, rice pudding, and molded milk jellies or blancmange.*

LEMON SAUCE

A fairly thick sauce which looks a little like jam. Just a few spoonfuls will be enough to add an extra taste to baked pears or to moisten a chocolate cake if it is a little dry.

Time: 20 minutes
Very easy

1 cup sugar
4 tbsp hot water
peel of 1 lemon, grated
½ cup lemon juice
2½ tbsp orange juice
2 egg yolks
1 tbsp kirsch

Heat the sugar and water until it just reaches boiling point, stirring constantly. Add the grated lemon peel and lemon and orange juice, and stir before removing from the heat. Beat the egg yolks in a bowl with the kirsch; continue beating while adding the sugar syrup in a very thin stream. Strain and serve in a sauceboat.

• • •

SUGAR AND WATER FROSTING

This is one of the quickest and simplest ways to decorate a cake or small pastry.

Time: 5 minutes
Very easy

1 cup confectioners' sugar
2½ tbsp water
few drops food coloring e.g. cochineal, etc. (optional)

51

Sift the sugar into a bowl and use a wooden spoon to add the water a little at a time. The white frosting should be very thick but still spreadable. Use a coloring of your choice if you like.

• • •

ROYAL FROSTING

This bears some resemblance to fondant frosting but is much less trouble to make. Use for piping a design with a very small tube.

Time: 10 minutes
Very easy

1 egg white
1¾ cups confectioners' sugar
2 tsp lemon juice

Beat the egg white until stiff, adding the sugar a little at a time. Add the lemon juice.

Cover the bowl with a damp cloth if the frosting is not to be used immediately.

• • •

FONDANT FROSTING

A sugar paste with a gleaming finish used to cover cakes; liqueur or chocolate can be added for flavor. More complicated than the preceding recipes for frostings but well

CONFECTIONERS' SUGAR

This extremely fine, highly refined powdered sugar is put to all sorts of uses in bakery. Very little is sufficient to sweeten cream, or to add to beaten egg whites for meringue. Used for uncooked frostings and general decoration.

worth the trouble, fondant frosting keeps well if not used immediately.

Time: 20 minutes
Easy

scant ½ lb cube sugar
2½ tbsp water
½ tsp cream of tartar

Place the sugar in a saucepan with 2 tbsp water. Add the cream of tartar and boil, skimming the surface frequently. Cook to the small or soft ball stage (241–244° F). Lightly sprinkle a marble slab or suitable work surface with iced water and pour the syrup onto this. When it has cooled a little, slide a spatula (a short wide one) underneath the edges and tip the thickening fondant over toward the center; work all the way round the edge in this way and repeat until the fondant whitens and becomes opaque. Use your hands to work the fondant into a ball; this will keep well in a large sealed jar. When it is time to use it, warm in a saucepan ready for spreading.

• • •

LIQUEUR FROSTING

Another simple recipe. Choose a liqueur which will match or complement the flavor of the cake you are to frost; use Grand Marnier flavored frosting for an orange cake and Crème de Menthe, Tia Maria or Kahula for a chocolate cake.

Time: 5 minutes
Very easy

scant 1 cup confectioners' sugar
1 tbsp liqueur of your choice
1 tbsp water

Sift the sugar into a bowl and add the liqueur a little at a time followed by the water. Mix thoroughly to make a very smooth spreadable frosting.

• • •

CHOCOLATE FROSTING

A shiny, satiny frosting, which is perfect for chocolate cakes and profiteroles.

Time: 10 minutes
Very easy

SUGAR-FROSTED FRUIT
■ If you want a smooth, glassy coating, dip the fruit in a sugar syrup made by melting 2 cups sugar in ½ cup liqueur topped up to 4 cups with water. Boil for 1 minute then add a pinch of cream of tartar diluted with 1 tbsp water. Cook to hard crack stage (approx. 300°F). Leave to dry after dipping.

2 oz (2 squares) baker's chocolate or fine unsweetened chocolate
scant 1 cup confectioners' sugar
2 tbsp water

Break the chocolate into pieces and melt over hot water, stirring continuously. Add the sugar, mix well, then stir in the water a few drops at a time. Remove from the heat and continue stirring until the frosting has cooled and thickened a little. Frost the cake and leave to grow cold and set.

SUGAR-FROSTED FRUIT

20 minutes
Very easy

2 lb mixed fruit
2 cups sugar

Pick over the fruit and rinse in iced water. Dry gently. Melt scant ½ cup of the sugar in ¼ cup water; leave to cool completely. Place the remaining sugar in a wide bowl. Dip the fruit in the sugar syrup and then in the sugar in the bowl. Arrange the fruit in rows on a marble slab or work surface to set and dry.

CUBE SUGAR

Useful in patisserie and ice cream making: when the rough cubes are rubbed against orange or lemon peel they absorb the essential oils. They are then melted in a little water and the resulting syrup gives a strong, true flavor.

The pastries in this chapter are made with the two basic ingredients of flour and butter but eggs, sugar, finely grated lemon or orange peel, water, and chocolate are also added according to which is best suited to achieve a certain texture or the desired flavor. The resulting mixtures are used to make delicious, melt-in-the-mouth pies, tarts, flans, petit fours, and cookies. The combination of a fairly high proportion of sugar and butter with the flour gives a pastry which is very tender and friable, easy to cut and all too easy to eat; this sweet egg pastry, also known as pâte sucrée, is very quick to make and requires no magic pastrycook's touch to be successful. Pie dough is straightforward but perhaps "good pastry hands" do play a part in achieving an excellent result; it can be made with or without sugar depending on whether it is to be used for sweet or savory dishes.

SWEET EGG PASTRY I (PÂTE SUCRÉE)

Suitable for all sweet tarts, this pastry should be worked quickly and can be frozen. Thaw for at least 3 hours at room temperature before you try to roll it out and use it. If it is a little cold still, roll out with a wine bottle full of hot water.

Time: 20 minutes + resting time
Easy

2½ cups all-purpose flour
scant ½ cup sugar
½ cup + 2 tbsp (1¼ sticks) softened (not melted) butter
3 egg yolks
peel of 1 lemon, grated
pinch salt
1 extra tbsp butter
1 extra tbsp flour

Sift the flour in a mound onto a marble pastry slab, make a well in the middle, and place the sugar and the softened butter cut into very small pieces in it, together with the egg yolks, grated lemon peel, and salt. Blend until the dough is soft and smooth. (Do this in an electric mixer, using the dough or pastry hook if you prefer.) Shape into a ball, wrap in floured waxed paper or saran wrap; leave to rest in a cool place for 30 minutes. Roll out on the pastry slab (between two layers of waxed paper to help prevent it sticking). Grease a pie shell not more than 1¼ in deep and 10 in in diameter with the extra tbsp butter, sprinkle with the extra 1 tbsp flour, tipping out excess, and line with the pastry. If baking "blind" (i.e. without a filling),

□ *At its best, sweet egg pastry should be friable and melt in the mouth. It is the basic pastry used for tarts and pies, little teatime pastries and many types of cookies (using cookie cutters of all shapes and sizes).*

□ *Classic sweet egg pastry (pâte sucrée), for which all your ingredients, including the eggs and the butter, should have reached room temperature before you start work, is made as follows: sift the flour and a pinch of salt into a mound on a pastry slab (preferably marble) or into a large mixing bowl; make a well in the middle and place the sugar, egg yolks, softened butter, and a little finely grated orange or lemon peel in it. (The quantities may vary from those given in the basic recipe on this page, but the proportions remain the same.) If the pastry dough is too dry, add 1 tbsp water. Prepare the dough in advance so that it can rest for at least 30 minutes before it is needed. Make it the day before if you prefer, wrap in saran wrap or waxed paper and keep in the refrigerator. It can also be frozen.*

□ *Once the ingredients have been mixed together, press down on the mixture with the base of your palm and push it away from you, crushing it as you go, working all the dough in this way. Repeat two or three times so that the mixture is well blended. Roll out with waxed paper above and below the dough, or press into a flan ring on a cookie sheet (work with waxed paper between your fingers and the dough). It should not be very thin or it will disintegrate too easily when cooked or may burn. An even cooking temperature is all-important; position toward the top of the oven, preheated to 350°F.*

□ *Chocolate, almonds, filberts etc. can be added to the dough (when it becomes Milanese, Viennese, Neapolitan, Roman, etc.), or it can be made less rich by omitting some (or all) of the eggs and substituting water. The cooking temperature remains the same.*

□ *Pie dough or pâte brisée is similar to sweet egg pastry: the ingredients remain the same except for the sugar, very little or none of which is used and pie dough is used for both sweet and savory preparations. Pie shells are often baked empty, in which case prick the surface with a fork, cover with greaseproof paper and fill with dried beans before baking. It is a good idea to grease even nonstick baking pans with butter and even give them a dusting of flour if you want to ensure that the tart slides out cleanly when cooked.*

prick the surface all over with a fork; cover with a circle of waxed paper and fill with dried navy beans. Bake for about 40 minutes at 350° F. Remove beans and paper for the last 10 minutes of cooking.

• • •

SWEET EGG PASTRY II

Less rich than the previous recipe, it can be put to exactly the same uses.

Time: 20 minutes + resting time
Easy

2½ cups all-purpose flour
scant ½ cup (1 stick) butter
½ cup sugar
1 egg
peel of 1 lemon, grated
pinch salt

Sift the flour in a mound onto a marble pastry slab or work surface, add the softened butter, cut into small pieces, the sugar, the whole egg (beaten with a fork for a few seconds), lemon peel, and salt. Combine thoroughly while working the dough for as short a time as possible. Leave to rest in a cool place wrapped in floured saran wrap for 30 minutes before using as required (see previous recipe). Do not roll out too thinly.

• • •

SWEET PIE DOUGH (PÂTE BRISÉE)

If you omit the sugar, this pastry can also be used for

PINEAPPLE TART
■ Sweet pie dough (pâte brisée) could be substituted for this sweet egg pastry. If fresh pineapple is unavailable use canned, well drained, and patted fairly dry with paper towels.

savory pies, flans, and cocktail snacks, with various fillings of meat, vegetables, fish etc.

Time: 20 minutes
Easy

2½ cups all-purpose flour
½ cup + 2 tbsp (1¼ sticks) butter
2 tbsp sugar
pinch salt
3 tbsp cold water

Sift the flour onto a marble pastry slab, make a well in the middle and place the softened butter, cut into very small pieces in it, together with the sugar and the salt. Rub in quickly using the tips of your fingers until the butter has absorbed all the flour. Add the water, mix briefly by hand or in a mixer with the dough hook attachment, then shape into a ball; wrap in saran wrap and place in the refrigerator for 30 minutes. Roll out between waxed paper and use to line a greased and floured pie shell pan not more than 1¼ in deep, 10 in in diameter. If baking without a filling, prick the surface of the bottom all over with a fork, cover with a circle of waxed paper, and fill with dried beans. Bake for 40 minutes at 350° F. Remove the paper and beans for the last 10 minutes.

• • •

PINEAPPLE TART

Time: 1 hour
Easy

1 quantity Sweet Egg Pastry II (see page 56)
2 tbsp Graham cracker or plain cookie crumbs

SWEET EGG PASTRY

Excellent for sweet pies, flans, and tarts: the sugar gives a friable, slightly crumbly texture, while the eggs act as a binding agent. It is not kneaded and benefits from not being worked too much. Quantities given on this page are for a large pie pan.

1 lb all-purpose flour
2 tbsp confectioners' sugar
2 tsp salt
1¼ cups (2½ sticks) sweet butter, worked at room temperature until soft
2 whole eggs or 4 egg yolks

Have the butter at room temperature for 1–2 hours and work briefly with a wooden spoon to soften. Sift the flour, a pinch of salt and all the sugar into a mound on a marble slab or work surface.

Make a well in the center, place the butter in it, and break the eggs on top of the butter. Use your fingertips to combine the butter and eggs, just enough to mix properly.

Use a spatula or broad-bladed knife to scoop the surrounding dry ingredients into the very soft butter and egg mixture in the center; "cut" the ingredients into one another, still using a knife.

Continue sliding the knife under the outer edges of the mixture and scooping into the center. You should end up with a mixture which breaks into very large, moist-looking crumbs. If it is too dry to absorb all the flour and will not bind together quite well when pressed, add a very few drops of cold water.

Work the pastry very briefly and shape lightly into a ball; wrap in saran wrap or foil and chill for 30 minutes in the refrigerator.

1 pineapple weighing about
  2¼ lb
1 cup brandy
1 tbsp confectioners' sugar
10 glacé, candied, or canned
  cherries
6 canned apricots
1 orange
1 banana

Follow the method given in the recipe for Sweet Egg Pastry II. Grease and flour a 10-in pie pan and line with the pastry; sprinkle the cookie crumbs evenly over the bottom. Peel, core, and slice the pineapple. Peel the orange, divide into sections, and carefully remove the thin skin. Slice the banana (sprinkle with a little lemon juice to prevent discoloration if wished). Arrange the pineapple in the pie shell; bake for 40 minutes at 350° F. Transfer to a plate; heat the brandy, sprinkle over the pineapple, and flame. Sprinkle confectioners' sugar over the sliced apricots and arrange on top, together with the cherries, orange sections, and banana.

• • •

BANANA TART

Use fresh fruit instead of the prunes for a change, e.g. apples, apricots, cherries, or peaches.

Time: 1 hour 30 minutes
Easy

1 quantity Sweet Egg Pastry I
  (see page 56)
4 bananas
2 pears
½ cup white wine
6 pitted prunes
6 tbsp sugar

FLOUR

Store flour in an airtight container. Soft-wheat or cake flour contains more starch and less gluten than hard-wheat bread flour or all-purpose flour. Do not use quick-mixing or self-rising flour for the recipes in this book. (For these we calculate that 1 cup holds 4 oz all-purpose flour. Cornstarch has no gluten content, so it is always mixed with other flours for baking.

peel of 1 lemon, cut into thin strips

Peel the bananas and cut into rounds; peel the pears, and cut into small pieces. Cook them in the wine with the prunes, sugar and lemon peel for about 20 minutes over gentle heat. Drain well. Make the pastry following the recipe on page 56; reserve one third of it. Use two thirds of the pastry to line the pie pan. Fill with the fruit, making a level layer. Roll out the remaining pastry, cut into narrow strips and cover the fruit with a lattice pattern. Bake for 40 minutes (400° F) in a hot oven.

• • •

CUSTARD PIE

The basic filling for this pie is a thick custard which can be flavored with a few drops of coffee essence or 1 tbsp very strong black coffee, or with grated lemon or orange peel or liqueur of your choice.

Time: 1 hour 15 minutes
Easy

1 quantity Sweet Egg Pastry I
  (see page 56)
1 quart milk
2 egg yolks
½ cup sugar
¼ cup all-purpose flour
1 tbsp butter
1 egg white

Make 1 quantity of the Sweet Egg Pastry I recipe. Grease a 10-in pie pan with butter, dust with flour and line with the pastry. Bake "blind" with a filling of beans on waxed paper for 40 minutes at 350° F. Heat the milk very slowly to boiling point. While it is heating, beat the egg yolks with the sugar until very pale and greatly increased in volume; add the flour. Continue beating as you pour in the hot milk in a very thin stream. Cook the custard in a saucepan over very low heat, stirring all the time, until it boils. Add the butter to the thickened custard and stir until it has cooled completely; fold in the stiffly beaten egg white; transfer the pie shell to a serving plate, spoon the custard into it, and serve.

• • •

AMARETTO TART

You can use crisp macaroons or ratafias instead of amaretti; the crumbled cookies soak up moisture from the pear purée which might otherwise stop the pastry from cooking properly and make it soggy.

Time: 1 hour
Easy

1 quantity Sweet Egg Pastry
  II (see page 56)
2¼ lb pears
½ cup sugar
juice of 1 lemon

2 egg yolks and 1 egg white
2 cups finely crumbled
  amaretti

Make the pastry and set it to rest in a cool place. Peel and core the pears, slice, and bake with a little water, half the sugar, and all the lemon juice in a heatproof dish in the oven. Push through a sieve or purée in a blender. Cook, stirring continuously, until the purée has thickened considerably. Beat the two egg yolks with the remaining sugar. Beat the egg white and fold gently but thoroughly into the yolk and sugar mixture. Line the pie pan with the pastry, cover the bottom with the cookie crumbs, and spoon the purée on top of them. Cover with the fluffy egg mixture. Bake for about 40 minutes at 350° F; take care that the topping does not become too brown.

• • •

CHERRY PIE

Use Kentish Red or Bing cherries for this recipe.

Time: 1 hour 15 minutes
Easy

1 quantity Sweet Egg Pastry I
  (see page 56)
2¼ lb cherries
½ cup sugar
peel of 1 lemon
2 cloves
pinch cinnamon
1 cup good white wine
1 whole egg and 1 egg yolk
1 tbsp flour
few drops vanilla extract
2 extra tbsp sugar or 2 tbsp
  vanilla sugar
1 cup milk

Pit the cherries and cook for 15 minutes with half the sugar, the lemon peel, cloves, cinnamon, and white wine. Remove the cherries with a slotted spoon. Line a greased and floured 10-in pie dish with the pastry. Beat the egg and extra yolk for 5–10 minutes with the remaining sugar and the 2 tbsp vanilla sugar or use the 2 extra tbsp sugar and vanilla extract. Add the flour a little at a time.

Beat in the hot milk, adding it gradually in a thin stream. Cook the custard until it thickens (it should coat the back of a wooden spoon, a strip remaining clear after running a finger down the back of the spoon). Allow to cool a little before pouring into the pie shell; cover with the cherries and cook for 40 minutes at 350° F.

• • •

QUEEN OF PUDDINGS

Time: 1 hour
Easy

1 quantity Sweet Egg Pastry I
    (see page 56)
1 cup marmalade
12 ladyfingers
1 cup Grand Marnier
2 egg whites
½ cup sugar
pinch salt

Line a 10-in greased and floured pie dish with the sweet egg pastry. Prick the bottom with a fork, cover with waxed

paper, and weight down with dried beans. Cook at 350° F for 30 minutes. Remove from the oven and allow to cool before covering the surface with an even layer of marmalade. Dip the ladyfingers in the Grand Marnier, and lay on top of the marmalade layer. Beat the egg whites until stiff, adding the salt after the first minute or two and the sugar when the whites are firm. Continue beating until glossy. Use a pastry bag and fluted tube to cover the pie with the meringue topping. Bake for about 10 minutes at 350° F or until the meringue is pale golden brown. Serve immediately.

• • •

FIG AND LEMON TART

"White figs" – small, very sweet, tender, and full of flavor are best for this recipe, but small "black" figs will also give good results. Larger, less sweet varieties are not so suitable.

Time: 1 hour
Easy

1 quantity Sweet Egg Pastry I (see page 56)
2¼ lb figs (not too ripe)
½ cup sugar
juice and grated peel of 1 lemon
2 cups finely crumbled sponge cake
1 cup whipping cream

Let the pastry rest for 30 minutes in the refrigerator before you roll it out into a

circle. Grease a 10-in pie pan or flan ring with a little butter, lightly dust with flour, and line with the pastry. Peel off the thin outer skin of the figs, cut them in half (from stalk to base) and place in a bowl with the sugar, lemon juice, and peel. Leave to stand for 1 hour. Sprinkle a generous layer of sponge cake crumbs all over the bottom of the pie shell. Arrange the figs on the cake crumbs, cut side uppermost. Bake at 350° F for about 40 minutes. Allow to cool before decorating with rosettes of piped whipped cream.

• • •

SWEET CHESTNUT TART

Chestnut jam looks a little like a thick paste; substitute sweetened chestnut purée (available in cans) if you prefer.

Time: 1 hour
Easy

1 quantity Sweet Egg Pastry II (see page 56)
1¼ cups sweet chestnut jam
1 tbsp unsweetened cocoa powder
2 tbsp brandy
1 tbsp apricot or peach jam
1 tbsp sugar
¾ cup marrons glacés, finely chopped

APPLE AND CUSTARD FLAN

■ *Apples which retain their shape when cooked should be selected for this type of pie: Russet, Granny Smith, Pippin, or Golden or Red Delicious.*

Allow the pastry 30 minutes' resting time in the refrigerator, then prepare the filling. Combine the chestnut jam, the cocoa powder, and the brandy. Grease the pan with a little butter and dust lightly with flour before lining with three quarters of the pastry. Fill with the chestnut jam mixture and smooth the surface. Cut the remaining pastry into thin strips with a fluted pastry wheel and arrange in a lattice over the filling. Cook in a preheated oven for 40 minutes at 350° F. Melt the apricot or peach jam with the sugar and brush this over the whole surface of the pie (lattice included) as soon as it comes out of the oven. Place the chopped marrons glacés in each square of the lattice and allow to cool before serving.

•   •   •

APPLE AND CUSTARD FLAN

Time: 30 minutes
Easy

1 quantity Sweet Pie Dough (see page 56)
1 lb Reinette, Cox's, or Blenheim apples
2 egg yolks
½ cup sugar
1 tbsp all-purpose flour
1 cup milk

Follow the recipe on pages 56–57 for the pastry, combining the ingredients as quickly as possible; use this to line a 10-in pie pan. Peel and core the apples, cut into thin slices, and arrange, slightly overlapping, in the pie shell. Beat the eggs vigorously with the sugar; when pale and frothy beat in the flour followed by the hot milk, adding this a little at a time. Pour this custard all over the apples. Bake at 350° F for 40 minutes. Serve warm or cold.

•   •   •

ALMOND TART

Time: 1 hour
Easy

1 quantity Sweet Pie Dough (see page 56)
2 egg whites
½ cup sugar

1⅔ cups peeled almonds
⅓ cup pine nuts

Make the pastry and leave in the refrigerator for 30 minutes. Roll out a circle sufficient to line a 10-in pie pan and leave a ½-in overlap hanging over the sides. Chop the almonds very finely. Beat the egg whites until stiff but not dry, then fold in the sugar, almonds, and pine nuts. Fill the pie shell with this mixture. Fold the overlapping pastry over the edge of the tart, pinching together in little pleats all the way round (see apple tart illustration opposite). Cook for 40 minutes at 350° F. If the pastry shows signs of browning too quickly, place a piece of foil or waxed paper on top.

PRUNE TART

Use "no soak" California pitted prunes for this recipe. If the prunes you use do need soaking, however, you could save time by simmering them in the wine for 10 minutes.

Time: 1 hour + extra time if prunes are soaked
Easy

1 quantity Sweet Pie Dough
 (see page 56)
1⅔ cups prunes
1¾ cups good-quality sweet
 dessert wine
1 cup apricot jam
2 tbsp Cointreau
1 tbsp confectioners' sugar

If the prunes need soaking, leave to stand overnight in the white wine. Make the pastry (see recipe on pages 56–57),

wrap, and leave to rest for 30 minutes in the refrigerator. Pit the prunes if necessary. Roll out the pastry ⅛–¼ in thick and line a lightly greased 10-in pie pan with it. Mix the apricot jam with the Cointreau and spread over the bottom of the uncooked pie shell. Arrange the prunes on top. Cook for 40 minutes at 350° F. Wait until the tart is completely cold before serving, sprinkling with the confectioners' sugar at the last minute.

GREENGAGE TART

Greengages keep their shape and release little juice in cooking; the ladyfingers will absorb what little there is.

Time: 1 hour
Easy

1 quantity Sweet Pie Dough
 (see page 56)
12 greengages
2 cups crumbled ladyfingers
2 egg yolks
¼ cup sugar
2 tbsp all-purpose flour
1 tbsp butter

2–3 drops vanilla extract
scant 1 cup milk
1 tbsp confectioners' sugar

Prepare the sweet pie dough. Blanch the greengages in boiling water for a few seconds, peel them, cut in half and remove pits. Set the fruit aside in a covered dish in a cool place. Roll out the pastry and line a prepared 10-in pie pan with it, pricking the bottom with a fork before sprinkling with the crumbled sponge fingers. Set aside with the greengages. Make the custard: beat the yolks and sugar very thoroughly, beat in the sifted flour a little at a time, followed by the softened (not melted) butter, the vanilla extract, and the hot milk. Spread the greengages out over the layer of crumbs, pour over the custard, and cook for 40 minutes at 350° F. Serve warm or cold, sprinkled with the confectioners' sugar at the last minute.

CITRUS FRUIT

These are indispensible in cake making and general confectionery. Small quantities of the fragrant and pervasive essential oils contained in their peel provide a wonderful flavor. Lime can be used instead of lemon (its juice and peel go further). Only the peel of citron is used. Kumquats, miniature orange-like fruits native to China, can be used to great decorative effect.

LEMON CUSTARD TART

Time: 1 hour
Easy

1 egg and 1 egg yolk
4 tbsp sugar
grated peel and juice of 2
    lemons
generous 1 cup heavy cream
1 quantity Sweet Pie Dough
    (see page 56)
1 tbsp confectioners' sugar

Beat the egg yolks and sugar
until very pale and greatly
increased in volume. Beat in
the lemon peel and juice. Cook
over hot water, stirring
continuously until the mixture
thickens. (If it comes near to
boiling point it will curdle and
you will have to start again.)
Set aside; when completely
cold, whip the cream and the
egg white in separate bowls
until very firm. Fold first the
cream, then the egg white into
the lemon mixture, using a
metal spoon in order to lose as
much air as possible from the
mixture. Line the prepared pie
pan with the pastry. Spoon in
the filling, giving the pan a
couple of quick turns to help
level the filling. Cook for up to
40 minutes at 350° F. Serve
warm or cold, with a last-
minute dusting of sifted
confectioners' sugar.

• • •

ORANGE FLAN

Time: 1 hour
Easy

1 quantity Sweet Egg Pastry
    II (see page 56)
½ cup peeled almonds
vanilla extract
¾ cup sugar
3 oranges
4 tbsp toasted breadcrumbs
1 egg and 1 egg yolk
2 tbsp sugar

While the prepared pastry is
resting in the refrigerator,

64

LEMON CUSTARD TART
■ *The filling is an extremely light and delicate mousse. Very thin strips of orange peel can be used instead of the lemon slices as decoration but boil them first for a few minutes and allow to dry.*

ORANGE FLAN
■ *This can also be prepared with lemons, Seville (bitter) oranges, or grapefruit.*

prepare the filling. Toast the almonds in a medium oven until pale golden brown. Place ½ cup sugar, ½ cup water and 2–3 drops vanilla extract in a small saucepan and simmer for about 10 minutes. Peel the oranges and extract the sections from the inner membrane, keeping them as intact as possible. Cut some of the peel into very thin, short strips (about 2 tablespoonfuls) add to the sugar syrup, and boil for a further 5 minutes. Remove from the heat and allow to cool. Using a pestle and mortar (or a blender) pound or grind the almonds very finely (using ordinary ground almonds will not give the same taste) together with the 2 tbsp sugar. Roll out the

ORANGE

Perhaps the most widely used fruit in cakes, pastries, and desserts. Available all the year round, from the very sweet, almost oval summer oranges, to the slightly bitter and very distinctive taste of the varieties available in winter. The peel, grated and fresh or candied, is invaluable in pastry making and confectionery.

pastry and line a 10-in pie pan; sprinkle an even layer of breadcrumbs over the base. Trim off any extra pastry around the sides. Beat the whole egg and the extra egg yolk with the remaining sugar (¼ cup) and 2 drops vanilla extract for 5 minutes before combining with the almond paste. Spread this mixture out evenly in the pie shell and place in a moderate oven (350° F) for 40 minutes. Remove from the oven. When the flan has cooled a little, sprinkle all over with the orange syrup. Arrange the orange sections as shown below and serve.

EASY STRAWBERRY TART

Time: 1 hour
Easy

1 quantity Sweet Egg Pastry II (see page 56)
1 cup best-quality raspberry preserve
2–2½ cups wild, or very small cultivated strawberries
1 tbsp confectioners' sugar

Grease a 10-in pie pan lightly with butter and dust lightly with flour before lining with the prepared pastry, rolled out

in a circle wide enough to leave about ¾ in hanging over the edges. Trim to an even border all round, then tuck the overlapping edges inward to form a border round the edge of the pan (see illustration on page 66). Place a circle of waxed paper over the bottom of the pie shell, weighed down with dried beans and bake for 30 minutes at 350° F. Remove the paper and beans. Spread a layer of raspberry preserve over the bottom of the pie

shell, fill with the strawberries, and dust with sifted confectioners' sugar.

•   •   •

STRAWBERRY & KIRSCH CUSTARD TART

Choose medium-sized cultivated strawberries for this tart and arrange them with their pointed ends uppermost.

*Time: 1 hour 30 minutes
Easy*

½ tbsp gelatin powder
1 quantity Sweet Egg Pastry I
   (see page 56)
2 eggs
4 tbsp sugar
1 tbsp all-purpose flour
1 cup milk
1 cup whipping cream
scant ½ cup strawberry jam
2 tbsp kirsch (cherry liqueur)
2½–3 cups strawberries

Follow the manufacturer's instructions for dissolving the gelatin. Roll out the prepared

pastry and line a 10-in pie pan, crimping the edges to make a decorative border. Prick the bottom with a fork and bake at 350° F with waxed paper and beans weighting it down for the first 30 minutes; remove these and bake for a further 10 minutes. Beat 1 whole egg and 1 yolk with the sugar until pale and frothy, then add the flour and beat in the hot milk in a thin stream. Cook over low heat, stirring continuously, until the mixture has thickened a little; draw aside from the heat and add the prepared gelatin. When completely cold, fold in the remaining egg white, stiffly beaten, the whipped cream, and the kirsch. Fill the pie shell with this mixture, level with a spatula, and arrange the strawberries on top. Melt the

66

sieved strawberry preserve with 1 tbsp kirsch; when almost cold use as a glaze, brushed gently over the strawberries.

SUGAR PIE

A very sweet, but delicate dessert. The sugar is lightly caramelized.

Time: 1 hour
Easy

1 quantity Sweet Egg Pastry II (see page 56)
1 cup sugar (fine cane sugar if available)
¼ cup (½ stick) butter
1 tbsp all-purpose flour

Roll out the prepared pastry and use to line a prepared 10-in pie pan. Sprinkle ⅔ cup sugar over the base of the pie shell; dot with very small pieces of butter, spaced at fairly regular intervals. Dust evenly with sifted flour. Sprinkle the remaining sugar evenly on top of the flour. Bake in a preheated oven at 350° F for about 40 minutes. Serve warm, not hot.

• • •

BLUEBERRY AND APPLE PIE

Rinse wild fruit well in cold water before you use it. When fresh berries are not available, use frozen.

Time: 1 hour
Easy

1 quantity Sweet Pie Dough (see page 56)
1 cup blueberry preserve
3 Reinette, Cox's, or Blenheim apples
1 cup blueberries
¼ cup sugar
1 egg white

Rest the pastry for 30 minutes in the refrigerator wrapped in saran wrap. Meanwhile, prepare a 10-in pie pan by greasing it with butter and dusting lightly with flour. Roll out the pastry and use about two thirds of it to line the pan, reserving the offcuts and remaining pastry for a lattice. Spread the preserve over the base of the pie shell. Peel, core, and slice the apples very thinly; arrange in concentric circles, working from the outside toward the center, with the slices slightly overlapping one another. Sprinkle the berries on top, followed by the sugar. Cut the remaining pastry into thin strips; using the palm of your hands, roll these gently to make them look like lengths of spaghetti and arrange in a lattice design over the pie. Beat the egg white very lightly with a fork and use a pastry brush to spread this glaze over the lattice and any exposed pastry. Bake for 40 minutes at 350° F. Serve cold.

CANDIED FRUIT AND NUT TART

If you do not have any homemade candied fruit (see recipe on page 27) a wide selection can usually be found in good food stores and delicatessens. Different combinations of fruit may be used for this dessert.

Time: 1 hour
Easy

⅓ cup seedless white raisins
1 quantity Sweet Egg Pastry I (see page 56)
2 eggs
½ cup sugar
1 tbsp all-purpose flour
¼ cup (½ stick) butter, melted
1 cup almonds, very finely chopped or ground
1¼ cups filberts, very finely chopped or ground
1 cup mixed candied fruit
peel of 1 lemon, grated
1 tsp confectioners' sugar

Soak the rasins in lukewarm water. Line a prepared 10-in pie pan with the pastry, allowing an extra ¾ in "hem" all round. Beat the eggs with the sugar until pale and fluffy, then add, one by one, the sifted flour, the melted butter, the well drained raisins, the chopped candied fruit, and the grated lemon peel. Spread this filling out in an even layer in the pie shell and fold the spare border of pastry over the edge of it, pinching together at intervals. Bake for 40 minutes in a moderate oven (350° F). Allow to cool completely and dust with the confectioners' sugar just before serving.

• • •

PEAR AND CHOCOLATE PIE

This happy marriage of pears and chocolate makes this a delicious dessert.

Time: 1 hour 30 minutes
Easy

3 Bartlett or Conference pears
1 cup sugar
1 quantity Sweet Egg Pastry I (see page 56)
2 egg yolks
1 cup milk
4 oz (4 squares) good bakers' or semisweet chocolate
2 tbsp light cream
finely grated orange peel (optional)

Peel and quarter the pears, removing the cores. Dissolve half the sugar in ½ cup water in a small saucepan. Bring to a boil, add the pears, cut into fairly thin lengthwise slices. Simmer for 10 minutes. Make the pastry, following the

PUMPKIN PIE
■ Canned unseasoned
pumpkin (drain before
weighing) will save time and
trouble. If you do use fresh
pumpkin, peel it and remove
the seeds together with the
fibrous section which encloses
them before baking in the
oven.

recipe on page 56. Beat the egg yolks with the remaining sugar for 5–10 minutes then add the hot milk in a thin stream, beating constantly with a wooden spoon. Cook in a double boiler, stirring continuously until the custard coats the back of the wooden spoon. Draw aside from the heat. Remove the pears from the syrup with a slotted spoon. Boil the sugar syrup until it starts to turn a very pale golden brown. Beat this sugar syrup into the custard. Roll out the pastry and line a 10-in pie pan with it. Place a piece of waxed paper over the pie shell, weight down with dried beans, and bake for 30 minutes in a moderate oven (350° F). Remove the paper and beans for 10 more minutes' cooking. Allow to cool then fill with the custard, and arrange the pear slices in circles on top. Melt the chocolate, broken into small pieces, with the cream; allow to cool slightly before spooning over the pear slices shortly before serving. Sprinkle grated orange peel over the pie as a decoration, if wished.

• • •

PUMPKIN PIE

Time: 1 hour 30 minutes
Easy

1¾ cups cooked pumpkin flesh
  or canned (unsweetened
  and unflavored) pumpkin,
  drained
1 quantity Sweet Egg Pastry
  II (see page 56)
10 crumbled amaretti cookies
  or crisp macaroons
½ tsp cinnamon
½ tsp ground nutmeg
2 crumbled cloves or ¼–

½ tsp ground cloves
generous 1 cup milk
2 eggs
½ cup sugar
1 cup whipping cream

Sieve the pumpkin flesh or put it through a ricer. Line a pie pan or shallow pie dish with the pastry. Prick the bottom with a fork and bake for 20 minutes at 350° F. Heat the pumpkin in a saucepan over moderate heat with the fine cookie crumbs, spices, and milk, stirring continuously with a wooden spoon until the mixture has thickened considerably. Draw aside from the heat; beat the eggs with the sugar and stir into the pumpkin mixture. Fill the pie shell evenly with this, making a ribbed design on the surface with a fork (see illustration on the right). Return the pie to the oven for a further 20 minutes, still at 350° F. Allow to cool before serving. A decoration of piped whipped cream is optional.

• • •

POMEGRANATE PIE

Pomegranates have an interesting, slightly acid flavor. The ancient Persian custom of using their fleshy seeds or juice in chicken, game, and fish dishes has recently become fashionable in Western cooking.

Time: 1 hour + standing time
Easy

4 pomegranates
2 cups good-quality red wine
½ cup sugar
1 clove
½ cup flaked almonds

CINNAMON
■ One of the oldest spices known to man, its distinctive flavor and aroma can enhance a variety of cakes and desserts.

1 quantity Sweet Egg Pastry I
(see page 56)

Peel the pomegranates; extract the seeds, taking care not to include any of the bitter membrane which encloses them. Place in a bowl with the wine, sugar, and clove and leave to stand for at least 6 hours. Drain off the wine. Line a greased and lightly floured pie pan with the pastry, cover with waxed paper, weight down with dried beans, and bake for 30 minutes in a preheated moderate oven (350° F). Discard the paper and beans and place the pomegranate seeds and the flaked almonds in the pie shell. Return to the oven for a further 10 minutes.

• • •

GRAPE AND CHOCOLATE TART

These flavors complement each other well. As an alternative sliced oranges could be teamed with the chocolate or, in summer, fresh raspberries.

Time: 1 hour
Easy

scant ½ cup sugar
1¾ cups all-purpose flour
½ cup (1 stick) butter
1 cup unsweetened cocoa
    powder
1 egg
1 cup raspberry preserve
¾ lb grapes, peeled and
    seeded
2 tbsp lemon juice

Mix half the sugar with all the flour, all but 1 tbsp of the softened but not melted

butter, the cocoa powder, and the egg. Work until it forms a smooth, homogenous ball. Use the remaining butter to grease a pie pan and line with the prepared pastry. Place a circle of waxed paper over the base, weight it down with dried beans and bake "blind" for 30 minutes at 350° F. Remove the beans and paper and, when cold, place the grapes in a single layer over the base. Cook the remaining sugar with the lemon juice in a saucepan until it is a pale golden brown, then pour immediately while still boiling all over the grapes. Serve when completely cold.

• • •

MELON TART

Choose very fragrant melons for this dessert; the best are the late summer Charentais or netted melons.

Time: 1 hour
Easy

1 quantity Sweet Pie Dough
(see page 56)
1 or 2 melons, weighing
approximately 2¼ lb in all
¼ cup sugar
1 cup sweet dessert wine
(e.g. Muscat de Beaumes
de Venise or California
Muscat)
peel of 1 lemon, grated
3 eggs

Once the dough is made, leave it to rest in a cool place for 30 minutes. Cut the melon or melons in quarters, scoop out and discard the seeds and surrounding fibrous matter, then cut the flesh away from the skin, dice it, and place in a saucepan with the sugar,

RHUBARB TART
■ A large-leaved perennial at its best for cooking purposes in late spring when the stalks are sweet and tender.

wine, and grated lemon peel. Cook, uncovered, for about 20 minutes, pour off any excess liquid, then push through a sieve and mix with the lightly beaten eggs. Roll out the pastry and line a prepared 10-in pie pan with it. Fill with the melon purée and bake for 40 minutes at 350° F. Allow to cool before serving.

• • •

RHUBARB TART

Time: 1 hour
Easy

1 quantity Sweet Pie Dough
   (see page 56)
1 lb tender pink rhubarb stems
½ cup sugar
1 vanilla bean or a few drops
   vanilla extract
⅔ cup ground almonds

Follow the recipe on page 56 for the pastry. Wash the rhubarb stalks well (if not very young and tender, peel off the pink outer skin) and chop into short lengths. Cook the sugar, vanilla bean (or extract) and ½ cup water in a saucepan for a minute or two before adding the rhubarb. Simmer gently for 20 minutes; it should be very tender. Remove the rhubarb chunks with a slotted spoon and allow to cool completely. Remove the vanilla bean if used. Boil the liquid left in the pan until it reduces to an extremely thick syrup. Grease a 10-in pie pan with butter, line with the pastry, and sprinkle the ground almonds all over the base. Place the cooked

rhubarb in a layer on top and
cover with the syrup. Place in
a preheated moderate oven
(350° F) and bake for about 40
minutes. Serve cold with
sweetened whipped cream to
counteract the acidity of the
rhubarb.

• • •

PEACH PIE

*Peaches and amaretti cookies
or macaroons are a perfect
match. Substitute apricot
halves for the peaches if you
prefer. Canned fruit may be
used when good fresh produce
is scarce.*

*Time: 1 hour
Very easy*

1 quantity Sweet Pie Dough
   (see page 56)
4 peaches
½ cup sugar
8 small amaretti or ratafia
   cookies
½ cup whipping cream

Make the pastry. Wash and
dry the peaches, but do not
peel. Cut in half and remove
the pits. Grease a 10-in pie
pan with a little butter, dust
with flour, and line with the
pastry. Sprinkle 1 tbsp sugar
over the base; arrange the
peaches in the pie shell, cut
side uppermost and place a
ratafia or amaretto snugly in
each hollow in place of the pit.
Sprinkle with the remaining
sugar and cook in a moderate
oven (350° F) for 40 minutes.
Serve when cold, decorated
with rosettes of piped whipped
cream.

FIG AND
BLACKBERRY
TART

*Ideally this dessert should be
made in late summer when
blackberries are fully ripe.
Frozen fruit may, however, be
substituted.*

*Time: 1 hour + standing time
Easy*

12 ripe figs
1 cup sweet dessert wine
   (e.g. California Muscat)
24 ripe blackberries
1 quantity Sweet Egg Pastry I
   (see page 56)
½ cup heavy cream
½ cup confectioners' sugar

Peel the figs carefully, slice
lengthwise in half with a very
sharp serrated knife, and place
in a shallow bowl or dish. Pour
the wine over the figs and
leave to soak for 12 hours.

When it is time to make the
tart, rinse the blackberries
thoroughly in cold water and
spread out to dry on a clean
cloth or paper towels. Grease
and lightly flour a 10-in pie pan
and line with the pastry,
pricking the base with a fork.
Place a circle of waxed paper
over this, weight with beans
and bake blind for 30 minutes
at 350° F. Remove the paper
and beans and return to the
oven for a further 10 minutes.
Set aside to cool. Whip the
cream, sweetening with the
sugar, spread an even layer
over the cold pie shell, and
arrange the drained figs and
the blackberries on top.

• • •

JAM TART

*The addition of baking powder
to the Sweet Egg Pastry makes
it extra light and soft. It is
important to use the very best
(preferably homemade) apricot
jam you can find for this recipe.*

*Time: 1 hour
Easy*

1 quantity Sweet Egg Pastry I
   (see page 56)
1 tbsp baking powder
1½ cups finest-quality apricot
   jam or preserve

Make the pastry following the
recipe on page 56, sifting the
baking powder with the flour.
Roll out the pastry and use
about three quarters of it to
line a 9½-in pie pan. Spread
the apricot jam evenly over
the bottom. Use the remaining
pastry, cut into strips with a
fluted pastry wheel, to form a
wide lattice covering the tart.
Bake for 40 minutes at 350° F.
Allow to cool before serving.

• • •

71

APPLE TART

For the Sweet Egg Pastry:
2½ cups all-purpose flour
½ cup sugar
½ tsp salt
scant ½ cup (1 stick) butter
2 egg yolks
1 egg for glazing

For the filling:
2¼ lb peeled, cored, thickly sliced apples
½ lemon
½ cup sugar
pinch nutmeg
½ tsp cinnamon
2 tbsp all-purpose flour or cornstarch
2 tbsp orange juice

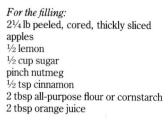

Make the Sweet Egg Pastry following the method given on page 56. Peel, core, and cut the apples into thick slices into a bowl of cold water to which the juice of half a lemon has been added.

Cut off just under half the dough ball, roll out and line a greased and floured pie pan.

Roll out half the remaining pastry to between ⅛–¼ in thick and use a fluted pastry wheel to cut it into strips about ¾ in wide.

Drain the apples and cook these with the sugar, nutmeg, and cinnamon until tender. Add 1–2 tbsp water if necessary. Remove from heat.

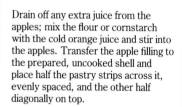

Drain off any extra juice from the apples; mix the flour or cornstarch with the cold orange juice and stir into the apples. Transfer the apple filling to the prepared, uncooked shell and place half the pastry strips across it, evenly spaced, and the other half diagonally on top.

Glaze with beaten egg.

Roll out the remaining pastry to a circle, cut a large hole out of the center and set aside; place the large circular lid over the pie. Pinch the edges together.

Use a decorative pastry cutter to cut pieces out of the small remaining disk of pastry.

Place these on the pie lid as shown bottom right and brush the entire surface with the egg glaze. Bake in a preheated oven at 350° for 40 minutes or until done.

APPLE AND ALMOND PIE
■ *Choose varieties of apples and pears which release very little water when cooked for this pie to prevent the shell becoming soggy.*

APPLE AND ALMOND PIE

Time: 1 hr 15 minutes
Easy

3 apples
2 pears
3 tbsp sugar
peel of 1 lemon, grated
1 quantity Sweet Pie Dough (see page 56)
1 cup very finely chopped or ground almonds
⅓ cup roasted slivered and/or whole almonds for decoration

Peel, core, and slice the apples and pears; cook gently with the sugar, lemon peel and 2 tbsp water in a covered saucepan. Make the pastry and use two thirds of it to line the base and sides of a prepared pie pan. Fill the uncooked pie shell with the cooked apple and pear mixture, then sprinkle with the very finely chopped or ground almonds. Roll out the remaining pastry and use for the pie lid, pinching firmly together all round the edges (alternatively, use a pastry wheel). Prick the top pie crust in several places with a fork (to let steam escape as it bakes) and cook in a moderate oven (350° F) for 40 minutes. Sprinkle the cooked pie with roasted almonds and serve immediately.

• • •

KIWI TART

The kiwi fruit has become enormously popular. Not only beautiful to look at when sliced, with a delicate sweetness, it is also very rich in vitamin C.

Time: 1 hour 20 minutes
Easy

1 quantity Sweet Egg Pastry I
   (see page 56)
2 egg yolks
¼ cup sugar
¼ cup all-purpose flour
1 cup milk
8 kiwi fruit
2 tbsp Cedrina (citron-
   flavored) liqueur or 1 tbsp
   lime or lemon juice and
   1 tbsp brandy
¼ cup apricot jam, sieved

Make the pastry, roll out, and
line a prepared pie pan. Cover
this with waxed paper and fill
with dried beans; bake at
350° F for 30 minutes.
Remove the beans and paper
and bake for another 10
minutes. Set aside to cool
completely. Beat the egg
yolks with the sugar for 5–10
minutes before adding the
flour and then beat in the
boiling milk in a thin stream.
Cook over very low heat,
stirring continuously, until the
mixture thickens. Peel two
kiwi fruits, remove the hard
stalk end and blend to a purée
with the liqueur; stir this into
the custard. Pour the custard
into the pie shell; cut the rest
of the kiwi fruit into thin slices
and arrange on top of the
custard so that they overlap a
little. Melt the jam and use it
to glaze the surface of the kiwi
fruit.

•   •   •

COCONUT MERINGUE PIE

Time: 1 hour
Easy

1 quantity Sweet Egg Pastry
   II (see page 56)
2 eggs and 1 extra yolk
½ cup sugar
1 tsp potato flour, cornstarch,
   or arrowroot
½ cup heavy cream
2⅓ cups shredded coconut

Follow the recipe on page 56
for the pastry. Roll out and
line a prepared pie pan. Beat
the three egg yolks with the
sugar until very pale and
greatly increased in volume;
stir in the sifted potato flour,
then fold in the whipped cream
followed by the two stiffly
beaten egg whites and the
coconut. Fill the pie shell
evenly with this mixture and
bake at 350° F for 40 minutes.
Allow to cool before serving.

•   •   •

PECAN AND APPLE PIE

*Pecan and apple is a classic
combination of complementary
flavors and textures.*

Time: 1 hour 20 minutes
Easy

1 quantity Sweet Egg Pastry I
   (see page 56)
5 apples (Golden Delicious or
   Jonathon)
2 eggs
½ cup sugar
½ cup heavy cream
peel of 1 lemon, grated
1 cup pecan nuts

COCONUT MERINGUE PIE
■ *Fresh coconut flesh is juicy and has a wonderful aroma. Failing this, use shredded coconut from your local foodstore, available all the year round.*

Make the pastry. Peel, core, and slice the apples; cook gently with 1 tbsp water until very soft. Push through a sieve or process in a blender. Beat the egg yolks thoroughly with the sugar; add the apple purée, cream, and lemon peel then fold in the stiffly beaten egg whites. Line a greased pie pan with the pastry, sprinkle the coarsely chopped pecan nuts over the base and then fill the pie shell with the apple mixture, smoothing the surface with a spatula. Bake for 40 minutes in moderate oven (350° F).

•   •   •

APPLE MERINGUE PIE

Sprinkle finely crumbled cookies over the base of the pie shell so that it does not become sodden with juice from the apples as they cook.

Time: 1 hour
Easy

1 quantity Sweet Egg Pastry I
    (see page 56)
4 apples (Golden Delicious or
    Jonathon)
¼ cup sugar
2 tbsp butter
2 egg whites
1 cup confectioners' sugar
pinch salt

Make the pastry, leave to rest, roll out, and use to line a greased pie pan. Peel, quarter, and core the apples and cut into slices; arrange these slices in the pie shell, sprinkle first with the sugar and then with the melted

butter. Bake for 20 minutes at 350° F. Beat the egg whites and salt until stiff but not dry and grainy; beat in the confectioners' sugar and continue beating for a few more minutes. Using a pastry bag and fluted tube, pipe the meringue all over the apples and bake in the same moderate oven for a further 20 minutes.

•   •   •

RISING AGENTS

Yeast is a living fungus which needs moisture, warmth, and sweetness to function and introduce air into all sorts of baked goods. Baking powder is an American invention: bicarbonate of soda mixed with a mild acid such as cream of tartar, or, for modern double-action powder, with tartaric acid and acid sodium pyrophosphate.

GRAPE TART

Time: 1 hour
Easy

1 quantity Sweet Egg Pastry I
    (see page 56)
2 eggs
¼ cup sugar
1 tsp flour
1 cup milk
1½ lb very sweet grapes
    (Muscat or Thompson
    seedless)
½ cup grape jelly

Make the pastry and leave to rest. Roll out; line a greased pie pan. Bake blind in a hot

1 cup milk
⅔ cup sugar
2 tbsp water
grated peel and juice of 1
    lemon
3 tbsp butter
4 tbsp brandy

Make the pastry and leave to rest. Roll out and line a prepared pie pan. Bake blind covered with a circle of waxed paper and weighted down with dried beans. Bake at 350° F for 30 minutes, then remove the paper and beans, and return to the oven for 10 minutes. Beat the egg yolks with ¼ cup of the sugar until pale and frothy, add the grated lemon peel and the flour. Beat in the hot milk a little at a time, then cook, stirring continuously, in the top of a double boiler until the mixture coats the back of the spoon well. Peel the bananas, slice into rounds and mix gently in a bowl with the lemon juice. Melt the butter in a wide saucepan, add the bananas, and sprinkle them with 3 tbsp of the brandy; cook for 1 minute. Spread the custard out over the base of the cold pie shell and cover with the bananas. Cook the remaining sugar with the 2 tbsp water until golden brown; add the remaining brandy and quickly sprinkle the caramel over the bananas. Serve immediately.

•   •   •

oven (400° F) for 30 minutes. Remove the waxed paper and the dried beans and return to the oven for a further 10 minutes. Leave to cool. Beat the egg yolks vigorously with the sugar, add the flour, and then pour in the hot milk in a thin stream, beating all the time. Cook over low heat or in a double boiler, stirring constantly, until thick. Wait until this custard is cold before folding in the stiffly beaten egg whites. Spread the custard evenly in the pie shell and cover with the grapes. Melt the grape jelly over low heat and use to glaze the grapes.

•   •   •

BANANA CARAMEL TART

Speed is of the essence when it comes to pouring the caramel over the bananas; it hardens very quickly once off the heat. A little lemon juice will help to keep it workable.

*Time: 1 hour 15 minutes
Easy*

1 quantity Sweet Pie Dough
    (see page 56)
3 bananas
2 egg yolks
¼ cup all-purpose flour

MASCARPONE TART

Mascarpone is a thick, white, creamy cheese with a high fat content. It is made by adding citric acid to cream.

76

RASPBERRY TART
■ *A straightforward recipe which can be used for blackberries, red currants, gooseberries, blueberries, or strawberries. The fruits can be arranged in a circular arrangement (spiral or concentric) for greater visual effect.*

Time: 1 hour
Easy

1 quantity Sweet Pie Dough
    (see page 56)
1¼ cups mascarpone
pinch cinnamon
2 eggs
4 tbsp sugar
½ cup light cream
4 tbsp brandy
8 amaretti cookies or crisp
    macaroons
4 oz (4 squares) semisweet
    chocolate

Grease a pie pan with butter and line with the dough. Push the mascarpone through a sieve and combine in a bowl with the cinnamon, the beaten egg yolks and sugar, the cream and brandy. Stir in the crumbled amaretti. Fill the pie shell with this mixture and bake for about 40 minutes in a moderate oven (350° F). Leave to cool before removing from the pan. Place on a serving plate and decorate the surface with grated chocolate, before serving.

•   •   •

RASPBERRY TART

Time: 1 hour 30 minutes
Easy

1 quantity Sweet Pie Dough
    (see page 56)
1 cup heavy cream
½ cup confectioners' sugar
few drops vanilla extract
1 lb raspberries
½ cup red currant jelly
1 tbsp kirsch

Make the pastry and leave to rest for 30 minutes before rolling out and use to line a 10-in pie pan. Prick the bottom with a fork and bake blind,

removing the waxed paper and dried beans before it is set aside to cool. Beat the cream until stiff, adding the sugar and vanilla a little at a time in the later stages of beating. Spoon into the pie shell, making sure it is smooth and level. Mask completely with the raspberries. Warm the red currant jelly gently with the kirsch, sprinkle over the raspberries, and serve.

•   •   •

DRIED FRUIT TART

For a stronger taste, soak the dried fruit for 12 hours in brandy, omit the wine and do not boil the fruit.

Time: 1 hour
Easy

1 quantity Sweet Pie Dough
    (see page 56)
6 pitted prunes
6 dried apricots
6 dried figs

⅓ cup seedless white raisins
1 cup good-quality white wine
½ cup chopped walnuts
1 lemon
¼ cup sugar
¼ cup (½ stick) butter
1 cup heavy cream

Make the pastry. Place all the dried fruit in a deep, narrow saucepan with the white wine; bring to a boil, cover, and cook for 5 minutes. Drain off the

wine, and pat the fruit dry with kitchen towels. Chop the prunes, figs, and apricots coarsely and mix them with the raisins, walnuts, grated lemon peel, sugar, and melted butter. Use two thirds of the pastry to line a greased 9½-in pie pan. Fill with the dried fruit and cut thin strips of the remaining pastry with a fluted pastry wheel for a lattice top. Bake for 40 minutes at 350° F. Allow to cool before decorating with rosettes of piped whipped cream.

• • •

SEEDLESS WHITE RAISINS
■ Soak in warm water for at least half an hour before using; drain, gently squeeze out any liquid and spread on kitchen towels to remove excess moisture when it is time to use them.

PEAR AND RAISIN PIE

Time: 1 hour
Easy

1 quantity Sweet Egg Pastry I (see page 56)
4 pears (Bartlett or Conference)
⅔ cup seedless white raisins
1 tsp cinnamon
peel of 1 lemon, grated
¼ cup sugar
1 cup raspberry preserve

Soak the raisins in water for about 1 hour. Make the pastry, allow it the usual resting time then roll out and line a prepared 10-in pie pan. Spread the raspberry preserve evenly over the base. Cut the pears in quarters, peel, core, and slice. Arrange the slices, slightly overlapping, on top of the raspberry preserve and sprinkle with the well drained seedless white raisins, the cinnamon, grated lemon peel, and the sugar. Bake in a moderate oven (350° F) for 40 minutes or until golden brown.

• • •

CINNAMON RICE FLAN

Use short-grain pudding rice for this recipe, either Carolina rice or, if it is available (the outstanding quality is worth the higher price) imported Italian Maratelli rice.

Time: 1 hour + standing time
Easy

⅓ cup seedless white raisins
2 tbsp rum
½ cup short-grain rice
2¼ cups rich milk
½ cup sugar
generous pinch ground cinnamon
few drops vanilla extract or 1 vanilla bean
2 egg yolks
1 quantity Sweet Egg Pastry I (see page 56)

Soak the seedless white raisins in the rum for about 1 hour. Bring 2 quarts lightly salted water to a boil in a large saucepan and sprinkle in the rice; once the water has returned to a full boil, cook the rice for 5 minutes. Drain. Heat the milk to boiling point with the sugar, cinnamon, and vanilla. Sprinkle the rice into the milk and cook very slowly for 45 minutes by which time there will be very little liquid left in the pan. (If a vanilla bean is used, remove it now.) Draw aside from the heat and allow to cool a little before stirring in the raisins and the egg yolks. Line a greased ovenproof flan dish with the Sweet Egg Pastry and fill with the rice, smoothing the surface so it is level. Place in a preheated oven (350° F) and cook for 40 minutes.

• • •

RICE

Use short-grain rice for the recipes in this book. This type of rice is rich in starch and the grains will cling together and give a creamy consistency when cooked. Italian *Arborio* rice has more flavor than Carolina rice and is also more absorbent.

FILBERT TART

Drier in consistency than most of the previous recipes and full of flavor. Serve with a jug of fresh pouring cream or homemade chocolate custard (see page 41), made with a little more milk than usual.

Time: 1 hour
Easy

1 quantity Sweet Egg Pastry II (see page 56)
4 tbsp peach or apricot jelly or sieved jam
2 egg whites
1 cup confectioners' sugar
2 cups filberts

Make the pastry and leave to rest in a cool place for a while before rolling out to line a greased pie pan. Melt the jelly over low heat and sprinkle 2 tbsp of it over the base of the pie shell. Beat the egg whites until firm and continue beating as you add the sugar a little at a time. Add the very finely chopped nuts. Bake in a moderate oven (350° F) for 40 minutes. Cool before glazing the top with the remaining jelly. Serve warm or cold.

• • •

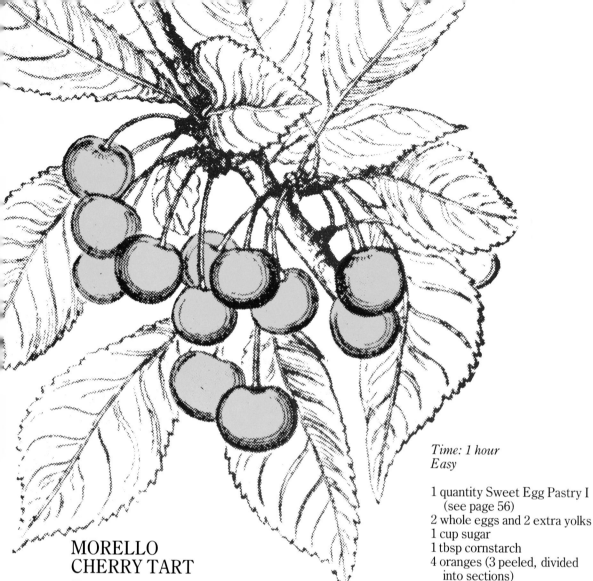

sugar syrup a few at a time, in a skimmer or slotted ladle. As soon as the sugar syrup comes back to a boil, draw the ladle out of it and let the excess syrup drain back into the pan before lowering the next batch into it. Let the sections cool. Cover the base of the pastry with the cold egg mixture and arrange the orange and lemon sections alternately on top. Melt the jelly (sieved marmalade or red currant jelly would be suitable) with the brandy and sprinkle this glaze over the fruit.

• • •

MORELLO CHERRY TART

You can use cooked (and sweetened) fresh or frozen Morello cherries instead of canned, or substitute peaches, apricots, black cherries or chopped fresh pineapple.

Time: 1 hour
Easy

1 quantity Sweet Pie Dough
  (see page 56)
2 egg yolks
¼ cup sugar
¼ cup all-purpose flour
1 cup milk
2¼ lb canned Morello cherries

Line a greased 10-in pie pan with the pastry. Cover with waxed paper, fill with dried beans, and bake for 30 minutes at 350° F. Remove the paper and beans and return to the oven for a further 10 minutes. Set aside to cool. Beat the egg yolks with the sugar until pale and

fluffy, beat in the flour a little at a time, followed by the hot milk, pouring it in very slowly. Stir continuously over low heat until the custard thickens. Allow to cool a little before pouring into the pie shell. Drain the cherries well, pit, and arrange on top of the custard filling.

• • •

ORANGE AND LEMON TART

Desserts made with citrus fruits are refreshing and rarely taste too sweet. Take care not to include any of the bitter white pith with the orange and lemon sections.

Time: 1 hour
Easy

1 quantity Sweet Egg Pastry I
  (see page 56)
2 whole eggs and 2 extra yolks
1 cup sugar
1 tbsp cornstarch
4 oranges (3 peeled, divided into sections)
4 lemons (3 peeled, divided into sections)
½ cup fruit jelly
1 tbsp brandy

Line a prepared pie pan with the pastry. Using waxed paper and dried beans as a "filling," bake the shell blind for 30 minutes at 350° F; remove the paper and beans and return to the oven for a further 10 minutes. Leave to cool completely. Beat the eggs (and the extra yolks) with ¼ cup of the sugar, add the cornstarch, followed by the juice of 1 lemon and 1 orange. Stir constantly over low heat until the mixture has thickened. Carefully peel off the thin inner skin from the orange and lemon sections. Melt the remaining sugar with 2 tbsp water, simmer for 5 minutes, skimming off any foam from the surface. Lower the sections into the boiling

CINNAMON TART

Time: 1 hour
Easy

2⅔ cups all-purpose flour
½ cup sugar
1 tbsp baking powder
2 egg yolks and 1 egg white
½ cup + 2 tbsp butter
1 tbsp Marsala
2 tsp ground cinnamon
1 tsp ground ginger
salt

Sift the flour in a mound onto a marble slab or into a large mixing bowl. Make a well in the center and place the egg yolks in it with the softened butter cut into very small pieces, the Marsala, cinnamon, ginger, and a pinch of salt. Mix these ingredients gently round in the well with a wooden spoon or the tips of your fingers and allow gradually to combine with the flour. When combined, shape the pastry into a ball, wrap in waxed paper, and chill in the refrigerator for 30 minutes.

CINNAMON TART
■ *Cinnamon is sold in sticks (rolled pieces of bark) or finely ground, when some of its aroma is lost. Root ginger, also used in this recipe, is widely available in shops.*

Roll out and place in a 10-in pie pan. Using a pastry brush, coat the pastry thinly with the very lightly beaten egg white; bake for 40 minutes at 350° F. Allow to cool before serving.

• • •

CARAMELIZED FRUIT TART

Wild fruit has more flavor than cultivated produce, enhancing tarts and other desserts with its wonderful aroma and color. Use frozen fruit when fresh is not available.

Time: 1 hour
Easy

1 quantity Sweet Egg Pastry I
   (see page 56)

2 eggs
1 cup sugar
¼ cup all-purpose flour
1 cup milk
½ cup blueberries
½ cup wild strawberries
½ cup blackberries
½ cup raspberries
¼ cup red currants
2 tbsp lemon juice

Make the pastry and leave to rest. Roll out and line a prepared 10-in shallow pie pan with it; cover with waxed paper, fill with dried beans, and bake "blind" for 30 minutes at 350° F. Remove the paper and beans and bake for a further 10 minutes. Beat the egg yolks with ¼ cup sugar for about 5 minutes; add the flour and then add the hot milk in a very thin stream, beating all the time. Stir over low heat until the custard thickens. Leave to cool while you wash and prepare the fruit, drying it gently but thoroughly with paper towels. Spread the custard over the bottom of the pie shell and cover with the fruit. Melt the remaining sugar with the strained lemon juice; cook until pale golden brown and then pour quickly over the fruit while it is still boiling hot.

• • •

CHERRY AND RICOTTA TART

Time: 1 hour
Easy

1 quantity Sweet Pie Dough
   (see page 56)
2 eggs
½ cup sugar
1¾ cups ricotta cheese
½ cup candied cherries
1 tbsp rum or brandy
small pinch cinnamon

Follow the recipe for the pastry. Beat the egg yolks with the sugar until pale and increased in volume and then beat in the ricotta cheese a little at a time. Add the drained cherries, the brandy, and cinnamon. Fold in the stiffly beaten egg whites. Roll out the pastry and use to line a 10-in pie pan lightly greased with butter. Fill with the ricotta mixture. With the blunt edge of a large kitchen knife, press lightly to mark out spokes radiating from the center of the filling. Bake at 350° F for 40 minutes. This pie is better the day after it is made.

• • •

PERSIMMON PIE

If you like cinnamon, sprinkle a teaspoonful over the top of this pie: it goes well with the persimmons and with the oranges.

Time: 1 hour 30 minutes
Easy

4 very ripe persimmons
4 tbsp brandy
1 quantity Sweet Pie Dough
   (see page 56)

½ cup sugar
¼ cup potato flour
1 cup boiling water
2 egg yolks
peel of 1 orange, grated
6 tbsp orange juice
1½ tbsp butter
¼ cup candied orange peel
pinch salt

The persimmons should be squashy to the touch; rinse, pull off the stem, cut the fruit vertically in half, and sprinkle the cut surfaces with brandy. Leave to stand, cut sides uppermost for about 30 minutes. Make the pastry, roll it out and line a greased 10-in pie pan, cover with waxed paper and weight with beans. Bake blind for 30 minutes in a moderate oven (350° F), remove paper and beans, and bake for a further 10 minutes. While the pie shell is cooling, mix the sugar and the potato flour in a small saucepan and then beat in the boiling water, adding it in a very thin stream. Cook for 10 minutes over low heat, stirring constantly. Draw aside from the heat. Beat the egg yolks briefly and then stir quickly into the thickened mixture in the saucepan. Return to a low heat and stir for 2 minutes. Remove from the heat and add the orange peel and juice and the butter; stir well. Pour this mixture into the pie shell, smooth with spatula, place the persimmons on top, cut side uppermost, sprinkle them with strips of candied orange peel, and serve.

•　•　•

Successful puff pastry, it is sometimes said, distinguishes the truly gifted pastrymaker from the merely competent. Provided you follow every stage and do not feel tempted to take short cuts or substitute guesswork for careful measuring, there is no reason why you should not become one of the experts. Few cooks ever tire of the miracle which occurs each time the raw puff pastry is placed in the oven, emerging a short while later as a featherlight work of art.

PUFF PASTRY

Puff pastry is used for a wide range of desserts and pastries. It needs care and practice, so do not be discouraged if you produce the occasional batch which is not quite as successful as it could be. Each time you make puff pastry, give it your full concentration, having first refreshed your memory as to the hints given in this and other cookery books.

Time: 30 minutes + resting times
Fairly easy

2 cups + 2 tbsp white strong or medium strong flour or all-purpose flour
pinch salt
1 cup (2 sticks) sweet butter, at room temperature
½–1 cup cold water

Sift 2 cups of flour with the salt onto a marble pastry slab or work surface, or into a large bowl. Make a well in the center and add sufficient water to make a fairly stiff dough (but still quite soft) working it with the tips of your fingers. Work in just over 1½ tbsp of the butter. When the dough is well mixed, knead lightly until it has lost some of its elasticity, wrap in saran wrap and place in the refrigerator to rest for 30 minutes.

• • •

□ *To prevent the lower layers of puff pastry sticking to your baking sheet or pan, grease with butter even if they are supposed to be nonstick and then sprinkle with flour; turn the sheet or pan over and shake gently to get rid of any loose flour. Another precaution is to ensure that your filling does not leak out or overflow during cooking.*

□ *If baking an unfilled puff pie shell, prick the surface all over with a fork to release any air trapped between the pan and the pastry which would expand as it heats; you can also weight down the bottom with greaseproof paper or parchment and beans.*

□ *Almond shells are hard and time-consuming to break open, releasing the kernel, still in its covering of thin brown skin. This skin is quickly removed once the kernels have been placed in boiling water for a minute or two. Usually almonds are sold blanched and peeled, ready for use.*

□ *Soak seedless white raisins in warm (not hot) water for about 30 minutes before using them; this will make them swell and double in size. If you are in a rush, use hot water, but do not leave the raisins in it for more than a few minutes.*

ROUGH PUFF PASTRY

This pastry uses less butter than puff pastry; it can replace it in the same recipes, but will be less light and delicate.

Time: 30 minutes + resting times
Fairly easy

2½ cups + 2 tbsp strong or medium strong flour or all-purpose flour
1 tsp salt
½ cup + 2 tbsp (1¼ sticks) butter
cold water

Using the above ingredients, carry out exactly the same procedure as for Puff Pastry.

• • •

APRICOT AND MACAROON PIE

Time: 1 hour 25 minutes
Fairly easy

1 quantity Puff Pastry or Rough Puff Pastry (see pages 86–7)
⅓ cup seedless white raisins
6 ripe apricots
scant ½ lb very small crisp macaroons, preferably amarettini or ratafias
1 egg
¼ cup sugar
¼ cup melted butter
3 tbsp cornstarch
1½ cups fresh ricotta cheese
peel of ½ lemon, grated
pinch salt
angelica

Grease a 10-in pie pan with a little butter, and dust lightly

*APRICOT AND
MACAROON PIE*
■ *Macaroons made with
apricot kernels (amaretti) are
the natural complement to
their fruit; here they serve a
practical purpose as well by
absorbing the juices released
by the fruit while cooking.*

with flour; roll out the pastry
and line the pan. Place in the
refrigerator to keep cold. Soak
the seedless white raisins in
warm water. Wash the
apricots, cut neatly in half, and
remove the pit. (Well drained,
canned apricots may be used.)
Crumble half the macaroons
coarsely. Beat the egg yolk
with the sugar in a bowl until
pale and frothy, beat in the
melted butter, the cornstarch,
ricotta, grated lemon peel and
the salt, and combine
thoroughly; fold in the stiffly
beaten egg white. Cover the
bottom of the pie shell with
half the crumbled macaroons;
place the apricots on top,

spoon in the ricotta mixture,
level with a spatula and cook
for 45 minutes at 350° F.
When cold, decorate with the
remaining macaroons, the
drained and dried raisins, and
slivers of angelica. (A few
extra apricot halves could be
added if wished.)

• • •

PINEAPPLE PIE

*Fresh pineapple is normally
available all the year round; if
unavailable, canned pineapple
may be substituted. Drain and
pat dry with paper towels.*

*Time: 1 hour 10 minutes
Fairly easy*

1 quantity Puff Pastry (see
   page 86)
2 yolks and 1 egg white
½ cup sugar
1¾ cups ricotta cheese
2 tbsp butter
8 slices fresh pineapple,
   peeled and cored
few drops vanilla extract
1 small piece angelica

Roll out the pastry and use to
line a lightly greased and
floured 10-in pie pan. Chill in
the refrigerator for 1 hour
before resting.
Beat the egg yolks with the
sugar until pale and fluffy;
push the ricotta through a
sieve and beat into the egg
mixture; beat in the melted
butter, 1 tbsp pineapple juice
and 2–3 drops vanilla extract.
Chop 6 of the pineapple slices,

TRADITIONAL PUFF PASTRY

These quantities are for a large pie pan; the recipes in this chapter normally call for the quantities given on page 86.

Makes about 2¼ lb
1 lb strong or medium strong flour
2 tsp salt
1 lb sweet butter
½-scant 1 cup cold water

Sift the flour and salt into a large bowl. Add a little cold butter and rub into the flour. Add sufficient cold water to make a stiff but still fairly soft dough. Shake a little flour inside a plastic bag and place the dough ball inside; place in the refrigerator.

Remove the pastry after 30 minutes (or longer). Spread a sheet of waxed paper on the marble slab or work surface, put the butter on top (straight out of the refrigerator), and cover with another sheet of nonstick parchment. Roll the butter to a thickness of ¾ in.

Take the pastry out of its bag, place on the lightly floured marble slab or work surface; roll out in a square sheet ⅜–¼ in thick; this will be sufficiently large to completely enclose the butter when the corners are folded over toward the center, overlapping one another like an envelope. As you roll out the pastry, turn it frequently.

Peel off the top parchment from the butter and place it in the center of the pastry square; peel off the second piece of paper.

Fold the four corners towards the center, enclosing the butter. Press the surrounding margin gently with the rolling pin.

Roll the envelope lightly until it acquires a rectangular shape, the length of which should be three times its width.

Fold one end over so that its edge comes two thirds of the way up the rectangle; fold the other end over so that its edge is level with the first fold; this will give you 3 layers of pastry.

Repeat these last two steps. Remember to give a half turn to the pastry after each complete process so that you are rolling it in a different direction each time. Place the pastry in its floured bag and return to the refrigerator for 30 minutes (it must be chilled and rested after each full turn). Do two more full turns and your puff pastry will be ready for use.

APPLE FLAN
■ This flan can be made with
other fruit; pears or bananas
would be particularly
suitable.

drain off excess liquid, and stir into the mixture. Fold in the stiffly beaten egg white. Take the pie shell from the refrigerator; prick the bottom lightly all over with a fork and spoon in the filling. Bake at 400° F for 30 minutes.
Pat the remaining 2 pineapple slices dry with paper towels, cut into small, neat pieces and use to decorate the tart, together with small strips of angelica.

•   •   •

APPLE FLAN

Time: 1 hour 15 minutes
Fairly easy

1 quantity Puff Pastry (see page 86)
2 whole eggs and 2 extra yolks
⅔ cup sugar
¼ cup all-purpose flour
1 cup milk
3 Golden Delicious apples
¼ cup (½ stick) butter, melted
⅔ cup ground almonds
1 tbsp vanilla sugar

Roll out the pastry and line a prepared 10-in flan dish or pie pan. Prick the bottom lightly with a fork and chill in the refrigerator for 30 minutes. Beat the two extra egg yolks with ½ cup of the sugar until pale and frothy; beat in the sifted flour followed by 1 whole egg. Continue beating for 10 minutes, then beat in the hot milk, adding it in a very thin stream. Stir this custard continuously with a wooden spoon over low heat; continue cooking for 2 minutes (still stirring) after it has come to a gentle boil. Allow to cool

RASPBERRIES
■ An engraving taken from a nineteenth-century botanical treatise. Frozen or fresh raspberries may be turned into cordials, jellies, and preserves.

before spooning into the pie shell. Level the surface with a spatula.

Peel and core the apples, slice thinly and arrange, slightly overlapping, in concentric circles on top of the custard. Place in the oven, preheated to 415° F for the first 10 minutes, then reduce the temperature to 350° F and cook for a further 20 minutes. Remove from the oven. Mix the remaining sugar with the melted butter and the remaining egg; pour this mixture all over the surface of the hot flan, sprinkle the ground almonds on top and return to the oven for 10 minutes or until the top turns golden brown. Allow to cool before sprinkling the vanilla sugar over the surface. (If you have no vanilla sugar, plain sugar may be substituted.)

· · ·

PEACH AND ALMOND PIE

This refreshing, creamy dessert can be made with other summer fruits, such as apricots, strawberries, or raspberries.

Time: 1 hour 20 minutes
Fairly easy

1 quantity Puff Pastry or
　Rough Puff Pastry (see
　pages 86–7)
2¼ lb ripe peaches
1 cup sugar
4 eggs
2–3 drops vanilla extract
½ cup (1 stick) butter, melted
20 blanched almonds

Roll out the pastry, line a prepared 10-in pie pan, pricking the bottom lightly with a fork. Chill in the refrigerator for 30 minutes. Peel the peaches, cut in half, and remove the pits. In a food processor blend 4 peaches with the sugar, all the eggs, the vanilla, and melted butter until very smooth. Cut the remaining two peaches into slices and arrange in the pie shell. Place the whole almonds

in the available spaces and cover with the peach mixture. Cook for 35–40 minutes at 400° F.

· · ·

BERRY GATEAU

Time: 1 hour 10 minutes
Fairly easy

1 quantity Puff Pastry or
　Rough Puff Pastry (see
　pages 86–7)
1 lb mixed berry fruits
　(raspberries, strawberries,
　and blueberries)
½ cup granulated cane sugar
1 cup all-purpose flour
¼ cup red currant jam or jelly
⅔ cup sugar
½ cup + 2 tbsp butter

Once you have made the pastry, rinse the fruit in cold water, dry, mix in a

nonmetallic bowl with the cane sugar, and leave to stand for 1 hour.

Roll out the pastry into a thinner sheet than usual and use a flan ring to cut out three identical circles of pastry. Grease 1 very large or three medium-sized cookie sheets lightly with butter, dust with flour, shaking off any excess, and place the circles of pastry on them; bake at 400° F for 20 minutes or until pale golden brown, risen, and crisp.

Mix the flour in a bowl with the ordinary sugar; cut the softened butter into very small pieces and rub into the flour mixture, using your fingertips. You should end up with a granular mixture, like the topping for fruit crumble puddings. Allow the cooked pastry to cool completely before sprinkling one circle with one third of the crumble mixture; place one third of the mixed fruit on top. Place the second pastry circle over the

BERRY GATEAU
■ *Frozen berries or fruits of the forest can be used when these berries are out of season; leave to thaw slowly at room temperature for about two hours.*

fruit, follow with another layer of crumble and another of fruit. Cover with the last pastry circle and the remaining crumble mixture; finish with a layer of the red currant jelly, and arrange the remaining berries on top.

• • •

BANANA CREAM SLICE

Mix the bananas with a little lemon juice to prevent discoloration.

*Time: 1 hour 20 minutes
Fairly easy*

1 quantity Puff Pastry (see page 86)
½ cup sugar
1 cup water
2 egg yolks
1 cup (2 sticks) butter
2 tbsp vanilla sugar (or 2 extra tbsp sugar and few drops vanilla extract)
2 very ripe bananas
1 tbsp maraschino liqueur
¾ cup flaked or slivered almonds

Roll out the pastry and cut into 4 rectangles of identical size and just over ⅛ in thick. Grease a large cookie sheet lightly with butter, dust with flour, and place the pastry shapes on it, evenly spaced out. Prick their surfaces lightly with a fork and bake for 20 minutes (or until golden brown and cooked) at 400° F. Set aside to cool.

Heat the sugar and water in a heavy saucepan and boil until the large thread stage is reached. Turn off the heat. Beat the egg yolks energetically as you add the very hot sugar syrup, pouring it onto them in a very thin stream; continue beating until the mixture has cooled completely. Beat the butter with the vanilla sugar (or with the extra sugar and the vanilla extract). Process the peeled, sliced bananas to a smooth cream in a blender or food processor, then combine thoroughly with the butter and sugar. Add the egg mixture a little at a time, and the maraschino few drops at a time, beating well after each addition.

Spread out one third of this mixture over the top of one of the pastry rectangles; place another rectangle on top. Repeat this operation twice, finishing with a pastry lid. Roast the almonds in the oven (5 minutes at 400° F), taking care that they do not burn. Allow to cool and sprinkle over the top and sides of the slice.

• • •

STRAWBERRY DELIGHT
■ Tiny woodland strawberries
can be found at high-quality
stores or growing wild: they
have a wonderful taste and
scent. Cut cultivated
strawberries in quarters as a
substitute.

SPONGE AND RAISIN DESSERT

*Layers of sponge cake
alternating with puff pastry
make this dessert even lighter
and more delicate than usual.
Chocolate can be used to flavor
the pastry cream for a change.*

*Time: 1 hour 15 minutes
Fairly easy*

1 quantity Puff Pastry or
   Rough Puff Pastry (see
   pages 86–7)
½ cup seedless white raisins
½ cup Grand Marnier
1 quantity Pastry Cream (see
   page 44)
1 round sponge cake 8½–9 in
   in diameter (see page 146)
confectioners' sugar

Divide the puff pastry in half
and roll out both halves to
form circles to match the size
of your sponge cake. Place
these two pastry rounds on a
prepared cookie sheet and
cook in a hot oven (400° F) for
20 minutes or until done.
Soak the seedless white
raisins in warm water for
about 10 minutes. When soft
and plump, drain them, dry
with paper towels and place in
a cup with 2 tbsp of the Grand
Marnier.
Make the pastry cream; when
it has cooled completely, drain
the raisins and stir into the
pastry cream. Place one of the
puff pastry circles on a serving
plate and spread with half the
pastry cream; cover with the
sponge cake. Sprinkle the
remaining Grand Marnier over
the surface of the sponge,
then spread with the rest of
the cream. Top with the last
pastry circle and dredge with a
little sifted confectioners'
sugar.

92

PASTRY COOK'S KNIFE
■ Sixteenth-century French
engraving. An ivory-handled
knife such as this would have
been used for cutting and
serving cakes and other
confections.

PUFF PASTRY

CREAM

Tepid cream takes a very long
time to become thick when
beaten. Save time and energy
by chilling it for an hour or two
beforehand. Egg whites,
conversely, become firm and
snowy much more quickly if
they reach room temperature
before you beat them. A pinch
of salt or sugar before you
start can hasten the process.

STRAWBERRY DELIGHT

Time: 1 hour 20 minutes
Fairly easy

1 quantity Puff Pastry or
 Rough Puff Pastry (see
 pages 86–7)
2 egg yolks
½ cup sugar
¼ cup all-purpose flour
1 cup milk
generous ½ cup whipping
 cream
2–2½ cups wild strawberries
 or very small cultivated
 strawberries
1 tbsp confectioners' sugar

Divide the pastry into quarters
and roll each quarter out to
matching squares; place these
on a large prepared cookie
sheet and bake for 20 minutes
at 400° F.
Beat the egg yolks with the
sugar until pale and fluffy.
Beat in the flour, followed by
the very hot milk, adding a
little at a time. Cook, stirring
continuously, over low heat
until the custard thickens. Set
aside to cool. When cold fold in
the stiffly beaten cream.
Rinse and dry the

strawberries (if cultivated
strawberries are used, hull
them). Spread one third of the
custard over a pastry square;
sprinkle one third of the
strawberries onto the custard;
cover with the second pastry
square. Repeat this layering
process until you have used all
the custard, strawberries, and
pastry squares, ending with a
pastry square "lid," and dust
the surface lightly with sifted
confectioners' sugar.
Decorate the center of the
pastry lid with few extra
strawberries if wished.

• • •

NECTARINE FLAN

*The cornflakes absorb the juice
released by the nectarines as
they cook, preventing the pastry
case from becoming sodden.*

Time: 1 hour 10 minutes
Fairly easy

1 quantity Puff Pastry or
 Rough Puff Pastry (see
 pages 86–7)
4 nectarines
¼ cup butter
½ cup sugar
¼ cup all-purpose flour
2 eggs
1 cup milk
6 tbsp crumbled cornflakes

Roll out the pastry and line a
greased and lightly floured
round pie pan. Chill in the
refrigerator for 30 minutes.
Wash and peel the nectarines,
cut the flesh away from the
pits, and dice. Soften the
butter by beating it; beat in
the sugar, add the flour, and
continue beating for 5
minutes. Add the eggs,
beating them in one at a time;
lastly, beat in the hot milk,

adding it in a thin stream. Take the pie shell out of the refrigerator, sprinkle the crushed cornflakes all over the base, and arrange the diced nectarines on top in an even layer. Cover with the custard and cook for 40 minutes at 400° F.

• • •

RASPBERRY AND CHOCOLATE FLAN

Chocolate goes very well with many varieties of fruit, particularly with raspberries, oranges, and pears.

Time: 1 hour 25 minutes
Fairly easy

1 quantity Puff Pastry or
    Rough Puff Pastry (see
    pages 86–7)
4 eggs
½ cup sugar
1 tsp vanilla extract
¼ cup all-purpose flour
2 tbsp butter
1¾ cups milk
½ lb raspberries
4 oz (4 squares) semisweet
    chocolate or fine bakers'
    chocolate

Grease a 10-in flan dish or pie pan with butter and dust lightly with flour. Roll out the pastry to a circular shape just over ⅛ in thick and sufficient in diameter to overlap the edges of the pan by ½–¾ in. Prick the bottom lightly with a fork and chill for 30 minutes in the refrigerator.
Place two whole eggs and two egg yolks in a bowl (the remaining two whites will be used later) with the sugar and vanilla. Beat very thoroughly

□ *White sugar (granulated, superfine, and confectioners') is produced from the sugarbeet. Vanilla sugar is very useful when making cakes, desserts, and cookies; you can make your own by burying a vanilla bean in a jar of sugar and leaving it, tightly stoppered, for a week or two. Cane sugar is less widely available; coarse or fine cane sugar, light or dark, is commercially produced. It has a better flavor than ordinary sugar but less sweetening power.*

□ *Lemons and oranges are almost invariably treated with diphenyl by large-scale producers to improve their keeping qualities. Ideally, select fruit which you know has not been treated when using the skin, otherwise boil for a minute or two in water, change the water and boil again; repeat this operation a third or even fourth time.*

□ *When cooking a tart with a fresh fruit filling, it is a good idea to line the bottom of the shell with very thin cookies or ladyfingers, so that any juice released during cooking will not make the shell cook unevenly or become soggy.*

□ *Make sure that you know whether your oven temperature is accurate when baking cakes and pastry; preheat conventional ovens and check the equivalent cooking times for convection ovens: cooking times can vary by as much as 5 minutes for every 30 minutes' baking time.*

□ *Use a very sharp serrated knife to cut cooked puff pastry or sweet egg pastry: you will end up with a far neater result. Other types of pastry will cut perfectly well with an ordinary cake slice or broad-bladed knife.*

□ *Baking pans, pie shell pans, flan rings etc. vary greatly in size and capacity. When using puff pastry or sweet egg pastry a wide pan, no more than 1 in deep, is normally used. If you use a flan ring or a baking sheet or a pan with a removable base, it will be much easier to extract the cooked pastry.*

for 5–10 minutes. Stir in the flour, the softened butter and combine well before beating in the hot milk a little at a time. Fold in the stiffly beaten egg whites.
Spread the raspberries out in the bottom of the pie shell and cover with the frothy custard mixture. Fold the spare border of pastry toward the center of the flan, pleating it as you go (see illustration on page 62). Place in the oven, preheated to 400° F and cook for 20 minutes; place a flat sheet of aluminum foil loosely on top of the flan, reduce the heat to 320° F and cook for a further 40 minutes, or until the flan is done.
Melt the chocolate with 2 tbsp water over hot water and use a teaspoon to dribble it all over the surface of the flan.

• • •

MORELLO CHERRY FLAN

Time: 1 hour 30 minutes
Fairly easy

1 quantity Puff Pastry or
   Rough Puff Pastry (see
   pages 86–7)
scant ½ cup butter
½ cup sugar
1 cup ground almonds
1 tsp all-purpose flour
3 eggs
3 tbsp rum
1¼ lb Morello cherries
6 ladyfingers
½ cup red currant jelly

Roll out the pastry, line a prepared 10-in flan dish or pie pan with it and prick the bottom with a fork; set aside in the refrigerator for 30 minutes. Work the softened butter with a wooden spoon, then beat in the sugar followed by the ground almonds, and the flour. Add the eggs one at a time; stir in 2 tbsp of the rum.
Pit the cherries and crumble the ladyfingers into the bottom of the chilled pie shell. Place the cherries in a layer on top, spoon the almond mixture over them, level with a spatula, and bake for 30 minutes at 400° F, then cover the flan with a flat sheet of foil and continue cooking for a further 20 minutes.
Melt the red currant jelly with the remaining 1 tbsp rum over low heat; sprinkle over the surface of the flan as soon as it comes out of the oven. Serve cold.

• • •

DIPLOMAT
■ Mascarpone is a delicious full-fat cream cheese with a fresh, delicate taste. Cocoa powder, sugar, and a little brandy can be added if wished.

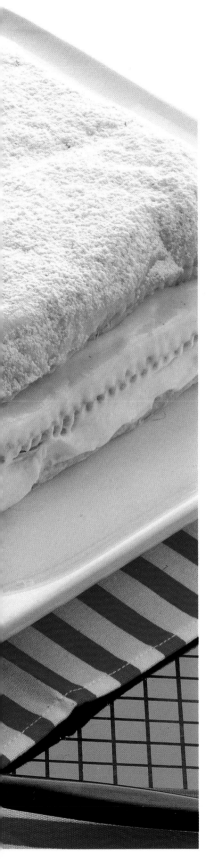

DIPLOMAT

Time: 1 hour
Fairly easy

1 quantity Puff Pastry or Rough Puff Pastry (see pages 86–7)
1–2 tbsp confectioners' sugar
2 eggs
4 tbsp sugar
1 cup mascarpone (or similar fresh cheese)
½ cup whipping or heavy cream
2 slices Sponge Cake, cut to size (see page 146)
½ cup very strong black coffee
½ cup brandy

Roll out the pastry into a large sheet and cut into 4 neat, matching rectangles; place these on a prepared cookie sheet; chill for 30 minutes before baking in a hot oven (400° F) for 20 minutes. Remove the pastry from the oven and sprinkle the surface of each rectangle with sifted confectioners' sugar before leaving to cool.
Beat the egg yolks with the sugar for 10 minutes; add the mascarpone, combining it thoroughly; fold in the stiffly beaten cream.
Place one of the pastry rectangles on a serving plate; dip one of the slices of sponge cake carefully in the coffee and brandy (mixed together) and place on top of the pastry. Cover with one third of the mascarpone cream. Place another pastry layer on the cream; follow with the second dipped sponge slice, more cream, another layer of pastry, the remainder of the cream and finally, a lid of the last pastry layer.

MANGO TART

The mango is a delicious, highly flavored, and scented fruit, which should be eaten very ripe.

Time: 1 hour 15 minutes
Fairly easy

1 quantity Puff Pastry or Rough Puff Pastry (see pages 86–7)
2 very ripe mangoes
3 egg yolks
juice of 1 lemon
1 cup confectioners' sugar
¼ cup all-purpose flour
½ cup heavy cream
1 cup milk
2 tbsp butter

Roll out the pastry and line a lightly greased and floured 10-in pie pan with it. Prick the bottom in several places with a fork and chill in the refrigerator for 30 minutes. Peel the mangoes, cut the flesh away from the pit and place the flesh in a food processor with the lemon juice and ¼ cup of the sugar. Blend to a smooth purée.
Beat the egg yolks very thoroughly with the remaining sugar; when pale and frothy beat in the flour, the cream and lastly the hot milk. Cook over low heat, stirring constantly, until this custard mixture thickens. Remove from the heat and stir in the softened butter and the mango purée; stir well.
Cook the pie shell for 20 minutes at 400° F; take out of the oven, spoon in the mango filling, and return to the oven for a further 20 minutes, or until done. Allow to cool before serving.

CHESTNUT SLICE

Whole marrons glacés (candied chestnuts) are expensive, so buy them only for decoration; use the marron débris (broken marrons) for other purposes (available in the food departments of large stores or in good delicatessens).

Time: 1 hour 15 minutes
Fairly easy

2¼ cups crumbled marrons glacés
½ cup brandy
1 quantity Puff Pastry or Rough Puff Pastry (see pages 86–7)
1 cup mascarpone cheese (or similar fresh cheese)
¾ cup chestnut preserve or sweetened chestnut purée
4 oz (4 squares) bitter chocolate
6 whole marrons glacés
1 tbsp confectioners' sugar

Place the crumbled marrons glacés in a bowl with the brandy. Roll out the pastry to a thickness of just over ⅛ in, cut into 4 identical rectangles, place these on a greased and lightly floured cookie sheet, and prick the surface of each one in several places with a fork. Bake at 400° F for 20 minutes or until done. Remove from the oven and leave to cool.
Mix the mascarpone (or similar cheese) with the marron preserve or purée; melt the chocolate over hot water and then stir into the chestnut cream. Drain off the brandy from the crumbled marrons and stir these into the mixture. Spread one third of the chestnut cream on one of the pastry rectangles, and

cover with a second rectangle.
Repeat this operation twice
more, ending with a rectangle
of pastry for the "lid,"
sprinkled with the sifted
confectioners' sugar and with
the whole chestnuts arranged
in a line down the center.

• • •

BRANDIED PRUNE TART

*Make your own brandied
prunes: pack glass jars loosely
with pitted prunes, and fill up
with good-quality brandy. Seal
tightly and leave for 1 month
before using.*

Time: 1 hour
Fairly easy

1 quantity Puff Pastry or
   Rough Puff Pastry (see
   pages 86–7)
20 brandied prunes
6 tbsp sugar
4 eggs
¼ cup all-purpose flour
pinch salt
½ cup heavy cream

Roll out the pastry and line the
base and sides of a pie pan as
usual, having first lightly
greased the pan with butter
and dusted it with flour. Chill
in the refrigerator for 30
minutes.
Drain off all the brandy from
the prunes. Beat all but 1 tbsp
of the sugar in a bowl with the
eggs, and add the flour and
salt. Beat in the cream. Prick
the bottom of the uncooked
pastry case with a fork. Fill
with a layer of prunes and
cover these with the egg,
flour, and cream mixture.
Bake at 400° F for 40 minutes.
About 5 minutes before the

tart is done, sprinkle the
remaining sugar over the
surface; it will then caramelize
during the remainder of the
cooking time.

• • •

LEMON LAYERED DESSERT

Time: 1 hour
Fairly easy

1 quantity Puff Pastry or
   Rough Puff Pastry (see
   pages 86–7)
2 egg yolks
½ cup sugar
3 tbsp all-purpose flour
1 cup milk
2 lemons
½ cup (1 stick) butter
1 tbsp confectioners' sugar

Divide the pastry dough into
three equal portions and roll
these out to form three circles
of pastry 7 in in diameter.
Lightly grease a large cookie

sheet (or three smaller cookie
sheets) with butter, dust with
flour (shaking off excess), and
arrange the pastry circles
ready for baking; prick their
surfaces with a fork and place
in a hot oven (400° F) for 20
minutes. While the pastry is
baking, beat the egg yolks
with the sugar until pale and
greatly increased in volume;
add the flour; beat in the hot
milk, adding it a little at a time.
Add the grated peel of the two
lemons and cook over low
heat, stirring continuously,
until the mixture has
thickened. Add the lemon
juice and continue stirring.
Remove from the heat and
allow to cool.
Beat the butter until pale and
creamy and add it, a spoonful
at a time to the cold custard,
stirring well after each
addition. Spread half this
custard filling over a puff
pastry circle; cover with a
second circle; top with the
remaining filling and place the
third pastry round in position.
Sprinkle the surface with
sifted confectioners' sugar and
serve.

• • •

COCONUT CREAM PIE

*Fresh coconut forms part of
many fruit based desserts;
shredded coconut keeps well
and may be used in a variety of
cakes and desserts.*

Time: 1 hour 10 minutes
Fairly easy

1 quantity Puff Pastry or
   Rough Puff Pastry (see
   pages 86–7)
1 cup shredded coconut
½ cup sugar
few drops vanilla extract
2 tbsp cornstarch
½ cup heavy cream
3 eggs
6 ladyfingers

Roll out the pastry and use it
to line a prepared 10-in pie
pan. Place the lined pan in the
refrigerator for 30 minutes.
Mix the coconut in a bowl with
the sugar, vanilla extract, and
cornstarch. Work in the
cream. Stir in the lightly
beaten egg yolks, then fold in
the stiffly beaten egg whites.

LEMON LAYERED DESSERT
■ *If time is short, use stiffly beaten cream instead of the special pastry cream. Do not forget to add the finely grated lemon peel.*

Take the pie pan from the refrigerator, cover the base with a layer of crumbled ladyfingers, and then fill the shell with the coconut cream mixture. Bake for 20 minutes at 400° F, then reduce the heat to 350° F and continue cooking for a further 20 minutes or until done.

• • •

PEACH CREAM PIE

In summer, use fresh peaches, cooked with sugar and water.

Time: 45 minutes
Fairly easy

1 quantity Puff Pastry or Rough Puff Pastry (see pages 86–7)
14 oz net (drained) weight canned peach halves
2 eggs
¼ cup sugar
3 tbsp cornstarch
1 cup water
1 cup heavy or whipping cream

Roll out the pastry to a thickness of just over ⅛ in, forming a single neat rectangle. Place on a prepared cookie sheet and cook at 400° F for 20 minutes or until done. Cut this large rectangle into 4 smaller rectangles and leave to cool.

Liquidize the peaches in a blender or food processor to form a smooth thick purée. Beat the egg yolks with the sugar until pale and fluffy; dissolve the cornstarch in the water, stir well, and combine with the eggs and sugar; stir in the peach purée. Cook this mixture over low heat, stirring

carefully, until it has thickened.

Spread one third of the peach mixture on one of the pastry rectangles; place another pastry rectangle on top and continue layering in this way, ending up with a pastry "lid" on top; use a pastry bag and fluted tube to pipe a decoration of stiffly beaten cream on the top (and sides if wished).

• • •

RHUBARB AND RAISIN TART

Time: 1 hour 10 minutes
Fairly easy

1 quantity Puff Pastry or
    Rough Puff Pastry (see
    pages 86–7)
2¼ lb tender rhubarb
2 eggs
½ cup sugar
1 cup heavy cream
⅓ cup seedless white raisins

Roll out the pastry and line a greased and floured 10-in pie pan. Use a fork to prick the bottom lightly. Place in the refrigerator to chill for 30 minutes. Cut off every trace of the leaves from the rhubarb and if the stalks are not very young and tender, peel off their outer layer; cut into very short pieces and cook in boiling water for 2 minutes, then drain very thoroughly. Beat the eggs with the sugar, cream, and drained seedless white raisins. Spread the rhubarb pieces evenly over the bottom of the pie shell. Cover with the egg and cream mixture. Cook for 20 minutes at 400° F; place a piece of foil on top of the tart to prevent it

RHUBARB AND RAISIN
TART
■ The rhubarb plant grows
wild in its native habitat in
Asia and medicinal rhubarb
has long been used as a
purgative. The young, tender
stalks can be used for jellies
and other preserves as well as
for many desserts.

coloring too much and reduce
the heat to 350° F; cook for a
further 20 minutes or until
done. Remove the foil and
serve warm.

• • •

LEMON CREAM TART

*Lemons are used a great deal
in patisserie; the peel is
particularly useful because of
the essential oil it contains,
imparting a delicate yet intense
aroma to everything it flavors.
Try to buy lemons which have
not been treated with chemical
sprays.*

Time: 45 minutes
Fairly easy

1 quantity Puff Pastry or
    Rough Puff Pastry (see
    pages 86–7)
6 egg yolks
½ cup sugar
scant ½ cup butter
½ cup + 2 tbsp lemon juice
1 tbsp finely grated lemon peel

Roll out the pastry and line a
prepared 10-in pie pan. Prick
the bottom with a fork and
bake in a hot oven (400° F) for
20 minutes or until done. Beat
the egg yolks in a heatproof
bowl with the sugar until pale
and greatly increased in
volume. Still using a whisk,
beat in the softened butter in
small pieces, followed by the
lemon juice. Place the bowl
securely over a pan of gently
simmering water and continue
beating while cooking until the
mixture thickens (do not
overheat or it will curdle).
Remove from the heat and stir
in the grated lemon peel.
When cold, pour into the
cooked and cooled pie shell.

RHUBARB

This perennial plant, originally
native to Tibet, is now widely
grown and used for preserves
and pie fillings. Available from
the very early spring until
early summer. Only the stalks
are used in cooking, preferably
when they are pinkish and
tender. The leaves must not
be used.

Place a round slice of lemon,
with all the peel and pith
removed in the center, and
serve.

• • •

BLUEBERRY CREAM SLICE

*If blueberries are not available,
use suitable substitutes such as
cherries, raspberries, or diced
pieces of larger fruits. Canned
blueberries may also be used for
this recipe.*

Time: 1 hour
Fairly easy

1 quantity Puff Pastry or
    Rough Puff Pastry (see
    pages 86–7)
1 quantity Chantilly Cream
    (see page 48)
1 lb blueberries
1 tbsp confectioners' sugar

Roll out the pastry to the
shape of a rectangle; place this
on a lightly greased and
floured cookie sheet; bake at
400° F for 20 minutes or until
done. Immediately after
removing from the oven, cut
the cooked pastry into 4 equal

parts. Leave to cool.
Make the Chantilly Cream; if
using canned blueberries drain
very thoroughly. Spread one
third of the cream on one of
the pieces of pastry, place one
third of the fruit on top; cover
with another pastry piece.
Continue layering, ending up
with a final piece of pastry.
Chill in the refrigerator until it
is time to serve (do not
assemble more than 2 hours
before required). Dust with
icing sugar just before
serving.

• • •

APPLE AND BLUEBERRY PIE

*An early autumn treat, when
both apples and berries are ripe.
Frozen berries can be used;
leave to thaw at room
temperature for 2 hours before
using.*

Time: 40 minutes
Fairly easy

1 quantity Puff Pastry or
    Rough Puff Pastry (see
    pages 86–7)
½ cup blueberry jam
½ cup sugar
1 lb apples, peeled, cored, and
    very thinly sliced
½ lb blueberries

Roll out the pastry to a slightly
larger circle than is needed to
line a prepared 10-in pie pan
and pinch in the extra fullness
all round to give a ¾-in high
edge (alternatively, use a
fairly deep pie dish). Spread
the jam over the bottom and
sprinkle half the sugar over it.
Layer all the apple slices on
top of this in a single layer.
Top with the blueberries, and
sprinkle the remaining sugar

on top. Bake in a hot oven (400° F) for about 40 minutes or until done. Allow to cool before removing from the pan (if used). This pie is best served cold.

· · ·

BLACKBERRY FLAN

Always use very ripe blackberries or they will be unpleasantly acidic. The wild berries usually have more flavor but need thorough washing. Fresh strawberries or raspberries could be substituted.

Time: 45 minutes
Fairly easy

1 quantity Puff Pastry or Rough Puff Pastry (see pages 86–7)
1 cup heavy cream
½ cup confectioners' sugar
few drops vanilla extract
1 lb blackberries
3 tbsp blackberry jelly or other fruit jelly
2 tbsp kirsch

Roll out the pastry and use to line a 10-in greased and floured pie pan. Prick the bottom with a fork; use a pastry crimper or a pastry wheel with a ribbed boss to

give a decorative edge if you wish. Place in the oven, preheated to 400° F, for 25 minutes or until golden brown. Set aside to cool. Beat the sifted confectioners' sugar and the vanilla into the cream; continue beating until stiff. Spoon this into the cold pie shell and completely cover with the washed and dried blackberries. Melt the jelly over very low heat; stir in the kirsch and sprinkle over the blackberries. Serve without too much delay.

· · ·

RICOTTA PIE

Time: 1 hour 15 minutes
Fairly easy

1 quantity Puff Pastry or Rough Puff Pastry (see pages 86–7)
2 cups fresh ricotta cheese
2 tbsp pine nuts, lightly roasted
2 tbsp flaked or slivered almonds
2 tbsp finely diced citron peel
1 tbsp all-purpose flour
3 eggs
¾ cup sugar
1 tbsp orange liqueur (e.g. Curaçao, Grand Marnier) or brandy

Grease a 10-in pie pan lightly with butter as usual, dust with flour, shaking off excess. Roll out the pastry and line the pan, prick the bottom lightly with a fork in several places

RICOTTA PIE
■ Cows' milk ricotta is best for desserts and cakes. The ewes' milk variety has a pleasant but slightly intrusive taste. A covered pie is illustrated but an open pie is just as good.

BANANA AND CREAM LAYERED PASTRY
■ For a less rich dessert, omit the butter from the pastry cream, or use mascarpone (or a similar cream cheese) instead.

and chill in the refrigerator for 30 minutes.
Have the ricotta at room temperature and stir it well, both before and after adding the pine nuts, the almonds, and the candied peel. Sprinkle the sifted flour into the bowl and stir thoroughly.
Beat the eggs with the sugar until pale and creamy before combining with the ricotta mixture. Add the liqueur or brandy and transfer this filling to the pie shell. Bake at 400°F for 40 minutes or until done.

• • •

kirsch, mix well, and leave to stand for 30 minutes. Beat the egg yolks very thoroughly with the sugar; beat in the sifted flour and then the hot milk, adding this in a thin stream as you beat. Stirring constantly, cook the custard over low heat until it thickens. Draw aside from the heat and leave to cool to room temperature. Beat the butter until pale and creamy, then beat the custard into it 1 tbsp at a time (using an electric beater or wire whisk). Spread half the custard on top of one of the pastry circles. Drain any excess kirsch from

the sliced bananas and place half of these on top of the custard. Place another pastry circle on top and then use up the rest of the custard and the banana slices, finishing with a pastry lid. Chill until you are ready to serve the gateau, giving the top a dusting of confectioners' sugar at the last minute, adding extra banana slices and some orange sections with rosettes of piped whipped cream for decoration if wished.

• • •

RASPBERRY MERINGUE PIE

This straightforward dessert is exceptionally light and delicate and looks wonderful if you pipe the meringue with a fluted pastry tube.

Time: 1 hour
Fairly easy

1 quantity Puff Pastry or Rough Puff Pastry (see pages 86–7)
1 lb raspberries
½ cup sugar

BANANA AND CREAM LAYERED PASTRY GATEAU

Time: 1 hour
Fairly easy

1 quantity Puff Pastry or Rough Puff Pastry (see pages 86–7)
2 bananas
2–3 tbsp kirsch
2 egg yolks
½ cup sugar
3 tbsp all-purpose flour
1 cup milk
½ cup butter
1 tbsp confectioners' sugar

Divide the pastry dough into three equal parts and roll each of these out into a circle 7 in in diameter; prick their surfaces lightly with a fork and place on greased and floured cookie sheets in a preheated oven (425°F) for 20 minutes. Leave to cool. Once the pastry is in the oven, peel the bananas, slice into a bowl; add the

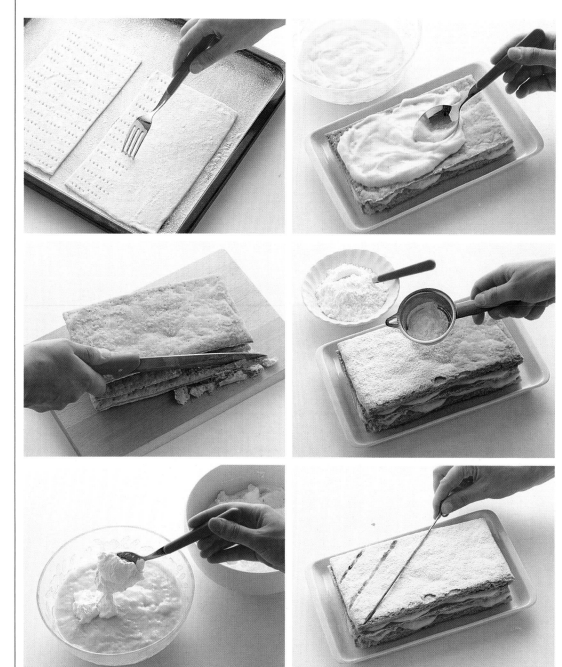

One of the most classic examples of puff pastry use; we have used three layers of pastry with pastry cream in between. Only successful, light puff pastry is suitable for this purpose.

For 1 slice measuring approx. 6 x 8 in you will need:
1¼ cups Pastry Cream (see page 44)
½ cup well chilled whipping cream
6 tbsp confectioners' sugar
¾ lb Puff Pastry (see pages 86 and 88)

Roll out the puff pastry into a rectangle ⅛ in thick. Cut into 3 identical pieces and place each of these on a greased cookie sheet. Prick the surface with the tines of a fork. Cover the pastry and chill in the refrigerator for 30 minutes, then bake at 425° F for 20 minutes or until the pastry is crisp, well risen and pale golden brown.

Leave to cool; trim off any uneven edges with a very sharp knife. Fold the stiffly beaten cream into the pastry cream if you prefer a lighter filling. Spread the filling thickly on 2 of the pastry rectangles; assemble the slice, placing the plain pastry on top. Dust the top layer with the sifted confectioners' sugar.

Heat a skewer until very hot and press against the sugar to form diagonal markings as decoration (hold with an oven cloth).

3 egg whites
1¼ cups confectioners' sugar

Roll out the pastry and use it to line a prepared 10-in pie pan; prick the bottom with a fork and place in the refrigerator for 30 minutes. Rinse the raspberries in cold water, drain, and dry on paper towels; place them in a bowl and sprinkle with the sugar. Leave to stand.
Bake the pie shell for 20 minutes (or until cooked and pale golden brown) at 400° F. Remove from the oven and leave to cool. Beat the egg whites until very stiff, add the confectioners' sugar and beat until glossy. Spread the raspberries in the pie shell. Use a pastry bag and large fluted tube to pipe the meringue so that it completely covers the raspberries. Return to a very hot oven (490° F) for up to 10 minutes to set and lightly brown the meringue.

· · ·

RICOTTA AND CANDIED FRUIT LAYERED PASTRY

If you have not candied your own fruit (see recipe on page 27) you should find a good selection in the better delicatessens or luxury food stores, often imported from France. Orange flower water is also sold by many delicatessens.

Time: 50 minutes
Fairly easy

1 quantity Puff Pastry or
   Rough Puff Pastry (see

pages 86–7)
2 cups fresh ricotta cheese
1¾ cups confectioners' sugar
1 cup or ½ lb mixed candied
   fruits
1 tbsp orange flower water
½ cup whipping cream

Roll out the pastry in a rectangle or square; the sheet should be just under ¼ in thick. Lightly grease a large cookie sheet with butter, dust lightly with flour, place the pastry on it and place in the oven, preheated to 425° F. Cook for 10 minutes at this temperature before reducing the heat to 350° F for a further 5–8 minutes (the pastry should be crisp and pale golden brown). Using a sharp knife, cut the pastry horizontally into three sections (the layers usually separate easily once the knife is inserted).
Beat the ricotta thoroughly with all but 1 tbsp of the confectioners' sugar. Add the candied fruit, cut into fairly small pieces, and stir in the orange flower water. Fold in the stiffly beaten cream gently but thoroughly. Place the first pastry layer carefully on a flat serving plate; spoon half the

filling onto it, making sure it is level; place another pastry layer on top, then a layer of the remaining filling and top with the last rectangle or square of pastry, and sprinkle the remaining confectioners' sugar over the top.

· · ·

MARTINIQUE FRUIT FLAN

You can use bananas, pawpaw, kiwi fruit, or any other tropical fruit instead of pineapple.

Time: 1 hour 15 minutes
Fairly easy

8 slices fresh pineapple
½ cup Grand Marnier
1 quantity Puff Pastry or
   Rough Puff Pastry (see
   pages 86–7)
1 whole egg and 2 egg yolks
½ cup sugar
¼ cup all-purpose flour
1¾ cups milk
1 cup whipping cream

Place the peeled and cored slices of pineapple in a bowl, pour the Grand Marnier over them and leave to stand. Roll out the pastry and use to line a prepared 10-in pie pan. Prick the bottom in several places with a fork and set aside in the refrigerator for 30 minutes. Drain the Grand Marnier from the pineapple slices and cut these into small pieces. Beat the whole egg and the two extra yolks very thoroughly with the sugar; beat in the flour, followed by the hot milk, adding this in a thin stream as you beat. Cook

over very gentle heat, stirring continuously, until the custard thickens. Drain the pineapple and add to the custard. Stir well.
Cook the pie shell at 400° F for 20 minutes. Remove from the oven and fill with the pineapple custard mixture; reduce the heat to 350° F, and return to the oven for a further 20 minutes. Let the flan cool completely before decorating with piped whipped cream.

· · ·

MOCHA CREAM DESSERT

Time: 1 hour
Fairly easy

1 quantity Puff Pastry or
   Rough Puff Pastry (see
   pages 86–7)

MOCHA CREAM DESSERT

■ Buttercream is used for many classics of the patisserie repertoire: teamed with various types of sponge cake and with meringue. The yolks can be omitted and an Italian meringue mixture used instead: pour the hot sugar syrup slowly onto the stiffly beaten egg whites while whisking.

½ cup sugar
¼ cup water
2 egg yolks
1 tsp good-quality instant
coffee
1 cup (2 sticks) butter
2–3 drops vanilla extract
confectioners' sugar
few roasted coffee beans
(optional)

Divide the dough into three equal parts and roll each out to form a circle 7 in in diameter; prick the surface of the pastry with a fork and transfer to a cookie sheet greased lightly with butter and dusted with flour as usual; cook in a preheated oven (400° F) for 20 minutes. Mix the sugar with the water and boil in a small saucepan until the large thread stage is reached.
Beat the eggs vigorously as you pour the boiling hot sugar syrup onto them in a thin stream; continue beating until they become pale and reach the "ribbon" stage (i.e. when you lift the whisk above the bowl a flat unbroken ribbon of mixture will fall from it, folding as it hits the mixture in the bowl). Continue beating until the mixture is completely cold. Dissolve the coffee in 2 tbsp water. Beat the butter until pale and creamy and work into the egg yolk and sugar mixture a little at a time, alternating the additions with the vanilla and the coffee, added a drop at a time. Spread one third of this coffee filling on the first pastry circle; cover with another pastry round and cover this in turn with more coffee mixture and with the third piece of pastry. Spread the remaining coffee mixture all over the top and dust with confectioners' sugar (or a mixture of cocoa powder

and confectioners' sugar) and decorate with real coffee beans or chocolate replicas.

●   ●   ●

FILBERT CREAM

If you feel like a change from filberts, you can use almonds, pistachio nuts, or roasted pine nuts instead.

Time: 1 hour
Fairly easy

1 quantity Puff Pastry or
   Rough Puff Pastry (see
   pages 86–7)
2 cups filberts
1 cup milk
2 egg yolks
½ cup sugar
3 tbsp all-purpose flour
1 tbsp confectioners' sugar

Divide the pastry dough into three equal portions and roll these out to form three circles

7 in in diameter; transfer to a prepared cookie sheet and place in a preheated oven (400° F). Cook for 20 minutes. Pour the milk into a blender or liquidizer, add 1⅓ cups of the nuts and blend thoroughly. Pour into a saucepan and bring to boiling point.
Beat the egg yolks with the sugar for 5–10 minutes, add the flour and then beat in the hot milk and nut mixture. Stir over low heat until the custard thickens. Remove from the heat. Chop the remaining nuts fairly finely and stir half into the cold custard mixture. Spread half the custard on one pastry circle, place the second pastry circle on top and cover in turn with the remaining custard. Place the last round of pastry on top and decorate

with a sprinkling of confectioners' sugar and the remaining chopped nuts.

●   ●   ●

FRUIT AND CREAM PIE

Once an exotic rarity, kiwi fruit have now become almost an everyday fruit. Rich in vitamin C, they are not only delicious but beautiful as well, when sliced and used for decoration.

Time: 1 hour 10 minutes
Fairly easy

1 quantity Puff Pastry or
   Rough Puff Pastry (see
   pages 86–7)
2 egg yolks
½ cup sugar
few drops vanilla extract
3 tbsp all-purpose flour
1 cup milk
1 cup heavy cream
1 tsp confectioners' sugar
3 kiwi fruit
½ lb small strawberries
2 tbsp fruit jelly
1 tbsp Grand Marnier or
   Curaçao

Roll out the pastry and line a 10-in prepared pie pan or use a flan ring placed on a cookie sheet; prick the bottom in several places with a fork and set aside in the refrigerator for 30 minutes. Beat the egg yolks with the sugar and the vanilla until pale and greatly increased in volume; add the flour and then beat in the hot milk, adding it in a thin stream. Stir continuously over low heat until the mixture thickens. Set aside to cool. Beat the cream until stiff with the confectioners' sugar and fold into the cold egg and milk mixture. Cook the pie shell in a preheated oven at 400° F for 20 minutes. Remove the pie shell carefully from its pan; when cold spoon the filling into it.

Peel the kiwi fruit, slice into fairly thick rounds, and cut these rounds into quarters. Rinse and dry the strawberries. Arrange the fruit on top of the filling and glaze with red currant or other fruit jelly, melted with the liqueur.

• • •

STRAWBERRY CREAM GALETTE

In place of the strawberry frosting, you could pipe rosettes of sweetened whipped cream for decoration.

Time: 50 minutes + standing time
Fairly easy

1 lb strawberries
½ cup sugar
½ cup kirsch
1 quantity Puff Pastry or Rough Puff Pastry (see pages 86–7)

1 pint heavy or whipping cream
2¼ cups confectioners' sugar
few drops vanilla extract
1 cup best-quality strawberry jam

Wash, dry, and hull the strawberries, cut them in half and place in a bowl with ½ cup sugar and the kirsch; leave to stand for 2 hours, after which drain off all the syrupy juice and reserve.
Roll out the pastry in a rectangle just under ¼ in thick. Place on a cookie sheet which has been lightly greased with butter and dusted with flour and cook for 10 minutes at 425° F, then lower the heat to 350° F, and cook for a further 5–8 minutes or until the pastry is crisp and golden brown. Cut the pastry horizontally into three sections (the pastry leaves will probably separate quite easily of their own accord once you have inserted the knife).
Beat the cream with 1 cup of the confectioners' sugar and flavor with the vanilla. Spread a thin layer of jam on the first pastry layer, then spread a quarter of the cream on top. Press half the strawberries

gently into the cream and cover with the same quantity of cream as you spread below them. Cover with a second pastry layer, repeat the cream and stawberry arrangement, topping with a "lid" of the last pastry layer. Dissolve the remaining confectioners' sugar in 4 tbsp of the reserved syrupy strawberry juice over low heat, to make a frosting. Pour the frosting over the pastry top and spread evenly with a spatula.

• • •

CHOCOLATE AND PISTACHIO SLICE

Chocolate and pistachio nuts go extremely well together. Pistachio is a very versatile flavoring: wonderful for ice creams and desserts and equally effective in savory galantines, stuffings, and pâtés.

Time: 1 hour
Fairly easy

1 quantity Puff Pastry or Rough Puff Pastry (see pages 86–7)
2 cups shelled pistachio nuts (not salted)
1 cup milk
2 egg yolks
½ cup sugar
3 tbsp all-purpose flour
7 oz (7 squares) semisweet chocolate or finest baker's chocolate
1 cup heavy cream
1 tbsp confectioners' sugar

Roll out the pastry into a rectangle just under ⅛ in thick. Place on a greased and floured cookie sheet, prick the surface here and there with a fork and place in the

refrigerator for 30 minutes. Grind the pistachios in a food processor. Heat the milk to boiling point, stir in the pistachio nuts and cook over very low heat, stirring constantly, for 3–4 minutes. Beat the egg yolks with the sugar until pale and frothy, add the flour and then mix in the hot milk and nut mixture. Cook over low heat, stirring, until the mixture thickens. Add the chocolate, broken into small pieces, stirring until it has melted completely. Pour into a bowl and leave to cool completely, stirring from time to time.
Beat the cream with 1 tbsp confectioners' sugar until stiff and fold into the cold custard mixture. Bake the pastry in a preheated oven (400° F) for about 20 minutes. Cut it into four identical rectangles. Spread one third of the pastry cream onto each of three pastry pieces; place these one on top of the other, placing the last plain pastry rectangle on top; sprinkle this "lid" with confectioners' sugar and serve.

• • •

RUM CREAM GATEAU

Time: 45 minutes
Fairly easy

1 quantity Puff Pastry or Rough Puff Pastry (see pages 86–7)
3 eggs
6 tbsp sugar
1 cup mascarpone (or similar fresh cheese)
1 cup cookie crumbs
½ cup rum

CHOCOLATE AND PEAR SLICE
■ *Drained canned apricot halves or canned orange or pineapple slices also go well with chocolate. The illustration shows how a "lid" can be made with the pastry cut out to leave a hollow for the filling, like a large vol-au-vent.*

Roll out the pastry into a sheet large enough to cut out 2 circles 7½–8 in in diameter; place these on a prepared cookie sheet, brush them with one lightly beaten egg yolk as a glaze, and leave to stand in a cool place for 30 minutes before baking at 400° F for 20 minutes.

Meanwhile, make the filling: beat the remaining 2 egg yolks with the sugar for about 10 minutes, beat in the mascarpone, then fold in the stiffly beaten egg whites. Mix the fine crumbs with the rum (place your cookies in the food processor to obtain really fine crumbs); spread the resulting paste over the surface of one of the cooked pastry rounds when it has had time to cool.

Spread half the mascarpone filling over the rum and cookie mixture, place the other pastry circle on top and cover with the remaining mascarpone cream.

• • •

CHOCOLATE AND PEAR SLICE

Time: 50 minutes
Fairly easy

1 lb drained, canned pears
1 quantity Puff Pastry or Rough Puff Pastry (see pages 86–7)
4 tbsp pear jam

7 oz (7 squares) semisweet chocolate or fine bakers' chocolate
2 egg yolks
½ cup sugar
1 cup heavy cream or whipping cream

Roll out the pastry and line a greased and floured 10-in pie pan with it. Prick the bottom in several places with a fork and set aside in the refrigerator for 30 minutes.

Spread the pear jam (or other jam such as apricot or raspberry) over the base of the uncooked chilled pie shell and place in the oven, preheated to 400° F for 20 minutes.

Melt the chocolate gently over hot water. Beat the egg yolks with the sugar until pale and increased in volume; beat in

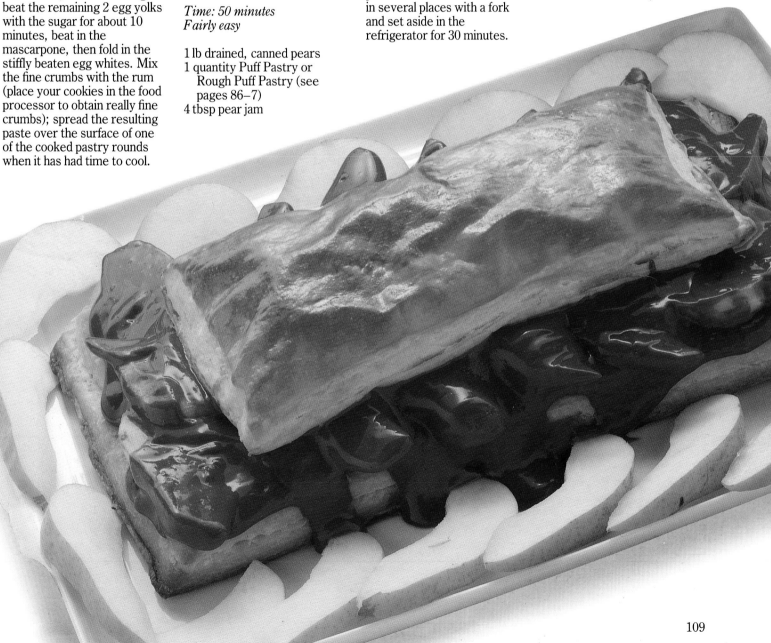

ORANGE MOUSSELINE
DESSERT
■ The orange mousse filling,
made with gelatin, is quick
and easy to make. Other
jellies or preserves can be
used instead of marmalade,
provided they go well with
oranges.

the melted chocolate a little at
a time when the mixture has
cooled a good deal, using an
electric beater or wire whisk.
Whip the cream until stiff and
combine half of it with the
chocolate and egg mixture.
Arrange the well drained
pears in a single layer in the
bottom of the pie shell. Cover
with the chocolate mixture and
keep cold until it is time to
serve the dessert. Decorate
with the remaining whipped
cream, piped into rosettes and
with small pieces of fresh fruit
(e.g. raspberries,
strawberries, orange
sections) if wished.

• • •

ORANGE
MOUSSELINE
DESSERT

Time: 1 hour
Fairly easy

1 quantity Puff Pastry or
    Rough Puff Pastry (see
    pages 86–7)
1 cup best-quality marmalade
2 tbsp Grand Marnier
1 tbsp gelatin powder
1 cup fresh orange juice
1 cup heavy or whipping
    cream
1 orange
1 tbsp confectioners' sugar

Roll out the pastry to a
rectangle, just over $\frac{1}{8}$ in thick.
Lightly grease a cookie sheet
with butter and dust with
flour, place the pastry on it,
and prick lightly at regular
intervals over its surface.
Place in the refrigerator for 30
minutes. Put the marmalade in
the blender with the Grand
Marnier and process until
smooth.
Prepare the gelatin according

to the manufacturer's instructions, and dissolve it completely in the hot orange juice (it should never be allowed to boil nor should boiling liquid be used) and then stir this hot liquid into the marmalade and Grand Marnier mixture very thoroughly. Whip the cream until stiff, combine with the orange mixture and place in the refrigerator.
Cook the pie shell at 400° F for 20 minutes, allow to grow completely cold before cutting into 4 rectangles. Spread one third of the orange mousse on a piece of pastry, cover with pastry and continue layering, finishing with a pastry lid; decorate this with a dusting of confectioners' sugar and orange sections, their thin membrane carefully removed.

• • •

SEMOLINA CHIFFON PIE

A rich dessert best served at the end of a light supper: serve hot or warm, as it acquires a heavy consistency when cold.

Time: 1 hour 15 minutes
Fairly easy

1 quantity Puff Pastry or
    Rough Puff Pastry (see
    pages 86–7)
⅓ cup seedless white raisins
1 cup milk
½ cup semolina
½ cup sugar
2–3 drops vanilla extract
2 eggs
¾ cup mixed candied fruit
1 tbsp peach brandy

Roll out the pastry and line a prepared 10-in pie pan, pricking the bottom with a fork. Place in the refrigerator for 30 minutes. Soak the seedless white raisins for 10 minutes in warm water, then drain and dry them.
Bring the milk to a boil. Sprinkle the semolina into the hot milk, reduce the heat and cook, stirring continuously, for 15 minutes. Stir in the sugar and add the vanilla extract. Remove from the heat, leave to cool a little before stirring in the egg yolks, the candied fruit and seedless white raisins, and the peach brandy. Set aside to cool further. Beat the egg whites until stiff, fold into the semolina, and spoon into the pie shell, smoothing the surface level. Bake at 400° F for 40 minutes or until done.

• • •

MANDARIN RICE PIE

Use short-grain (pudding) rice, the best you can buy (imported Italian Arborio rice is ideal, Carolina rice is also suitable); rinse briefly in cold water before cooking to wash away a little of
the starch or the rice will be mushy when cooked.

Time: 2 hours
Fairly easy

1 quantity Puff Pastry or
    Rough Puff Pastry (see
    pages 86–7)
½ cup short-grain (pudding)
    rice
¾ cup diced mixed candied
    fruit
3 tbsp mandarin liqueur
1 quart milk
½ cup sugar
2 eggs
1 tsp cinnamon
1 oz (1 square) semisweet
    chocolate, grated

Roll out the pastry and line a prepared 10-in pie pan. Prick the bottom with a fork and place in the refrigerator for 30 minutes before baking.
Boil the rice in a large pan of water for 5 minutes; drain. Mix the candied fruit with the liqueur and set aside. Bring the milk to a boil with the sugar, sprinkle in the rice; reduce the heat and cook over very low heat, stirring frequently, for about 1 hour or until very tender. Remove from the heat, allow to cool a little before stirring in the egg yolks, candied fruit, liqueur, and cinnamon. Fold in the stiffly beaten egg whites. Spoon the rice filling evenly into the pie shell and place in the oven, preheated to 400° F for about 40 minutes or until done. When cold, sprinkle the chocolate over the surface and serve.

• • •

111

Many cakes are baked with yeast or a similar raising agent, which makes them increase in volume during cooking. Fresh yeast should be dissolved in water or milk (scalded and then left to cool to 85–90° F). Temperature is all-important, so work in a warm room out of draughts.

Dry yeast comes in ¼-oz packages, each containing 1 tbsp. This is supposed to be equivalent to a cake of compressed fresh yeast, which weighs 1 oz, but you may find that slightly less dry yeast will do the work of 1 cake of fresh yeast. Dry yeast should be dissolved in lukewarm water or milk at about 100–108° F.

Baking powder is a comparatively recent invention, introduced in the United States in the nineteenth century; double-acting baking powder (which needs heat before it will work effectively rather than just moisture) has taken a lot of the rush out of cake mixing.

ALMOND BRIOCHES

For a delectable breakfast there is little to beat fresh brioches, served warm with homemade apricot or raspberry jam.

Time: 1 hour + rising time
Fairly easy

½ cake compressed fresh
   yeast or 1 package (¼ oz)
   dry yeast
½ cup + 1 tbsp milk
1¾ cups unbleached all-
   purpose flour
1 cup ground almonds
4 egg yolks
½ cup very fresh sweet butter
¼ cup sugar
pinch salt
1 whole egg

Have all your ingredients at warm room temperature before you start. Scald the milk then allow to cool to correct temperature (see box insert on this page) in a small bowl; add the yeast and leave to stand for 10 minutes before stirring very gently. Mix with 1 cup of the flour and shape into a soft ball; leave this to stand in the bowl in a warm place (around 80° F) covered by a cloth, for 30 minutes. Place the rest of the sifted flour and the ground almonds in a mound in a large mixing bowl, make a well in the center, and place the small dough ball in it together with the 4 egg yolks, soft (but not melted) butter, sugar, and salt. Mix well with a wooden spoon and when the dough starts to leave the sides of the bowl cleanly, transfer to an unfloured pastry board and knead energetically. The dough should be soft and elastic at this stage. Pull up

□ *The use of raising agents began with yeast when man first discovered how to make leavened bread. From these humble beginnings increasingly elaborate and consistent baked products gradually developed. It is best not to use too highly refined flour for yeast baking: strong or unbleached flour will contain the necessary high amount of gluten which produces good results with yeast. Other ingredients such as milk, fats, eggs, and many others are added to enrich the mixture.*

□ *The action of yeast is produced by tiny microorganisms which cause the sugars contained in cereal flour to ferment, giving off gases which inflate the dough and cause it to rise. Yeast loves warm, moist conditions and will only remain active within a narrow temperature range. With the exception of some yeast doughs (certain brioche doughs among them) a yeast based dough is not usually refrigerated as this halts fermentation. If too much yeast is used the baked goods will smell too highly of it and will not necessarily be any lighter; over-proving can lead to yeast cakes being too crumbly. It is best to adhere closely to the recommended times and quantities.*

□ *Fresh yeast is grayish-beige in color, smooth on the surface yet easily crumbled, with a strong, sweet, and pleasant smell. Place the fresh yeast in warm milk or water, but do not crush it with a spoon as this will destroy some of the yeast cells. It will soon dissolve and start to froth, showing that it is active. If added to liquid which is too hot, the yeast will not ferment properly and, over a certain temperature, will die. If the liquid is too cold, the yeast will remain inert but will not be killed.*
Fresh yeast will keep in the refrigerator for only a few days before starting to lose its efficacy; it can, however, be successfully frozen.
Dry yeast which sometimes has vitamin C added and is then called accelerated yeast can tolerate slightly hotter liquids and needs longer to reactivate and start frothing. Many cooks feel that dry yeast does not give quite such a good flavor or consistency to baked goods.

□ *Baking powder acts on a different principle and is a much more recent discovery. When moistened and heated it releases a gas which aerates the mixture or batter.*

and away from the work surface, flip the dough over and punch down again several times.
Pull off pieces about the size of a golf ball. Press down on one side of each ball with the side of your hand, making a sawing motion to produce a "neck" and a small "head" (see step by step illustrations on page 118). Pick up by the head and place in small brioche molds, greased with butter; press the head down into the brioche and leave to rise in a warm place, covered with a clean cloth, for about 2 hours or until doubled in volume. (You can arrange the brioche dough on a greased cookie sheet or in muffin pans if you do not have the traditional fluted brioche molds.)
Beat the whole egg and brush carefully over the upper surfaces of the brioches, taking care that none trickles down into the molds if these are used. Place in a preheated oven (400° F) for 20 minutes or until done and golden brown (test by pushing a thin skewer or cocktail stick deep into a brioche; if it comes out clean, they are ready).

• • •

EMILIAN BRIOCHE

An Italian recipe which originally called for lard or rendered pork fat; butter is used here.

Time: 1 hour + rising time
Easy

1¾ cups unbleached all-
   purpose flour
¼ cup sugar
peel of 1 lemon, grated
3 eggs
¼ cup sweet butter

SAVARIN
■ *As an alternative to the decoration shown below, fill the center with piped whipped cream or with a fruit sauce.*

1 cake compressed fresh yeast or 1 package (¼ oz) dry yeast
½ cup + 1 tbsp lukewarm milk (scalded and cooled to the correct temperature)
1 tbsp olive oil
2 tbsp nibbed sugar
pinch salt

Sift the flour into a mound on the pastry board, add the sugar and the grated lemon peel. Make a well in the middle and place 2 eggs, the

EGGS

Eggs keep for up to one month if refrigerated; they can also be frozen, providing they have been separated first.

soft (but not melted) butter cut into small pieces, the salt and the yeast dissolved in the lukewarm milk. Combine the ingredients by hand (stir the ingredients in the center with your index finger or slightly cupped hand or use a wooden spoon if you prefer: they will gradually take up the flour) and then knead for 10 minutes. Leave to rise in a covered bowl set in a warm place for 30 minutes; pull out into a sausage, shape this into an S-shape and place on a lightly oiled cookie sheet. Beat the remaining egg and brush the surface of the brioche dough with it, concentrating on the top. Sprinkle the nibbed sugar onto the glaze and bake in a preheated oven (400° F) for 30 minutes or until done.

•   •   •   •

SAVARIN

Time: 1 hour + rising time
Easy

1 cake compressed fresh
    yeast or 1 package (¼ oz)
    dry yeast
½ cup + 1 tbsp lukewarm milk
3 cups unbleached all-purpose
    flour
2 eggs
½ cup (1 stick) + 2 tbsp
    butter
pinch salt
¼ cup sugar
For the syrup:
½ cup + 2 tbsp water
¼ cup sugar
½ cup + 2 tbsp kirsch
½ cup apricot jam

Dissolve the yeast in the
lukewarm milk. Sift the flour
into a large mixing bowl,
forming a mound; make a well
in the center and place the
milk and yeast and eggs in it.
Combine the ingredients
thoroughly to make a fairly
soft dough. Cover the bowl;
leave to rise and almost double
in volume in a warm place for
about 1 hour.
Beat the butter until very soft
and creamy, work into the
risen dough together with the
sugar and salt. Lift up the
dough with the tips of your
fingers (it will stretch and then
leave the bowl quite easily)
and knock down back into the
bowl 4 or 5 times.
Grease the inside of a ring
mold with butter and dust
lightly with flour. Shape the
dough into a long sausage
shape, and place in the mold.
Leave to prove until the dough
has risen considerably in the
mold (about 30–40 minutes).
Do not overprove or the
texture of the savarin will be
too crumbly when baked.

Bake at 425° F for 10 minutes,
then turn the heat down to
350° F and bake for a further
30 minutes or until well risen
and golden brown. Turn the
savarin upside down and
unmold into a fairly deep dish.
While the savarin is baking,
prepare the sugar syrup: boil
the water and sugar over
moderate heat for a few
minutes while stirring; add the
kirsch and remove from the
heat as soon as the syrup
returns to a boil. Pour evenly
all over the savarin and leave
to soak up most of the syrup.
Transfer the savarin and any
remaining unabsorbed syrup
to a serving plate. Melt the
jam over hot water (sieve it if
you wish) and brush over the
surface of the savarin as a
glaze.

• • •

BRIOCHE RING

Time: 1 hour + rising time
Easy

1 cake compressed fresh
    yeast or 1 package (¼ oz)
    dry yeast
½ cup + 1 tbsp lukewarm milk
1¾ cups unbleached all-
    purpose flour
½ cup (1 stick) butter
1 tbsp sugar
few drops vanilla extract
4 eggs
pinch salt
3 canned peaches
½ cup whipping cream

Dissolve the yeast in the
lukewarm milk and leave to
stand for 10 minutes. Mix in
just enough flour to make a
very soft dough ball which will
just hold its shape. Leave to
stand, covered, in a warm
place for 30 minutes.

BRIOCHE RING
■ Brioche dough can be left
to rise before being baked in
a ring mold, which lends itself
to effective decoration. The
ring can be sliced horizontally
in half and filled with cooked
fruit or pastry cream.

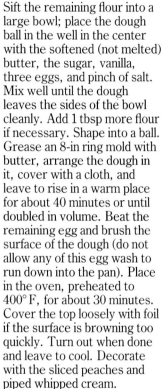

Sift the remaining flour into a large bowl; place the dough ball in the well in the center with the softened (not melted) butter, the sugar, vanilla, three eggs, and pinch of salt. Mix well until the dough leaves the sides of the bowl cleanly. Add 1 tbsp more flour if necessary. Shape into a ball. Grease an 8-in ring mold with butter, arrange the dough in it, cover with a cloth, and leave to rise in a warm place for about 40 minutes or until doubled in volume. Beat the remaining egg and brush the surface of the dough (do not allow any of this egg wash to run down into the pan). Place in the oven, preheated to 400° F, for about 30 minutes. Cover the top loosely with foil if the surface is browning too quickly. Turn out when done and leave to cool. Decorate with the sliced peaches and piped whipped cream.

• • •

VENETIAN YEAST CAKE

Nibbed sugar (very small irregular pieces of sugar, often vanilla-flavored, see illustration on page 119) is used to decorate this cake, which can be made in a large mold or several smaller molds.

Time: 1 hour + rising time
Easy

1 cake compressed fresh
    yeast or 1 package (¼ oz)
    dry yeast
scant ½ cup lukewarm milk
2¾ cups unbleached all-
    purpose flour
⅔ cup sugar
5 egg yolks and 1 whole egg
pinch salt

¼ cup orange flower water
½ cake compressed fresh yeast or ½ package (⅛ oz) dry yeast
2¾ cups unbleached all-purpose flour
¾ cup + 2 tbsp (1¾ sticks) sweet butter
2 tbsp sugar
1 tsp salt
3 eggs
To glaze:
1 egg, lightly beaten

Mix the yeast with the slightly warmed orange flower water and ½ cup of the flour. Cover and leave in a warm place until doubled in bulk.

Beat the butter (softened at room temperature) until light and creamy.

Sift the remaining flour into a mixing bowl, then stir in the sugar and salt. Combine with the eggs. When the dough is smooth and well blended, work in the ferment which has been left to rise.

Work in the butter. Cover and leave the dough to rise in a warm place until doubled in bulk (about 10 hours).

Lightly oil (or grease with butter) small brioche molds. Knock down the brioche dough, break off pieces about the size of a golf ball, large enough to half fill each mold. This will allow space for the dough to rise once more when proved.

Use the method described on page 114 and illustrated on this page to "saw" a neck and head for the brioche.

Place the molds, evenly spaced out, on a cookie sheet or roasting pan. Cover with a cloth and leave to prove until doubled in bulk. Brush with beaten egg (do not allow any to trickle down inside the mold) and bake for 10–20 minutes at 450° F until done.

Serve at once or leave to cool.

RAISIN BRAID
■ *Dough similar to brioche dough is braided before baking. Seedless white raisins can be replaced by finely diced candied peel.*

1 cup (2 sticks) butter
2 tbsp clear (runny) honey
2 tbsp nibbed sugar

Leave the yeast to dissolve and start foaming in the lukewarm milk in a small bowl. Sift the flour into a large mixing bowl; add the sugar, 4 egg yolks, the salt, the softened butter (cut into small pieces), and the honey; mix well with a wooden spoon. Add the milk and yeast and stir until the dough leaves the sides of the bowl cleanly. It should be smooth and velvety, elastic, and soft.
Place the dough in a lightly floured bowl; cut a cross in the center of the top, cover with a thick cloth or towel and leave to rise in a warm place for about 2 hours. Punch down the dough and knead briskly for 15 minutes; press the dough into a rounded, slightly flattened dome shape and place on a greased and floured cookie sheet. Beat the one

remaining egg yolk and the whole egg together and brush over the surface of the dough. Sprinkle the nibbed sugar onto the egg wash and bake at 400° F for 35 minutes or until done. Let the cake cool thoroughly on a rack before cutting and serving.

•   •   •

RAISIN BRAID

Time: 1 hour + rising time
Easy

½ cup seedless white raisins
1 cake compressed fresh yeast or 1 package (¼ oz) dry yeast
½ cup + 1 tbsp lukewarm milk
3½ cups unbleached all-purpose flour
3 eggs
¼ cup sugar
scant ½ cup lard

peel of ½ lemon, grated
1 tbsp nibbed sugar
pinch salt

Soak the seedless white raisins in warm water for 15–20 minutes; drain thoroughly and dry.
Dissolve the yeast in the lukewarm milk in a small bowl; add ½ cup flour and mix to form a small dough ball; leave this to rise in a warm place, covered by a towel. Sift the remaining flour onto the work surface in a mound; make a well in the center and place 2 eggs, the sugar, lard, grated lemon peel, seedless white raisins, and salt. Combine all these ingredients, add the dough ball, and work together to an even, soft, and elastic

dough. Shape into a ball and place in a large, lightly floured bowl; cut a cross in the top of the dough, cover with a heavy cloth or two kitchen towels and leave to rise for 2 hours, or until doubled in volume. Punch down the dough and knead before dividing into 3 identical long sausages; braid these loosely and leave to prove on a prepared cookie sheet for up to 1 hour. Glaze with the remaining, lightly beaten, egg; sprinkle with the nibbed sugar and bake at 400° F for 30 minutes or until done.

•   •   •

MOLASSES BREAD

Originally a Scottish specialty and very quick to make since it

MOLASSES

A liquid residue produced when crude brown sugar is made (almost always cane sugar). Dark, very sweet, and rich in iron, molasses is quite frequently used in baking. Treacle is partly decolorized molasses, usually sweeter and therefore useful in sweet sauces.

HONEY BREAD

Time: 1 hour + rising time
Easy

1 cup lukewarm milk
1 cake compressed fresh
   yeast or 1 package (¼ oz)
   dry yeast
1 lb 1 oz (4¼ cups) unbleached
   all-purpose flour
¼ cup sugar
2 tbsp clear (runny) honey
pinch salt
peel of 1 lemon, grated
¼ cup (½ stick) + 1 tbsp
   butter
1 egg
1 tbsp nibbed sugar

Dissolve the yeast in the lukewarm milk. Sift the flour in a mound onto the work surface; make a well in the center and place the sugar, honey, salt, grated lemon peel, the soft butter cut into small pieces, and the yeast and milk mixture in it. Combine all these ingredients very thoroughly. Shape into a ball, place in a bowl and cover with a cloth; leave to stand in a warm place until doubled in volume; punch down, knead again, and shape into 2 oval

needs no rising time. It keeps very well, wrapped in foil in an airtight tin. This quantity is sufficient for about 10 people.

Time: 1 hour 15 minutes
Very easy

4 cups all-purpose flour
1 tsp baking powder
pinch salt
¼ cup sugar
1 tsp cinnamon
1 tsp nutmeg
½ tsp ground cloves
1 cup pitted chopped dates
1 cup finely chopped walnuts

½ cup molasses
1 cup (2 sticks) butter
4 eggs
½ cup milk

Sift the flour, baking powder, and salt into a large mixing bowl and stir in the sugar and spices. Mix in the dates and walnuts. Melt the molasses with the butter in a saucepan over low heat and then stir a little at a time into the ingredients in the bowl. Add the lightly beaten whole eggs and stir in gently using a wooden spoon. The mixture should be firm but soft; add a very little milk if necessary.

Grease a fairly shallow rectangular baking pan with butter and dust lightly with flour; transfer the batter into it and place in a preheated oven (350° F) to bake for 30 minutes, then reduce the heat to 320° F and bake for a further 30 minutes.

BUTTER PAT
■ *Used to shape butter and make ridged patterns on its surfaces. Eighteenth-century engraving.*

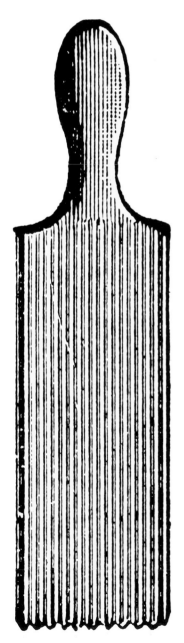

shapes; place one across the other (see illustration left) and leave to prove until almost doubled in volume; brush with the lightly beaten egg. Bake at 400° F. When nearly done, sprinkle quickly with nibbed sugar and finish baking. Serve cold.

GRAPPA BREAD PUDDING

If grappa is unavailable, you could use brandy or applejack but the taste and aroma will not be quite as distinctive.

Time: 1 hour + soaking time
Very easy

¾ lb piece stale bread
2¼ cups hot milk
10 amaretti cookies, crisp macaroons, or ratafias
1 tsp vanilla extract
1 cup sugar
1 egg
¼ cup grappa or alternative spirit
1 lemon
1 cup seedless white raisins
½ cup candied citron peel
1 tbsp unsweetened cocoa powder
⅔ cup pine nuts
½ tsp baking powder
1–2 tsp butter

Slice the bread, cut off the crusts, and place in a large bowl; pour the hot milk all over it and break the bread up with a fork, mixing well; leave to stand for 10–12 hours. Work well by hand until smooth and all the bread has been broken into tiny pieces. Add the crumbled amaretti, vanilla, sugar, the whole egg, grappa, the juice and grated peel of the lemon, the soaked and drained seedless white raisins, the citron peel cut into small dice, the cocoa powder, and all but 1 tbsp of the pine nuts. Mix very thoroughly, adding the sifted baking powder last of all.
Grease a 9-in soufflé dish, fill (about ⅔–¾ full) with the mixture and sprinkle the remaining pine nuts over the surface. Bake at 350° F for 1

hour when the top should have turned golden brown.

• • •

RUM BABA

Classic rum baba calls for yeast but you can save time by using 1 tbsp baking powder instead, in which case you can use the "softer" all-purpose flour which contains less gluten than unbleached flour.

Time: 1 hour + rising time
Easy

1 cake compressed fresh yeast or 1 package (¼ oz) dry yeast
1 cup lukewarm milk
2¾ cups unbleached all-purpose flour
1 cup sugar
¼ cup (½ stick) butter
4 eggs
4 tbsp rum
1 cup whipping cream

Place the yeast in the lukewarm milk and leave for 10 minutes to dissolve and start foaming. Work into the sifted flour in a large bowl, add half the sugar, the softened butter and the eggs and mix well; leave to rise until doubled in volume. Punch down and knead; place in a greased 8-in diameter baba

HONEY

The flavor and aroma of honey depends on the bees' source of nectar. Acacia honey is very light and delicate and does not crystallize, unlike other varieties. Chestnut blossom honey is strong and dark; orange flavor honey is milder. There are many other types, including heather, rosemary, and clover.

(ring) mold and bake at 400° F for 25 minutes or until done. Boil the remaining sugar with ½ cup water for 6 minutes; remove from the heat and stir in the rum. When the baba cake is cooked, turn the mold upside down and release the baba into a fairly deep flat-bottomed dish. Spoon the syrup evenly over the baba, leave for a while to soak it up, then transfer carefully to a serving plate with any unabsorbed syrup. Decorate with piped whipped cream and serve.

APRICOT BABA

This baba is served with apricot sauce; you can add a little rum to the sauce if you wish.

Time: 1 hour + rising time
Easy

1 Rum Baba (see page 121)
1½ cups apricot jam

Once the baba has been soaked with the rum syrup, sieve the apricot jam into a saucepan, add 2 tbsp water, and heat slowly until very hot. Pour into a jug and serve piping hot with the rum baba.

• • •

CANDIED FRUIT BABA

Time: 1 hour + rising time
Easy

1 Rum Baba (see page 121)
⅔ cup candied fruits, finely
   chopped
1 cup whipping cream
2 tbsp liqueur of your choice
   (optional)

When the baba has been turned out onto a serving plate and soaked with the rum syrup, whip the cream until stiff, fold in the candied fruit and the liqueur if used; spoon into the central well of the baba.

• • •

RAISIN AND NUT BREAD

Time: 1 hour + rising time
Easy

½ cake compressed fresh
   yeast or ½ package (⅛ oz)
   dry yeast

½ cup lukewarm water
⅓ cup seedless white raisins
3 cups unbleached all-purpose
   flour
1½ tbsp sugar
4 eggs
⅓ cup pine nuts
pinch salt
¾ cup (1½ sticks) butter

Dissolve the yeast in the lukewarm water. Soak the raisins in warm water for 10 minutes, then drain and dry. While they are soaking, start making the dough: sift ¾ cup flour in a mound, make a well in the center, and pour the yeast and warm water into it. Mix gradually into the flour, shape into a soft dough ball, cover the bowl with a towel, and leave to rise in a warm place for 20 minutes. Sift the remaining flour into a large mixing bowl, make a well in the center to accommodate the sugar, 3 eggs, pine nuts, raisins, and salt. Combine these ingredients by hand, gradually adding small pieces of the softened butter and, lastly, work in the dough ball. Knead thoroughly to obtain a smooth, homogenous dough. Leave to rise in a warm place until doubled in volume. Punch down and knead briefly. Shape into a large, dome shaped bun (see illustration on the right). Place on a greased and lightly floured cookie sheet and leave to prove for 35–40 minutes. Place in a preheated oven at 400° F and bake for 30 minutes. Brush the sweet bread quickly with the remaining, lightly beaten, egg and return to the oven for a further 10 minutes, or until done.

PINE NUT CAKE

Chopped pine nuts give a pleasant flavor and appearance to this cake, contrasting with the dark chocolate cake.

Time: 1 hour
Easy

2¾ cups all-purpose flour
2 tsp baking powder
½ cup sugar
1 cup unsweetened cocoa
   powder
pinch salt
pinch cinnamon
⅔ cup pine nuts
½ cup (1 stick) butter
1 cup milk
2 tbsp rum
peel of 2 oranges, grated

Sift the flour and baking powder into a large mixing bowl; add the sugar, cocoa powder, salt, cinnamon, and the coarsely chopped pine nuts; stir in the melted butter, milk, rum, and the grated orange peel. Mix very thoroughly for 5 minutes; the mixture should be smooth and quite stiff. Add a very little warm milk if it is too stiff or dry.
Grease an 8½-in cake pan, dust lightly with flour, shaking off any excess, and spoon the cake batter into it. Bake at 400° F for 40 minutes or until a thin skewer comes out clean when inserted into the middle of the cake.

• • •

CARROT AND ALMOND CAKE

Time: 1 hour 20 minutes
Very easy

1 lb carrots
6 eggs

RAISIN AND NUT BREAD
■ *Served on high days and holidays. At Eastertime the seedless white raisins and almonds can be omitted and six painted hardboiled eggs placed on top of the cooked bread as a suitable decoration.*

5 tbsp lukewarm water
1½ cups sugar
juice of 1 lemon
2 tbsp rum
1¼ cups all-purpose flour
1 tbsp baking powder
4 cups ground almonds or 2
    cups very finely chopped
    blanched almonds
1–2 tsp butter

Peel the carrots, and grate finely. Beat the egg yolks thoroughly with the 5 tbsp lukewarm water, then gradually beat in the sugar, the lemon juice, and rum. Beat the egg whites until very stiff and fold into the mixture. Quickly add the sifted flour and baking powder, the almonds and, finally, the carrots. Stir well. Grease an 8½-in cake pan with butter, dust with flour, and spoon the cake batter into it. Bake for 1 hour at 350° F. Remove from the oven, leave to cool, then turn out and serve.

• • •

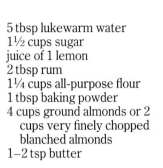

FRESH FRUIT CAKE

Other fruit, such as bananas, kiwi fruit, pineapple etc. can be used when in season.

Time: 2 hours
Easy

1 apple
2 small pears or 1 large pear
½ lb pitted cherries
4 apricots
1 tbsp seedless white raisins,
    soaked in warm water
½ cup candied fruit
¾ cup all-purpose flour

1 tsp baking powder
⅔ cup sugar
pinch salt
4 eggs
1 cup (2 sticks) butter
1½ cups raspberry jam

Peel, core, and dice the apples
and pears then cover with a
cloth. Dice the candied fruit
very finely and mix with 1 tbsp
flour. Sift the remaining flour
with the baking powder into a
bowl and mix with the sugar
and salt. Beat the eggs in a
blender for 2–3 minutes, and
pour into the flour and sugar
mixture; stir and then beat for
up to 10 minutes with an
electric beater, longer if using
a whisk.
Melt the butter and beat into
the batter. Stir in the candied
fruit and then the fresh fruit.
Have a 7-in deep cake pan
ready greased with butter and
dusted lightly with flour; pour
the batter into it and place in a
cold oven; turn on the oven,
set at 340° F, and cook for 1½
hours or until a thin skewer
inserted deep into the cake
comes out clean. Leave to
cool a little before turning out.
Heat the raspberry jam with
2 tbsp water: dribble a little of
this decoratively over the cake
if wished; serve the rest in a
jug with the cake.

• • •

SPECIAL FRUIT
CAKE

*This rich fruit cake is
substantial and filling; ideal
for afternoon tea.*

Time: 1 hour
Very easy

1¼ lb apples
1 lb pears
1 tbsp sugar
½ cup walnut pieces
⅓ cup peeled almonds
½ cup dried figs
½ cup candied orange or
    citron peel
⅓ cup seedless white raisins
2 eggs
½ cup all-purpose
    flour
1 tsp baking powder
1–2 tsp butter
1 tbsp fine breadcrumbs

Peel, core, and slice the
apples and pears and cook
gently in a saucepan with the
sugar and 1 cup water, stirring
from time to time. Chop the
walnuts, almonds, dried figs,
and the candied peel into very

small pieces. Soak the
sultanas in warm water for 10
minutes, drain and dry. Sieve
the apples and pears into a
large mixing bowl when very
tender.
Beat the eggs and stir into the
fruit purée, followed by the
flour and baking powder,
sifted together; mix well. Stir
in the candied fruit or peel, the
sultanas, figs, almonds, and
walnuts.
Grease a fairly deep cake pan
with butter, sprinkle with the
breadcrumbs, spoon in the
cake batter, and bake at
350° F for 1 hour or until done.
(Test by inserting a skewer
into the center: if it comes out
clean, the cake is done.)

• • •

125

CHESTNUT JELLY ROLL

Time: 45 minutes
Easy

1 tbsp butter
4 eggs
½ cup sugar
1½ cups all-purpose flour
1 tsp baking powder
pinch salt
1 tbsp vegetable, groundnut,
  or sunflower seed oil
1¾ cups chestnut jam or
  sweetened chestnut purée

Grease a jelly roll pan. Break the eggs into a bowl and beat well; beat in the sugar a little at a time, followed by the sifted flour, baking powder and salt, and lastly the oil. Transfer the batter to the prepared baking pan, smooth level with a spatula and bake for 40 minutes at 350° F. Spread a damp cloth out flat on a work surface, turn the cooked sponge cake out onto it, spread carefully but quickly with the chestnut jam and then roll up. Leave the jelly roll to cool on a cake rack. Slice and serve with pouring cream if wished.

• • •

FEATHERLIGHT SPONGE CAKE

Do not be tempted to skimp on the beating when preparing this cake or it will not be as airy as it should be.

Time: 20 minutes
Easy

½ cup + 2 tbsp butter
½ cup + 2 tbsp sugar

3 eggs
1¼ cups all-purpose or soft
  cake flour
1 tsp baking powder
2 oranges
1 cup confectioners' sugar

Beat the butter in a warmed mixing bowl with a wooden spoon until light and creamy. Beat in ½ cup + 2 tbsp sugar a little at a time. Beat in the eggs one at a time. Stir in the sifted flour and baking

CHESTNUT JELLY ROLL
■ *Jelly rolls can be served as desserts as well as with coffee.*

powder, followed by the juice and grated peel of 1 orange. Fold in the stiffly beaten egg whites. Transfer this batter to a greased and floured 8½-in cake pan and bake at 350° F for 50 minutes or until done. While the cake is baking make the frosting: melt the confectioners' sugar with the juice of the remaining orange over low heat. This should be quite thick yet easily spreadable and become smooth when left to stand. Remove the cake from the oven and leave to cool. Turn out onto a serving plate and spread the frosting evenly over the top, adding decoration of your choice.

• • •

MEXICAN CAKE

The olive oil gives a distinctive taste to this cake, enhanced by the lemon peel.

Time: 1 hour
Very easy

1¾ cups all-purpose flour
1 tsp baking powder
pinch salt
½ cup (1 stick) butter
1 cup sugar
3 eggs
1 cup filberts, finely chopped
¼ cup olive oil
½ cup milk
peel of 1 lemon, grated

Sift the flour together with the baking powder and salt. Have the butter at room temperature so it is soft enough to beat easily with the sugar until pale and creamy. Separate the eggs and reserve the whites. Beat the yolks one at a time into the butter mixture, then add the other ingredients a little at a time, starting with some of the flour. Beat the egg whites until stiff and fold into the batter.
Grease a 10-in cake pan with butter, dust lightly with flour, and transfer the cake batter to it. Bake at 350° F for about 50 minutes or until done.

• • •

CHESTNUTS

These ripen in autumn and have many uses in cakes, desserts, and confectionery. They can be roasted, boiled, preserved in syrup, candied, or ground to a paste (sweetened or unsweetened) and canned, or left whole and dried.

CHOCOLATE JELLY ROLL

Time: 1 hour
Easy

5 eggs
⅔ cup sugar
1 cup all-purpose flour
1 tsp baking powder
½ cup + 1 tbsp butter
2 tbsp unsweetened cocoa
  powder
½ cup confectioners' sugar
2 tbsp maraschino liqueur
1 cup whipping or heavy
  cream

Beat the egg yolks very thoroughly with the sugar; add the flour sifted with the baking powder and stir well. Fold in the stiffly beaten egg whites. Transfer the mixture to a jelly roll pan, smoothing it level with a spatula (it should be about ⅜ in thick). Bake at 350° F for 40 minutes or until done. Remove from the oven; turn out carefully onto a damp cloth and roll up; leave to cool. Beat the butter until creamy and then beat in the sifted cocoa and confectioners' sugar; Add the maraschino a little at a time, then fold in the stiffly beaten cream. Unroll

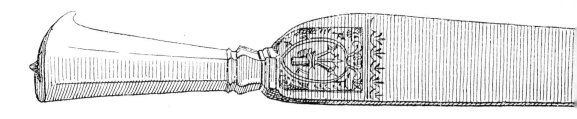

the cake, removing the cloth; spread the surface with half the chocolate mixture. Roll up again, spread with the remaining chocolate cream, and serve.

• • •

MASCARPONE CAKE

A very simple cake. If mascarpone (an Italian fresh cream cheese) is unavailable, use very soft fresh cream cheese.

Time: 1 hour
Very easy

3 eggs and 2 extra egg yolks
½ cup sugar
2¾ cups all-purpose flour
1 tsp baking powder
½ cup milk
1 cup mascarpone
¼ cup very strong black coffee
few coffee beans (optional)

Beat 3 egg yolks very thoroughly with half the sugar; stir in the sifted flour and baking powder, followed by the milk, then fold in the stiffly beaten egg whites. Use a mixing spatula or metal spoon to combine all the ingredients evenly. Grease a cake pan, dust lightly with flour, and spoon in the cake batter. Bake at 350° F for 50 minutes or until a skewer comes out clean when inserted into the center of the cake. Remove from the oven and turn out; when cold cut horizontally in half. Beat the remaining egg yolks with the rest of the sugar until pale and fluffy, beat in the mascarpone and the coffee. Place one half of the sponge cake on a serving plate, spread with half the coffee mixture, place the other sponge half on top and top with the remaining coffee cream, smoothing with a spatula. Chill before serving, and decorate with coffee beans if wished.

• • •

CHERRY AND CHOCOLATE CAKE

The taste of unsweetened chocolate can be enhanced by the fresh sweetness of many varieties of fruit.

Time: 1 hour 30 minutes
Easy

1 lb cherries
1 cup sugar
3 whole eggs and 3 extra yolks
pinch salt
few drops vanilla extract

1¾ cups all-purpose flour
1 cup potato flour or
   cornstarch
½ cup unsweetened cocoa
   powder
1 tsp baking powder
¼ cup (½ stick) butter,
   melted

Wash and dry the cherries, remove their stalks, and pit using a cherry pitter so as not to break them up too much. Heat them with 2 tbsp water and ¼ cup of the sugar. The moment they show signs of coming to a boil, remove from the heat and leave to cool. Place the eggs and extra yolks, the salt, remaining sugar, and vanilla in the top of a double boiler and beat very thoroughly indeed, preferably with a hand-held electric beater. Place over gently simmering water and beat until the mixture is thoroughly warmed but do not overheat or it will curdle. Remove from the heat and continue beating until cold. Place the flour, potato flour (or cornstarch), cocoa powder, and baking powder in a sieve and sift a little at a time into the mixture, stirring well after each addition. Lastly, add the melted butter and the well-drained cherries. Grease a deep, rectangular cake pan (approx. 9½ × 6 in) and fill three-quarters full with the cake mixture. Place in the oven preheated to 400° F and bake for 1 hour, reducing the temperature in stages after the first 30 minutes (reduce by 20° F every 10 minutes but do not reduce below 320° F). Turn out the cake and serve.

• • •

ORANGE CAKE

A full-flavored, light cake: a baking powder version of a baba. You can add Grand Marnier to the syrup to give it a little extra kick.

Time: 1 hour
Very easy

5 eggs
1 cup sugar
4 oranges
1¾ cups all-purpose flour
½ tsp baking powder
½ cup granulated or cube
   sugar

Beat the eggs with the first quantity of sugar for up to 10 minutes (you will save time and energy by preparing this batter in the large bowl of your electric mixer, at medium speed) then beat in the grated peel of the 4 oranges, followed by the flour sifted with the baking powder (add a little at a time, beating after each addition). Beat in the melted butter.
Grease a 10-in cake pan with butter and transfer the batter to it. Bake at 350° F for 45 minutes or until a thin skewer inserted in the cake comes out clean. Turn out and leave to cool. Heat the juice of the 4 oranges with the granulated or cube sugar until it has completely dissolved and boil for 5 minutes over fairly high heat. Pierce the cake at regular intervals with the tines of a fork, pour the syrup slowly all over it and serve.

• • •

JAM CAKE

An Italian recipe which originally called for grape preserve (mostarda d'uva), a northern Italian specialty. Use your favorite homemade or high-quality jam.

Time: 1 hour
Very easy

2¾ cups all-purpose flour
½ tsp baking powder
2 eggs
½ cup sugar
¼ cup (½ stick) butter
peel of 1 lemon, grated
¼ cup milk
1¾ cups jam of your choice

Sift the flour and baking powder into a large mixing bowl; make a well in the center and pour the lightly beaten eggs into it, followed by the sugar, melted butter, grated lemon peel, and milk. Mix gradually into the flour to give a soft consistency which will just hold its shape. Divide into two portions, one slightly larger than the other.
Grease an 8½-in cake pan with butter and sprinkle with flour. Spread out the larger portion into an even layer of the cake batter in the bottom of the pan; spread half the jam on top, then cover this in turn with the rest of the batter, and finish with a layer of the remaining jam.
Bake at 400° F for 50 minutes or until done.

APPLE AND COCONUT
CAKE
■ *Coconut is a very popular
ingredient in many cake and
dessert recipes: it goes well
with a wide variety of fruit.*

APPLE AND POTATO CAKE

*Potatoes often replace part of
the flour content in many
recipes; they add lightness to a
cake, just as potato flour does.*

*Time: 1 hour
Easy*

1 boiled floury potato
2 eggs
¼ cup sugar
1¾ cups all-purpose flour
1 tsp baking powder
peel of 1 lemon, grated
½ cup milk
3 Golden Delicious apples
2 tbsp butter
1 tbsp confectioners' sugar

Peel the potato while it is still
very hot and push through a
sieve or use a ricer. Beat the
eggs very well with the sugar.
Sieve the flour with the baking
powder and stir into the egg
mixture; add the potato, the
grated lemon peel, and the
milk. Mix to a smooth
consistency. Have a 10-in
cake pan ready greased with a
very little butter and sprinkled
with flour; transfer the cake
batter to it. Level the surface
with a spatula. Peel, core, and
slice the apples thinly,
arranging them in slightly
overlapping concentric circles
on top of the cake batter.
Distribute the remaining
butter over the surface in very
small pieces and bake at
350° F for 45 minutes or until
done and golden brown on top.
Sprinkle the top with the
confectioners' sugar before
serving.

• • •

APPLE AND COCONUT CAKE

*Time: 1 hour
Very easy*

½ cup (1 stick) butter
½ cup sugar
3 eggs
peel of 1 lemon, grated
1¼ cups shredded coconut
1¼ cups all-purpose flour
½ tsp baking powder
3 Golden Delicious apples

Have the butter at room
temperature so that it is soft
and beat until pale and creamy
with the sugar; beat in the egg
yolks, one at a time. Stir in the
grated lemon peel and half the
coconut, followed by the sifted
flour and baking powder. Fold
in the stiffly beaten egg
whites.
Place this mixture in a greased
and floured 8½-in cake pan.
Smooth the surface with a
spatula; quickly peel, core,
and slice the apples and press
lightly into the top of the cake
batter. Sprinkle with the
remaining coconut and bake at
400° F for 40 minutes or until
done. Leave to cool before
serving.

• • •

APPLE, PEAR, AND PEACH CAKE

As an alternative to the jam sauce that accompanies this cake, you could serve a sauce made with liquidized peaches sweetened with sugar.

Time: 1 hour 15 minutes
Very easy

generous ½ cup all-purpose
   flour
1 tsp baking powder
8 tbsp sugar
4 eggs
pinch salt
1 cup (2 sticks) + 2 tbsp
   butter
4 tbsp water
2 pears
2 apples
4 peaches
1 cup peach jam

Sift the flour with the baking powder into a mound in a large mixing bowl, make a well in the center and place the sugar, eggs, and salt in it and, last of all, the melted butter. Mix quickly, then add the water and the peeled, cored, and diced pears and apples and 2 of the peaches, peeled, pitted, and diced.
Place the cake batter in a greased and lightly floured 10-in cake pan and bake at 350° F for 1 hour or until done. This cake is best served warm, with peach sauce: peel and pit the 2 remaining peaches and melt the jam. Liquidize the fruit and jam, and pour into a jug or sauceboat.

. . .

RICOTTA AND ORANGE CAKE

You can make this cake with lemon, lime, or mandarin instead of orange.

Time: 1 hour 15 minutes
Very easy

1 cup ricotta
1 cup sugar
3 eggs
1¾ cups all-purpose flour
½ tsp baking powder
juice and grated peel of ½
   orange
2 tsp butter

Push the ricotta through a sieve into a large mixing bowl and combine it very thoroughly with the sugar. Mix in the egg yolks one at a time. Stir in the sifted flour and baking powder, followed by the orange juice and grated peel. Fold in the stiffly beaten egg whites and transfer the batter to a greased and lightly floured 8½-in cake pan. Bake at 350° F for 1 hour or until done.

. . .

Seedless white raisins, candied fruit, and candied peel make this large bun popular with children.

½ cup milk
3 tbsp pure almond flour or very finely ground almonds
1¼ cups all-purpose flour
1½ tbsp baking powder
½ cup sugar
1 whole egg and 1 egg yolk
¼ cup softened butter
4 drops vanilla extract
⅓ cup diced candied peel and cherries
½ cup seedless white raisins, soaked in warm water and drained
generous pinch each cinnamon and ginger

For the rum frosting:
¼ cup confectioners' sugar
rum

For decoration:
1 tbsp coarsely chopped walnuts
1 tbsp diced candied peel or chopped candied fruit

Mix the milk with the almond flour or ground almonds in a bowl, then combine with the sifted flour and baking powder, the sugar, egg yolk, softened butter, the whole egg, and vanilla.

When the dough is smooth and evenly mixed, place on a lightly floured pastry board, sprinkle with the spices and knead in.

Flatten the dough a little by hand; sprinkle with the fruit and shape the dough into a ball, enclosing the fruit.

Grease a ring mold with butter.

Shape and stretch the dough, making a hole in the middle, to form a ring which will fit in the mold. Bake in a preheated oven at 400° F for 30 minutes.

Turn out and leave to cool. Make the rum frosting (see page 52) and trickle over the top of the cake (it will run down the sides a little). Sprinkle with the walnuts and candied fruit or peel before the frosting sets.

BUTTER MOLD
■ Italian engraving dating
from the nineteenth century.

YEAST BAKING AND RAISED CAKES

PINEAPPLE UPSIDE-DOWN CAKE

If you wish to use peaches or apricots instead of pineapple, omit the cinnamon and use a few drops of vanilla extract instead.

Time: 1 hour 15 minutes
Very easy

7 slices drained canned
   pineapple
2 eggs
2¼ cups unrefined brown cane
   sugar
½ cup milk
½ cup (1 stick) butter
3¼ cups all-purpose flour
1½ tbsp baking powder
½ tsp cinnamon
7 maraschino cherries

Remove excess moisture from the pineapple slices with paper towels. Beat the eggs with 1½ cups of the sugar, beat in the milk followed by half the butter, melted. Sift the flour with the baking powder and cinnamon into the bowl and stir into the egg mixture. Melt the remaining butter in a pan over moderate heat and pour into the base of a 10-in square cake pan, tilting the pan so that the base is evenly coated. Sprinkle over the remaining sugar. Place a layer of pineapple slices in the pan (cut some of the rings if necessary to fit), filling the central holes with maraschino cherries. Cover evenly with the cake batter and bake for 50 minutes at 350° F. Immediately the cake comes out of the oven, cover with a serving plate and turn upside down, releasing the cake. Serve warm.

•   •   •

BUTTER

The fat most widely used in baking, patisserie, and confectionery. Sometimes it must be clarified: heated gently to separate the ingredient which burns at low temperatures, the white casein subsequently discarded. Butter can then be used for frying.

CRUNCHY CHOCOLATE CAKE

The crushed cookies forming the base of this dessert or cake can be replaced by the same volume of chopped (not ground) filberts, which add a special taste.

Time: 1 hour
Very easy

⅔ cup almonds
½ cup (1 stick) butter
½ cup sugar
4 oz (4 squares) semisweet
   chocolate or bakers'
   chocolate
1 tsp baking powder
¼ cup potato flour or
cornstarch
⅔ cup crushed Graham
   crackers

Clean the almonds if necessary by rubbing with a cloth but do not peel them. Chop finely in the food processor but do not grind to a paste. Have the butter at room temperature, soft enough to beat until pale and creamy with the sugar. Stir in the almonds, followed by the finely grated chocolate and three egg yolks. When thoroughly combined, fold in the stiffly beaten egg whites.

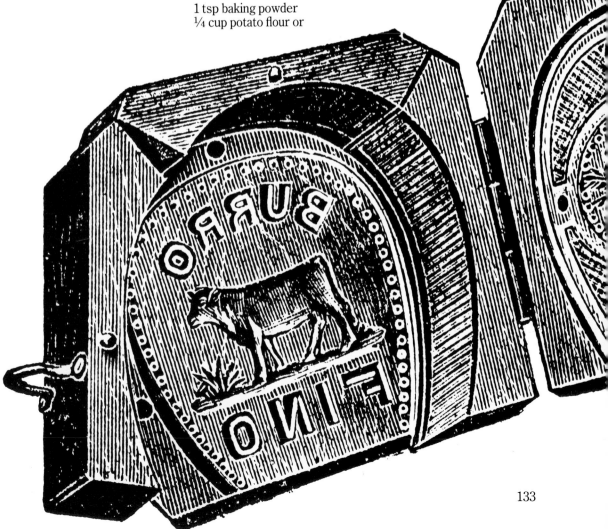

SWEET BUN RING WITH
FRUIT FILLING
■ This yeast dough ring is
soaked with sugar syrup like a
baba. It can be horizontally
cut in half and filled with more
fruit.

Sift the baking powder and potato flour together into the bowl and stir gently but thoroughly into the batter using a mixing spatula. Grease a 10-in cake pan with butter; cover the bottom with a layer of the cracker crumbs; cover with the cake batter and bake at 350° F for 50 minutes.

• • •

SWEET BUN RING WITH FRUIT FILLING

Time: 1 hour
Very easy

1 cake compressed fresh
    yeast or 1 package (¼ oz)
    dry yeast
½ cup lukewarm milk
2¾ cups unbleached all-
    purpose flour
½ tsp salt
2 tbsp sugar
4 eggs, separated
½ cup (1 stick) + 2 tbsp
    butter, melted
For the fruit filling:
4 oranges
1 cup sugar
¼ cup kirsch
½ lb white grapes

Place the yeast in the lukewarm milk (scalded and allowed to cool to the correct temperature). Leave for 10 minutes to dissolve. Place the flour, salt, and sugar in a large mixing bowl; make a well in the middle, and pour the yeast and milk into it, followed by the egg yolks. Work into the flour gradually, adding the stiffly beaten egg whites a little at a time. Mix very thoroughly before adding the melted butter. The dough should be soft and rather

sticky. Knead for 10 minutes. Shape into a slightly flattened ball and leave to rise in the bowl, covered by a cloth or towel until it has doubled in volume.
Punch down the risen dough, knead briefly and place in a greased and lightly floured 8½-in ring mold. Leave to prove for 30 minutes in a warm, draught-free place and then bake for 20 minutes at 425° F.

• • •

BRAN BUN

A high-fiber sweet bun, perfect for breakfast, with coffee or tea.

Time: 1 hour
Very easy

1 cup low-fat natural yogurt
1¼ cups wheat bran
2 cups all-purpose flour
½ tsp baking powder
2 eggs
peel of 1 lemon, grated
½ cup sunflower seed oil
2 cups sugar

Place the yogurt in a mixing bowl, add the bran, the flour sifted with the baking powder, the lightly beaten eggs, the lemon peel, the sunflower seed oil, and the sugar. Mix well and transfer to a greased and floured 10-in cake pan. Bake at 350° F for 50 minutes or until done.

• • •

134

CHOCOLATE WALNUT CAKE

Filberts can replace the walnuts in this recipe, if preferred.

*Time: 1 hour 30 minutes
Very easy*

1 cup (2 sticks) butter
4¼ cups potato flour
1 tsp baking powder
2 eggs
1 cup sugar
1 cup unsweetened cocoa
   powder
1 cup milk
1 tsp vanilla extract
pinch salt
1 cup walnut halves

Melt the butter in a saucepan over very low heat; remove from the heat and stir in the sifted potato flour and baking powder, mixing thoroughly so that the mixture is smooth and well blended. Stir in the lightly beaten eggs adding a little at a time; add the sugar and the cocoa powder and moisten with a little of the milk. Add the vanilla and salt, followed by more milk. Continue adding milk until the batter is thick, creamy, and will just hold its shape; it should not be liquid. Transfer the batter to a prepared 8½-in deep cake pan. Press the walnut halves lightly into the surface of the cake and bake at 350° F for 1 hour or until done. Leave to cool before turning out, and place nut side uppermost on a serving plate.

•   •   •

ALMONDS

To peel almonds, blanch them in boiling water for a few seconds to loosen their skins. Roasting almonds in the oven for a few minutes heightens their flavor.

MARZIPAN CAKE

Homemade marzipan is quite time-consuming to make, so buy the very best you can afford from your grocer or delicatessen.

*Time: 1 hour 30 minutes
Easy*

2¾ cups all-purpose flour
1 tsp baking powder
⅔ cup finely chopped or
   ground almonds
few drops vanilla extract
1 cup sugar
½ cup + 2 tbsp butter
3 egg yolks and 2 egg whites
2 tbsp plum jam
1 tbsp unsweetened cocoa
   powder
8 amaretti, ratafia cookies, or
   small macaroons
2 tbsp Cointreau or orange
   flower water
1 apples
1 pear
¾ lb or 1½ cups marzipan

Sift the flour and baking powder together onto a working surface, add the almonds, half the sugar (½ cup), and the softened butter cut into very small pieces. Add the egg yolks to the mixture

135

APPLE
■ *Engraving taken from a nineteenth-century botanical work. Apples keep well if stored stem downward in a cool, well ventilated place.*

greased and floured 10-in cake pan and bake at 350° F for 50 minutes or until done.

•   •   •

APPLE BREAD

A sweet bread which can be served at breakfast time or as a teatime treat for children.

Time: 1 hour 30 minutes
Very easy

1 cake compressed fresh
    yeast or 1 package (¼ oz)
    dry yeast
½ cup lukewarm milk
½ cup sugar
2¾ cups all-purpose flour
½ cup (1 stick) butter
pinch salt
1 cup seedless white raisins
1 lb apples
juice of 1 lemon
1 cup sieved apricot preserve

Add the yeast to the lukewarm milk with 1 tbsp of the sugar and leave to stand for 10 minutes. Sift the flour into a large mixing bowl, add the milk and yeast, and combine with the flour to form a smooth dough. Cover and leave in a warm place to rise for 30 minutes. Soften the butter at room temperature then beat. Punch down the dough, then work in the softened butter, the sugar, and the salt. Knead well; roll out with a lightly floured rolling pin and use to line a prepared 10-in cake pan or flan case. Leave to prove in a warm place for 20 minutes. Soak the seedless white raisins in warm water until plump, then drain well. Peel, core, and thinly slice the apples, sprinkle with the lemon juice, and spread evenly

CORN MEAL CAKE

Time: 1 hour
Very easy

1 quart milk
½ vanilla bean or 3–4 drops
    vanilla extract
pinch salt
1 cup fine milled corn meal
½ cup (1 stick) butter
½ cup sugar
3 eggs, separated
1 tsp baking powder

Heat the milk to boiling point with the vanilla bean (or extract) and salt. Sprinkle in the corn meal, stirring continuously. Remove from the heat and stir in the butter, sugar, egg yolks, and baking powder. Wait until the mixture has cooled further before folding in the stiffly beaten egg whites.
Transfer the batter to a

followed by 3–4 drops vanilla extract. Mix well, shape into a ball, wrap this in foil, and chill for 30 minutes. Mix the jam in a bowl with the cocoa powder, the finely crumbled amaretti, and the liqueur.
Grease and flour a 10-in cake pan (preferably with a removable base). Use your knuckles to press the dough out into an even layer covering the bottom of the pan. Spread the jam and cocoa mixture on top and cover with the peeled, cored, and sliced apple and pear. Place in a preheated oven, at 350° F and bake for 20 minutes.
Beat the two egg whites until stiff, then beat in the remaining sugar. Remove the

cake from the oven and spread the meringue over the top. Return to the oven, reducing the heat to 300° F, and bake for 20–25 minutes more. The meringue should be golden brown; if it colors too quickly, gently reduce the heat again. While the cake is cooking, roll out the marzipan and cut out leaf shapes, draw a veining pattern with a knife, and arrange the leaves on the surface of the cake after it has been removed from the cake pan.

•   •   •

CORN MEAL CAKE
■ Very fine, white cornstarch
is invaluable for cake making.
Potato flour can be used
instead.

over the dough. Sprinkle the raisins on top and bake at 350° F for 50 minutes or until done. Remove from the oven and spread the apricot jam carefully over the top; serve while still hot.

• • •

POTATO CAKE

For an even lighter consistency, use 1 cup potato flour instead of the boiled potatoes.

Time: 1 hour
Very easy

2 floury potatoes
6 tbsp butter
1 cup sugar
¼ cup unsweetened cocoa
   powder
1 whole egg and 1 extra yolk
1¾ cups all-purpose flour
2 tsp baking powder
½ cup milk
pinch salt
4 tbsp chopped walnuts
2 tbsp confectioners' sugar
½ cup flaked or slivered
   almonds

Boil the potatoes, drain, then sieve or put through a ricer while still very hot. Have the butter at room temperature so that it is soft enough to beat until pale and creamy with the sugar; stir in the cocoa powder and the potatoes. Add the egg yolks one at a time, mixing well. Sift the flour with the baking powder and salt then alternate additions of this and the milk to the mixture. Add the walnuts; fold in the stiffly beaten egg white. The mixture should be evenly blended and smooth. Transfer

to a greased and lightly floured 10-in cake pan. Bake at 350° F for 50 minutes or until done. Turn out of the tin, dust with sifted confectioners' sugar, sprinkle with the almonds, and serve.

• • •

MANDARIN CAKE

For a lower fat content, use ricotta, quark, or any low-fat fresh cheese and add 2 tbsp mandarin liqueur for a more pronounced taste.

Time: 1 hour 15 minutes
Very easy

¼ cup seedless white raisins
   or seeded raisins
2¾ cups all-purpose flour
2 tsp baking powder
½ cup water
⅔ cup sugar
peel of 1 mandarin or

tangerine, coarsely grated
   or shredded
1 egg
pinch salt
½ cup cream cheese (e.g.
   mascarpone or quark)
2 amaretti cookies or small
   crisp macaroons

*CINNAMON AND
COCONUT CAKE*
■ *Northern and Central
European cake and cookie
recipes often employ spices;
spices also play a very
important role in Middle
Eastern confectionery.*

2 tbsp strong black coffee
3 tbsp butter

Soak the seedless white raisins in warm water until plump, then drain. Sift the flour and baking powder into a large mixing bowl; stir in the water a little at a time until you have a fairly firm dough. Add ¼ cup of the sugar, the mandarin peel (grated or cut into very thin, short strips), the egg, and salt. Work together with a wooden spoon or with the dough hook attachment in an electric mixer for 15 minutes. Mix the cream cheese, ¼ cup of the sugar, the seedless white raisins, the crumbled amaretti, and the cold black coffee. Grease an 8½-in cake pan with a little butter, and dust lightly with flour. Cover the base with a layer of half the dough; place a layer of all the cream cheese mixture on top and finish with a layer of the remaining dough. Distribute the butter, in small flakes, all over the top and sprinkle with the remaining sugar. Bake at 350° F for 1 hour or until done.

• • •

CINNAMON AND COCONUT CAKE

*Time: 1 hour
Very easy*

1 cup sugar
2 eggs, separated
½ cup (1 stick) butter
1¾ cups all-purpose flour
1 tsp baking powder
1 tsp cinnamon
pinch salt
1 cup milk
1 piece fresh coconut flesh

Beat the sugar and egg yolks together with a whisk until pale and increased in volume. Beat the butter (softened at room temperature), adding it in small pieces. Stir in a little of the flour at a time, sifted together with the baking powder, alternating with small quantities of the milk. Beat the egg whites until stiff and fold into the mixture. Transfer to a greased and floured 10-in cake pan and bake at 350° F for about 50 minutes. Turn out and decorate with strips of fresh coconut (see illustration on the left), finely cut with a potato peeler or cheese slicer.

• • •

IMPERIAL CAKE

Nougatine or almond brittle is used for this cake. To save time you can use bought nut toffee or nougat.

*Time: 1 hour 15 minutes
Fairly easy*

3 eggs, separated
3 tbsp boiling water
few drops vanilla extract
¾ cup sugar
¾ cup all-purpose flour
2 tbsp baking powder
½ cup potato flour
3 tbsp unsweetened cocoa
  powder
For the filling:
2 cups Pastry Cream (see
  page 44)
⅔ cup sweet butter, at room
  temperature
1 tbsp confectioners' sugar
For the topping:
2 tsp butter
½ cup sugar
1¼ cups finely chopped
  almonds
almond oil

Beat the egg yolks with a wire whisk (or use an electric beater) and then beat in the boiling water; continue beating as you add a total of ½ cup of the sugar a little at a time, until the mixture is like a pale, fluffy cream. Beat the egg whites until very stiff and beat in the remaining sugar. Spoon the egg whites on top of the egg yolk mixture, then sift the flour, baking powder, and the cocoa together on top of the egg whites. Fold these ingredients gently but thoroughly into one another using a mixing spatula. Grease an 8½-in springform cake pan, line with waxed paper or nonstick silicone-treated paper; spoon in the

TUTTIFRUTTI CAKE

Time: 1 hour 30 minutes
Very easy

½ cup (1 stick) butter
½ cup sugar
4 eggs, separated
2¼ cups all-purpose flour
1 tsp baking powder
few drops vanilla extract
¼ cup milk
pinch salt
2 oranges
4 canned apricot halves
2 canned pears
½ cup canned cherries

batter and place in a preheated oven at 400° F for 30 minutes or until done. While the cake is baking, make the filling: prepare the pastry cream and while still hot, stir in the softened butter and the confectioners' sugar. Stir from time to time as the pastry cream cools to blend in the melting butter and sugar. Make the topping: melt the butter and sugar in a small

heavy-bottomed saucepan and cook until pale golden brown. Add the almonds and continue stirring over the heat until they turn golden brown. Lightly oil a large plate with almond oil and spread the hot nut and caramel mixture about ⅜-in thick. Leave until cold. Remove the cooked cake from its pan; cut it horizontally into 3 layers of equal thickness. Place one cake layer on the

serving plate, cover with a third of the filling, place the second cake layer on top, followed by half the remaining filling, then the final cake layer and use the rest of the filling to completely mask the cake. Chop the cold almond brittle into small pieces and sprinkle a thick layer over the top of the cake, pressing pieces against the sides of the cake.

• • • •

140

TUTTIFRUTTI CAKE
■ *You can either buy the canned fruit needed for this cake or can your own at home, following the recipes at the beginning of the book.*

STRAWBERRIES
■ *The sooner these are used after picking, the better. Once gathered and out of the sun they lose their vitamin content very quickly.*

juice of ½ lemon
4 tbsp apricot jam
¼ cup slivered or flaked
   almonds
6 tbsp raspberry or red
   currant jelly

Beat the butter (softened at room temperature) with the sugar until pale and creamy; beat in the egg yolks one at a time. Sift in the flour with the baking powder a little at a time, alternating this with the milk and vanilla extract. Beat the egg whites stiffly with the salt and fold into the cake batter.
Transfer to a prepared 10-in cake pan and bake at 350° F for 45 minutes or until done. While the cake is baking prepare the fruit: peel the oranges, divide into sections, and boil gently in the syrup drained from the apricots and pears. Leave to cool. Cut the apricots and pears into small pieces, halve the cherries, and place all together in a bowl; sprinkle with the lemon juice. Turn out the cake and when it is cold spread with the sieved apricot jam (warm this a little if necessary); press the almonds into this glaze. Drain all the fruit thoroughly and place on the top of the cake.
Boil the syrup drained from the fruit until reduced to 8 tbsp. Sieve the raspberry or red currant jelly into this syrup, stir, and leave to cool. Pour over the cake as a final glaze.

•   •   •

GLAZED STRAWBERRY CAKE

One of the simplest finishing touches to many cakes and desserts consists of melting jam in a small saucepan over low heat and then glazing the surface of the cake with this.

Time: 1 hour
Very easy

5 apples
2 cloves
½ cup dry vermouth
1 cup sugar
½ cup (1 stick) butter
4 eggs, separated
grated peel and juice of 1
   lemon
2¾ cups all-purpose flour
1 tsp baking powder
few drops vanilla extract
pinch salt
½ cup strawberry jam, sieved
½ cup confectioners' sugar
¾ lb strawberries
1 cup whipping cream

Peel the apples, cut them in half, and core them. Place in an ovenproof dish with the cloves, vermouth, and 6 tbsp of the sugar; cover with a lid or foil and cook for 30 minutes in a moderate oven (350° F), turning them once or twice. Make the cake: beat the butter (softened at room temperature) with the remaining sugar until pale and creamy; beat in the egg yolks one at a time, followed by the vanilla extract. Stir in the peel and the strained lemon juice; sift in the flour and baking powder and mix well. Beat the egg whites until stiff with the pinch of salt and fold into the batter.
Grease a 10-in deep cake pan

with butter; transfer half the batter to it, level before placing the drained apples on top (core side downward), and cover with the remaining batter. Bake at 350° F for 1 hour or until cooked. Remove the cake from the pan and leave to cool. Sieve the strawberry jam into a saucepan; melt gently with the confectioners' sugar and use to glaze the entire surface of the cake. Decorate the top with the strawberries and piped whipped cream and serve.

•   •   •

THREE-SPICE CAKE

The combination of cinnamon with cloves and nutmeg has always appealed to northern European tastes.

Time: 1 hour 15 minutes
Very easy

2 tbsp seedless white raisins
1 cup (2 sticks) butter
1 cup sugar
6 sugar cubes
1 orange

4 eggs, separated
2¾ cups all-purpose flour
1 tsp baking powder
1 cup candied fruit
2 tbsp brandy
1 tsp cinnamon
1 tsp nutmeg
½ tsp ground cloves
pinch salt

Soak the seedless white raisins in warm water. Have the butter at room temperature, soft enough to beat with the sugar until pale and creamy. Rub the sugar cubes hard against the peel of orange, then crush and add to the butter and sugar; beat well. (Alternatively, add an extra 2 tbsp to the first quantity of sugar and use 6 drops essential oil of orange.) Stir in the egg yolks one at a time, then the flour, sifted, with the baking powder. Drain the raisins, dry with kitchen towels, and mix with 2 tsp flour; add to the mixture. Cut the fruit into small pieces and stir in, followed by the brandy. Continue stirring for several minutes. Add the cinnamon, nutmeg, and cloves. Beat the egg whites with the salt until stiff and fold into the batter. Line an 8½-in cake pan with waxed paper. Transfer the cake batter into it and bake at 350° F for 1 hour or until done.

• • •

HIGHLAND CAKE

Another cake made with corn meal (see also page 136), mixed here with amaretti and almonds, and enriched with candied fruit and seedless white raisins.

Another cake made with corn meal (see also page 136)

GRAPE AND WHITE RAISIN CAKE
■ The Italian grappa liqueur in this cake gives it quite a strong, dry flavor. Use kirsch or other fruit-based liqueurs if you prefer a less unusual taste.

Time: 1 hour
Very easy

⅓ cup seedless white raisins
2 cups fine milled corn meal
1 tsp baking powder
½ cup (1 stick) + 2 tbsp
  butter
6 crumbled amaretti cookies
  or small macaroons
2 eggs, separated
⅓ cup finely chopped almonds
peel of 1 lemon, grated
½ cup candied fruit, finely
  chopped
pinch salt

Soak the seedless white raisins in warm water until plump; drain, dry, and shake with 2 tsp flour. Sift the corn meal into a mixing bowl with the baking powder; combine with the butter (softened at room temperature) the crumbled amaretti, and the

SALT

Salt is an important ingredient in most cakes and breads: it is used partly to enhance flavor and also because it strengthens the gluten content of the flour.

egg yolks. Add the almonds, lemon peel, candied fruit, then the raisins. Beat the egg whites stiffly with the salt and fold into the cake batter. Grease a 10-in cake pan with butter, dust lightly with flour, and transfer the batter into it. Bake at 350° F for 50 minutes.

• • •

GRAPE AND WHITE RAISIN CAKE

Time: 2 hours
Very easy

½ cup seedless white raisins
1 cup blanched almonds
1 cup sugar
6 eggs
½ cup fine milled corn meal
½ cup all-purpose flour
1 tsp baking powder
¼ cup potato flour or
  cornstarch
pinch salt
½ cup (1 stick) + 2 tbsp
  butter
3 tbsp grappa
½ lb black grapes
2 tbsp grape jelly

Soak the raisins in warm water. Roast the almonds in a moderate oven (350° F) until pale golden brown. Grind or process them with ¼ cup sugar. Beat the eggs well with the remaining sugar in the top of a double boiler; place over gently simmering water and continue beating until the mixture is lukewarm, then remove from the heat and continue beating (with a wire whisk or electric beater) until very soft and fluffy. Stir in the flour and baking powder sifted together, the potato flour, salt, ground almonds, the drained and dried seedless white raisins, the softened butter, and finally the grappa. Mix thoroughly and place in a prepared 10-in cake pan. Bake at 350° F for 1 hour or until done. Turn out. Halve the grapes and remove the seeds; arrange on top of the cake and glaze with the melted grape jelly.

• • •

CHESTNUT CAKE WITH RUM FROSTING

Time: 2 hours
Easy

2¼ lb sweet chestnuts
1 tsp baking powder
1 cup milk
½ cup sugar
3 eggs, separated
1 cup confectioners' sugar
few drops vanilla extract
2 tbsp rum

If you use whole fresh chestnuts, boil them for 10 minutes then remove their tough outer skin carefully. Boil for another 30 minutes and then peel off the thin inner skin. Push through a fine sieve while still hot into a mixing bowl. Stir in the baking powder, cold milk, sugar, and egg yolks. Beat the egg whites until stiff and fold gently but thoroughly into the mixture.
Grease a 10-in cake pan with butter, line with waxed paper and spoon in the mixture, smoothing it level with a spatula. Bake at 350° F for 45 minutes or until done. When the cake has cooled, turn out onto a serving plate. Make the frosting by adding the sifted confectioners' sugar to the rum; stir in the vanilla. Spread over the top of the cake, smoothing with a warmed spatula.

• • •

143

These cakes owe none of their lightness to baking powder; they were enjoyed long before that raising agent was invented and certainly from the late Middle Ages onward. One of their most important ingredients costs nothing: air, which we incorporate when beating the eggs, butter, cream, and other ingredients, adding lightness with every turn of the whisk. Such fragile but delicious creations can still make the cook's heart beat faster. Their surface should be pressed gently with the fingertips to test for doneness: if the imprint of fingertips remains, the cake needs a little more baking, if the sponge springs back and the impression vanishes, the cake is done.

CLASSIC SPONGE CAKES AND GATEAUX

CLASSIC SPONGE CAKE

Time: 1 hour 15 minutes
Easy

6 eggs, separated
1¼ cups confectioners' sugar
peel of 1 lemon, grated
1¼ cups very fine white cake
   flour
1–2 tsp butter

Place the egg yolks in a bowl and start beating, adding the sugar a little at a time as you beat (use a wire whisk or a hand-held electric beater). Continue beating until the mixture becomes so pale that it is nearly white.
Beat the egg whites until very stiff; fold into the egg and sugar mixture a little at a time (use a mixing spatula or a large shallow spoon rather than a wooden spoon for this). Add the grated lemon peel, and before you stir it in, sift the flour into the bowl. Stir in slowly and gently with the spatula or a wooden spoon, making sure the ingredients are well mixed.
Grease a 9½-in cake pan with butter, dust with flour, and shake off any excess. Transfer the sponge batter into it; level the surface gently and place in

□ *The sponge cakes in this chapter owe their lightness to air being incorporated at various stages by vigorous beating: as much as one third of the bulk of the batter when it is placed in the oven is air; no raising agent is involved. Preparation of the classic sponge cake starts off with egg yolks or butter being beaten with sugar, until very pale and fluffy. All ingredients should be at room temperature before you start preparation.*

□ *Many cooks swear by beating egg whites in the special semispherical copper mixing bowls (harmless acid produced in a reaction with the copper stablizes the egg whites and means that they achieve greater bulk and firmness). These cake batters are very soft and fluffy, almost of pouring consistency: they must be treated gently, using a spatula for folding in beaten egg whites and combining delicate mixtures. Have your cake pans prepared before you start: grease lightly with butter and dust lightly but evenly with sifted flour, tipping the pan upside down and tapping it to get rid of any excess flour. Once the cake batter is in the pan, level the surface very gently with a spatula or broad bladed knife.*

□ *After removing the cake from the oven, let it stand in the pan for a few minutes to "set" before unmolding while still warm. Run a very sharp broad knife around the inside of the cake pan if necessary to loosen the edges of the cake. This type of sponge cake freezes well; defrost for 3 hours before using. Sponge cakes lend themselves to all sorts of uses: they can form the basis of flans, trifles, charlottes, bombes, and other molds as well as layer cakes, gateaux, and many other sweet dishes.*

the oven, preheated to 350° F for 1 hour or until done (press lightly on the middle of the surface of the cake with your fingertips: if the cake feels firm and springs back leaving no mark, it is baked; if the impression made by your fingers remains, cook for a little longer).

•   •   •

MADELEINE SPONGE CAKE

This sponge has the advantage of cooking satisfactorily in a very thin layer (as little as ⅜ in); it can also be cut into diamond shapes and sprinkled with confectioners' sugar. Often baked in traditional little Madeleine molds (greased lightly with butter and dusted lightly with flour), this sponge forms the basis of many desserts and gateaux.

Time: 1 hour 15 minutes
Easy

6 egg yolks
⅔ cup sugar
1 cup very fine white cake
   flour
¼ cup sweet butter
pinch baking soda
peel of 1 lemon, grated
4 egg whites
1 tbsp confectioners' sugar

Beat the egg yolks with the sugar until they are white and fluffy, sift in the flour and combine with the egg mixture, continuing to beat for 15 minutes. Add the butter (melted over hot water), the soda, and the grated lemon peel; mix well and then fold in the stiffly beaten egg whites. Grease a 9½-in cake pan with butter, dust lightly with flour,

GENOA SPONGE CAKE
■ This is the most widely used
of the various types of sponge
cake, indispensable for a very
wide range of desserts and
cakes.

CLASSIC SPONGE CAKES AND GATEAUX

and transfer the batter to it. Place in the oven, preheated to 350° F, and bake for 1 hour or until done. Turn out onto a cake rack to cool, sprinkle with the confectioners' sugar, and serve.

• • •

GENOA SPONGE CAKE

One of the most versatile and generally useful of all the classic sponges: for cakes, elaborate gateaux, lining charlotte molds, and countless other confections.

Time: 1 hour 15 minutes
Easy

⅔ cup sugar
peel of 1 lemon, grated
5 eggs
1 cup + 2 tbsp fine white cake
    flour or all-purpose flour

Warm a medium-sized mixing bowl which will fit snugly over a pan containing a little simmering water. Place the sugar, grated lemon peel, and the whole eggs in the warm bowl and beat very vigorously. Place the bowl over the hot water and continue beating (use a hand-held electric whisk or a balloon whisk) until the mixture has warmed through; do not overheat or it may curdle. Remove the bowl from above the hot water and continue beating until the mixture has become soft and frothy. Sift the flour into the bowl, mixing gently but thoroughly with a wooden mixing spatula or spoon. Transfer to a greased 9½-in cake pan and bake at 350° F for 30 minutes or until done.

• • •

148

SAVOY SPONGE

Another versatile type of sponge, delicious either filled with pastry cream or other creams, or soaked or sprinkled with liqueurs.

Time: 1 hour 15 minutes
Easy

6 eggs, separated
1½ cups sugar
¾ cup potato flour or cornstarch
¾ cup all-purpose flour
few drops vanilla extract

Beat the egg yolks with the sugar until very pale and greatly increased in volume. Beat in the vanilla extract. Sift the two types of flour together into the bowl, stirring as you do so. Fold in the stiffly beaten egg whites.
Grease a cake pan 9½ in in diameter and at least 2–2½ in deep with butter; transfer the cake batter to it and place in the oven, preheated to 350° F;

bake for 1 hour or until done. The cake should be well risen and pale golden brown on top. (Test by pressing with your fingertips; see Classic Sponge recipe on page 146).

• • •

SPONGE CAKE WITH APPLE SAUCE

Time: 1 hour 15 minutes
Very easy

6 eggs, separated
1 cup sugar
juice and grated peel of 1 lemon
7 tbsp potato flour
pinch salt
1 tbsp confectioners' sugar
2 apples
¼ cup sugar
½ cup water
1 cup natural unsweetened yogurt
1–2 tsp butter
2 tbsp all-purpose flour

Place the egg yolks in a bowl, and add the sugar and the lemon juice. Beat with a wooden spoon until pale and frothy and increased in volume; by this time the sugar should have dissolved completely. Sift the potato flour and stir into the egg mixture, a little at a time: add the salt and, finally, fold in the stiffly beaten egg whites gently but thoroughly.
Grease a 9½-in cake pan with butter, dust lightly with flour, and place the cake batter in it. Bake at 350° F for 50 minutes or until a thin skewer pushed deep into the center of the cake comes out clean.
Turn the cake out onto a serving plate; dust the top by sifting the icing sugar onto it.

Make the apple sauce: peel, core, and slice the apples. Cook with ¼ cup sugar, the water, and the grated lemon peel until very tender. Push through a sieve. Return to the saucepan and cook slowly until the purée has thickened considerably. Leave until cold before mixing well with the yogurt. Transfer to a bowl or jug and serve with the cake.

• • •

WALNUT AND CREAM CAKE

You can make a very thick hot chocolate sauce for this cake in place of the cream if it is more to your taste.

Time: 1 hour 15 minutes
Very easy

4 eggs, separated
1 cup sugar
1¾ cups walnuts, preferably blanched and peeled
3 tbsp fine cake flour or all-purpose flour
7 oz (7 squares) semisweet or bitter chocolate, grated
½ cup milk
1 cup heavy or whipping cream (well chilled)
1 tbsp sugar

Beat the egg yolks very thoroughly with the sugar until pale; chop the walnuts very finely (or grind fairly coarsely in a food processor) and add them to the mixture, followed by the flour, chocolate, and the milk. Fold in the stiffly beaten egg whites carefully but thoroughly.
Transfer this batter to a greased 24-in diameter ring mold and bake at 350° F for 1 hour or until done. Beat the cream with the confectioners' sugar until stiff.

149

CARROT CAKE RING

The kirsch-flavored buttercream can be omitted if preferred, and kirsch-flavored frosting included instead. The kirsch buttercream, if used, can be made in advance.

1–2 carrots weighing approx. ¼ lb
¼ cup sugar
3 egg yolks
6 tbsp all-purpose flour
½ cup almond flour or ⅔ cup finely ground almonds
1 tbsp grated lemon peel
1 tbsp lemon juice
3 egg whites
For the kirsch buttercream:
2 tbsp sugar
¼ cup sweet butter
1 egg yolk
1 tbsp kirsch
For the Chantilly cream:
1 cup heavy or whipping cream
¼ cup confectioners' sugar
To moisten the cake:
¼ cup Cointreau

Grease a ring mold with butter and dust lightly with sifted flour, shaking out any excess.

Cut the top off the carrots, peel, and grate finely; you will need ⅔ cup (loosely packed) grated carrot.

Beat the sugar and egg yolks until very pale and fluffy, beat in the all-purpose flour and cook very gently over hot water to thicken.

Remove from the heat; stir in the carrot, almond flour, or ground almonds, grated lemon peel, and finally the lemon juice.

Beat the egg whites stiffly.

Fold the egg whites into the cake batter gently but thoroughly.

Spoon half this cake batter into the ring mold; make sure it is evenly distributed. Have the kirsch buttercream ready prepared and spread in an even layer on top of the cake batter. Spread the remaining cake batter on top.

Bake at 350° F for 45 minutes or until done. Turn out and, leaving "upside down," brush the top of the cake with the Cointreau. Decorate with piped Chantilly Cream (see page 48).

ORANGE
■ The heavier the orange, the more juice it contains Those with smooth, thin peel are the best juicing fruit.

CLASSIC SPONGE CAKES AND GATEAUX

Turn out the cake (leave upside down as is usual for this type of cake) and when cold fill the central well with the cream.

• • •

MARGUERITE SPONGE CAKE

A very soft, moist, and digestible cake which is put to a wide variety of uses. It is a particularly suitable basis for children's cakes, when a sugar syrup, grenadine, or rose hip syrup could be sprinkled onto the cake.

Time: 1 hour
Easy

6 eggs, separated
6 tbsp boiling water
1½ cups sugar
few drops vanilla extract
2¼ cups all-purpose flour
1 cup cornstarch
¼ cup butter, melted but not hot
pinch salt

Beat the egg yolks, beat in the boiling water, and continue beating as you add a total of 1 cup of the sugar a little at a time. Beat in the vanilla. By this time the mixture should be very pale and soft. Add a small pinch of salt.
Beat the egg whites until very stiff; continue beating as you add the remaining sugar. The meringue mixture should be so firm that a knife cut through them leaves a distinct trace. Place the meringue on top of the yolk mixture but do not combine yet. Quickly sift the flour and cornstarch together into the bowl on top of the whites and sprinkle with the melted butter. Combine all

these ingredients gently but thoroughly.
Have a 9½-in springform cake pan ready greased with butter and dusted with flour and transfer the cake batter to it without delay. Place in the oven, preheated to 415° F and bake for 30 minutes or until done.

• • •

ORANGE ROLL

A good cake to serve for brunch or afternoon tea; the filling is very rich and satisfying.

Time: 1 hour 15 minutes
Easy

2¼ cups all-purpose flour
½ cup sugar
4 eggs
1 cup (2 sticks) butter
3 tbsp orange liqueur (e.g. Curaçao) or brandy
⅓ cup seedless white raisins
1 cup sweet dessert wine
1 cup walnuts
⅓ cup peeled almonds
⅓ cup candied orange and citron peel
1 tbsp stale or dry (not toasted) breadcrumbs
⅓ cup pine nuts
peel of 1 orange, grated
peel of 1 lemon, grated
1 tbsp confectioners' sugar

Mix the flour and sugar and heap up in a mound on the work surface. Make a well in the center and place into it 1 whole egg and 1 yolk and ½ cup of the butter (softened at room temperature and cut into small pieces). Combine quickly and briefly; add the orange liqueur or brandy and shape into a ball. Wrap in foil or saran wrap and chill in the least cold part of the

refrigerator (the salad crisper will do very well).
Make the filling: soak the seedless white raisins in the wine until plump. Chop the walnuts and almonds fairly finely (or grind coarsely in a food processor) and mix with the chopped candied peel. Fry the breadcrumbs until golden brown in the remaining butter. Drain the seedless white raisins and mix in a bowl with the nuts, peel, breadcrumbs, pine nuts, and the grated orange and lemon peel. Mix with 1 egg yolk and then with 1 white, stiffly beaten.
Roll out the chilled dough into a rectangle about 8 × 12 in; spread the prepared filling over its entire surface; roll up just as you would a jelly roll. Lightly grease and flour a cookie sheet and place the roll on it; brush with the remaining egg yolk and sprinkle with the

confectioners' sugar. Bake at 375° F for 45 minutes or until done.

• • •

RUM AND BANANA CAKE

Bananas and rum seem made for each other. When cooked in a cake the bananas provide a pleasantly moist consistency and an unmistakable flavor.

Time: 40 minutes
Very easy

1½ cups milk
⅔ cup sugar
2–3 drops vanilla extract
2⅓ cups stale bread, crusts removed
½ tsp cinnamon
grated peel and juice of 1 lemon
2 eggs, separated
¼ cup (½ stick) butter

APRICOTS
■ Nineteenth-century botanical engraving. To thicken and add flavor to your apricot preserve, add a few shelled sweet almonds before boiling it.

fold into the mixture. Grease and lightly dust with flour an 8½-in deep cake pan, place the cake batter in it and bake at 350° F for 45 minutes or until done. Turn the cake out of the pan, leave to cool, and decorate with the skinned orange sections and rosettes or piped whipped cream. Hand round the chocolate sauce separately in a bowl or jug.

• • •

and leave to cool. Fill the central well of the cake with the stiffly beaten cream and decorate with the chocolate sprinkles. Chill in the refrigerator until serving.

• • •

hour. Leave to cool before glazing the top with the apricot jam melted gently with the rum.

• • •

4 ripe bananas
1 cup apricot jam
3 tbsp rum

Bring the milk to a boil with the sugar and vanilla. Crumble the bread into a bowl and pour the hot milk over it. Add the cinnamon, lemon peel and juice, and the 2 egg yolks. Stir very thoroughly. Heat the butter over hot water until just melted and stir into the bread mixture. Add the thinly sliced bananas. Stir well. Beat the egg whites stiffly and fold into the bread and milk mixture. Grease an 8½-in soufflé dish with butter, dust with flour and fill about ⅔–¾ full with the mixture; set the dish in a roasting pan, pour sufficient boiling water into the pan to come about half way up the sides of the soufflé dish, and cook at 350° F for about 1

EXTRA-LIGHT SPONGE CAKE

Time: 1 hour
Easy

6 eggs, separated
1 cup + 2 tbsp sugar
1 cup potato flour or
    cornstarch
½ cup all-purpose flour
peel of 1 lemon, grated
1 quantity Chocolate Sauce
    (see page 50)
2 oranges
scant ½ cup whipping cream

Beat the egg yolks with the sugar until pale and increased in volume; sift in the flour and potato flour together while stirring; add the lemon peel. Beat the egg whites stiffly and

MANDARIN LIQUEUR CAKE

This cake can be served with homemade fruit ice cream or cooked fruit, with fresh strawberries or with cream.

Time: 1 hour
Easy

6 eggs, separated
½ cup sugar
3 tbsp fine breadcrumbs (not
    toasted or colored)
3 tbsp mandarin liqueur
1¼ cups potato flour or
    cornstarch
1 cup whipping cream
2 tbsp chocolate sprinkles

Beat the egg yolks with the sugar until pale and frothy, add the breadcrumbs and the liqueur; stir well. Fold in the stiffly beaten egg whites and then sift in the potato flour. Stir gently but thoroughly, preferably with a mixing spatula. The mixture should be very soft and fluffy; transfer it to a 9½-in diameter turban or ring tube mold, greased lightly with butter. Place in the oven, preheated to 350° F and bake for 50 minutes or until done. Unmold

EXTRA-LIGHT SPONGE
CAKE
■ The addition of cornstarch
makes this cake particularly
light. The lemon peel can be
replaced by orange peel, if
preferred, and a sprinkling of
cinnamon over the surface of
the cake is optional.

CLASSIC SPONGE CAKES AND GATEAUX

RED CHERRY CAKE

*Use firm red sweet cherries
such as Bing, not Morellos for
this cake. If fresh cherries are
out of season, use well drained
canned fruit.*

Time: 1 hour
Very easy

1 cup (2 sticks) butter
1 cup sugar
4 eggs
1¾ cups all-purpose flour
2¼ lb cherries
1 cup sieved cherry jam or
  jelly

Have the butter softened at
room temperature and work
with a wooden spoon until
very pale and creamy. Add the
sugar and beat well; beat in
the eggs one at a time and
then sift in the flour and stir
well. The mixture should be
soft and of an even
consistency; transfer it to a
10-in cake pan, lightly greased
with butter and dusted with
flour. Wash and dry the
cherries, remove their stalks,
pit them, and use to cover the
top of the cake completely.
Bake at 350° F for 50 minutes
or until the cake is cooked.
Melt the cherry jam or jelly
and sprinkle over the cherries.
Serve when cold.

• • •

CURAÇAO CAKE

*Orange flower can replace the
Curaçao in this recipe, if
preferred.*

Time: 1 hour
Easy

1 Marguerite Sponge Cake
  (see page 151)
¼ cup Curaçao
1 cup (2 sticks) butter
2¼ cups confectioners' sugar
1 orange
3 egg yolks
½ cup granulated or superfine
  sugar
½ cup water
few drops lemon juice

Cut the cooked Marguerite
sponge cake horizontally into
three layers. Sprinkle each
layer with a little Curaçao.
Beat the butter (softened at
room temperature) with ½
cup of the sifted confectioners'
sugar and then add the grated
orange peel. In a separate
bowl beat the egg yolks very
well with the granulated or
superfine sugar and then
combine the two mixtures and
use as the filling between the
layers of cake, leaving the
exposed surface of the top
layer for the frosting.
Make the frosting: mix the
remaining confectioners' sugar
with the water and lemon
juice. Spread this snowy white
frosting over the top of the
cake. Divide the oranges into
segments, peel off the thin
inner skins or membranes,
and arrange in a circle all
round the top of the cake on
top of the frosting. Chill before
serving.

• • •

*OLD-FASHIONED
ALMOND CAKE*
■ *Ideally chop your own
almonds and sieve them for
flavor and moisture. Do not
over-grind them if using a
food processor.*

OLD-FASHIONED
ALMOND CAKE

Time: 1 hour
Very easy

½ cup peeled whole almonds
　　or 1 cup ground almonds
4 egg yolks + 2 egg whites
1 cup + 2 tbsp sugar
1 cup butter
2 cups all-purpose flour
1 tbsp potato flour or
　　cornstarch

Chop the almonds very finely
if you are using whole nuts
(this gives a slightly better
consistency). Beat the 4 egg
yolks with the sugar until pale,
add the almonds and the
butter (melted over hot water)
and stir well. Sift in the flour
and potato flour together and
mix thoroughly. Beat the 2
egg whites until stiff and fold
into the mixture.
Pour the mixture into a
prepared 8½-in cake pan and
bake at 350° F for 50 minutes
or until a thin skewer inserted
deep into the cake comes out
clean.
For an especially attractive
finish, cover the entire cake
with a thin layer of chocolate
frosting (see pages 52–3) and
decorate with rosettes of
piped whipped cream.

•　　•　　•

RASPBERRY
SYRUP LAYER
CAKE

*Raspberry syrup can be
replaced by other fruit syrups
that go well with kirsch liqueur
(which is made from cracked
cherry pits).*

154

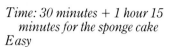

Time: 30 minutes + 1 hour 15 minutes for the sponge cake
Easy

1 Classic Sponge Cake (see page 146)
1¼ cups heavy or whipping cream
½ cup confectioners' sugar
½ tsp vanilla extract
4 tbsp kirsch
10 tbsp raspberry syrup or cordial
1½ lb strawberries

Bake the sponge cake in an 8-in cake pan for a little longer than stated in the recipe; cut the cake horizontally (and very carefully) into 4 equal thicknesses. Chill the bowl and whisk for 10 minutes in the freezer and then take the cream out of the refrigerator and beat with the sugar and vanilla until the cream is very firm but still looks velvety and smooth. Mix the kirsch with the syrup. Place a layer of sponge on a serving plate, sprinkle with a quarter of the syrup; cover with a quarter of the cream and a quarter of the strawberries. Continue the layers in this order, finishing with the last quarter of the strawberries. Chill until it is time to serve the gateau.

• • •

WHITE CHOCOLATE CAKE

Grate this chocolate with a cheese grater or one used for grating carrots into julienne strips (a mouli grater with the appropriate disk will do very well).

Time: 1 hour
Easy

RASPBERRIES

Like blackberries and such popular hybrids as boysenberries and loganberries, raspberries are very perishable and should be washed just before use. They are often sieved when used fresh in desserts, cakes, and for jelly making.

For the cake:
3 eggs
⅔ cup sugar
1 cup all-purpose flour
1 cup potato flour or cornstarch
1 cup unsweetened cocoa powder
½ tsp vanilla extract
¼ cup (½ stick) butter
1 cup finely chopped almonds
For the filling and topping:
2 egg yolks
½ cup confectioners' sugar
1 cup mascarpone (or similar fresh cheese) or very heavy cream
¼ cup chocolate flakes (preferably bitter chocolate)
3 tbsp Curaçao or Grand Marnier
¾ lb good-quality white chocolate

Beat the 3 whole eggs with the sugar very thoroughly; sift together the flour, potato flour, and cocoa powder, and stir into the eggs a little at a time. Stir in the vanilla and then the melted butter. Grease a 9½-in cake pan quite liberally with butter; sprinkle the chopped almonds all over the bottom and sides of the pan and carefully spoon in the cake batter. Bake at 400° F for 40 minutes or until done. While the cake is baking, make

the filling and topping: beat the 2 egg yolks with the confectioners' sugar until pale, stir in the mascarpone and the chocolate. When the cake is cold, cut horizontally in half; sprinkle the cut surfaces with the liqueur, spread half the cream on the lower cut surface, and replace the other half of the cake on top. Top with the remaining cream and grate the white chocolate all over it. Chill until you are ready to serve.

• • •

except for a few left whole (brush the areas where they are to go with a very little sieved apricot jam if wished to make them stay in place).

• • •

RASPBERRY-LAYERED MADELEINE CAKE

When fresh raspberries are unavailable, use frozen, thawed in advance for 2 hours at room temperature.

Time: 30 minutes + chilling time
Easy

1 Madeleine Sponge Cake (see page 146)
¾–1 lb fresh raspberries
¼ cup sugar
1 lb raspberry jam
½ cup raspberry liqueur
1½ cups whipping cream
1 tbsp confectioners' sugar

Bake the sponge cake in an 8½-in cake pan and when cold cut horizontally into 3 equal layers. Rinse and drain the raspberries; spread out to dry on paper towels. Reserve 12 for decoration. Crush the rest in a bowl with a fork and mix in the sugar followed by the

raspberry jam. Dilute the raspberry liqueur with ½ cup water, sprinkle over the three sponge layers, and then spread a quarter of the raspberry mixture over the cut surfaces of the bottom two layers, putting the cake together again as you do so. Spread the remaining raspberry mixture over the whole of the reassembled cake. Chill for 2 hours. Beat the cream with the confectioners' sugar and use a pastry bag and fluted tube to pipe rosettes of cream on the top of the cake; use the reserved raspberries to top some of these.

• • •

ANISETTE AND ALMOND CAKE

Time: 1 hour 20 minutes
Easy

9 eggs
1 cup + 2 tbsp sugar
3 cups ground almonds
1½ cups peeled whole almonds
4 tbsp anisette liqueur
½ cup potato flour or cornstarch
¼ cup all-purpose flour
¼ cup (½ stick) butter

Beat 3 whole eggs and 4 egg yolks with the sugar until pale and increased in volume. Beat in half the ground almonds. Sift in the potato flour and the all-purpose flour together and stir well. Add the butter (melted and cooled). When all these ingredients have been well blended, fold in 6 stiffly beaten egg whites, scooping the heavier mixture up from the bottom of the bowl to the top, until evenly combined. Transfer to a greased deep 10-in cake pan and place in the oven, preheated to 350° F; bake for 1 hour or until a skewer inserted deep into the cake comes out clean. Decorate with the remaining almonds, coarsely chopped

GENOA CAKE WITH PRALINE RUM CREAM

If you wish to save time, use finely chopped bought nougatine or nut toffee brittle instead of making the almond brittle yourself, or use Toblerone crunchy Swiss chocolate bars, chopped into small pieces.

Time: 50 minutes + 1 hour 15 minutes for the sponge cake
Easy

1 Genoa Sponge Cake (see page 147)
3 egg whites
⅔ cup sugar
1 cup (2 sticks) butter
¼ lb Praline (see page 25)
6 tbsp rum
1 cup flaked or slivered almonds
1–2 tbsp confectioners' sugar

Make the Genoa Sponge Cake. Beat the egg whites until stiff. Place the sugar in a saucepan, add ½ cup water, and boil until the syrup has noticeably thickened (or reached soft to hard ball stage, about 250° F). Pour this mixture slowly into the bowl containing the beaten egg whites as you beat continuously (use the large bowl of a food processor and use the egg beater attachment, on high speed or use a hand-held electric

ANISETTE AND ALMOND CAKE
■ *As its name suggests, anisette liqueur has a strong aniseed flavor. If anisette is hard to find, use 1 tsp aniseed seeds instead.*

beater). Continue beating until the meringue is completely cold. Beat the butter until it is pale and creamy; mix in the nut brittle pounded or processed to a powder (praline) and then fold in the meringue a little at a time. Cut the sponge cake horizontally into 3 sections. Sprinkle the cut surfaces with a little rum mixed with 3 tbsp water. Spread one third of the praline cream on the top of each of the 3 sections and then

reassemble the cake. Roast the almonds briefly in a hot oven until pale golden brown and when cold sprinkle over the cream topping.
Place strips of paper side by side on the top of the cake, leaving gaps between them the same as their width (¾ in). Using a very fine sieve, dust the top of the cake with the

confectioners' sugar and then carefully remove the strips of paper (see the illustration on page 145, where cocoa powder has been used in this way). Chill for a few hours before serving.

•   •   •

AMARETTO CAKE

Amaretto liqueur is quite sweet and gives a deliciously subtle almond flavor to cakes and desserts; substitute crushed amaretti cookies if you cannot find Amaretto.

Time: 1 hour + 1 hour 15

ALMONDS
■ Many receipes call for
these to be flaked or slivered
before they are used.

opted for chocolate sprinkles.)
Melt the confectioners' sugar
in 6 tbsp of boiling water and
1½ tbsp rum. Spread all but
3 tbsp of this smooth, slightly
runny frosting over the top,
uncovered sponge layer. Mix
the remaining frosting with the
cocoa powder and 1½ tbsp
rum. Place in a pastry bag with
a very small tube and pipe
concentric circles on the white
frosting.

. . .

BRIDAL CAKE

*This can be served as a
wedding cake with a difference,
increasing the recipe as
required and arranging layers
of sponge of decreasing
diameter one on top of the*

---

*minutes for the sponge cake
+ chilling time*
Easy

1 cup sugar
3 egg yolks and 1 whole egg
1 cup sweet butter
2–3 drops vanilla extract
¼ lb nougatine or Praline (see
  page 25)
1 Madeleine sponge cake (see
  page 146)
3 tbsp Amaretto di Saronno
  liqueur
½ cup flaked or slivered
  almonds
1 tbsp confectioners' sugar

Sprinkle ¾ cup of the sugar
into a small saucepan, add just
enough water to cover the
sugar and cook over moderate
heat until the syrup has
noticeably thickened (or
reached soft to hard ball stage,
about 250° F). Beat the egg
yolks briefly and continue
beating as you pour in the
syrup in a very thin stream.
Beat until the mixture is
completely cold. Beat the
butter (softened at room
temperature) until pale and
creamy, then combine with
the egg and sugar mixture and

the vanilla extract. Add the
toffee brittle (very finely
chopped) and mix well.
Place the cooked and cooled
sponge cake on a serving
plate; sprinkle with the
Amaretto liqueur and spread
with the butter cream. Chill
for about 3 hours. Beat the
whole egg with the almonds
and the remaining ¼ cup
sugar, spread out over the
topping of the cake, sprinkle
with the sifted confectioners'
sugar, and quickly place under
a heated broiler for 1–2
minutes. Leave to cool before
serving.

. . .

CHOCOLATE-
FILLED LAYER
CAKE

*You can either pipe designs on
this cake in melted chocolate
using a very narrow pastry tube
or buy chocolate sprinkles
instead. Use more kirsch
instead of alkermes if you
cannot buy this spicy
Mediterranean liqueur.*

Time: 1 hour + 1 hour 15

minutes for the sponge cake
Easy

2¼ cups milk
peel of 1 lemon, grated
3 egg yolks
6 tbsp sugar
¼ cup all-purpose flour
4 oz (4 squares) bitter
  chocolate
¼ cup (½ stick) butter
1 Marguerite Sponge Cake
  (see page 146)
4 tbsp kirsch mixed with 4 tbsp
  alkermes liqueur (or use
  8 tbsp kirsch)
2¾ cups confectioners' sugar
1 tbsp unsweetened cocoa
  powder
6 tbsp water
3 tbsp rum

Bring the milk and lemon peel
to a boil in a saucepan. Beat
the egg yolks with the sugar
until very pale; beat in the
flour and then the hot milk,
added in a thin stream as you
beat. Cook over low heat to
thicken, stirring all the time.
Add the chocolate in small
pieces, followed by the butter.
Keep stirring.
Cut the sponge cake
horizontally into 3 equal layers
and sprinkle with the liqueur
mixture. Spread half the
chocolate filling onto 2 of the
sponge layers then
reassemble the cake.
(Reserve a little of the filling,
see below, unless you have

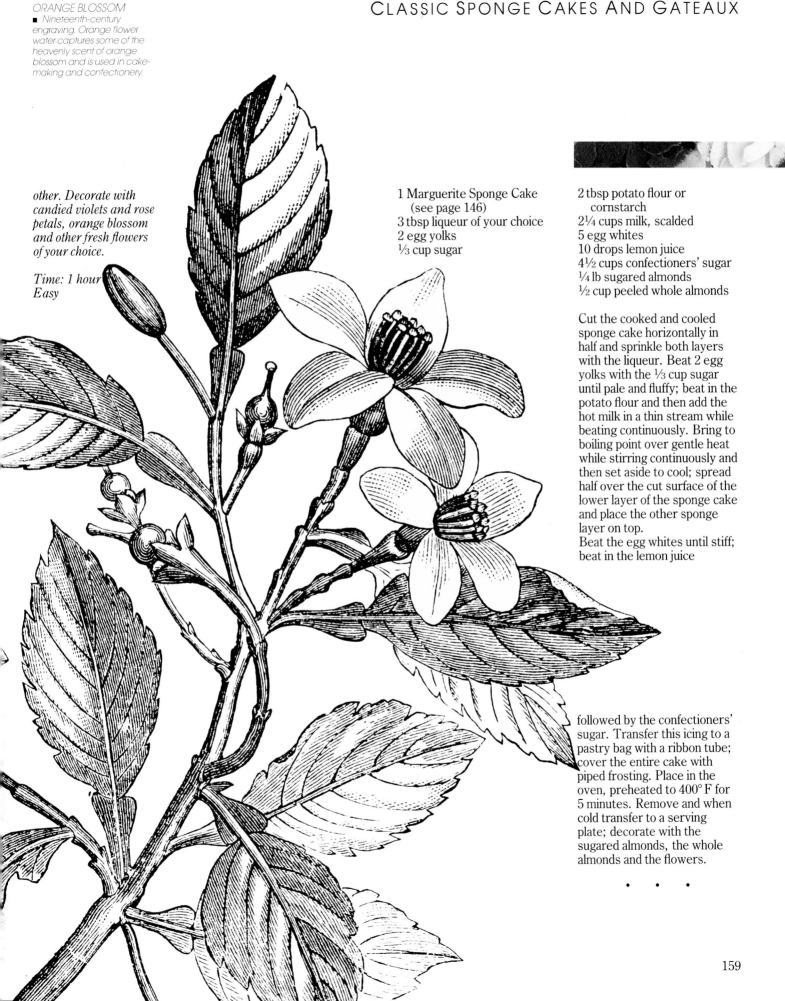

other. Decorate with candied violets and rose petals, orange blossom and other fresh flowers of your choice.

Time: 1 hour
Easy

1 Marguerite Sponge Cake
  (see page 146)
3 tbsp liqueur of your choice
2 egg yolks
⅓ cup sugar

2 tbsp potato flour or
  cornstarch
2¼ cups milk, scalded
5 egg whites
10 drops lemon juice
4½ cups confectioners' sugar
¼ lb sugared almonds
½ cup peeled whole almonds

Cut the cooked and cooled sponge cake horizontally in half and sprinkle both layers with the liqueur. Beat 2 egg yolks with the ⅓ cup sugar until pale and fluffy; beat in the potato flour and then add the hot milk in a thin stream while beating continuously. Bring to boiling point over gentle heat while stirring continuously and then set aside to cool; spread half over the cut surface of the lower layer of the sponge cake and place the other sponge layer on top.
Beat the egg whites until stiff; beat in the lemon juice followed by the confectioners' sugar. Transfer this icing to a pastry bag with a ribbon tube; cover the entire cake with piped frosting. Place in the oven, preheated to 400° F for 5 minutes. Remove and when cold transfer to a serving plate; decorate with the sugared almonds, the whole almonds and the flowers.

• • •

159

MARRON GLACÉ ROLL

This is not a difficult cake to make, it just needs care and the result is very rewarding.

¼ cup (½ stick) sweet butter
¼ cup sugar
¼ cup milk
½ cup + 2 tbsp fine cake flour or all-purpose flour
4 drops vanilla extract
5 eggs
For the filling:
1 cup whipping cream
2 tbsp confectioners' sugar
4 drops vanilla extract
5 oz marron glacé (candied sweet chestnut) pieces
To moisten and flavor the sponge cake:
¼ cup rum
¼ cup water

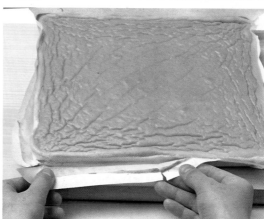

Melt the butter with the sugar over low heat; stir in half the milk; continue heating gently for a few minutes.

Add the flour and vanilla, stirring well. Draw aside from the heat and allow to cool a little before mixing in the whole egg very thoroughly, followed by the 4 yolks one at a time.

Stir in the rest of the milk; strain the batter through a fine sieve to eliminate any small lumps.

Leave to stand and cool completely before folding in the stiffly beaten egg whites gently but thoroughly.

Have a shallow rectangular baking pan ready greased and lined with waxed paper; pour the cake batter into it and level the surface with a spatula. Place in the oven, preheated to 330° F and bake for 30 minutes or until done and golden brown on top.

Remove from the pan, together with the waxed paper; leave to cool; remove the paper.

Beat the cream until stiff, add the vanilla and the confectioners' sugar; spread evenly over the surface of the sponge cake, stopping about ¼ in short of the edges and sprinkle with the coarsely crumbled or chopped marron glacé pieces. Roll up very carefully and not too tightly.

Wrap the sponge roll in waxed paper and chill for at least 30 minutes in the refrigerator.

Unwrap; mix in the rum and water and brush the surface of the cake with this mixture. To serve, cut into slices about 1 in thick.

MALAGA CAKE

Large juicy Muscatel or California raisins are best for this recipe. Buy the best chocolate (bakers' plain or fine bitter eating chocolate) you can afford.

Time: 1 hour 30 minutes + chilling time
Easy

¾ cup sugar
½ cup seeded raisins
½ cup + 2 tbsp rum
4 eggs
1¼ cups all-purpose flour
3 tbsp potato flour or cornstarch
1 cup unsweetened cocoa powder
1 tbsp grated orange peel
7 oz (7 squares) bitter chocolate
1½ cups whipping cream
1 cup confectioners' sugar
few drops vanilla extract

Place ½ cup water in a small saucepan with 6 tbsp of the sugar and bring to a boil. Add the raisins, cook for 5 minutes, then add the rum. Remove from heat and allow to cool.
Beat the eggs in a bowl with the remaining sugar (½ cup) and continue beating over hot (not boiling) water. When doubled in volume, remove from the heat and continue beating until cold. Sift in the flour, potato flour, and all but 1 tbsp of the cocoa powder, stir, then add the grated orange peel. Grease an 8½-in cake pan with butter and lightly dust with flour, turn the cake batter into it, and bake at 350° F for 50 minutes or until done. Melt 5 oz (5 squares) of the chocolate (broken into small pieces) over hot water.

Beat the cream until stiff with the confectioners' sugar and a few drops vanilla extract. Reserve one third of the cream and combine two thirds with the melted (and slightly cooled) chocolate.
Turn out the cooked cake and when cold cut horizontally into 3 layers. Spread one third of the raisin mixture over the lowest layer, followed by half the chocolate cream; repeat this with the next sponge layer. Sprinkle the remaining syrup over the top of the cake, decorate with the reserved cream and sprinkle with the remaining bitter chocolate, cut into slivers and the remaining, sifted, cocoa powder. Chill for 24 hours before serving.

• • •

CHESTNUT CAKE

The sweet chestnut season is short: marron glacé debris can be used instead, pushed *through a sieve and mixed with the rum and confectioners' sugar, but omit the butter.*

Time: 1 hour 30 minutes + chilling time
Easy

1 Genoa Sponge Cake, 9½ in in diameter (see page 147)
1¼ lb sweet chestnuts
1 cup + 2 tbsp sweet butter
2¼ cups confectoners' sugar
10 tbsp rum
½ cup sugar
1 cup Royal Frosting (see page 52)
10 marrons glacés (candied sweet chestnuts)

Make the sponge cake and leave to cool. Pierce the tough outer skins of the chestnuts, place in a saucepan of cold water and boil for 40 minutes from the moment the water comes to a boil. Peel off the outer and inner skins and sieve while still warm.

Using a wooden spoon, work the softened butter a small piece at a time into the chestnut purée. Add the confectioners' sugar, half the rum, and stir well. Cut the sponge cake horizontally into 3 equal layers. Dissolve the sugar in ¼ cup water over moderate heat and stir in the remaining rum. Sprinkle the sponge layers with this. Spread one third of the chestnut mixture over the 3 layers; reassemble the cake and chill for 2 hours. Cover with royal frosting, decorate with the marrons glacés, and serve.

• • •

PINEAPPLE AND ALMOND GATEAU

Time: 1 hour
Easy

1 Genoa Sponge Cake, 9½ in in diameter (see page 147)
10 slices canned pineapple

2 cups apricot jam
½ cup kirsch
1 cup peeled whole almonds
12 candied cherries
small piece angelica

Make the sponge cake and leave to cool. Drain the pineapple well, reserving the syrup; chop 5 of the slices coarsely and mix with 1½ cups of the apricot jam. Dilute the kirsch with ½ cup of the reserved syrup.
Cut the sponge cake horizontally into 3 equal layers. Sprinkle a little of the kirsch syrup on the lowest layer and cover with half the pineapple and apricot mixture. Cover with the second sponge layer and repeat the operation. Put the top layer in place, sprinkle with the remaining kirsch-flavored syrup and then glaze all over the top and sides with the remaining, sieved, apricot jam, gently warmed until it has melted.
Chop the almonds coarsely and roast very briefly in the oven, preheated to 400° F, until golden. Cut the remaining pineapple slices into small sections and use to decorate the top of the cake together with pieces of the angelica and cherries. Press the chopped almonds into the sides of the cake.

•   •   •

POLISH COFFEE CAKE

The preparation of this cake must start the day before you plan to serve it.

Time: 1 hour 30 minutes
Easy

POLISH COFFEE CAKE
■ *Make the sponge cake the day before you assemble the cake; freshly made sponges are very difficult to cut into layers.*

For the cake:
4 eggs
1 cup sugar
peel of 1 lemon, grated
1¾ cups all-purpose flour
For the filling:
½ cup sugar
½ cup very strong black coffee
3 egg yolks
½ cup + 2 tbsp sweet butter

Make the cake 24 hours in advance: beat the egg yolks with the sugar until pale, add the lemon peel, and continue beating until considerably increased in volume. Stir in the sifted flour a little at a time; fold in the stiffly beaten egg whites. Transfer the batter to a greased and lightly floured 8½-in cake pan and bake at 350° F for 1 hour or until done. Leave to cool before turning out.
The next day cut the cake horizontally into 3 equal layers and spread one third of the following coffee cream on each: heat the sugar and the coffee in a small saucepan over gentle heat until the mixture turns to a thick syrup. Beat the egg yolks and beat this hot syrup into them, adding a little at a time. Beat the softened (not melted) butter until pale and creamy and beat in the cooled egg and coffee mixture. Once you have reassembled the cake, chill it. Just before serving, decorate with roasted coffee beans and rosettes of piped whipped coffee cream if wished.

• • •

LEMON

One of nature's most versatile fruits and indispensable in patisserie for its juice and for its grated peel: the essential oil which the peel contains is even more aromatic and pervasive in flavor than that of the orange. The juice has a high iron content and can be sprinkled over certain fruits and vegetables to prevent discoloration.

PEANUT CAKE

The thin inner skin can be removed from peanuts very easily by rubbing gently.

Time: 1 hour 10 minutes + 1 hour 15 minutes for the sponge cake
Easy

3 egg yolks
½ cup sugar
¼ cup all-purpose flour
2¼ cups milk, scalded
½ cup + 2 tbsp butter
1 cup chopped unroasted, unsalted peanuts
1 Marguerite Sponge Cake (see page 151)
6 candied cherries
2 tbsp chocolate sprinkles

Beat the egg yolks with the sugar until pale and fluffy. Sift in the flour and stir gently. Beat in the hot milk a little at a time and cook gently over low heat, stirring continuously until the mixture has thickened somewhat. Leave to cool. Beat the softened butter and add it a little at a time to the cold custard mixture, stirring well. Stir in half the chopped peanuts. Cut

STRAWBERRY GATEAU
■ Choose your strawberries
for flavor, not size or color,
and make sure they are not
overripe.

the sponge cake horizontally into 3 equal layers, spread the first two with a quarter of the creamy mixture each, reassemble the cake, and spread the remaining cream all over the top and sides of the cake. Sprinkle the entire surface with the remaining peanuts, pressing them against the sides of the cake. Decorate the top with the halved cherries and chocolate sprinkles.

• • •

STRAWBERRY GATEAU

Time: 1 hour + 1 hour 15 minutes for the sponge cake + chilling time
Easy

1 Classic Sponge Cake (see page 146)
1¾ cups milk
1 vanilla bean or vanilla extract
3 egg yolks
½ cup sugar
3 tbsp all-purpose flour
3 tbsp liqueur of your choice
1¾ cups heavy or whipping cream
4 tbsp confectioners' sugar

Cut the sponge cake horizontally in half.
Pour the milk into a saucepan, add the vanilla bean if used, and bring to a boil. Remove the vanilla bean, beat the egg yolks with the sugar until pale and frothy. Beat in the vanilla extract (if used), the flour, and then the hot milk, adding this in a thin stream as you beat. Cook over low heat to thicken, stirring continuously. Leave to cool. Sprinkle the cut surface of the lower layer with half the liqueur and spread the custard on top. Lightly press half the strawberries (hulled) into the custard. Cover with the top layer of sponge and sprinkle this with the rest of the liqueur. Beat the chilled cream stiffly with the confectioners' sugar and spread over the top and sides of the cake. Decorate with the remaining strawberries. Chill in the refrigerator for about 4 hours before serving.

• • •

GRAPE GATEAU

Place the grapes in very hot water for a few seconds to make them easier to peel.

Time: 1 hour 10 minutes + 1 hour 15 minutes for the sponge cake
Easy

1 Marguerite Sponge Cake (see page 146) baked in a rectangular pan, approx. 8½ in × 9½ in
¾ cup sugar
3 egg yolks
1 cup + 2 tbsp butter
2 drops vanilla extract
⅓ cup Cointreau
½ cup grape jelly
1½ cups whipping cream
1 lb white grapes

Make the sponge cake, turn out, and leave to cool. Make the filling: bring ¼ cup water and the sugar to a boil and cook until the syrup has noticeably thickened (reaching the soft to hard ball stage, around 250° F). Beat the egg yolks briefly and continue beating vigorously as you pour in the boiling hot sugar syrup in a very thin stream or a little at a time (rather like adding the oil when making mayonnaise). Beat the softened butter until creamy and beat in a little at a time to the egg and sugar mixture. Add the vanilla extract. Cut the sponge cake horizontally in half and sprinkle both halves with the Cointreau. Spread the grape jelly over the lower layer and spread the filling on top. Cover with the other sponge layer; pipe the stiffly beaten cream through a fluted tube all over the cake and decorate with the peeled, seeded grapes.

• • •

165

CHERRY AND RICOTTA CAKE

Make your own candied cherries (see page 27) or buy them. You can also use well drained canned fruit.

Time: 50 minutes + 1 hour 15 minutes for the sponge cake
Easy

1 Genoa Sponge Cake (see page 147)
1¼ cups ricotta cheese
3 tbsp kirsch
½ tsp cinnamon
2½ cups + 2 tbsp confectioners' sugar
1 egg
¼ cup sugar
3 tbsp all-purpose flour
1 cup milk
1 cup glacé or candied cherries

Make the sponge cake and leave to cool. Beat the ricotta thoroughly with 1½ tbsp kirsch and the cinnamon; beat in half the confectioners' sugar, adding a little at a time. Beat the egg vigorously in a separate bowl with the granulated sugar, beat in the sifted flour followed by the hot milk (a little at a time). Cook, stirring continuously, over low heat to thicken. Leave to cool before beating in the ricotta mixture a little at a time. Cut the sponge cake horizontally in half; spread the ricotta mixture over the lower half, place the other sponge layer on top. Heat the remaining sugar over low heat with the remaining kirsch and cover the cake with this frosting. Decorate with the cherries before the frosting sets. Serve without too much delay.

• • •

GRAND MARNIER CAKE

A Grand Marnier-flavored sugar syrup is used to coat roasted or slivered almonds for a delicious and effective topping.

Time: 1 hour 30 minutes
Easy

1 Genoa Sponge Cake (see page 147)
For the filling:
¾ cup sugar
3 egg yolks
1 cup (2 sticks) sweet butter
few drops vanilla extract
2¼ cups slivered almonds
For the syrup:
½ cup sugar
1 cup water
½ cup Grand Marnier

Make the sponge cake and leave to cool. Prepare the filling: place all but 1 tbsp of the ¾ cup sugar in a saucepan, pour in ¼ cup water, and cook over moderate heat until the syrup has noticeably thickened (soft to hard ball stage, reached around 250° F). Beat the egg yolks and then beat in the hot sugar syrup a few drops at a time; when all the syrup has been added the mixture should be pale and frothy. Beat the softened (not melted) butter with the remaining 1 tbsp sugar and the vanilla extract and beat a little at a time into the egg mixture. Make the coating syrup for the almonds: dissolve the sugar in the water over moderate heat. When cold mix with the Grand Marnier.
Roast the almonds in a shallow baking pan at 400° F very briefly until pale golden brown; take out of the oven and immediately pour half the

ORANGE MARGUERITE SPONGE

■ *Use homemade clear fruit jellies, or buy them, for use as glazings to enhance fresh fruit toppings and prevent discoloration.*

sugar syrup over them, stir, and turn. Turn off the oven and return the almonds to it to dry a little, then remove and cool.

Cut the sponge cake horizontally into 3 sections. Sprinkle the lower two layers with the remaining Grand Marnier syrup; spread less than one third of the vanilla cream over them and replace the last layer on top. Spread the remaining vanilla cream all over the top and sides of the cake. Sprinkle all over with the almonds, sides included where the almonds should be lightly pressed into place. Chill.

• • •

ORANGE MARGUERITE SPONGE

*Time: 50 minutes + 1 hour 15
    minutes for the sponge cake
Easy*

1 Marguerite Sponge Cake
    (see page 146)
1¼ cups milk
peel of 1 orange, grated
3 egg yolks
½ cup sugar
1½ tbsp all-purpose flour
½ cup (1 stick) butter
3 tbsp Cointreau
For decoration:
2 oranges
½ cup apricot jam or preserve
¼ lb grapes

Make the sponge cake and while it is baking, prepare the filling: pour the milk into an electric blender with the grated orange peel and process at high speed. Pour into a saucepan and bring to scalding point (i.e. when bubbles appear all round the

inside edge of the pan). Beat the egg yolks with the sugar until very pale, beat in the flour and then the hot milk, adding this in a very thin stream as you beat. Cook over gentle heat to thicken, stirring continuously. Leave to cool. Beat the softened butter until creamy with a wooden spoon and add a little at a time into the cold custard mixture, stirring very gently but thoroughly.

Turn out the cake and when cold, cut horizontally in half. Sprinkle the Cointreau over the cut surface of the lower half and cover with the custard. Place the top sponge layer in position and decorate with the very thinly sliced oranges, slightly overlapping. Sieve the apricot preserve if necessary and melt gently: use to glaze over the orange slices. Use the grapes as extra decoration and serve.

• • •

RUM AND CHOCOLATE CAKE

Rum has been chosen to go with

the chocolate in this recipe but many other flavors go just as well, orange (Grand Marnier) or Crème de Menthe among them.

Time: 1 hour 30 minutes
Easy

For the cake:
1 cup walnut pieces
6 eggs, separated
½ cup sugar
1 cup all-purpose flour
1 tbsp butter
For the filling and decoration:
4 oz (4 squares) plain bakers'
　or fine bitter chocolate
3 egg yolks
½ cup sugar
¼ cup all-purpose flour
2¼ cups milk
1 cup (2 sticks) sweet butter
½ cup walnut halves
For the syrup:
1½ tbsp sugar
2 tbsp water
½ cup rum

Chop the walnut pieces very finely (or grind in a food

processor). Beat the 6 egg yolks with the sugar until pale and increased in volume. Sift in the flour, add the walnuts and stir well. Beat the 6 egg whites until stiff and fold into the mixture. Grease a 9½-in cake pan with butter, dust lightly with flour, and turn the batter into it. Bake at 350° F for 50 minutes or until done. Turn out onto a cake rack to cool. Make the filling and frosting: break the chocolate into pieces and melt gently over hot water. Beat the 3 yolks with the sugar until pale and frothy, add the flour and then beat in the hot milk; cook over low heat, stirring continuously to thicken. Stir in the chocolate and leave to cool. Beat the butter until soft and creamy; stir in the chocolate custard a little at a time.

Make the syrup: heat the sugar with the water until dissolved, stir in the rum. Cut the cake horizontally into 3 equal layers, sprinkle each

with one third of the syrup, and spread each with one third of the filling. Reassemble and decorate the top with the walnut halves.

• • •

CHOCOLATE BUTTERCREAM-LAYERED SPONGE

*Time: 30 minutes + 1 hour 15
　minutes for the sponge +
　chilling time*
Easy

1 Marguerite Sponge Cake
　(see page 146)
3 egg yolks
½ cup caster sugar
¼ cup all-purpose flour
2½ cups milk

CHOCOLATE
BUTTERCREAM-LAYERED
SPONGE
■ *Use ground pistachio nuts,
filberts, or almonds instead of
coffee if preferred.*

CLASSIC SPONGE CAKES AND GATEAUX

4 tbsp unsweetened cocoa
   powder
4 tsp instant coffee powder
½ cup + 2 tbsp butter
5 tbsp coffee liqueur (e.g. Tia
   Maria or Kahula)
3 tbsp brandy
few roasted coffee beans
   (optional)

Make the sponge cake and
leave to cool. Beat the egg
yolks with the sugar until pale;
stir in the sifted flour and then
beat in the hot milk, adding a
little at a time. Cook over low
heat, stirring constantly to
thicken.
Add the sifted cocoa and the
instant coffee to the hot
custard mixture away from the
heat, stir well, and leave to
cool. Beat the softened butter
until pale and creamy and
gradually add to the cold (not
chilled) custard.
Cut the sponge cake
horizontally into 3 equal
layers; sprinkle these with the
mixed coffee liqueur and
brandy. Spread two layers
with a quarter of the
buttercream mixture each,
then reassemble the cake.
Spread the remaining
buttercream all over the top
and sides of the cake.
Decorate with the coffee
beans. Chill for about 2 hours
before serving.

• • •

GENOA SPONGE WITH KIRSCH FILLING

*Morello cherries can be difficult
to find unless you grow your
own and they have a short
season. Buy canned Morellos
instead if fresh are
unavailable.*

*Time: 1 hour 10 minutes + 1
   hour 15 minutes for the
   sponge cake*
Easy

1 Genoa Sponge Cake (see
   page 147)
¾ cup sugar
¼ cup water
3 egg yolks
1 cup + 2 tbsp sweet butter
few drops vanilla extract
½ cup kirsch
1 lb fresh or canned Morello
   cherries
5 oz (5 squares) white
   chocolate (dessert
   chocolate, bakers', or
   couverture quality)

Make the sponge cake. Boil
the sugar and water until it has
thickened noticeably (reaching
the soft to hard ball stage, at
around 250° F). Beat the egg

yolks and continue beating vigorously as you add the hot syrup a very little at a time; continue beating until pale and considerably increased in volume. Beat the softened butter until creamy and stir a little at a time into the egg mixture. Stir in the vanilla extract, followed by 1½ tbsp kirsch.

Cut the sponge cake horizontally in half and sprinkle the two layers with a mixture of 6 tbsp kirsch and 6 tbsp of the syrup drained from the cherries (if using fresh fruit, simply make double the quantity of sugar syrup). Cover the lower layer with half the egg mixture and arrange the well drained cherries on top. Cover with the top sponge layer and frost the surface with the remaining egg mixture. Use a very sharp knife to make curls or shavings of white chocolate: decorate the top with a thick layer of these.

•   •   •

CLASSIC SPONGE WITH STRAWBERRIES

Sabayon sauce is the perfect foil for strawberries. This delicate concoction can be made with a sweet white wine or Madeira if you cannot buy Marsala.

Time: 1 hour 15 minutes + 1 hour 15 minutes for the sponge cake
Easy

1 Classic Sponge Cake (see page 146)
¾ lb strawberries
3 tbsp sugar

1 cup sparkling white wine
1 lemon
1 quantity Sabayon (see page 44)

Make the sponge cake and leave to cool. Place the strawberries in a bowl, sprinkle with the sugar and lemon juice, and pour the wine over them. Leave to stand for 1 hour.

Cut the sponge cake horizontally into 3 layers. Place the lowest on the serving plate, sprinkle with some of the juice and wine from the strawberries, placing a little less than half the fruit on top. Repeat for the next layer, adding one third of the zabaglione as the last layer of filling this time. Cover the topmost layer with the remaining zabaglione, decorate with a few strawberries, and serve.

•   •   •

FROSTED LAYER CAKE WITH CARAMELIZED WALNUTS

This delicious and impressive cake is perfect for a dinner party. Use strawberries in place of some or all of the walnuts if you wish.

Time: 1 hour 30 minutes
Easy

For the cake:
4 eggs, separated
1 cup sugar
4 oz (4 squares) bitter or unsweetened chocolate
1 cup + 2 tbsp all-purpose flour
For the filling:
1 cup walnuts
1 egg

½ cup sugar
½ cup (1 stick) sweet butter
3 tbsp brandy
For the frosting:
4 oz (4 squares) bitter or
    unsweetened chocolate
3 tbsp heavy cream
For the caramel:
½ cup sugar
3 tbsp water
½ tsp lemon juice
1 cup walnut halves
1 tbsp almond oil

Preheat the oven to 350° F.
Lightly grease a fairly deep 9-
in square cake pan with butter
and dust lightly with flour.
Beat the egg yolks with the
sugar until pale and increased
in volume. Break the
chocolate into small pieces and
melt gently over hot water
with 3 tbsp water. Stir into the
egg and sugar mixture. Add
the sifted flour and mix. Beat
the egg whites until stiff and
fold into the cake mixture with
a mixing spatula. Turn into the
cake pan, level the surface
gently, and bake for 45
minutes or until done.
Make the filling: break the
whole egg into a bowl, add the
sugar, and place over hot
water. Beat vigorously. Draw
aside from the heat. Have the
butter ready softened at room
temperature and beat until
creamy; combine with the egg
and sugar mixture. Add the
walnuts and brandy. Cut the
sponge cake horizontally into 3
layers; spread half the filling
over each of the first two
layers and reassemble the
cake, pressing down gently.
Cover with foil and chill in the
refrigerator for at least 3
hours.
Make the frosting: melt the
chocolate in small pieces over
hot water with the cream,
stirring constantly. Spread

CHOCOLATE

Extra cocoa butter is added to
pulverized dry cakes of
chocolate and refined by
"conching" (rolling the
chocolate mixture in a curved
trough) for fondant chocolate
which is usually bitter (little
sugar added) or semisweet. A
high fat content is necessary
for use in patisserie.

over the cake and return to
the refrigerator (uncovered).
Make the caramel: bring the
sugar to a boil with the water
over moderate heat in a wide
pan. When it turns pale golden
brown, add the lemon juice.
Have the walnuts ready
threaded onto thin wooden
skewers or satay sticks and
dip carefully in the caramel,
turning quickly once or twice.
Transfer to a plate, lightly
oiled with almond oil. When
the caramel has hardened,
finish decorating the cake with
the nuts, and chill until time to
serve.

•   •   •

CHOCOLATE AND FILBERT CAKE

*Unless you grate the chocolate,
it is best to melt it separately
(broken into pieces) over hot
water or melt 1 tsp butter with
it.*

Time: 45 minutes
Easy

8 eggs
1 cup + 2 tbsp sugar
pinch salt

1½ cups filberts
11 oz (11 squares) bitter or
  unsweetened chocolate,
  grated
2¼ cups whipping cream
3 tbsp confectioners' sugar
½ cup whipping cream

Beat the egg yolks with the
sugar and salt until pale and
fluffy. Chop the filberts very
finely or grind in a food
processor (do not overprocess
or they will become oily), add
them to the egg mixture with
half the grated chocolate. Fold
in the stiffly beaten egg
whites.
Divide this batter into 3 equal
parts and cook each in a
greased springform or
removable-base 8½-in cake
pan at 400° F for 20 minutes.
When the 3 thin layers of
sponge have been removed
from the pans and cooled,
assemble into a layer cake
with the stiffly beaten and
sweetened cream as filling.
Melt the rest of the chocolate
over gentle heat and spread
over the top, using a spatula
dipped in cold water. Pipe
rosettes with the smaller
quantity of cream, whipped
but unsweetened, to finish.

• • •

LEMON-FROSTED
CAKE

Time: 1 hour 20 minutes +
  chilling time
Easy

For the sponge cake:
4 eggs
½ cup sugar
few drops vanilla extract
1 cup + 2 tbsp all-purpose
  flour
2 tbsp butter, melted
¼ cup Grand Marnier

For the filling:
⅔ cup sugar
½ cup + 2 tbsp butter
2 lemons
4 eggs
For the frosting:
2¼ cups confectioners' sugar
juice of ½ lemon
¼ cup Grand Marnier
¼ lb raspberries

Preheat the oven to 350° F.
Break the whole eggs into a
bowl, place over hot water and
beat with the sugar until
greatly increased in volume.
Remove from the heat, add
the vanilla extract and
continue beating until cold. Sift
in the flour and fold in gently.
Mix in the melted butter a
little at a time and transfer the
batter to a prepared 9½-in
ring tube pan. Bake for 30
minutes or until done.
Remove from the oven and
place on a cake rack.
Make the filling: beat the
sugar very thoroughly with
the butter (softened at room
temperature, not melted).
Beat in the grated lemon peel,
followed by the lemon juice,
adding a little at a time. Lightly
beat the eggs and then beat
into the butter cream. Heat
over hot water, stirring
constantly, to thicken but do
not allow to approach boiling
point. Leave to cool. When
the cake is cold, turn out of
the pan and cut carefully into 3
layers. Sprinkle each layer
with just over 1 tbsp Grand
Marnier and spread the cold
lemon filling over the lower
two layers. Reassemble the
cake, wrap in foil, and chill for
12 hours.
Make the frosting, mixing the
confectioners' sugar with the
gently heated lemon juice and
Grand Marnier; it should be

thick but spreadable. Spread
all over the cake as smoothly
as possible and return to the
refrigerator for 2 hours.
Decorate with the raspberries
and serve.

• • •

CUBAN CAKE

Rum goes extremely well with
most fruit and particularly well
with pineapple. Use white rum
for this recipe.

Time: 50 minutes
Easy

1 Madeleine Sponge Cake
  (see page 146)
½ cup rum
½ cup sugar
¼ cup whipping cream
3 tbsp confectioners' sugar
1⅓ cups shredded coconut
10 slices canned pineapple

Make the sponge cake. Bring
the rum to a boil with the
sugar, then leave to cool. Beat
the cream until stiff with the
confectioners' sugar.
Cut the cold sponge cake
horizontally in half. Sprinkle
the rum syrup over the lower
half, spread with nearly half
the cream and sprinkle with
half the coconut. Place 4 well
drained slices of pineapple on
top. Cover with the second
layer and cover the cake with
the remaining cream.
Decorate with the remaining
pineapple slices and sprinkle
with the rest of the coconut.

• • •

LEMON-FROSTED CAKE
■ *Lemon enhances other flavors wonderfully. Fold a few raspberries carefully into the filling, if liked, before assembling the cake.*

CHOCOLATE-FROSTED MARZIPAN CAKE

If you do not make your own marzipan, best-quality ready-made marzipan will work well in this recipe.

*Time: 2 hours 15 minutes
Fairly easy*

1 vanilla bean or a few drops
 vanilla extract
¼ lb marzipan
1 cup confectioners' sugar
⅔ cup filberts, chopped
4 eggs
½ cup butter, softened
½ cup heavy cream
pinch salt
1 cup all-purpose flour
½ cup potato flour or
 cornstarch
2 tbsp apricot liqueur or
 apricot brandy
½ cup apricot jam
Chocolate Frosting (see pages
 52–53)
1 cup whipping cream

Grease an 8½-in cake pan with butter, dust lightly with flour, and chill in the refrigerator. Slit the vanilla bean lengthwise and scrape out all the sticky black seeds inside (alternatively, use 4 drops vanilla extract) and knead into the marzipan with ¾ cup of the confectioners' sugar. Roast the almonds briefly in the oven at 350° F until pale golden brown. Chop coarsely. Beat the egg yolks, then beat in the softened butter, cream, and salt. Combine with the marzipan until very smooth. Sift the flour and potato flour together into the mixture and stir well. Beat the egg whites until stiff with the remaining sugar and fold in, together with the filberts.

Turn the batter into the prepared pan and bake at 350° F for 50 minutes or until done. Turn out the cake and leave to cool on a rack. When cold, cut horizontally in half, sprinkle with the liqueur, and sandwich the apricot jam between the two layers. Coat the cake with the chocolate frosting and chill.

WHIPPED CREAM
■ To make successful
Chantilly cream, do not just
chill the cream: place the
bowl and the whisk (or beater
attachment) in the refrigerator
an hour beforehand.

ORANGE GATEAU

*If you suspect your oranges
have been treated with
fungicides (many are) pierce the
skins lightly all over with a fork
and boil them whole in several
changes of water so that they
are not bitter.*

*Time: 2 hours + 1 hour 15
  minutes for the sponge cake
  + chilling time*
Fairly easy

6 oranges
2 cups sugar
1 Genoa Cake (see page 147)
  made in a 9½-in pan
2¼ cups milk
½ vanilla bean (slit open) or 2–
  3 drops vanilla extract
6 egg yolks
3 tbsp cornstarch
2 tbsp all-purpose flour
¼ cup orange liqueur (e. g.
  Grand Marnier, Curaçao,
  etc.)
1 cup whipping cream

Cut the 6 oranges (do not peel) into very thin round slices. Make a syrup by heating 1½ cups of the sugar with 2¼ cups water. When the syrup comes to a boil, add the orange slices, cover, and simmer very gently for 2 hours. Set aside to cool. To make the Genoa cake: bring the milk to scalding point with the vanilla bean or the vanilla extract and 3 tbsp of the sugar. Draw aside from the heat and leave to stand for 10 minutes. Beat the egg yolks with the remaining sugar until pale, sift in the cornstarch and flour together, and mix well. Beat in the strained (if a vanilla bean is used) warm milk, adding it slowly in a thin stream. Bring to boiling point over low heat, stirring constantly, then reduce the heat and simmer while stirring for 3 minutes. Leave to cool. Cut the cake horizontally in half. Mix ½ cup of the orange syrup with the orange liqueur and sprinkle this on the two layers of cake. Beat the cream until stiff with the confectioners' sugar. Line the base and sides of a deep 9½-in cake pan with the most intact orange slices. Place a sponge layer snugly in the pan (trim a fraction around the edge if necessary to fit). Spread half the cream on top of the sponge, followed by all the custard mixture and place the second sponge layer on top. Tap the bottom of the pan gently a few times on the work surface to get rid of any air pockets. Chill in the refrigerator for 24 hours. To unmold the gateau, lower the pan carefully into very hot water for a few seconds then place a serving plate upside down on top of it; turn the plate the right way up holding the pan tightly against it and turn out. Cover the top completely with the remaining orange slices; whip the remaining cream and pipe decoratively, using a fluted tube. Serve.

• • •

Many of these internationally renowned desserts and puddings had humble beginnings in a farmhouse kitchen when plentiful, cheap local produce was used to provide a change from the usual plain fare. Many were only made to celebrate special occasions and they often reflect the climate and customs of their native lands. The apple pie which seems synonymous with the frugal and efficient housewives in the early days of European settlement in North America may well have been made to a recipe brought from England. Many traditional desserts owe their existence to inventive cooks wishing to enhance their basic materials; sometimes this involved adding spices as in Austria's *Apfelstrudel* which is also a good example of how skills developed, progressing from simple variations on bread to wafer thin pastry and eventually to the exquisite creations of French and Italian pastrycooks.

176

□ Many of these traditional cakes, desserts, and other confections were originally created by master pastrycooks at the royal courts and in the noble households of Europe to satisfy the demand for a more elaborate and refined type of patisserie. The famous Sachertorte is a good example: it was created in Prince Metternich's household in 1832 by a sixteen-year-old assistant cook named Sacher. Babas (sweet yeast cakes, usually soaked in flavored syrup) and Madeleines were created for a deposed king, Stanislas I of Poland, to sweeten what cannot have been too bitter an exile in France during the mid eighteenth century.

□ Each country seems to have developed a fairly distinctive type of cake and dessert cookery, some concentrating more on elaborate and refined patisserie than others. The strongest traditions have evolved in Italy, France, Austria, and Germany. In Italy, cakes and elaborate gateaux are usually only served at the end of a meal on special occasions: birthdays, celebrations, and such festivals as Christmas and Easter. They are also served and eaten with coffee, tea or chocolate in those cafés which employ experienced pastrycooks. Many Italian specialties have dense consistencies, made with nuts, dried fruit, and spices; others are light and delicately flavored.

□ Austrian pâtissiers have specialized in particularly luscious cakes, in many of which chocolate and whipped cream play an important part. At almost any time of day the tables of the excellent cafés in Vienna and other cities in Austria have their sweet-toothed patrons savoring mouthwatering gateaux and coupes, accompanied more often than not by cups of coffee or rich chocolate topped by more whipped cream. In Germany this school of patisserie is also popular albeit on a less magnificent scale.
In France few serious eaters would consider a substantial meal complete without some exquisite creation as a final course. Such delicate and tempting desserts as Crêpes Suzette, Tarte Tatin and all sorts of mousses and soufflés are the perfect dessert.

PANETTONE (Italy)

The traditional Milanese Christmas cake, light and airy and fragrant with candied citrus peel.

Time: 1 hour + rising time
Very easy
Serves 10

3½ cakes compressed fresh
    yeast or 3 packages
    (totaling ¾ oz) dry yeast
7½ cups unbleached all-
    purpose flour
½ cup seedless white raisins
6 whole eggs
¾ cup (1½ sticks) butter
¾ cup superfine sugar
1 tsp salt
½ cup candied citron peel
peel of 1 orange, grated

Add the yeast to ¼ cup warm water and leave to dissolve and start foaming. Mix with 1 cup of the flour, shape into a soft ball, and leave to rise in a bowl covered with a cloth in a warm place for 3 hours. Combine this dough ball (or ferment) with another 1 cup flour and leave to rise again for another 3 hours.
Soak the seedless white raisins in warm water until plump. Drain, dry, and sprinkle lightly with flour to coat. Combine the remaining flour with the eggs, melted butter, sugar, salt, and the risen dough ball.
Knead very thoroughly: the dough should be firm. Work in the diced candied peel, the seedless white raisins, and the orange peel. Leave to prove on a greased cookie sheet or large, greased charlotte pan until doubled in volume; if no pan is used, shape gently into a dome. Cut a cross in the top of the risen dough (about 1 in) and bake at 350° F for 1 hour or until done. Wait at least 24 hours before serving.

• • •

BUNET (Italy)

This pudding, which originates in the Piedmont region of northern Italy, is made with chocolate and amaretti and coated with caramelized sugar. Bake in a large pan or in small, individual molds.

Time: 40 minutes
Very easy

2 whole eggs and 4 extra yolks
1 cup sugar
¾ cup unsweetened cocoa
    powder
1¼ cups finely crumbled
    amaretti or ratafias or crisp
    macaroons
1 quart rich milk
3 tbsp rum

Beat the egg yolks and whites together with half the sugar;

KUGELHUPF
■ *A classic cake made with sweet yeast dough; delicious just as it is with coffee or sliced horizontally and filled with fruit preserve or jelly.*

add the sifted cocoa powder and the amaretti. Stir in a little of the milk at a time, alternating with the rum. Take care that no lumps form. Heat the remaining sugar in a small heavy saucepan until it is golden brown and quickly pour into a hot 8½-in cake or charlotte pan which will serve as a mold, tipping it quickly but carefully so that the caramel coats the inside well before it has a chance to harden. Pour the egg and milk mixture into this mold and place in a roasting pan half-filled with hot water at 350° F for 1 hour. Lower the mold carefully into a bowl of cold water and leave to cool. When cold, turn out and serve.

• • •

KUGELHUPF
(Austria)

Time: 1 hour + rising time
Easy

2¾ cups unbleached all-
  purpose flour
½ cake compressed fresh

yeast or ½ packet (⅛ oz) dry
  yeast
7–8 tbsp milk
4 eggs
½ cup sugar
peel of 1 small lemon, grated
½ cup (1 stick) 2 tbsp sweet
  butter
For the filling:
½ cup seedless white raisins,
  soaked
½ cup slivered almonds
1 tbsp confectioners' sugar

Sift the flour into a mound on the working surface; make a well in the center and place in it the yeast dissolved in the warm milk, the eggs lightly beaten with the sugar, and the grated lemon peel. Combine with the flour. The dough should have roughly the same slightly sticky consistency as brioche dough; pull up and away from the work surface several times (it should come away quite easily, stretching in the process) and flip over, slapping down against the

surface. Repeat several times. Place in a bowl, covered with a cloth or towel and leave to rise in a warm place until doubled in bulk. Knock down the dough and work in the softened butter in small pieces. Add the seedless white raisins (dried and shaken with a little flour) and the almonds. Knead for a few minutes, slapping down again in the same way as before. Grease and flour a 9½-in Kugelhupf (fluted tube) mold, place the dough in it, and leave to prove until doubled in bulk again.
Bake at 350° F for 1 hour or until done. Unmold and dust with the sifted confectioners' sugar.

• • •

CASTAGNACCIO
(Italy)

A specialty from Florence, once sold by street vendors; a few shops now sell fresh fried pieces of this chestnut cake.

Time: 1 hour
Very easy

½ cup seedless white raisins,
  soaked
2¾ cups chestnut flour
½ cup water
6–8 tbsp oil
1 tbsp finely chopped fresh
  rosemary
½ cup pine nuts
pinch salt

Drain the raisins and squeeze gently. Place the flour in a

179

large bowl, add the water, salt, 2 tbsp oil, and stir very thoroughly with a wooden spoon until smooth and creamy; add a very little more oil if necessary.

Add the raisins, rosemary, and pine nuts. Pour the remaining oil into a 10-in ovenproof dish, transfer the batter to this, and bake at 400° F for 20 minutes or until small cracks appear in the surface. Pour off any excess oil and place the chestnut cake on a serving plate.

• • •

CASSATA SICILIANA (Italy)

Time: 1 hour
Very easy

½ quantity Classic Sponge Cake recipe (see page 146)
1 cup sweet liqueur (such as Maraschino)
1 lb ricotta, sieved
½ cup sugar
2/3 tbsp finely chopped or grated bitter or semisweet chocolate
¾ cup mixed candied fruit and peel (cherries, orange, and citron peel)

½ teaspoon cinnamon
For the frosting:
¼ cup rum
¼ cup water
2¾ cups confectioners' sugar
1 cup whipping cream (optional)

Line a bombe mold or mixing bowl with saran wrap. Cut the sponge cake into thin slices, pour the liqueur into a shallow plate, and dip the slices briefly in it one at a time. Line the inside surface of the mold with the sponge cake, leaving no spaces. Combine the ricotta with the sugar; add the chocolate, the diced candied fruit, and the cinnamon. Stir thoroughly and spoon carefully into the lined mold, pressing down gently as you fill it. Cover the top with pieces of sponge cake and chill for at least 3 hours.
Heat the rum and water in a fireproof earthenware casserole or saucepan, stir in the confectioners' sugar with a wooden spoon, and cook until the mixture thickens and sticks to the spoon. Unmold the pudding onto a serving plate and cover the entire exposed surface with the frosting, then place it on the middle shelf of a preheated moderate oven, turning the cassata slowly: this will dry the icing and give it a sheen. Leave to cool. Decorate with rosettes of piped whipped cream.

• • •

STOLLEN (Germany)

A very substantial and very typical cake, traditionally served at Christmas.

Time: 1 hour 30 minutes
Easy

3 cups all-purpose flour
1 tsp baking powder
½ cup sugar
2 eggs
½ cup milk
1 cup + 2 tbsp (2¼ sticks) butter
¼ cup large California raisins
¼ cup seedless white raisins, soaked
2 tbsp currants
peel of 1 lemon, grated
½ cup slivered almonds
1 tbsp rum
¼ cup confectioners' sugar
pinch salt

Sift the flour and baking powder together into a large mixing bowl. Make a well in the center of the flour and place in it 6 tbsp of the sugar, the eggs, milk, and salt and combine with the flour. Have the butter ready softened at room temperature and add 1 cup (2 sticks) of it to the dough. Work into the dough by hand (or in a food mixer with the dough hook attachment), kneading until smooth and evenly blended. Add the drained, dried raisins, lemon peel, almonds, and the rum. Knead well.
Shape into an oblong loaf, transfer to a greased and floured cookie sheet, and bake for 15 minutes in an oven preheated to 320° F, then cover loosely with a piece of foil, increase temperature to 350° F and bake for another 45 minutes or until done. Place on a rack to cool. Melt the remaining butter and sprinkle over the Stollen, sprinkle with the remaining sugar and all the confectioners' sugar.

ZUPPA INGLESE (Italy)

The British who flocked to Florence in the late eighteenth century found this elegant dessert irresistible: foreign yet reminiscent of an old English trifle.

Time: 1 hour
Easy

2¼ cups milk
2 whole eggs and 3 extra yolks
½ cup sugar
¼ cup all-purpose flour
2 tbsp sweet butter
few drops vanilla extract
3 tbsp unsweetened cocoa powder
1 Classic Sponge Cake (see page 146)
1 cup alkermes or other liqueur of choice

Bring the milk to a boil. Beat the eggs and extra yolks with the sugar and sifted flour. Beat in the hot milk, adding half a very little at a time at first and then the rest in larger amounts. Place over low heat and bring to boiling point, stirring continuously. Remove from the heat.
Add the butter, stir well and pour half the custard into each of 2 bowls. Add the vanilla to one, the cocoa to the other, and stir well. Cut the sponge cake into slices, dip in the liqueur. Arrange alternate layers of sponge cake and custard in a large glass serving bowl, alternating the flavor of custard. Make the last layer of custard, half chocolate, half vanilla (the dividing line between the two colors does not have to be too neat). Chill in the refrigerator for a few hours before serving.

PLUM CAKE (Great Britain)

Time: 1 hour 30 minutes
Easy

½ cup seedless white raisins
⅔ cup mixed candied fruit and peel (cherries, orange, and citron)
3 tbsp rum
1 cup (2 sticks) butter
1¾ cups confectioners' sugar
6 eggs
1¾ cups all-purpose flour
few drops vanilla extract
½ cup potato flour or cornstarch
1 tsp baking powder
peel of ½ lemon, grated

Soak the raisins in warm water until plump; drain and squeeze gently before mixing with the diced cherries and candied peel in a small bowl. Add the rum and leave to stand until needed. Beat the butter (softened at room temperature) until creamy; beat in the sugar, the vanilla, and then the eggs, one at a time.
Sift in the flour, potato flour, and baking powder together and mix well. Stir in the lemon peel and the rum and candied fruit. Line a small rectangular pan (about 8 × 4 in) with waxed paper (or use a nonstick pan), turn the cake batter into it and bake at 400° F for 50 minutes or until done. When the cake is pale golden brown on top (about three quarters of the way through baking) grease a knife with a little butter and make a shallow slit lengthwise down the middle of the cake. Grease the knife again and make the slit much deeper. Return to the oven to finish baking.

Leave to cool, turn out, and remove the paper.

• • •

SCONES (Great Britain)

Scones are very versatile; seedless white raisins or a little cheese can be added to the dough. These plain ones can be served with butter alone, or jam and whipped cream as well.

Time: 1 hour
Easy

3 cups all-purpose flour
1½ tbsp baking powder
¼ cup sugar
¼ cup (½ stick) butter
1 egg
½ cup milk
1 tsp salt

Sift the flour and baking powder into a mixing bowl, add the salt and 3 tbsp sugar, and stir. Cut the butter (softened at room temperature) into small pieces, and rub in or "cut in" with a pastry mixer until the mixture resembles fine breadcrumbs. Do not overwork the mixture.
Beat the egg lightly in a small bowl, add ⅓ cup milk and mix into the flour and butter mixture. The scone mixture

should be stiff but soft. Add a very little more milk if it is too dry.

Roll out to about ¾ in thick and use a plain or fluted floured round cookie cutter (2 in in diameter) to cut out scones (or use a sharp knife and cut into 2-in squares and fold these in half to form triangles – do not press down). Use a little milk as glaze brushed on the top of the scones and sprinkle with the remaining sugar. Place on a lightly greased cookie tray and bake at 350° F for 25 minutes or until done. Serve hot or cold.

•　•　•

TARTE TATIN
(France)

Light, delicate, and delicious, this upside-down tart is best served warm with a separate bowl of whipped cream. It needs care to make well; choose apples which are not watery when cooked and which hold their shape well (Calville, Rennet, Granny Smith, or Golden Delicious).

Time: 1 hour 25 minutes
Fairly easy

2¼ cups all-purpose flour
scant 1½ cups sugar
1 egg
½ cup (1 stick) + 2 tbsp butter
4½ lb apples (see above)
2 tbsp vanilla sugar
pinch salt

Sift the flour in a mound on the working surface; make a well in the center and place ½ cup sugar in it with the salt, the whole egg, and ½ cup (1 stick) butter (softened at room

VANILLA
■ Flowers and fruit as shown in a plate from the eighteenth-century Encyclopédie *compiled by Diderot and D'Alembert.*

½ cup sugar
¼ cup water
2 tbsp gelatin powder
¾ lb Classic Sponge Cake (see page 146)
⅔ cup mixed candied fruit or peel
3½ oz (3½ squares) bitter or semisweet chocolate
1 cup sweet liqueur (e. g. maraschino)
2¼ cups heavy or whipping cream
3 tbsp confectioners' sugar

Make the chocolate custard: place the butter, cocoa powder, sugar, and the water in the top of a double boiler over gently simmering water and cook for a few minutes, stirring after the butter has melted to dissolve the sugar. Cut the sponge into long, rectangular, and fairly thin pieces (about ½ in thick). Finely chop the candied peel and the chocolate. Follow the manufacturers' instructions and dissolve the gelatin in ½ cup hot water; set aside to cool. Dip the sponge slices in the liqueur briefly and use to line a deep 8-in bowl or bombe mold. Leave no spaces between the slices.

Beat the cream stiffly, adding the confectioners' sugar and stir in the gelatin gently but thoroughly. Transfer half the cream to another bowl and fold in the chocolate custard mixture; fold the chopped fruit and chocolate into the remaining sweetened whipped cream.

Spoon the chocolate mixture into the lined bowl. Place the other half of the cream on top and level the surface with a palette knife. (The cream should come to within less than ½ in of the lip of the

sugar and the vanilla sugar. Cook carefully over gentle heat until the newly added sugar has caramelized if using a pan, or cover loosely with foil and cook at 400° F for 10 minutes. Roll out the chilled pastry dough and cover the apples snugly with it, pricking with a fork in several places. Cook in a preheated oven at 400° F for 30 minutes, then place a sheet of foil loosely on top, lower the temperature to 300° F and cook for 10 minutes more. Remove from the oven, place on a damp cloth and run a sharp knife all round the very edge of the pastry. Leave to "set" for 5 minutes. To ensure easy unmolding you can heat the bottom of the tin briefly over the burner (this is easier with gas) to liquefy the caramel, place a platter on top of the pie plate and turn upside down unmolding the tart so that the apples end up on top.

• • •

ZUCCOTTO (Italy)

*Time: 1 hour 10 minutes
Easy*

1 tbsp butter
6 tbsp unsweetened cocoa powder

it starts frothing, add ½ cup + 2 tbsp sugar and continue heating with care until the mixture caramelizes in the bottom of the pan. (If preferred, make this caramel in a saucepan and pour quickly into the bottom of a pie plate before it sets.) Peel, core, and slice the apples evenly, arrange on top of the caramel slightly overlapping and with the rounded sides hidden (so that these show when the tart is turned upside down later). Sprinkle with the remaining

temperature and cut into small pieces). Combine the ingredients quickly, do not overmix, and shape the resulting dough into a ball, wrap in foil or saran wrap, and chill in the refrigerator for 30 minutes.

Heat the remaining butter in a strong, shallow cake pan (about 10 in in diameter) until

ZUCCOTTO
■ A very rich and traditional Tuscan specialty. A perforated paper cover is often used when it is sprinkled with confectioners' sugar to achieve a decorative segmented pattern.

A classic French recipe from Alsace; if you cannot buy the traditional shell-shaped molds, use ordinary molds, or brioche or dariole molds. Madeleines are delicious plain, with a lemon frosting or with Chantilly cream.

¼ cup + 1 tbsp sweet butter
½ cup confectioners' sugar
2 egg yolks
3 tbsp dark (Jamaica) rum
2 egg whites
¼ cup + 2 tbsp fine cake flour or all-purpose flour
pinch salt
3 tbsp potato flour or cornstarch
3–4 drops vanilla extract
2 tbsp melted butter for greasing the molds

Dip a pastry brush in the 2 tbsp melted butter and brush the molds carefully with this.

Melt the first quantity of butter listed above over hot water. Set aside to cool.

Sift the confectioners' sugar, using a very fine sieve.

Mix the sugar, egg yolks, and rum in a bowl over hot water (or in the top of a double boiler). Stir, heating very gently, until the mixture thickens. Set aside to cool.

Beat the egg whites stiffly and fold in the sifted flour and salt.

Fold in the potato flour (or cornstarch), the vanilla, and the melted butter.

Stir in the sugar, egg, and rum mixture.

Ladle or spoon the cake batter into the molds. Holding the cookie tray level, tap the bottom gently down on the work surface to release any pockets of air trapped beneath the mixture. Bake in a preheated oven at 400° F for 10 minutes or until done. Remove from the oven, unmold the cakes, and spread them out to cool on a cake rack.

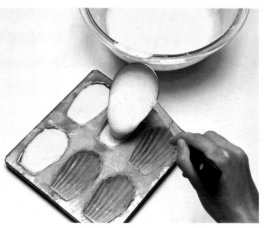

VANILLA BEANS
■ *Always use real vanilla extract, not artificial flavoring, if you cannot find the beans. The best Bourbon vanilla beans come from the island of Réunion.*

bowl.) Arrange a neat layer of liqueur dipped sponge slices on top, leaving no gaps. Chill for at least 6 hours in the refrigerator. Place a large round serving plate on top of the bowl and turn upside down, releasing the zuccotto onto the plate. Dust with sifted confectioners' sugar and serve at once.

• • •

MADELEINES
(France)

The classic molds for these delicate little sponge cakes so fondly remembered by the French novelist Marcel Proust are shell-shaped but any small cake molds can be used.

Time: 40 minutes
Easy

6 whole eggs and 3 extra yolks
2¾ cups confectioners' sugar
peel of 1 lemon, grated
1¾ cups all-purpose flour
1 cup cornstarch
1½ cups (3 sticks) butter

Beat the whole eggs with the yolks, sugar, and the lemon peel very thoroughly, until pale and frothy. Sift in the flour together with the cornstarch. Mix in the melted butter a little at a time. Ladle the mixture into well greased and floured madeleine molds and bake at 350° F for 20 minutes or until done. Leave

to set for 10 minutes after removing from the oven before unmolding. Store in an airtight tin to prevent them drying out. Serve cold with coffee or to accompany ice cream or fruit desserts.

• • •

ÎLE FLOTTANTE
(France)

Instead of one large "floating island" the beaten egg mixture can be poached in several heaped tablespoonfuls, thus creating "oeufs à la neige."

Time: 1 hour
Easy

2½ quarts milk
1 vanilla bean or a few drops vanilla extract
6 eggs
1½ cups sugar

Bring 2¼ cups of the milk to a boil with the vanilla bean (slit this lengthwise before adding to the milk) or with 4–5 drops vanilla extract. Leave to stand for 10 minutes if using a pod. Beat the egg yolks with ½ cup + 2 tbsp of the sugar until pale and frothy and continue

VANILLA

There is no satisfactory synthetic substitute for pure vanilla, which comes from a climbing orchid (*Vanilla planifolia*) native to central American tropical forests. Make your own vanilla sugar by placing one or more of these beans in a jar of sugar; seal tightly and leave for 2–3 weeks.

beating while adding the milk in a thin stream. Heat gently while stirring with a wooden spoon until the custard is thick enough to coat the back of the spoon.
Lower the pan (or top of double boiler) carefully into a bowl of cold water and stir for 5–10 minutes to avoid a skin forming as the custard cools. Beat the egg whites until firm, add ¼ of the sugar and continue beating until very stiff; add the rest of the sugar and beat for a few minutes longer.
Transfer this snowy egg white mixture to a pie plate which has been rinsed with cold water (and not dried

afterward). Bring the rest of the milk slowly to boiling point in a very wide saucepan and slide the mound of egg whites onto the surface. Poach for 2 minutes, then carefully turn over (there is no need to lift, the buoyancy of the milk will make the egg white easy to roll over) and poach for 2 minutes more.

Pour the vanilla custard into a deep glass bowl. Lift the egg whites from the milk with a very large slotted ladle; allow to drain, then place carefully on top of the custard. Serve immediately.

• • •

CHOCOLATE ÉCLAIRS (France)

These can be made in the shape of little round or oval buns or piped into large fingers. Coffee frosting can also be used.

Time: 1 hour 30 minutes
Easy

1 cup + 2 tbsp water
1 tbsp sugar
½ cup (1 stick) butter
1¼ cups all-purpose flour
4 eggs
1 tsp salt
For the pastry cream filling:
2¼ cups milk
few drops vanilla extract
5 egg yolks
½ cup sugar
¼ cup all-purpose flour
3 tbsp unsweetened cocoa
   powder
For the frosting:
1 cup Chocolate Frosting (see
   pages 52–3)

Boil the water with the salt, sugar, and butter in a saucepan. Pour all the flour at once into the pan and, without

delay, mix vigorously with a wooden spoon until the mixture is very thick and leaves the sides of the pan. Draw aside from the heat and continue beating for a minute or two. Beat the 4 eggs and add gradually to the mixture, beating very thoroughly between additions, until it is thick and glossy. Place the choux mixture in a pastry bag with a large plain tube. Lightly grease and flour one or more cookie sheets and pipe the choux mixture into well spaced out mounds or fingers about 1¼ in in diameter. Place in the oven, preheated to 350° F and bake for about 20 minutes or until well risen and dry and golden on the outside (take out one éclair if you wish, to check: if the inside is at all soggy, bake the rest for a little longer). On removing the éclairs from the oven, make a small slit in the sides to allow the steam to escape.

Make the pastry cream: bring the milk to a boil with 3–4 drops vanilla. Beat the eggs with the sugar until pale, add the flour, mix well, and then beat in the hot milk a little at a time. Heat gently, stirring continuously, until thick. Draw aside from the heat, beat in the sifted cocoa powder and leave to cool. Use a pastry bag and large tube again to pipe this filling into the éclairs. Melt the frosting over low heat, leave to cool a little, then drizzle a little over the top of each éclair. Serve without too much delay.

• • •

MUFFINS (Great Britain)

Time: 1 hour
Easy

1¾ cups all-purpose flour
2½ tsp baking powder
3 tbsp sugar
1 egg
¾ cup milk
6 tbsp (¾ stick) butter, melted
pinch salt

Sift the flour and baking powder into a mixing bowl; mix in the sugar and salt very thoroughly. Beat the egg thoroughly in a separate bowl, then beat the milk into it, followed by the melted but slightly cooled butter. Pour this liquid very slowly into the flour mixture, beating all the time. Grease muffin pans or small molds with butter and dust with flour. Fill them three-quarters full. Bake in an oven preheated to 415° F for 15 minutes or until a thin skewer pushed deep into a muffin comes out clean. Serve with butter and jam.

• • •

CLAFOUTIS (France)

The traditional recipe for this well-known sweet flan calls for cherries but in this version we have used apricots; small, thin-skinned (pitted) plums are also delicious, as are grapes. Add spices if you wish: a pinch of cinnamon or nutmeg.

Time: 1 hour 15 minutes
Easy

¼ cup (½ stick) butter
¾ cup sugar
1¾ lb ripe apricots
½ cup slivered almonds
4 eggs
2¼ cups milk

Use 2 tbsp butter to grease an ovenproof ceramic flan dish or a shallow 10-in removable-base cake pan. Sprinkle 2 tbsp sugar all over the butter. Wash and dry the apricots, cut in half, and remove the pits. Place in a single layer, cut side downward, covering the bottom of the dish or pan. Sprinkle the almonds over them.
Mix the flour in a bowl with the remaining sugar, stir in the lightly beaten eggs and then beat in the milk, adding a little at a time; beat well. Melt the remaining butter and beat into the batter. Pour this liquid batter over the apricots; place the flan in a preheated oven (350° F) and cook for

1 hour or until done (the batter should be soft but set and pale golden brown on top). Serve warm.

• • •

OMELETTE SOUFFLÉE (France)

The traditional finishing touch for these fluffy omelets is to press a very hot skewer gently against the surface of the cooked omelet, to leave parallel or crisscross lines as decoration.

Time: 40 minutes
Easy

4 egg yolks
¾ cup sugar
2–3 drops vanilla extract
5 egg whites
1 tbsp confectioners' sugar

Grease a soufflé dish with butter and dust with sugar, shaking out any excess. Beat

the egg yolks with ½ cup of the sugar and the vanilla extract until very pale and greatly increased in bulk. Beat the egg whites until just firm, add the remaining sugar, and continue beating until very stiff. Fold all but about 4 heaping tbsp of the meringue into the fluffy egg yolk mixture with a mixing spatula (to avoid crushing out any more air than necessary).

Turn this mixture into the soufflé dish and, with a pastry bag and large fluted tube, quickly pipe a decorative design on top. Sift the confectioners' sugar on top and place in the oven, preheated to 400° F, for 10 minutes or until the omelet is well risen and the top is pale golden brown. Serve immediately.

•   •   •

190

PASTIERA (Italy)

As whole-grain wheat is only available in some health food shops in the United States, ¾ cup of barley may be substituted for it; soak for 12 hours.

Time: 3 hours + standing time Easy

1 quantity Sweet Egg Pastry I or II (see page 56)
1 cup whole-grain wheat, hulled
1 cup rich milk
peel of 1 lemon, grated

1 cup sugar
pinch cinnamon
¾ lb fresh ricotta (sieved)
4 eggs
⅓ cup mixed candied peel (orange and citron)
1½ tbsp orange flower water
pinch salt
1–2 tbsp confectioners' sugar

Soak the wheat in a bowl of cold water for three days, changing the water every 24 hours.
Make the Sweet Egg Pastry as directed on page 56. Drain the wheat, place in a large pan of cold water, bring to a boil, and continue boiling for 15 minutes. Bring the milk to a boil in a saucepan with the grated lemon peel, 1½ tbsp of the sugar and a pinch of cinnamon. Drain the wheat and add to the milk. When the milk returns to a boil, lower the heat and cook very gently until the wheat has absorbed all the milk (use a double boiler to avoid the milk catching and burning if you wish). Leave to

PASTIERA
■ A traditional Neapolitan Easter treat: every family swears by its own version, handed down from generation to generation.

BUTTER
■ An essential ingredient in classic dessert cookery, its fat content varies from 84 to 88 percent.

TRADITIONAL DESSERTS

cool. Beat the ricotta in a large mixing bowl with a wooden spoon; beat in the egg yolks one by one, then the remaining sugar, a pinch of cinnamon (optional), lemon peel, finely diced candied peel, orange flower water, a pinch of salt and, finally, the cooked wheat. Stir thoroughly; leave to stand for 5 minutes before folding in the stiffly beaten egg whites.

Use about three quarters of the pastry to line the base and sides of a prepared pie pan or plate; turn the ricotta mixture into it, and smooth the surface level. Cut the remaining pastry into strips and place these in a lattice (see illustration opposite) on top of the filling. Bake at 350° F for 45 minutes or until done. Leave to cool before sprinkling with the sifted confectioners' sugar. This pie keeps well.

• • •

RIZ CONDÉ (France)

This is the very soft and creamy rice, often served with fruit.

Time: 45 minutes
Very easy

1 cup short-grain pudding rice
½ cup sugar
few drops vanilla extract
1 quart rich milk
pinch salt
¼ cup (½ stick) sweet butter
4 egg yolks

Sprinkle the rice into plenty of fast boiling water in a large pan and cook for 5 minutes after it has returned to a boil. Drain and place in a wide ovenproof

dish. Add the sugar, milk, and a pinch of salt. Cover with foil, tucking it in tightly all round the dish, and place in the oven, preheated to 400° F; cook for 25 minutes without lifting the foil. When done, remove the foil, stir in the butter, and then the egg yolks; use a mixing spatula to avoid crushing the rice grains. Serve hot without accompaniment or cold in a variety of desserts.

• • •

LINZERTORTE (Austria)

A traditional tart from the city of Linz, made with filbert or almond pastry; the nuts can be very finely chopped or ground, but the former method results in a better consistency.

Time: 1 hour 15 minutes
Easy

2¾ cups all-purpose flour
¾ cup sugar
pinch salt
½ cup water
½ tsp cinnamon
1 whole egg and 1 extra yolk
½ cup (1 stick) butter
6 drops almond extract
3 drops vanilla extract
2 cups very finely chopped or ground almonds
½ cup black cherry or raspberry preserve
1 tsp milk

Sift the flour and baking powder together onto a work surface. Make a well in the center of this mound and place in it the sugar, salt, water, cinnamon, 1 whole egg, the softened butter cut into small pieces, the almond and vanilla extract, and the chopped or

ground almonds. Stir these ingredients gradually into the flour with your slightly cupped hand, fingers closed. Shape into a ball and wrap in foil; chill for 1 hour in the refrigerator. Roll out half the pastry into a circle 8½ in in diameter and fit this snugly into a shallow greased pan of the same size (or place on a cookie sheet). Roll out the remaining dough and cut into ¼–½-in strips with a pastry wheel. Spread the jam over the pastry stopping ¼–½ in short of the edge all the way round.

Arrange the pastry strips in a grid pattern on top of the jam and place a strip all round the edge; press this border down lightly.

Beat the remaining yolk with the milk and brush this glaze over the pastry strips. Place in a preheated oven at 350° F and bake for 40 minutes.

• • •

FRANKFURTER KRANZ (Germany)

This ring-shaped cake has a

PLUM CAKE

An old English recipe. A richer version includes coarsely chopped almonds and pistachio nuts or filberts. This is a slightly richer and larger version of the recipe given on page 182.

1 cup (2 sticks) butter, softened at
    room temperature
2 cups confectioners' sugar
4 eggs
2 cups all-purpose flour
1 tbsp baking powder
½ tsp salt
1½ cups seedless white raisins
¼ cup rum
½ cup chopped candied cherries
    mixed with diced candied peel or
    candied fruit

Soak the seedless white raisins in the rum for about 30 minutes, stirring from time to time.

Beat the softened butter until pale and creamy in a large mixing bowl.

Beat in the confectioners' sugar (1 cup sugar can be used instead). Beat the egg whites stiffly and fold into the butter and sugar mixture.

Stir in the lightly beaten egg yolks; sift the flour, baking powder, and salt together, adding a little at a time to the bowl. Mix gently but thoroughly. Fold in the drained seedless white raisins and the candied fruit.

Grease a rectangular cake or loaf pan with butter, line with waxed paper (or use a nonstick pan) and transfer the cake batter into it. Level the surface with a spatula.

Bake at 350° F for about 1 hour or until a skewer pushed deep into the cake comes out dry and clean.

APPLES
■ *If you need to ripen fruit quickly, seal it in a plastic bag together with a ripe apple to accelerate the process.*

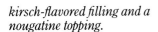

kirsch-flavored filling and a nougatine topping.

Time: 1 hour 15 minutes
Easy

½ cup (1 stick) butter
⅔ cup sugar
3 eggs
peel of 1 lemon, grated
1 cup all-purpose flour
1 cup potato flour or
    cornstarch
2½ tsp baking powder
For the filling and topping:
¾ cup sugar
3 egg yolks
1 cup (2 sticks) + 2 tbsp
    butter
2 tbsp confectioners' sugar
few drops vanilla extract
1½ tbsp kirsch
½ lb almond brittle or
    nougatine

Make the cake: have the butter softened at room temperature and beat with the sugar until pale and creamy, then beat in the eggs very thoroughly, one at a time. Stir in the grated lemon peel, then sift in the flour with the potato flour and baking powder. Mix well.
Grease a 9½-in ring or Kugelhupf mold lightly with butter, dust with a little flour and place the cake mixture in it; bake in the lower part of the oven at 350° F for 40 minutes or until done.
Make the filling and topping: sprinkle the sugar in an even layer in a saucepan, add just enough water to cover, and heat until the thread stage is reached. Beat the egg yolks very well; beat in the hot sugar syrup, trickling this down the inside of the bowl very slowly as you beat. Beat the softened butter until pale and frothy, add 2 tbsp

confectioners' sugar and a few drops vanilla extract. Beat in the egg and syrup mixture a little at a time. Add the kirsch a few drops at a time.
Cut the cake horizontally into 3 layers and spread the filling between the layers and on top. Pound the nougatine into very small pieces and sprinkle over the topping.

• • •

APPLE PIE (U.S.A. and Great Britain)

Still rated America's and Britain's favorite dessert, served on its own or with ice cream, custard or heavy cream.

Time: 1 hour 15 minutes
Easy

1 quantity Sweet Shortcrust
    Pastry or Sweet Pie Dough
    (see pages 56 and 57)
2¼ lb apples
¾ cup sugar
juice of ½ lemon
peel of 1 lemon, grated
1 cup whipping cream
1 tbsp confectioners' sugar

Grease a 10-in pie plate or deep pie pan with butter. Roll out half the pastry into a circle just under ¼ in thick, which will amply cover the base and sides and overlap the edges a little. Peel, core, and slice the apples quite thinly and arrange in the pie shell. Sprinkle with ⅔ cup of the sugar, the lemon juice, and grated peel.
Roll out the rest of the pastry to the same thickness and cover the pie with it; use a corrugated pastry wheel to trim off the overlapping edges and press the two layers

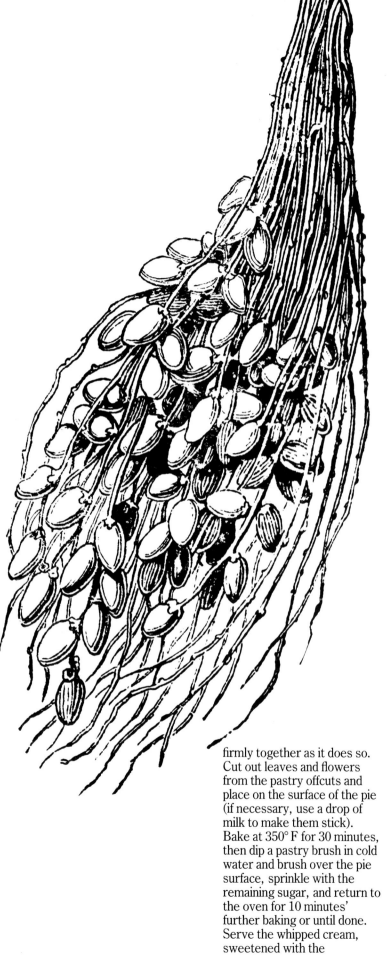

DATES
■ A cluster of ripening fruit (seventeenth-century engraving).

BLANC MANGER
■ This pudding owes its ethereal whiteness to the use of almond milk with the cream; almond milk is available in quality food stores and some delicatessens. Decorate with fresh fruit if preferred.

confectioners' sugar if wished, with the hot apple pie.

• • •

CHRISTMAS PUDDING (Great Britain)

This pudding should be made six months in advance as it improves with keeping; some people make their pudding a year in advance. Traditionally small silver coins (well boiled beforehand) or trinkets are hidden in the pudding. A sprig of holly is pushed into the top of the pudding for decoration; flame the pudding with brandy or rum at the table just before serving.

Time: 10 hours + keeping time Easy

½ cup chopped suet
1 cup sugar
¼ cup finely chopped or grated raw apple
½ cup diced candied orange peel
1 cup diced candied citron peel
2 cups currants, soaked
1 cup large California raisins (seeds removed)
1 cup chopped dates
3 tbsp raspberry jam
4 eggs
¾ cup all-purpose flour
3 cups fine soft fresh breadcrumbs
3 tsp cinnamon
generous pinch salt
generous pinch ground ginger
½ tsp allspice
pinch nutmeg
3 tbsp milk
¼ cup brandy
¼ cup sherry
½ cup dry white wine
For the hard sauce:
¾ cup (1½ sticks) sweet

butter
2¼ cups confectioners' sugar
1 egg yolk (optional)
¼ cup brandy
To add during storage:
1 cup brandy
For flaming:
½ cup brandy

Place the ingredients listed above up to and including the nutmeg in a very large mixing bowl. Mix well before adding the milk, brandy, sherry, and wine and stir very thoroughly. Cover and leave to stand in a cool place for 2 days. Grease a pudding bowl or mold (6–6½ in in diameter at the top) with butter and fill with the mixture, packing down firmly. Seal tightly with the pudding bowl lid or with a circle of waxed paper, covered with a canvas pudding cover or piece of canvas, and tie tightly with string to secure. Cook in a steamer over boiling water for 5 hours, topping up the boiling water at frequent intervals. Set the cooked pudding aside to cool completely. Turn out carefully and wrap in several layers of cheesecloth soaked in brandy. Store in a cool place (do not refrigerate), moistening the wrappings with more brandy over the following two weeks, after which it can be eaten, but will improve with further keeping. If keeping the pudding for a protracted period, remove the lid or coverings, pour in ½ cup brandy a little at a time, reseal and store in a cool place for 1 year or longer, adding a little more brandy at 6-monthly intervals if wished. When you are ready to eat the pudding, steam for 2–3 hours. While the pudding is being steamed make the hard sauce:

firmly together as it does so. Cut out leaves and flowers from the pastry offcuts and place on the surface of the pie (if necessary, use a drop of milk to make them stick). Bake at 350° F for 30 minutes, then dip a pastry brush in cold water and brush over the pie surface, sprinkle with the remaining sugar, and return to the oven for 10 minutes' further baking or until done. Serve the whipped cream, sweetened with the

Blanc-manger aux amandes (almond blancmange) is a classic French dessert. See page 197 for instructions on how to make almond milk. Grind peeled sweet almonds yourself if possible, as commercially prepared ground almonds have an inferior flavor.

1¼ cups confectioners' sugar
¾ cup cornstarch
1¼ cups hot milk
3 tbsp white Curaçao
1 cup heavy cream
½ cup almond milk (see page 197)

Sift the sugar and cornstarch together into a bowl (mixing sugar with cornstarch prevents it from forming lumps when cooked).

Slake the cornstarch by adding ½ cup of the milk. Stir well.

Add the remaining milk.

Stir the mixture well and immediately pour into a saucepan. Cook over gentle heat, stirring continuously, until the mixture has thickened.

Draw aside from the heat. Stir in the Curaçao. Add the cream; mix well.

Stir in the almond milk. Rinse a ring mold or small individual molds with cold water. Pour the blancmange mixture into them and chill in the refrigerator for several hours, until set.

beat the butter (softened at room temperature) until pale and creamy; beat in the sugar very thoroughly: the mixture should have a very light, almost fluffy consistency and be almost white. Beat in the brandy a teaspoonful at a time (do not add too quickly or too much, or the mixture will curdle). Place in a bowl and leave to set. (Refrigerate if made a day in advance.) Turn the pudding out onto a hot serving platter; heat the brandy (do not boil), pour over the pudding, and quickly set alight, shaking gently to encourage combustion. Each person takes a generous spoonful of hard sauce which will melt delectably on the helping of hot pudding.

•   •   •

BLANC-MANGER (France)

Time: 1 hour
Easy

1½ cups peeled whole sweet
   almonds
2 bitter almonds
1¾ cups water
1½ cups milk
½ cup sugar
3 tbsp gelatin powder
1 tbsp kirsch
1¾ cups heavy or whipping
   cream

Pound the almonds very finely (preferably using a pestle and mortar) and leave to stand in a large bowl in the cold water for 2 hours. Place a large piece of cheesecloth in a large sieve, place this in turn over a bowl, and pour the almond and water mixture into it; gather up the loose sides of the cheesecloth and twist increasingly tightly, forcing all the liquid out of the almond mixture into the bowl. Mix the sugar into this almond milk and stir for at least 5 minutes. Heat the milk to scalding point, remove from the heat and sprinkle in the gelatin; stir until it has completely dissolved. Mix into the almond milk and add the kirsch. Leave this mixture to cool and when it shows signs of beginning to set fold in the stiffly beaten cream.
Rinse a ring or decorative blancmange mold with cold water, and do not dry; fill with the mixture and chill in the refrigerator for about 8 hours. Turn out onto a plate and serve.

•   •   •

MOUSSE AU CHOCOLAT (France)

Very rich but very light, chocolate mousse should be served in small, individual dishes.

Time: 30 minutes
Easy

9 oz (9 squares) bitter
   chocolate
2¼ cups milk
¼ cup sugar
4 whole eggs and 1 extra
   white

Break the chocolate into small pieces and place, with the milk, in the top of a double boiler to melt. When the chocolate has completely melted, stir in the sugar, and turn off the heat. When the

CRÊPES SUZETTE
■ *A world-famous classic dessert which originated in France, where you can buy freshly cooked sweet or savory pancakes in sidewalk crêperies all day long. In the Crêpes Suzette shown below a fruit filling has been added to the traditional recipe.*

sugar has dissolved and the mixture has cooled a little, beat in the 4 egg yolks, one at a time. Leave to cool further. Beat the 5 egg whites very stiffly and fold very gently but thoroughly into the chocolate mixture. Transfer to a glass serving bowl and chill until just before serving.

• • •

LEMON CHIFFON PIE (USA)

Another firm favorite. Very thin strips of lemon peel can be sprinkled over the surface of the filling as a final garnish.

Time: 1 hour 15 minutes
Easy

1 quantity Sweet Egg Pastry I
   or II (see page 56)
6 egg yolks
1½ cups sugar
1¾ cups water
juice of 3 lemons
peel of 1 large lemon, grated
1½ tbsp gelatin powder
5 egg whites

Make the Sweet Egg Pastry and line a 10-in pie plate or a fairly deep pie pan with it. Cover with waxed paper, weight down with dried beans or rice, and bake at 350° F for 40 minutes or until done. Remove the beans and paper for the last 5 minutes.
Beat the egg yolks with the sugar until pale and fluffy; beat in the water, the lemon juice, and grated peel and cook gently in the top of a double boiler, stirring continuously; do not allow to reach boiling point or it will curdle.
Remove from the heat and sprinkle in the gelatin; make

sure this dissolves completely. Leave to cool and when showing the first signs of setting, fold in the stiffly beaten egg whites. Fill the cooked pie shell with this mixture. Chill before serving.

• • •

CRÊPES SUZETTE (France)

Time: 50 minutes
Easy

For the batter:
2¼ cups all-purpose flour
2 tbsp sugar
3 eggs
2¼ cups milk
3 tbsp Grand Marnier
½ cup (1 stick) sweet butter
pinch salt
For the sauce:
5 tbsp butter
10 sugar cubes
juice of 1 orange
½ cup Grand Marnier

In a blender on medium speed mix the flour with the sugar, lightly beaten eggs, milk, liqueur, and a pinch of salt. Add the melted butter a little at a time. Leave to stand for 1 hour. Grease a skillet (approx. 5–6 in in diameter) with butter and when the pan is hot, distribute a small ladleful (about 3 tbsp) of the pancake mixture over the bottom of the skillet, tip the pan quickly to distribute the batter very thinly. When the pancake is done on one side, turn and cook the other side. Transfer the pancake to a hot plate and keep warm (a good way is to transfer them straight to a very large platter, cover and keep hot over simmering water). The first pancake may not be perfect.

Continue cooking the pancakes until you have used up all the mixture, greasing the pan with a very little more butter when necessary. Make the sauce: while the batter is standing, rub the sugar cubes hard against the peel of the orange so that they absorb the essential oils contained in the peel. Crush these cubes and place in a very wide skillet, add the butter, and heat while stirring; add the orange juice and half the Grand Marnier. Heat the remaining Grand Marnier, sprinkle over the crêpes, and flame. Serve immediately.

• • •

PALACINKEN (Hungary)

These small individual sweet omelets are filled with pastry cream, jam, or whipped cream and chopped almonds.

Time: 35 minutes
Easy

9 eggs
4 tsp all-purpose flour
¼ cup milk
¼ cup (½ stick) sweet butter
2 tbsp sugar
½ quantity Pastry Cream (see page 44)
2–3 drops vanilla extract
¼ cup sieved raspberries
½ cup whipping cream

Separate the yolks from the whites of 6 eggs, placing in 2 separate bowls; break 3 whole eggs into the bowl containing the yolks and beat very well; beat in the flour and milk. Stir in the stiffly beaten 6 egg whites gently. Heat the butter in a very wide skillet (with ovenproof handles, suitable

for use in the oven) until it foams, sprinkle in the sugar, and pour in the egg and milk mixture. Reduce the heat and cook gently until the omelet starts to set. Place in a preheated oven at 350° F for 7–8 minutes.

Slip the omelet onto a hot serving platter; spoon the pastry cream (flavored with the vanilla) the raspberry purée, and stiffly beaten cream onto the omelet and fold carefully in half. Sprinkle with more sugar if wished and sear a design of parallel lines or a grid effect on the surface with a hot skewer or poker.

• • •

PRINZREGENTEN-TORTE (Germany)

This dessert has an extremely rich filling: in Germany it is usually eaten in the afternoon

with a cup of coffee. It is a good idea to serve such luscious layer cakes on their own rather than at the end of a large meal.

Time: 2 hours 30 minutes + chilling time
Fairly easy

½ cup (1 stick) butter
½ cup sugar
1 egg yolk
¾ cup all-purpose flour
½ cup cornstarch
1 tsp baking powder
½ cup milk
2 egg whites
For the filling:
7 oz (7 squares) bitter or semisweet chocolate
1 cup confectioners' sugar
1 large egg or 2 small eggs
2 tbsp butter
For the frosting:
1 cup Chocolate Frosting (see pages 52–3)

Have the butter softened at room temperature; beat it with the sugar until very soft and fluffy and then beat in the egg yolk. Sift the flour, cornstarch, and the baking powder together, adding a little at a time and alternating with a little milk. The batter should be soft but not too moist. Fold in the stiffly beaten egg whites.
Divide the batter equally between 5 shallow nonstick cake pans (or grease and line with nonstick paper) and bake in a preheated oven at 350° F for 10–12 minutes or until they are cooked and pale golden brown on top. Remove from the pans and leave to cool.
Make the filling: break the chocolate into small pieces and melt over hot water; stir in the sugar, remove from the heat,

and stir in the egg, followed by the softened butter, a small piece at a time. Beat thoroughly until cooler and spread on the cut surfaces of the 4 lower layers. Reassemble the cake. Cover the top layer (on which no chocolate mixture has been spread) with waxed paper, place a weight on top and chill for 24 hours in the refrigerator. Frost the top and leave to set before serving.

• • •

APFEL-STRUDEL (Austria)

Time: 1 hour 40 minutes
Fairly difficult

CINNAMON

Cinnamon is the dried bark of a tree native to Sri Lanka (*Cinnamomum zeylahicum*). This spice is sold in "sticks" or lengths of rolled bark or, more frequently, finely ground. Cinnamon keeps its strong, warm aroma for some time; use sparingly as a little goes a long way.

2¼ cups all-purpose flour
1 egg
½ cup sugar
pinch salt
½ cup (1 stick) + 2 tbsp butter
⅓ cup warm water
⅓ cup seedless white raisins
1¾ lb apples (see below)
1 cup fine breadcrumbs
⅓ cup pine nuts
peel of 1 lemon, grated
1 tsp cinnamon

1–1½ tbsp confectioners' sugar

Sift the flour into a large mixing bowl, make a well in the middle, and break the egg into it, adding 2 tbsp of the sugar, a pinch of salt, ¼ cup melted butter, and the warm water. Mix gradually into the flour, stirring with the closed fingers of your slightly cupped hand. The dough should be soft but not sticky. Knead the dough, slapping it against the work surface after you turn it over; shape into a ball and place a large, hot saucepan over it (not touching the dough) to create its own microclimate.
Soak the raisins in warm water for 10 minutes, drain, and dry on kitchen towels. Peel, core, and thinly slice the apples. Fry the breadcrumbs in ¼ cup butter. Roll out the pastry with a rolling pin to less than ⅛ in thick, thinner if possible, without breaking it. You should be able to just see the outline of your fingers placed beneath it. Spread the apples, raisins, pine nuts, and breadcrumbs all over the surface, leaving a ¾-in border uncovered all round the edge. Mix the remaining sugar with the cinnamon and grated lemon peel and sprinkle all over the fruit and nuts. Roll out the pastry, pinching the ends closed. Place on a large greased cookie sheet and sprinkle with the remaining, melted, butter. Bake at 320° F for 1 hour. Turn off the oven and leave the Strudel in it for 15 minutes as it gradually cools. Dust with the sifted confectioners' sugar and serve warm.

• • •

CROQUEM-BOUCHE (France)

These little choux pastry buns are stuck together with caramel in the shape of a pyramid on the serving plate. They are often filled with Chantilly Cream with more caramel drizzled onto them. Take care not to touch the caramel with your fingers.

Time: 1 hour 10 minutes
Easy

2¼ cups water
1 cup (2 sticks) + 2 tbsp
   sweet butter
1 tsp salt
2¼ cups all-purpose flour
8 eggs
For the caramel:
1 cup sugar
1 tsp lemon juice
1½ tbsp water

Make the choux pastry: place the water, butter, and salt in a saucepan and bring to a boil. Draw aside from the heat and pour all the sifted flour in at once. Without delay beat vigorously until the mixture forms a smooth ball and leaves the sides of the pan cleanly. Warm over gentle heat, stirring continuously, for 1 minute. Transfer the choux dough to a bowl and beat in the first egg very thoroughly indeed; it will take a little time to combine with the mixture which will suddenly "tighten" when the egg is properly mixed in. Beat in the remaining eggs equally thoroughly, one at a time. The choux pastry dough should now be very smooth and glossy.
Pipe the dough into small walnut-sized mounds, well spaced out on cookie sheets very lightly greased with butter and dusted with a little flour. Bake in a preheated oven at 400° F for 20–25 minutes.
Make the caramel: heat the sugar, lemon juice, and water until it turns a pale golden color. Turn off the heat; using a fork, dip each cooked choux ball on one side in the caramel and build up a pyramid, using the caramel as the "glue." A very little will suffice to hold the edifice together. Heat the remaining caramel briefly and trickle over the top and down the sides of the pyramid. Serve immediately.

•   •   •

SAINT HONORÉ (France)

Time: 2 hours 30 minutes
Fairly easy

1 quantity Sweet Egg Pastry I
   (see page 56)
20 small choux buns (see left)

For the filling:
1 cup milk
3 drops vanilla extract
3 egg yolks
½ cup sugar
3 tbsp cornstarch
4 egg whites
For the caramel:
1 cup sugar
⅓ cup water

Make the Sweet Egg Pastry as instructed on page 56 and use to line a 10-in pie pan. Bake this "blind."
Make the filling: bring the milk to a boil with the vanilla. Beat the egg yolks with 2 tbsp of the sugar; beat in the cornstarch and then the hot milk, adding this a little at a time. Heat in the top of a double boiler, stirring constantly, to thicken somewhat; do not allow to boil. Turn off the heat but keep hot. Beat the egg whites until stiff, preferably in an electric mixer with the whisk attachment.
Heat the remaining sugar

SAINT HONORÉ
■ *For an alternative version, split a Classic Sponge Cake (see page 146) in two horizontally, and spread some filling in the middle. Reassemble the cake and* cover the top and sides with more filling. Place the choux buns around the outer edge, and pipe any remaining filling over the top of the cake, if wished.

listed under the filling ingredients in a pan with 3 tbsp water and boil until the soft ball stage is reached (i.e. when a drop of syrup dropped into a cup of iced water forms a soft, malleable ball). Trickle this syrup slowly down the inside of the mixer bowl as you beat on high speed; beat for a few minutes more after all the syrup has been added. Add

the hot pastry cream to this mixture, beating on medium speed as you do so. Leave to cool.
Make the caramel by boiling the sugar and water together until the syrup turns a pale golden color. Dip the bottom of each choux bun in the caramel and attach the bottom to the edge of the pie shell, positioning them very close to

each other all round the edge. Fill the pie shell with the filling and chill. Serve within 24 hours.

• • •

BAYERISCHE ORANGENCREME (Germany)

Bavarian creams are named after their native region in southern Germany. This delicate, digestible dessert from the capital of Bavaria, Munich, can be made with chocolate, coffee, strawberries, and many other flavors.

Time: 45 minutes
Easy

1 cup milk
grated peel and juice of 1
    orange
3 egg yolks
½ cup sugar
3 tbsp all-purpose flour
2 tbsp gelatin powder
2¼ cups whipping cream
12 skinned orange sections

Put the milk and the grated orange peel in a blender and process at high speed; pour

into a saucepan and heat to boiling point. Beat the egg yolks with the sugar until pale, beat in the sifted flour and then the milk, adding a little at a time. Pour into the top of a double boiler and heat, stirring constantly, until thickened somewhat; do not allow to boil. Draw aside from the heat and sprinkle in the gelatin powder, which must dissolve completely. Stir well and leave to cool. Add the orange juice and when cold, fold in the stiffly beaten cream.

Fill an 8½-in ring or Bavarois mold with the mixture and chill in the refrigerator for at least 8 hours. Turn out onto a chilled serving plate and decorate with the orange sections.

• • •

SOUFFLÉ AU GRAND MARNIER (France)

The French have perfected the art of making soufflés, be they sweet or savory. The perfect soufflé should reach the table well risen, golden brown on top and fluffy except for a creamy center.

Time: 1 hour
Easy

1 cup finely crumbled
   amaretti, ratafias or crisp
   macaroons
peel of 1 orange, grated
3 tbsp butter
¼ cup + 2 tbsp all-purpose
   flour
1 cup milk, heated to boiling
   point
6 tbsp sugar
¼ cup Grand Marnier
4 egg yolks
6 egg whites

Lightly grease a 1½–2 quart soufflé mold with butter, dust with sugar, shaking out any excess, and tie a waxed paper collar round the dish if wished. Place the amaretti crumbs in a bowl and mix with the Grand Marnier and the grated orange peel. Melt the butter in a saucepan, stir in the flour, and then pour in all the hot milk at once, beating vigorously to keep the mixture smooth. As soon as the sauce shows signs of coming to a boil, remove from the heat, and add the sugar, the amaretti, Grand Marnier, and orange peel mixture. Stir well. Beat in the egg yolks one at a time. Fold in 1 tbsp of the very stiffly beaten egg whites and then fold this mixture into the rest of the beaten whites. Transfer to the prepared soufflé dish and place in a preheated oven at 400° F for 20 minutes or until done. Serve immediately.

• • •

KIRSCHEN-TORTE (Germany)

A luscious cake with an abundance of ripe cherries topped with pastry cream. If ripe, really sweet cherries are not available, use canned fruit.

Time: 1 hour 30 minutes
Easy

1 quantity Sweet Egg Pastry I
   or II (see pages 56–7)
1 lb washed, dried, and pitted
   cherries
½ cup (1 stick) + 1 tbsp
   butter
¾ cup sugar
4 egg yolks
6 egg whites
¾ cup slivered almonds
1 cup all-purpose flour
1 tbsp confectioners' sugar

APRICOTS
■ *This fruit will complement
and enhance almost any
type of dessert or cake.*

TRADITIONAL DESSERTS

Make the pastry and use to line the bottom and sides of a lightly greased and floured 10-in pie pan. Fill the pie shell with the cherries. Beat the softened butter with 6 tbsp of the sugar until very pale and creamy; beat in the egg yolks one at a time. Beat the egg whites until stiff and fold the almonds and sifted flour into them. Combine the two mixtures gently but thoroughly and spread out over the cherries. Bake at 350° F for 40 minutes or until done. Leave to cool, then sprinkle with the confectioners' sugar.

• • •

ZABAGLIONE
(Italy)

A classic Venetian dessert. Marsala was enjoyed by the Venetians as far back as the "Serenissima" republic.

*Time: 20 minutes
Easy*

6 egg yolks
6 tbsp sugar
1 tbsp warm water
⅔ cup sweet Marsala

Place the first 3 ingredients in a heatproof bowl. Beat vigorously with a balloon wire whisk for up to 15 minutes or until foamy and increased in volume. (If you use a hand-held electric whisk this will only take about 8 minutes.) Place the bowl over gently simmering water (the bottom of the bowl should not touch the water) and continue beating briskly as you add the Marsala in a thin trickle. Carry on beating, scraping the sides and bottom with the whisk

every so often to prevent the mixture cooking too much nearest the heat source; when the mixture forms soft mounds and has tripled in bulk, spoon immediately into tall glasses and serve immediately. Zabaglione can also be served cold, in which case a stiffly beaten egg white should be folded into the finished mixture.

• • •

SHORTBREAD
(Great Britain)

As a variation on the classic Scottish recipe we have added marzipan, adding lightness and flavor. Use shop-bought marzipan, unless you usually make your own.

*Time: 1 hour
Easy*

½ cup (1 stick) + 2 tbsp
    butter
1½ tbsp marzipan
1 cup confectioners' sugar
2¾ cups all-purpose flour

Have the butter and marzipan softened at room temperature and work them together with a wooden spoon; combine thoroughly with the confectioners' sugar. Sift in the flour a little at a time, mixing well after each addition. Lightly grease a shallow rectangular, square or round cake pan and press the shortbread mixture out in it with your fingers or the back of a wooden spoon; it should be between ½–¾ in thick. Bake at 350° F for about 30 minutes or until very pale golden brown.

• • •

DACQUOISE (France)

Similar to a Vacherin, but a little more complicated to make, and richer, with a buttercream filling. The meringue has almonds and filberts added to it.

Time: 1 hour 40 minutes
Fairly easy

8 egg whites
pinch salt
1 cup sugar
few drops vanilla extract
1⅔ cups ground almonds
1 cup roasted slivered
    almonds
1 cup finely chopped (not
    ground) filberts
butter
2 cups Buttercream (see page
    38)
1 tbsp confectioners' sugar

Beat the eggs and salt until firm, then beat in the sugar a little at a time, continue beating until stiff. Fold in the ground almonds and chopped filberts, using a mixing spatula so as not to crush air out of the meringue (scoop up the mixture from the bottom of the bowl and fold over on the top). Lightly grease three 8½-in shallow cake pans and divide the meringue equally between them or pipe out on nonstick silicone-treated paper. Level out gently. Bake in the oven at only 140° F for 2 hours, leaving the oven door very slightly ajar, or until the meringue has set and dried, not colored. Make the buttercream, following the recipe on page 38. Carefully remove the meringue from the pans and spread half the buttercream thickly over each of two layers. Place the layers on top of one another, finishing with a plain layer. Sprinkle this with the roasted almonds and sifted confectioners' sugar.

• • •

VACHERIN (France)

This meringue dessert is filled with Chantilly cream. Great care is needed to have the oven at exactly the right temperature for a successful meringue case. Keep the oven door open a little while it is baking.

Time: 2 hours 40 minutes
Fairly easy

8 egg whites
1 lb confectioners' sugar
1 cup Chantilly cream (see
    page 48)

Beat the egg whites until firm; add the sugar and continue beating until very stiff and glossy. Grease two ring molds lightly with butter, dust lightly with flour, and fill with the meringue mixture. Bake at 140° F for 2 hours or until the meringue has dried and set without coloring. Remove the meringue from the two molds with great care. Place one ring on a serving plate, spread Chantilly cream on top and place the second ring on it. Decorate with the remaining cream and serve.

• • •

SACHERTORTE
■ Probably the most typical
example of the famed
Viennese patisserie tradition,
originally created in a café
next door to the Sacher Hotel.

TRADITIONAL DESSERTS

SACHER-TORTE (Austria)

Time: 1 hour 40 minutes
Easy

5 oz (5 squares) bitter or
  semisweet chocolate
½ cup (1 stick) + 2 tbsp
  butter
½ cup + 2 tbsp sugar
pinch salt
6 eggs
For the filling:
½ cup best-quality apricot jam
For the frosting:
¾ lb Chocolate Frosting (see
  page 52–3)

Make the cake: break the
chocolate into small pieces and
melt gently over hot water
with 1½ tbsp water. Have the
butter softened at room
temperature and beat in a
bowl with the sugar and pinch
salt. Beat in the melted
chocolate, followed by the egg
yolks, beating these in very
thoroughly one at a time. Fold
in the stiffly beaten egg
whites; sift in the flour and fold
gently but thoroughly into the
mixture. Spoon this batter into
a 9½-in springform or
removable-base cake pan lined
with very lightly buttered
waxed paper. Place in a
preheated oven at 320° F for 1
hour or until done.
Remove the cake carefully
from the pan and when cold
cut horizontally in half; spread
the apricot jam over the
bottom layer, place the second
layer on top and cover the top
and sides completely with the
chocolate frosting.

• • •

PANPEPATO (Italy)

A very filling traditional Italian confection made with candied fruit and spices.

Time: 50 minutes
Very easy

2 cups firmly packed brown
 sugar
1 oz (1 square) chocolate
2¼ cups finely chopped
 walnuts
¾ lb (scant 2 cups) mixed
 candied fruit, cut into small
 pieces
1 lb (2⅔ cups) peeled whole
 almonds
pinch nutmeg
pinch cinnamon
approx. ¼ lb ice cream wafers

Heat the brown sugar and chocolate over moderate heat, stirring constantly and thoroughly to prevent the sugar catching and burning. Remove from the heat and immediately stir in the walnuts, fruit, whole almonds, and spices. Spread the mixture out on the work surface, roll out until it is about ⅜ in thick, and cut into rhomboids or diamond shapes. Place on wafers in an ovenproof dish. Bake for 30 minutes at 350° F. Remove from the oven and sprinkle sparingly with cinnamon.

•   •   •

FUDGE CAKE (USA)

A perennial favorite which is very simple to make.

Time: 1 hour 40 minutes
Easy

1 Genoa Sponge Cake baked
 in a 10-in pan (see page 147)
For the filling:
9 oz (9 squares) bitter or
 semisweet chocolate
pinch salt
2¼ cups confectioners' sugar
⅓ cup powdered milk
½ cup hot milk
few drops vanilla extract
½ cup (1 stick) + 2 tbsp
 butter

Make the sponge cake as directed. Break the chocolate into small pieces and melt over hot water; remove from the heat, transfer to a blender and add the salt, sugar, and powdered milk; process at medium speed for a minute or two, then blend in enough hot milk to result in a thick but easily spreadable mixture. Transfer to a bowl and stir in the softened (not melted) butter a little at a time. Cut the sponge cake in half, use half the chocolate fudge cream as the filling, put the top layer back in place, and use the rest of the fudge as frosting. Top with chocolate sprinkles if wished.

•   •   •

TORTA DOBOS (Hungary)

It is difficult to make this cake with a smaller quantity than given below, for 12 servings. This is a time consuming and elaborate but effective cake which could be served at the end of a special dinner party.

Time: 1 hour
Fairly easy
Serves 12

America's favorite cookies.

6 egg whites
¾ cup sugar
6 egg yolks
1¼ cups all-purpose flour
¼ cup melted butter
9 oz (9 squares) bitter or
    semisweet chocolate
3¼ cups Buttercream (see
    first recipe on page 38, use
    2 cups butter, 2 large egg
    whites, and 2¼ cups sugar)
For the caramel:
½ cup sugar
1 tsp butter
5 drops lemon juice

Lightly grease five 8½-in
springform or removable-base
cake pans with butter and dust
sparingly with flour, or use
shallow nonstick pans. Beat
the egg whites until firm; beat
in the sugar a little at a time.
Fold in the lightly beaten egg
yolks and the sifted flour;
gently stir in the melted
butter, adding it a few drops at
a time. Distribute the batter
evenly between the 5
prepared pans: it should not
be more than ⅛ in deep. Bake
in a preheated oven at 400° F
for 8–10 minutes. Make the
buttercream and keep at room
temperature. Break the
chocolate into pieces and melt
over hot water; leave to cool
and then beat into the
buttercream mixture.
Carefully remove the cakes
from their pans and spread a
quarter of the chocolate filling
over the 4 lower layers;
assemble into a 5-tier layer
cake. Heat the sugar with the
butter and lemon juice until it
turns a pale golden color, then
pour quickly all over the
surface of the top of the cake;
spread out immediately if
necessary with a spatula
dipped in water. Have a very
sharp large knife ready
greased with butter and waste

no time in cutting the cake into
12 sections, before the
caramel has time to set hard.

• • •

KRAPFEN (Austria)

Time: 3 hours 30 minutes
Fairly easy

1 cake compressed yeast or 1
    package (¼ oz) dry yeast
approx. 1 cup lukewarm milk
4½ cups unbleached all-
    purpose flour
2 eggs
½ cup (1 stick) butter
pinch salt
½ cup sugar
sunflower oil for deep frying
1 cup jam of choice or Pastry
    Cream (see page 44)

Have all the ingredients at
warm room temperature
before you start. Scald the
milk and then leave to cool to
lukewarm before pouring ½
cup of it into a small bowl,
adding the yeast. Leave to
dissolve and start foaming.
Combine with 2 cups of the
flour. Shape this very soft
dough into a ball (known as the
ferment) leave in the bowl and
gently pour in sufficient warm
water to amply cover the
dough ball. Leave to stand in a
warm place for 20 minutes or
until the ferment floats to the
surface of the water.
Sift the remaining flour onto
the work surface forming a
mound. Make a well in the
center and in it place the
dough ball with the eggs,
softened butter cut into small
pieces, salt, 2 tbsp sugar, and
6 tbsp lukewarm milk.
Combine all these ingredients:
the dough should be very soft
but not sticky. If it is not soft
enough, add very little more

warm milk.
Place the dough in a lightly
floured bowl, cover with a
towel, and leave to rise in a
warm place for 1½ hours or
until doubled in bulk. Use a
lightly floured rolling pin to roll
out the risen dough in a sheet
¾ in thick and use a ¾-in plain
round doughnut or cookie
cutter to cut out as many disks
of dough as you can, placing
these on a lightly greased and
floured (or nonstick) cookie
sheet. Cover the Krapfen with
a towel and leave to prove in a
warm place for 1 hour.
Heat the oil carefully in a
deep-fryer until it is very hot.
Lower the Krapfen into the fat
a few at a time and fry in
batches. Alternatively shallow
fry, turning once. Drain well
after removing from the fat
(use a frying basket or slotted
spoon) and place on kitchen
towels. Make a small
horizontal slit with a very
sharp serrated knife, large
enough to insert about 2 tsp of
jam or pastry cream. Sprinkle
with the remaining sugar and
serve.

• • •

BROWNIES (USA)

*The ever popular brownie has a
well deserved place as one of*

Time: 1 hour
Very easy

4 oz (4 squares) bitter or
    semisweet chocolate
1 cup (2 sticks) butter
4 eggs
1 cup sugar
6 drops vanilla extract
2 cups all-purpose flour
1 tsp baking powder
2 cups chopped walnuts

Break the chocolate into small
pieces and melt over hot
water with the butter. Beat
the eggs with the sugar, add
the vanilla, and stir in the
chocolate and butter mixture.
Sift in the flour with the baking
powder a little at a time,
stirring after each addition.
Mix in the walnuts.
Grease a shallow rectangular
or square cake pan or a cookie
sheet with butter and dust
lightly with flour. Spread the
brownie mix out in the tray or
on the sheet; it should be
about ¾ in thick. Bake in a
moderate oven (340° F) for 40
minutes or until done. Leave
to cool for a few minutes and
cut into 2-in squares.

Many of these desserts and confections originated in European cafés and restaurants and can be eaten on their own at any time of day (with a cup of coffee, tea or chocolate or something a little stronger) while others are best served at the end of a meal. They vary from mousses to milk puddings and charlottes: all are easily eaten with just a dessertspoon since they are soft and delicate.

RUM CREAM MOLD WITH ORANGES

Other citrus fruits can be used very successfully following this recipe: tangerines, mandarins, lemons or limes are best. When using lemons or limes increase the sugar content.

Time: 30 minutes + setting time
Easy

4 oranges
1 cup sugar
1 tbsp butter
2¼ cups half-and-half
3 tbsp powdered gelatin
4 egg yolks
½ cup rum

Wash the oranges thoroughly, dry, and cut into fairly thin round slices. Melt ½ cup sugar with 1½ tbsp water in a saucepan and cook until pale golden in color, then reduce the heat to very low or keep hot over simmering water. Dip the orange slices one by one in the caramel; place on a large lightly oiled or greased plate. Place the half-and-half in a saucepan and bring to a boil. Beat the 4 egg yolks with the remaining sugar until very pale and frothy; beat in the hot half-and-half. Pour this mixture into the saucepan used for heating the half-and-half and cook slowly to thicken. Remove from the heat and sprinkle in the gelatin; make sure this has dissolved completely, then beat in the rum. Stir frequently as the mixture cools. Rinse out a mold (a 1-quart capacity charlotte mold is ideal) and chill for 6–8 hours.
Dip the mold briefly in hot water, place a serving plate on

□ Most, if not all, the desserts in this chapter have very light, soft consistencies and are best eaten with a spoon. They can be served in small, individual dishes or glass coupes, and decorated with piped stiffly beaten cream or fruit or, in the case of charlottes and other molded desserts which are left to set in the refrigerator, turned out on a serving dish. Remember to rinse the inside of the mold with cold water before filling it with the mousse, Bavarian cream or jellied mixture. When making a charlotte it is sometimes advisable to brush the inside of the mold with a thin film of sweet almond oil.

□ When these desserts have to be cooked in their molds, it is best to place the mold in a fairly large pan (a roasting pan will do) of hot water. An easy method is to place the mold in the pan, place it securely on a shelf in the oven and use a kettle carefully to pour in sufficient boiling water to come two-thirds of the way up the sides of the mold. The pan can then be slid very slowly further back on the oven shelf.

□ When the mold has been in the oven for about 20 minutes (depending on the recipe) a sheet of foil can be loosely placed on top of the mold so that the surface does not become leathery or dry. Many molded puddings rely mainly on gelatin to ensure that they set firmly and unmold successfully.

top and turn the mold upside down on the plate, releasing it. Cover the surface of the rum cream mold completely with the caramelized orange slices and serve.

• • •

SPICED MOLASSES MOLD

Time: 1 hour 30 minutes
Easy

1 quart milk
1 cup cornstarch
½ cup (1 stick) butter
3 tbsp molasses
generous pinch ground ginger
1 tsp cinnamon
4 whole eggs and 1 extra white
1 cup confectioners' sugar
3 tbsp brandy
pinch nutmeg
1 cup heavy or whipping cream
salt

Mix the cornstarch with 1 cup of the milk and bring the rest

of the milk to a boil. Add the cornstarch and cold milk to the hot milk, stirring continuously, and continue cooking while stirring for 10 minutes. Remove from the heat; stir in 1½ tbsp of the butter, the molasses, ginger, cinnamon, a pinch of salt, and 4 lightly beaten eggs.

Grease an 8½-in mold lightly with butter and fill with the mixture. Place in a roasting pan containing hot water and cook at 320° F for 1 hour. Prepare the brandy sauce: with a hand-held electric beater beat the remaining butter with the confectioners' sugar over hot water until very pale and fluffy. Remove from the heat and beat in the brandy and nutmeg. When the mixture is cold, fold in 1 stiffly beaten egg white. Lastly, fold in the stiffly beaten cream. Turn the hot molasses mold out onto a heated serving plate and spoon the brandy sauce all round its base.

• • •

PINEAPPLE AND MARASCHINO COUPE

This dessert can be decorated by piping whipped cream through a fluted tube all over the surface, or served with a fresh fruit purée as a sauce. If maraschino cherries are unavailable, substitute canned cherries.

Time: 45 minutes + standing time
Easy

2¼ cups water
1 cup sugar
6 fresh pineapple slices

For the jellied custard:
4 egg yolks
1 cup sugar
2¼ cups milk
2 tbsp gelatin
1 Classic Sponge Cake (see page 146)
3 tbsp maraschino
¾ cup maraschino cherries

Boil the sugar and water together for 20 minutes. Remove from the heat. Cut each slice of pineapple into 4–6 pieces and add to the syrup.

213

Leave to stand for 3 hours. Beat the egg yolks with the sugar until pale and frothy; beat in the milk and heat slowly over very gently simmering water to thicken while stirring continuously (run a finger through the custard coating the back of the wooden spoon and if the trace remains clear, it is ready): do not allow to boil or the mixture will curdle. Take the double boiler off the heat and sprinkle the gelatin into the custard. Make sure this dissolves completely; stir well.

Cut the sponge cake into fairly thin slices; mix the maraschino with ½ cup of the syrup in which the pineapple has been soaking, dip the sponge slices briefly in this, and line a charlotte mold or similar type of mold neatly with them, leaving no gaps (but not overlapping any of the slices). Spoon a layer of the custard into the lined mold; drain the pineapple very thoroughly and place a layer of these pieces over the custard layer; top with a layer of sponge slices; continue layering in this order until all three components have been used up, finishing with a custard layer; level with a spatula and top with the cherries.

Chill for at least 3 hours before serving, preferably longer. Use a sharp knife and pastry slice when serving so that each helping emerges as a slice, surrounded on 2 sides by an edging of sponge cake.

• • •

CHOCOLATE SOUFFLÉ
■ *An economical, light and delicious dessert. Other spices can be substituted for cinnamon if preferred.*

CHOCOLATE AND POTATO SOUFFLÉ

Time: 1 hour 30 minutes
Very easy

1 lb floury potatoes
2 tbsp butter
2 tbsp all-purpose flour
¼ cup unsweetened cocoa
    powder
1 cup milk
½ cup sugar
pinch cinnamon
peel of 1 lemon, grated
4 eggs, separated

Wash but do not peel the potatoes; boil until very tender, drain, peel, and push through a sieve (or use a potato ricer) while still hot. Mix the potato in a saucepan with the butter; sift in the flour and cocoa powder together, and stir well over moderate heat. Stir in the milk a little at a time. Mix until thoroughly blended, then add the sugar, cinnamon, and lemon peel. Draw aside from the heat and allow to cool a little before beating in the egg yolks. Beat the egg whites stiffly and fold into the potato mixture. Grease 6 ramekins with butter, spoon the chocolate soufflé mixture into them, and place in a preheated oven (400° F) to bake for 20 minutes or until done. Serve immediately.

GELATIN

Gelatin is available in leaf or powdered form, and is used to set molded desserts. For the best results, always follow the manufacturer's instructions. Agar-agar or isinglass can be used as substitutes.

CHOCOLATE MASCARPONE DESSERT

A simple, yet elegant dessert. If mascarpone is not available, substitute very light fresh cream cheese (fromage frais) or quark. Sugar and water frosting can replace the cream topping.

Time: 1 hour 30 minutes
Very easy

¼ cup butter
3 cups dry breadcrumbs
½ cup sugar
7 oz (7 squares) bitter or
    semisweet chocolate
1¾ cups mascarpone
3 eggs, separated
¼ cup all-purpose flour
1 cup whipping cream
pinch salt

Melt the butter in a saucepan and mix in the breadcrumbs and 2 tbsp of the sugar. Sprinkle the base and sides of a 10-in cake pan with this mixture. Break half the chocolate into small pieces and melt slowly over hot water. Sieve the mascarpone, mix with the salt, half the remaining sugar, and the lightly beaten egg yolks. Beat in the melted chocolate. Beat the egg whites until firm; add the remaining sugar and continue beating until stiff. Mix gently but thoroughly with the mascarpone mixture using a wire whisk. Stir in the flour and ½ cup of the cream, stiffly beaten. Spoon this mixture carefully into the prepared pan and bake at 300° F for 1 hour. Turn off the oven but do not open the door, so that the

215

BANANAS
■ Nineteenth-century
engraving. Bananas have a
high vitamin content and are
very nutritious.

dessert cools very slowly.
Allow about 2 hours after
turning off the oven before
taking out the dessert; it
should be completely cold
before you unmold it. Beat the
remaining cream stiffly and
pipe decoratively around the
base and top of the dessert;
grate the rest of the chocolate
and sprinkle over it.

. . .

BREAD AND BUTTER PUDDING

*Never use very fresh bread for
this type of pudding; slightly
stale bread is easier to slice
thinly and absorbs the moisture
more evenly.*

*Time: 2 hours 30 minutes
Very easy*

½ cup currants or seedless
   white raisins
6 thin slices white or finely
   textured brown bread from
   a large loaf
3–4 tbsp butter, softened at
   room temperature
½ cup sugar
2¼ cups rich milk
1 cup light cream
small piece lemon peel (no
   pith)
4 eggs

Soak the currants or seedless
white raisins in cold water for
30 minutes to soften and
plump up; drain and squeeze
out excess moisture.
Spread the butter sparingly
over the bread slices; cut off
the crusts; cut into fingers
about 1½ × 3½ in or smaller if
wished. Grease a 9-in soufflé
mold with butter. Arrange
slices of bread in a single layer
to loosely cover the bottom of
the mold, buttered side

uppermost. Sprinkle with a
little sugar and some of the
currants or seedless white
raisins. Continue layering in
this way until all the
ingredients have been used
up, ending with a sprinkling of
sugar and currants or seedless
white raisins.
Mix the cream and milk with
any remaining sugar (add a
small pinch of nutmeg if
wished) and heat to scalding
point with the lemon peel.
Draw aside from the heat and
stir in the lightly beaten eggs.
Pour gently into the soufflé
mold and leave to stand for 1
hour.
Cook at 350° F for 1 hour or
until the pudding has risen up
in the soufflé dish and the top
is crisp and pale golden brown
(if preferred, bake in a
roasting pan containing hot
water but the top will not be
so crisp). Place the soufflé
mold on a serving plate with a

table napkin underneath it and
serve at once.

. . .

BANANA CREAM DESSERT

*Thick cream or pastry cream
(see page 44) can replace the
ricotta for a richer dessert;
decorate with strawberries
when in season.*

*Time: 10 minutes
Very easy*

4 ripe, unblemished bananas
juice of ½ lemon
1½ cups ricotta, sieved
½ cup sugar
½ cup heavy cream
⅓ cup Cointreau
6 canned apricot halves

Sieve the bananas and sprinkle
immediately with the lemon
juice (or reduce to a purée in a
blender with the lemon juice);

STRAWBERRIES,
ORANGES, AND LEMONS
■ When using citrus peel
make sure you leave all the
bitter white pith behind.

LIGHT DESSERTS

combine thoroughly with the
ricotta before stirring in the
sugar, cream, and Cointreau
very thoroughly with a
wooden spoon. The mixture
should be smooth and light.
Spoon into small, deep glass
dishes or coupes and chill for 2
hours in the refrigerator.
Decorate with the well-drained
apricot halves and serve.

• • •

STRAWBERRY MERINGUE MOLD

*Very simple and quick to
prepare; for a last-minute
dessert, use shop-bought
meringues.*

*Time: 10 minutes + time for
making the meringues
Very easy*

2¼ cups heavy or whipping
cream
¼ cup confectioners' sugar
8 meringues (see page 321)
¼ cup sugar
¾ lb strawberries
juice of ½ lemon

Line the base and sides of a
cake pan (preferably
springform) or soufflé mold
with silicone-treated nonstick
paper. Chill the cream well;
beat 1½ cups of it with
1½ tbsp of the confectioners'
sugar until very stiff.
Crush the meringue coarsely
and fold into the whipped
cream; place this mixture in
the prepared cake pan;
smooth the surface level with
a spatula and place a circle of
nonstick paper on top. Chill in
the coldest part of the
refrigerator (do not freeze) for
at least 2 hours. Rinse, dry,
and hull the strawberries;
place in a bowl and sprinkle
with the lemon juice and

sugar. Chill.

Just before serving, turn out the cream and meringue mold carefully onto a serving plate, removing the paper. Drain the strawberries and place on top of the mold; pipe the remaining cream, stiffly beaten and sweetened with the remaining confectioners' sugar, in a decorative pattern around the sides of the mold, using a fluted tube.

• • •

ALMOND AND MARRON GLACÉ CREAM GATEAU

For a change, arrange the sponge cake in alternate layers with the cream mixture in a mold (starting and ending with a sponge layer); chill for several hours and then unmold onto a serving plate.

Time: 20 minutes + 1 hour 15 minutes for the sponge cake
Easy

1 egg, separated
¼ cup sugar
½ cup mascarpone
1 cup marron glacé (candied chestnut) pieces (sold as marron débris)
3 tbsp maraschino or similar sweet liqueur
3 amaretti cookies or small crisp macaroons
1 cup whipping cream
1 Classic Sponge Cake (see page 146)
few whole marrons glacés or candied violets

Beat the egg yolk with all but 1½ tbsp of the sugar until pale and frothy; beat in the mascarpone. Stir in the chopped marron glacé pieces, 3 tbsp of the liqueur and the

218

crushed amaretti. Beat the egg white until stiff and fold into the egg, sugar and marron glacé mixture, then fold in the stiffly beaten cream. Chill in the refrigerator. Bring the remaining liqueur to a boil with ½ cup water and the remaining sugar. Cut the sponge cake into 3 layers; moisten each with a third of the syrup when it has cooled; spread a third of the cream mixture on each and reassemble the cake. Place the whole marrons glacés or candied violets on the top. Chill until ready to serve.

• • •

COCONUT BAVARIAN CREAM

*Time: 1 hour + chilling and
    setting time*
Easy

1 cup shredded coconut
2 tbsp gelatin powder
2¼ cups milk
4 eggs, separated
½ cup sugar
few drops vanilla extract
1 cup heavy or whipping
    cream
pinch salt

Spread the coconut out in a cookie sheet and bake in a moderate oven for a few minutes until very pale golden brown. Heat the milk to boiling point, draw aside from the heat and sprinkle in the gelatin. Make sure this dissolves completely, stirring well.
Place the egg yolks in a bowl, add the sugar and salt and beat with a wooden spoon until pale and fluffy. Beat in the hot milk and gelatin, adding a little at a

time. When the sugar has dissolved, stir in the vanilla, and leave to cool. Beat the egg whites stiffly; beat the cream until stiff in a separate bowl. When the milk and gelatin mixture is cold and just beginning to show signs of setting, stir in the coconut. Fold in the cream, then the egg whites; transfer to a rectangular mold which has been rinsed with cold water. Chill for several hours until completely set. Unmold just before serving (dip a cloth or towel in hot water, wring out and wrap round the mold to loosen, if necessary).

• • •

MASCARPONE BAVARIAN CREAM

*Although technically a fresh
cheese, mascarpone tastes more
like slightly acidulated thick
cream with a hint of natural
lactose sweetness; it is very
smooth and melts in the mouth.
Store and treat as fresh cream.
For a lower-fat substitute, use
ricotta.*

*Time: 30 minutes + chilling
    and setting time*
Very easy

3 tbsp seedless white raisins
1 whole egg and 2 extra yolks
1¼ cups mascarpone
½ cup sugar
3 tbsp pine nuts
3 tbsp shelled pistachio nuts
    (not roasted or salted)
3 tbsp rum
3 tbsp sweet white wine
½ lb ladyfingers

Soak the seedless white raisins in a bowl of warm water so that they plump up and soften. Mix the 3 egg

STRAWBERRY BAVARIAN
CREAM
■ Fruit-flavored Bavarian
cream molds make a perfect
dessert for a summer dinner
party. Apricot, raspberry, or
pear Bavarois (and other
flavors) can be made with this
recipe.

yolks one at a time into the mascarpone, stir in the sugar, and then beat thoroughly with a balloon whisk until light and aerated. Beat the egg white stiffly and fold gently into the mascarpone mixture. Add the well-drained seedless white raisins, the pine nuts, and pistachios.

Mix the rum and white wine together and dip the ladyfingers briefly in this as you use them to line an 8½-in deep rectangular mold or charlotte mold. Fill the lined mold with the mixture; level the surface and cover with greaseproof or waxed paper. Chill for at least 6 hours before unmolding and serving.

• • •

STRAWBERRY BAVARIAN CREAM

Time: 1 hour
Easy

2¼ lb strawberries
½ cup + 2 tbsp sugar
2 tbsp butter
3 tbsp gelatin powder
4 egg yolks
1 cup milk
1 cup whipping cream

Rinse the strawberries, dry and cook very gently with half the sugar in a covered saucepan. When mushy, push through a sieve. Beat the egg yolks energetically with the remaining sugar while heating the milk to scalding point; beat in the hot milk a little at a time. Heat gently to thicken while stirring continuously, do not allow to reach boiling point. Draw aside from the heat and sprinkle in the gelatin, making sure this dissolves totally; stir well. When cold, combine with the strawberry purée. Beat the cream stiffly and fold into the strawberry mixture. Rinse an 8½-in mold with cold water and fill with the strawberry cream. Chill for a few hours to set. Unmold onto a plate shortly before serving.

• • •

CHOCOLATE BAVARIAN CREAM

Time: 1 hour + setting time
Easy

2¼ cups milk
peel of 1 orange, grated
3 tbsp gelatin powder
5 oz (5 squares) bitter or
    semisweet chocolate
4 egg yolks
1 cup sugar

2¾ cups whipping cream
3 tbsp Grand Marnier
few roasted coffee beans
   (optional)

Place the milk and orange peel in a saucepan and bring to boiling point. Grate or chop the chocolate, place in a bowl over hot water, and add 1 cup of the hot milk to it. Leave to melt.
Beat the egg yolks with the sugar until pale and frothy; stir the milk and melted chocolate thoroughly and then gradually beat into the egg and sugar mixture; beat in the remaining hot milk a little at a time. Place over very low heat (or in a double boiler) and stir continuously with a wooden spoon until the custard coats the back of the spoon. Draw aside from the heat and sprinkle in the gelatin; make sure this dissolves; stir well. Strain through a fine sieve into a bowl and leave to cool. Beat all but ½ cup of the cream stiffly and fold into the cold chocolate mixture. Pour the Grand Marnier into a ring mold and tip this way and that so that the inner surface of the mold is moistened. Fill with the chocolate cream and chill in the coldest part of the refrigerator for at least 6 hours.
Shortly before serving, unmold onto a plate; fill the central well with the remaining cream, stiffly beaten, and decorate with a few coffee beans.

•   •   •

DIPLOMAT PUDDING

Rice puddings are straightforward and always popular; this is just one of the hundreds of variations on rice pudding.

Time: 1 hour + chilling time
Easy

2¼ cups milk
½ cup sugar
½ cup pudding (short-grain) rice
1 cup unsweetened cocoa powder
1 cup whipping cream
1 Classic Sponge Cake (see page 146) using half quantities of listed ingredients
3 tbsp liqueur of choice

Bring the milk slowly to boiling point with the sugar and sprinkle in the rice; cook

EGGS

To test for freshness, lower an egg into a small bowl of cold water; if it lies at the bottom it is fresh, if it floats it is bad.

221

COFFEE BAVARIAN
CREAM
■ Made to the same recipe
as chocolate Bavarian
cream, substituting half a cup
of very strong, best-quality
coffee for the chocolate. In
both cases coffee beans
make an effective
decoration. Always use the
best ingredients for flavoring
and avoid cheap synthetic
substitutes.

slowly, stirring frequently, until the rice has absorbed all the milk and is very tender (use a double boiler if preferred). Draw aside from the heat and stir in the sifted cocoa powder.

Beat half the cream stiffly. Cut the sponge cake into slices; arrange a layer of these in a mold, sprinkle with a little liqueur, and cover with a layer of the rice, followed by a layer of whipped cream and continue layering until all the rice and sponge cake have been used up. Tap the bottom of the mold on the work surfaces to make the contents settle as you fill it. Chill for several hours, until just before serving; unmold and decorate with the rest of the cream, stiffly beaten and piped through a fluted tube.

• • •

VANILLA PUDDING

This delicate and digestible dessert can be chilled in a ring mold, unmolded just before serving and the central well filled with a chocolate or fruit sauce.

Time: 1 hour + chilling time
Very easy

3 tbsp gelatin powder
1 cup peeled whole almonds
½ cup sugar
2¼ cups milk
1½ tsp vanilla extract
2¼ cups whipping cream
¾ lb blueberries

Place the almonds, 3 tbsp of the sugar, ½ cup of the milk and ¼ cup water in a blender and process until the mixture

becomes a smooth thin paste. Bring the rest of the milk to a boil, remove from the heat, sprinkle in the gelatin and make sure this dissolves completely. Stir well. Add the vanilla and the almond mixture, stir, and leave to cool slowly. When cold and just beginning to set, fold in the stiffly beaten cream. Rinse an 8½-in mold with cold water and fill with the vanilla and almond cream; chill for several hours. Unmold shortly before serving with a fresh sauce of the sieved blueberries (use a nonmetallic sieve).

• • •

AMARETTO CREAM DESSERT

The chocolate sprinkles can be replaced with grated bitter chocolate or chopped, roasted filberts or almonds.

Time: 15 minutes
Very easy

1 cup whipping cream
½ lb amaretti or crisp macaroons
1 cup fresh ricotta cheese, sieved
¼ cup sugar
3 tbsp rum
½ cup chocolate sprinkles

Beat the cream stiffly. Reduce the amaretti to a coarse powder in the food processor (or crush). Beat the ricotta and sugar together with a wooden spoon until light and well blended. Stir in the amaretti and the rum. Fold in the whipped cream. Spoon into individual deep glass dishes or glasses; sprinkle the

chocolate on top and chill until it is time to serve.

• • •

RASPBERRY AND OATMEAL CREAM

When raspberries are unavailable, diced melon can be substituted.

Time: 15 minutes + soaking time
Very easy

1 quart milk
1½ cups quick-rolled oats
1 cup filberts
3 tbsp sugar
generous pinch salt
6 tbsp raspberry or red currant jelly
½ lb raspberries

Soak the oats in the cold milk overnight. Finely chop (or process) the filberts, reserving 6 whole nuts for decoration. Place the oats and milk in a saucepan with the sugar and salt and bring to a boil; reduce the heat and cook for 10 minutes, stirring frequently. Draw aside from the heat and stir in the chopped or ground filberts and the raspberry or red currant jelly. Spoon into small heated bowls, top with the washed and dried raspberries, and decorate each serving with a filbert.

• • •

CHOCOLATE AND ORANGE RICOTTA PUDDING

Ricotta can be dense and difficult to mix with other ingredients unless it is first

sieved and beaten with a wooden spoon.

Time: 20 minutes
Easy

1 cup fresh ricotta cheese, sieved
3 tbsp sugar
3 tbsp Grand Marnier
½ lb (8 squares) bitter chocolate
12 amaretti or ratafia cookies
2¼ cups whipping cream
¼ cup confectioners' sugar

Beat the ricotta in a large bowl with a wooden spoon until soft; mix in the sugar a little at a time, followed by the Grand Marnier. Chop the chocolate and melt over hot water, then stir into the ricotta mixture. Stir in the finely crumbled or processed amaretti. Beat the cream until stiff and fold all but approx. 1½ cups (measured when beaten) into the ricotta mixture.

Heap up on a serving plate in a dome shape, smoothing the surface with a spatula (or transfer to a glass bowl) and decorate with the remaining cream, piped with a fluted tube into rosettes all over the surface. Chill.

• • •

CINNAMON GNOCCHI

These very light, subtly spiced gnocchi can also be served with a fresh fruit purée (sieved peaches or apricots) spooned over them just before they are placed in the oven. If a sauce is added, omit the butter and sprinkle the cinnamon over the fruit sauce.

Time: 40 minutes
Very easy

ORANGE AND RAISIN PANCAKES

Pour the milk, cream, and Grand Marnier into a bowl; sift in the flour, sugar, and salt, stirring well.

Beat the egg yolks and white very thoroughly before combining with the batter.

Leave to stand for about 1 hour.

Melt the butter over hot water and stir into the batter just before making the pancakes.

Heat a skillet with a little oil or clarified butter. Add a small ladleful of batter (3–4 tbsp); quickly tip the pan this way and that to distribute the batter thinly and evenly.

Fry until pale golden brown on the underside, then turn and fry the other side. Repeat until all the batter has been used up.

Orange pancakes: mix the butter, sugar, grated peel, and brandy in a small saucepan. Cook over low heat until thickened. Spread each pancake with about 1 tbsp. of this filling, roll up, and arrange on a heated serving plate. Peeled, sliced fresh or cooked oranges can be used for decoration or as additional filling.

Raisin pancakes: soak the raisins in the brandy for 30 minutes; cook the butter and sugar together in a small pan until the sugar has completely dissolved. Add the seedless white raisins together with the brandy, and continue cooking gently for a few minutes, stirring well. Sprinkle a little of this mixture on each pancake; roll up and sprinkle with the remainder.

*ORANGE AND RAISIN
PANCAKES*
■ *See the step-by-step recipe
on the opposite page. Right:
the finished pancake ready
for serving.*

2¼ cups milk
1 cup cream
6 egg yolks
½ cup sugar
1 cup cornstarch
peel of 1 lemon, grated
pinch salt
1 tsp cinnamon
3 tbsp butter

Heat the milk and cream together to scalding point. Beat the egg yolks with all but 2 tbsp of the sugar. Stir in the cornstarch, lemon peel, and salt, using a wooden spoon. Add the hot milk and cream a little at a time, mixing well. Place the bowl over boiling water and bring to a boil, stirring continuously. Pour the thickened mixture into a wide shallow straight-sided dish: it should be approx. ⅜ in deep. Leave to cool and set; use a 2-in plain round cookie cutter or glass dipped in cold water to cut out as many disks as possible and transfer these to a buttered ovenproof pan. Sprinkle with the cinnamon and the melted butter; heat for 10 minutes at 400° F and serve hot.

•   •   •

CHOCOLATE MERINGUES

Serve these as classic meringues with the cream sandwiched between them or pipe into two disks, using the cream as a filling between these two layers; decorate with piped cream and cherries.

*Time: 2 hours 15 minutes
Easy*

6 egg whites
5 cups confectioners' sugar
½ cup unsweetened cocoa powder
1 tbsp butter
1 tbsp all-purpose flour
1¼ cups whipping cream

Beat the egg whites until very firm; continue to beat as you add the sifted confectioners' sugar (reserve ¼ cup for later use) a little at a time and the sifted cocoa. Grease a sheet of foil with butter and dust with flour; use to cover a cookie sheet. Use a pastry bag and large fluted tube to pipe the meringue mixture into large rosettes on the cookie sheet. Sift the remaining sugar directly onto the uncooked meringues, dusting them lightly with it; blow away as much loose sugar which falls onto the greased and floured foil as possible. Bake at 200° F, keeping the oven door slightly ajar for about 2 hours, so that the meringues dry out and set but do not color. Remove from the foil and leave to cool. Beat the cream stiffly and sandwich the meringues together in pairs with the cream in the middle.

•   •   •

CHOCOLATE TRUFFLE DESSERT

This is a very rich and filling dessert which forms quite a hard outer shell and a very soft, luscious interior. Add a little crème de menthe or rum to the melted chocolate instead of the orange peel if you wish.

*Time: 1 hour 30 minutes
Easy*

14 oz (14 squares) bitter chocolate
1 cup (2 sticks) butter

COFFEE
■ A sprig from the bush showing flowers and fruits in various stages of development (eighteenth-century engraving).

Combine 2–3 tbsp of the stiffly beaten egg whites with this mixture, then fold into the remaining beaten whites. Preheat the oven to 480° F. Line a mold with greaseproof or waxed paper lightly greased with melted butter on the exposed side; fill with the chocolate mixture. Cook for 15 minutes, then lower the temperature to 350° F for another 15 minutes' cooking. When the dessert has cooled, unmold, remove the paper, and chill for at least 24 hours. Beat the sifted cocoa powder with the softened butter; pipe decoratively over the dessert and serve.

• • •

COFFEE AND ALMOND PUDDING

Time: 30 minutes + chilling time
Very easy

1 cup peeled whole almonds
1 cup (2 sticks) butter, softened
½ cup sugar
4 egg yolks and 1 egg white
⅓ cup confectioners' sugar
1 cup very strong black coffee
1 cup sweet dessert wine (e.g. Muscat de Beaumes de Venise or California Muscat)
½ lb ladyfingers

Spread the almonds out on a cookie sheet and place in a moderate oven for a few minutes to color lightly. Chop finely. Beat the butter with the sugar until very pale and creamy. Beat in the egg yolks one at a time. Beat 1 egg

peel of 1 orange, finely grated
½ cup sugar
¼ cup kirsch
3 eggs, separated
¼ cup unsweetened cocoa powder
½ cup (1 stick) butter, softened at room temperature

Chop the chocolate into small pieces and melt over hot (not boiling water) with 1 cup (2 sticks) butter and the orange peel.
Allow the chocolate to cool a little before stirring in the sugar and the kirsch. Stir in the egg yolks one at a time.

COFFEE CHARLOTTE MALAKOFF
■ *Ladyfingers are not difficult to find in good foodstores if you do not wish to make your own. Chocolate-flavored custard makes a pleasant alternative to coffee.*

white stiffly and continue beating while adding the sifted confectioners' sugar; fold this into the butter mixture together with half the almonds.

Mix the coffee with the wine and dip the ladyfingers in this one at a time, using them to cover the bottom of a wide glass bowl; spoon a layer of the prepared mixture on top; cover with another layer of dipped ladyfingers; continue layering until the ingredients have been used up ending with the egg and butter mixture. Sprinkle the remaining almonds on top. Chill for a few hours before serving.

• • •

COFFEE CHARLOTTE MALAKOFF

Slices of Classic Sponge Cake (page 146) can replace the ladyfingers to lend body and firmness to this simple but delicious dessert. Decorate with rosettes of cream and coffee beans after unmolding.

Time: 2 hours
Very easy

1 quart milk
2¼ cups heavy cream
1 cup very strong black coffee
½ lb ladyfingers, crumbled
¼ lb amaretti or crisp
   macaroons, crumbled
3 eggs
½ cup sugar
pinch salt
1 tbsp sweet almond oil
whipped cream and coffee
   beans (optional)

Heat the milk, cream, and coffee together in a saucepan to scalding point (do not allow

to boil). Draw aside from the heat then sprinkle in the crumbled sponge fingers and amaretti. Beat the eggs lightly with the sugar, add a small pinch of salt, and combine with the contents of the saucepan. Lightly oil a charlotte mold with the almond oil; fill with the coffee mixture; place the mold in a roasting pan and add sufficient boiling water to come about 1 in up the sides of the mold. Bake at 350° F for 1½ hours or until a thin skewer inserted deep into the

dessert comes out clean. Remove from the oven and leave to cool. Unmold carefully onto a serving plate. Decorate with whipped cream and coffee beans, if wished.

• • •

MARSALA PUDDING

This can also be served as a charlotte: line a charlotte mold neatly with ladyfingers, fill with the Marsala mixture, and chill for several hours; unmold to serve.

Time: 40 minutes + chilling time
Very easy

6 hardboiled egg yolks
1 cup mascarpone
½ cup sugar
2–3 drops vanilla extract
3 tbsp maraschino
1 cup sweet Marsala
1 Classic Sponge Cake (see
   page 146)
½ cup unsweetened cocoa
   powder

Hardboil 6 eggs; run plenty of cold water onto the hot eggs to cool quickly. Extract the yolks and crush with a fork in a bowl; mix with the mascarpone (which should be at room temperature). Add the sugar and vanilla and stir very thoroughly until creamy, adding the maraschino a little at a time.

Rinse the inside of a glass soufflé mold with a little of the Marsala; place a layer of half the sponge cake, thinly sliced, in the bottom of the mold; moisten with some more of the Marsala. Cover with a layer of half the egg and mascarpone mixture. Cover with the rest of the sponge slices, dipped into the Marsala. Add the sifted cocoa to the rest of the mascarpone mixture and stir well. Spread over the sponge cake layer, smooth level, and chill the dessert for at least 12 hours before serving.

• • •

STREGA DESSERT

Strega is an Italian liqueur made with herbs; this dessert can also be made with any other sweet liqueur.

*Time: 20 minutes + chilling
   time*
Very easy

2 cups ricotta, sieved

1 cup sugar
½ cup Strega or liqueur of
   choice
1 tbsp vanilla extract
⅓ cup candied fruit or peel
¼ lb (4 squares) bitter or
   semisweet chocolate
1 Classic Sponge Cake (see
   page 146)
4 oz (4 squares) white
   chocolate

Beat the ricotta and sugar with a wooden spoon; stir in half the liqueur and the vanilla. Transfer half this mixture to another bowl and combine with the candied fruit or peel and the chopped dark chocolate.

Cut the sponge cake into thin slices and arrange in a layer in the bottom of a serving bowl; sprinkle with some of the remaining liqueur and cover with a layer of half the plain ricotta mixture; follow with another layer of sponge cake moistened with the liqueur; place half of the ricotta which was mixed with the fruit and chocolate on top and continue layering until all the ingredients have been used up, ending with a layer of sponge cake. Decorate the surface with white chocolate curls (shave off the chocolate with a broad-bladed sharp knife). Chill well.

• • •

CHOCOLATE PEARS

Time: 30 minutes
Very easy

6 firm pears
½ cup sieved raspberry jam
4 eggs, separated
½ cup sugar
8 oz (8 squares) bitter or

CHOCOLATE PEARS
■ A simple but visually stunning end to a meal. Sliced kiwi fruit are an exotic alternative to pears.

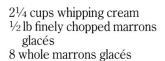

semisweet chocolate
2¼ cups milk
3 tbsp confectioners' sugar

Peel the pears and place them in an ovenproof pan. Melt the raspberry jam gently and sieve, covering each pear with 1½ tbsp of the jam. Cook at 350° F for about 30 minutes or until the pears are tender. Place the egg yolks in a small saucepan, beat with the sugar until pale and frothy; chop the chocolate and melt over hot water; stir into the egg mixture; beat in the milk a little at a time. Heat over hot water, stirring continuously, to thicken somewhat; do not allow to boil. Draw aside from the heat and leave to cool. Beat the egg whites until firm, continue beating while adding the confectioners' sugar and fold into the chocolate mixture. Dip the pears in this mixture so that it completely coats them; leave until the covering has set and then decorate with strawberries (optional) as illustrated (left).

• • •

MARRON GLACÉ MOUSSE

Marron glacé pieces cost much less than the whole perfect candied chestnuts. Substitute coarsely crumbled amaretti if preferred.

Time: 30 minutes + chilling time
Very easy

4 egg yolks
½ cup sugar
1½ tsp potato flour or cornstarch
2¼ cups hot milk
2 tbsp gelatin powder

2¼ cups whipping cream
½ lb finely chopped marrons glacés
8 whole marrons glacés

Beat the egg yolks with the sugar until pale and frothy. Stir in the potato flour or cornstarch and then add the hot milk a little at a time. Heat over very low heat or gently simmering water to thicken; do not allow to boil. Draw aside from the heat and sprinkle in the gelatin. Stir well until completely dissolved. Leave to cool, stirring from time to time. Beat half the cream until stiff, fold in the chopped marrons glacés, and then fold this into the cold custard mixture. Rinse the inside of a charlotte mold with cold water; do not dry. Fill with the mixture and chill for at least 6 hours. Carefully unmold the mousse onto a serving plate; beat the remaining cream and pipe over the mousse; decorate with the whole marrons glacés.

• • •

CHOCOLATE DELIGHT

For a more elegant presentation, chill this dessert for several hours in a bombe mold and then unmold.

Time: 20 minutes
Very easy

2 cups ricotta, sieved
¼ cup unsweetened cocoa powder
½ cup sugar
3 tbsp liqueur of choice
1 cup finely crushed amaretti
1 cup whipping cream
⅓ cup confectioners' sugar

229

RASPBERRIES AND RED
CURRANTS
■ All the edible berry fruits
provide a valuable source of
vitamins besides being
delicious.

Place the sieved ricotta in a bowl and beat with a wooden spoon until soft and light; stir in the sifted cocoa powder, the sugar and the liqueur a little at a time. Add the amaretti and mix well.

Beat the cream, fold in the sifted confectioners' sugar, and combine half this sweetened whipped cream (reserve the rest for decoration) with the ricotta mixture. Heap up in a mound on a serving plate, smoothing the surface with a spatula. Pipe the rest of the whipped cream in small rosettes all over the surface of the dessert.

• • •

RASPBERRY AND SEMOLINA DESSERT

If frozen raspberries are used for this recipe, sieve all of them, and reserve half this purée with which to surround the base of the semolina mold.

Time: 1 hour
Easy

2¼ cups milk
1 cup sweet white wine
½ cup semolina
peel of 1 lemon, grated
½ cup sugar
¾–1 lb raspberries
2 egg whites
pinch salt

Heat the milk, wine, and salt to boiling point. Sprinkle in the semolina while stirring continuously to avoid lumps forming. Cook for 20 minutes over gentle heat. Remove from the heat, stir in the lemon peel and half the sugar;

leave to cool. Place the raspberries in a bowl and sprinkle with the rest of the sugar; chill in the refrigerator. Beat the egg whites stiffly and fold into the semolina; push half the raspberries through a nonmetallic sieve and stir these gently into the semolina. Rinse out a mold with cold water and fill with the semolina mixture. Chill for several hours before unmolding. Surround with the remaining raspberries.

• • •

ORANGE BREAD PUDDING

Use bread from a slightly stale white loaf for this pudding.

Time: 1 hour 30 minutes
Very easy

2¼ cups milk
½ lb white bread
½ cup seedless white raisins
juice of 2 oranges
4 eggs
peel of 1 orange, grated
½ cup sugar
1 tbsp butter
1½ cups marmalade
3 tbsp rum
⅓ cup water
pinch salt

Heat the milk gently until warm. Cut the crusts off the bread and cut into cubes; place in a large bowl and pour the warm milk over it. Leave to stand for about 10 minutes. Soak the seedless white raisins in warm water.
Stir the strained orange juice into the bread and milk; mix well; add the drained and squeezed seedless white raisins, lightly beaten eggs, orange peel, sugar, and salt

and stir thoroughly. Grease a mold with the butter and fill with the bread mixture. Stand in a roasting pan; add sufficient boiling water to the pan to come halfway up the mold and bake for 1 hour at 350° F or until a skewer pushed deep into the pudding comes out clean and dry. Melt the marmalade with the rum and water; heat, stirring with a wooden spoon, for 1 minute. Unmold the pudding onto a heated serving plate and pour the hot sauce over it.

• • •

MERINGUE LAYER DESSERT

Pipe the meringue using a fairly large plain tube, starting from the center and working outward to form a disk; dip a spatula in cold water and smooth the surface.

Time: 2 hours
Fairly easy

7 egg whites
2¾ cups confectioners' sugar
4 drops lemon juice
¾ cup walnut pieces
½ lb strawberries
2¼ cups whipping cream
¼ cup sugar
approx. ¼ lb sponge cake
    (bought or homemade, see
    page 146)
3 tbsp brandy
pinch salt

Chill the egg whites before starting to beat on low speed; continue beating as you add the salt, lemon juice, and, a little at a time, the sifted confectioners' sugar. Increase the speed setting and beat until very stiff and glossy. A knife cut through the meringue mixture should leave a clear trace.
Place a sheet of nonstick paper on a cookie sheet and draw 2 circles 8 in in diameter. Use a pastry bag and tube (see above) and pipe out 2 disks of meringue; refill the pastry bag when necessary. Smooth. Place in the oven at 140° F with the door slightly ajar to dry out very slowly and harden. This will take about 1–1½ hours. Leave to cool when done.
Chop the walnuts finely (do not grind). Hull the strawberries. Beat the cream stiffly, adding the granulated sugar. Place a meringue layer on a serving plate; cover with half the cream; top with half the strawberries, all the walnuts, and the sponge cake (crumbled and moistened with the brandy). Place the other meringue layer on top and spread the remaining cream over the top and sides of the cake. Chill for 2 hours before serving.

• • •

RICE RING WITH FRUIT SAUCE

This dessert must be served piping hot as soon as it is ready. If you cannot be sure of using untreated (unsprayed) lemons, use a few drops of essential oil of lemon or pure lemon extract instead, or the rice may have a slightly bitter taste.

Time: 1 hour 30 minutes
Easy

1 lemon
1 cup pudding (short-grain)
    rice
1 quart milk
2–3 drops vanilla extract
4 eggs, separated
1 cup sugar
2½ tbsp butter

ORANGE MOUSSE

Quantities given are for 5 servings.

3 leaves isinglass or 1 tbsp gelatin powder
¼ cup hot (not boiling) water
2 egg yolks
¼ cup sugar
1¼ cups milk
¼ cup Grand Marnier
2 egg whites

For the orange sauce:
½ cup sugar
½ cup orange juice
2 egg yolks
1 cup heavy or whipping cream

Place the isinglass in the hot water in a small bowl and leave to soften. If using gelatin, remember to pour the hot water into the bowl first and then sprinkle the gelatin into it; make sure the gelatin has completely dissolved.

Beat the egg yolks with the sugar until very pale and frothy. Heat the milk to scalding point (below boiling point) and add to the egg and sugar mixture in a thin stream, beating continuously.

Stir in the liqueur and add the softened isinglass leaves or stir in the completely dissolved gelatin.

If isinglass is used, place the bowl in another, larger bowl containing very hot water and leave until the isinglass has completely dissolved. If gelatin has been used, set the bowl aside in a cool place until it is just beginning to thicken and set.

Beat the egg whites until stiff but not dry.

Fold the orange custard mixture gently into the egg whites (if isinglass is used you do not have to wait for it to show signs of setting).

Ladle into small molds, previously rinsed out with cold water, and leave to set in the refrigerator.

Make the orange sauce: Heat the sugar and orange juice gently until the sugar has completely dissolved.

Draw aside from the heat before beating in the egg yolks; continue beating vigorously until the mixture thickens somewhat.

Leave in a cool place and when cold, fold gently but thoroughly into the stiffly beaten cream.

To serve: unmold the orange mousses into a wide, flat-bottomed and fairly deep dish; pour the sauce evenly into the dish, between the mousses or all over them as you prefer.

2 peaches
2 pears
pinch salt

Boil the whole, unpeeled lemon until it is tender enough to push through a nonmetallic sieve. This will take some time.

Meanwhile, bring a large saucepan of lightly salted water to a boil and sprinkle in the rice; cook for 5 minutes, drain, and place in a saucepan with the milk and vanilla. Cook for about 20 minutes, stirring frequently, until all the moisture has been absorbed. Beat the egg yolks with half the sugar until pale and fluffy. Stir the lemon purée into the rice, followed by the egg mixture and 1½ tbsp butter. Fold in the stiffly beaten egg whites.

Use the remaining butter to grease a 9-in ring mold; fill evenly with the rice. Stand in a pan of hot water (which should come about half way up the side of the mold) and bake at 350° F for 1 hour or until done. Prepare the fruit sauce: peel, pit, and core the fruit; cut into small pieces and cook gently with the rest of the sugar, stirring frequently, for 10 minutes. Sieve. Turn the rice ring onto a hot serving plate and pour the hot fruit sauce into the central well. Serve immediately.

• • •

FLAMED APPLE CHARLOTTE

Time: 1 hour 30 minutes
Easy

½ cup seedless white raisins
6 apples (Calville, Rennet,

Granny Smith or Golden Delicious)
½ cup sugar
½ cup white wine
1 cup milk
½ lb slightly stale white bread
¼ cup (½ stick) butter
½ cup rum
½ cup pine nuts

Soak the seedless white raisins in warm water. Peel, core, and slice the apples into a saucepan. Sprinkle with half the sugar and all the wine, and add 1 cup water. Cook gently, uncovered, for about 15 minutes or until tender but not mushy. Drain, pouring the cooking liquid into a bowl. Add the milk to this liquid and dip the thinly sliced (about ¾ in thick) bread briefly in it before using some of it to line the bottom and sides of a well-buttered charlotte mold (use 1½ tbsp of the butter for this). Spoon a layer of apples into the mold, sprinkle some well-drained raisins and some pine nuts on top. Melt the remaining butter in a small saucepan; add the remaining sugar and half the rum. Sprinkle some of this liquid over the next layer, formed of a few slices of the remaining bread; continue layering and sprinkling in this way until all the ingredients have been used up, ending with a complete layer of bread. Press the contents of the mold gently and bake at 350° F, standing in a shallow pan of hot water, for 1 hour. Remove from the oven; leave to stand and "set" for 5 minutes. Unmold onto a very hot serving plate. Pour the heated rum over the charlotte and flame it.

• • •

FLAMED APPLE
CHARLOTTE
■ Flambéed desserts never
fail to impress. Heat the rum
well or it will not flame.

RICH CHESTNUT PUDDING

This dessert is delicious but rich; best served after a light main course.

Time: 2 hours + chilling time
Very easy

1¼ lb sweet chestnuts
2¼ cups milk
½ cup sugar
1 cup ricotta, sieved
1½ tbsp instant coffee powder
¼ cup unsweetened cocoa
  powder
3 tbsp liqueur of choice
small pinch salt

Remove the tough outer skin and boil the chestnuts in lightly salted boiling water until tender and slightly floury to the taste. Remove the thin inner skin while they are still hot. (Some people prefer to pierce the outer skin and remove it after the chestnuts have cooked.) Place the chestnuts in a saucepan with the milk and half the sugar; cook for 10 minutes, crushing the chestnuts with a fork as they cook to help them absorb the milk. Push through a sieve; if the mixture is not very thick indeed, cook a little longer after sieving.
Line a 10-in cake pan with greaseproof or nonstick paper; pack the chestnut mixture firmly into this, leveling the surface. Mix the ricotta with the coffee, sifted cocoa, remaining sugar and the liqueur. Beat well with a wooden spoon until smooth. Spoon on top of the chestnut layer, pressing down well to avoid air pockets. Smooth the surface and place a circle of non stick paper on top. Chill

for 6 hours or longer before unmolding onto a serving plate.

• • •

STRAWBERRY CHARLOTTE

A very light dessert; the strawberries could be mixed with more cream to make it richer.

Time: 20 minutes + standing and chilling time
Very easy

1 lb strawberries
⅓ cup sugar
3 tbsp kirsch or liqueur of
  choice
1 cup sweet white wine
1 cup orange juice
¾ lb ladyfingers
1 cup whipping cream

Rinse, dry, and hull the strawberries; slice them into a bowl and sprinkle with the sugar. Mix the kirsch with the wine and orange juice and pour over the fruit. Leave to stand for 1–2 hours. Drain, reserving the liquid, and dip the ladyfingers in this one by one as you use them to cover the bottom of a 10-in mold or straight-sided dish. Cover with a layer of strawberries and continue layering the sponge cake and fruit, ending with a sponge layer. Chill for at least 3 hours. Unmold onto a serving plate. Beat the cream stiffly and use a pastry bag and fluted tube to decorate the charlotte.

• • •

COFFEE CHARLOTTE

A jellied charlotte which looks most attractive.

Time: 20 minutes + chilling time
Very easy

3 tbsp gelatin powder
½ cup very strong black
  coffee
½ cup milk
½ cup sugar
5 oz ladyfingers
3 egg whites
1 cup heavy or whipping
  cream

Heat the coffee and milk together to scalding point; remove from the heat and sprinkle in the gelatin; allow this to dissolve completely,

stirring well. Stir in 2 tbsp of the sugar and leave to cool a little. Dip the ladyfingers briefly in this one by one and use them to line a charlotte mold.
Beat the egg whites until firm and continue beating as you gradually add the rest of the sugar until stiff and glossy. Beat the cream stiffly in a separate bowl. Mix the remaining coffee mixture gently into the cream and then fold into the meringue mixture; fill the lined mold with this. Chill for at least 2 hours until set firm. Unmold onto a serving plate; decorate with rosettes of stiffly beaten cream if wished.

• • •

RHUBARB CHARLOTTE

If rhubarb is too acid for your taste, try sweetening it with honey. Use only the stalks, never the leaves.

Time: 1 hour 30 minutes
Very easy

2¼ lb tender rhubarb stalks
1¼ cups sugar
¼ cup melted butter
½ lb slightly stale white bread, thinly sliced
1 cup milk

Wash and trim the rhubarb, dry well, and cut into ¾-in lengths. Cook gently in a nonmetallic saucepan, uncovered, with the sugar and 1 tbsp butter for about 20 minutes (if using honey ½ cup should be enough).
Grease a charlotte mold with a little butter. Trim the crusts off the bread slices and dip extremely briefly in the milk one at a time as you use them to line the bottom and sides of the mold. Sprinkle this lining with a little melted butter. Fill with the rhubarb and cover neatly with the remaining bread slices.
Sprinkle the remaining melted butter on top; cook at 350° F for 1 hour; the top should be crisp and golden brown. Allow to rest for a few minutes before unmolding carefully onto a heated serving plate.

• • •

CHERRY RICE RING

The central well could be filled with more cooked cherries or with a sauce (melt some cherry preserve gently with a little kirsch or maraschino).

Time: 1 hour 30 minutes
Very easy

1 cup pudding (short-grain) rice
1 quart milk

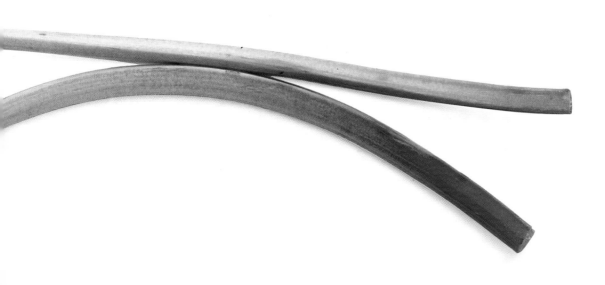

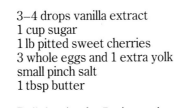

3–4 drops vanilla extract
1 cup sugar
1 lb pitted sweet cherries
3 whole eggs and 1 extra yolk
small pinch salt
1 tbsp butter

Boil the rice for 5 minutes in a large pan of lightly salted water; while it is cooking, bring the milk to a boil. Drain the rice and add to the milk. Flavor with the vanilla and cook over low heat until very thick and sticky, stirring frequently. Add half the sugar, mix well and leave to cool. Cook the cherries with the remaining sugar and ½ cup water for 10 minutes. Beat the eggs and the extra yolk together with a small pinch salt; stir into the rice. Grease a ring mold with butter; spoon a fairly deep layer of rice into the mold, followed by a layer of the drained cherries. Spoon in two more layers in the same way and then a final layer of rice. (You may prefer to have three layers only: rice, cherries, rice). Place the mold in a pan; pour in enough boiling water to come half way up the outside of the mold and cook in the oven at 350° F for 1 hour. When cold turn out the mold.

• • •

BANANA PUDDING

Take care when you start cooking the semolina or corn meal, as it can lump easily: stir quickly with a wooden spoon or beat with a wire whisk as you add it, or cook in a double boiler.

Time: 1 hour 30 minutes
Easy

1 quart milk
small pinch salt
1 cup semolina or corn meal
¼ cup (½ stick) butter
½ cup sugar
peel of 1 lemon, grated
4 eggs
2 bananas
juice of ½ lemon
1½ tbsp breadcrumbs

Bring the milk to a boil with the salt; sprinkle in the semolina or corn meal while stirring quickly; cook for 20 minutes, stirring almost continuously. Draw aside from the heat and stir in all but 1½ tbsp of the butter, all the sugar, and the lemon peel. Leave to cool a little before adding the lightly beaten eggs, one at a time, and stirring very thoroughly.
Slice the bananas and sprinkle with the lemon juice to

prevent discoloration. Use the remaining butter to grease a charlotte or soufflé mold; sprinkle the breadcrumbs all over the inside of the mold. Arrange the semolina and bananas in layers, starting and finishing with a semolina layer. Cook for 1 hour at 350° F, standing the mold in a roasting pan half-filled with boiling water. Turn out and serve.

• • •

RASPBERRY MOUSSE

Time: 20 minutes
Very easy

1 lb raspberries
1 cup whipping cream
½ cup sugar
1 cup mascarpone

Reserve ¾ cup of the raspberries for decoration; push the rest through a nonmetallic sieve. Beat the cream until firm, continue beating as you add the sugar, followed by the raspberry purée and the mascarpone. Spoon into a glass bowl or individual coupes and chill for 2 hours. Decorate with the reserved raspberries and serve.

• • •

STRAWBERRY PANCAKES

Time: 30 minutes
Very easy

1 cup all-purpose flour
3 tbsp sugar
pinch salt
3 eggs
generous 1 cup milk
½ cup (1 stick) butter
20 strawberries

Sift the flour into a large bowl; stir in the sugar and the salt. Continue stirring while adding the lightly beaten eggs and milk a little at a time, to give a thick pouring batter. Melt all but 1½ tbsp of the butter gently in a small saucepan; draw aside from the heat and allow to cool a little. Beat the melted butter into the batter. Grease a skillet approx. 6–6½ in in diameter with a little of the remaining butter. Heat the skillet; pour in ¼ cup batter, tipping the pan every which way to coat the base with a very thin layer of batter. Reduce the heat; turn the pancake when ready to cook on the second side. Slide onto a hot plate and repeat until all the batter has been used. Coarsely chop the strawberries; spoon onto the pancakes and then roll these up one by one, transferring them to a wide, shallow ovenproof pan greased with butter. Place in a preheated oven for 2–3 minutes at the hottest setting. Remove and serve.

• • •

APRICOT EGGS

Ideal for a summer lunch or brunch.

Time: 30 minutes
Very easy

½ cup sugar
½ cup water
6 large ripe apricots
1 large piece lemon peel
¾ lb mascarpone
3 tbsp butter
6 slices white bread from a
    small loaf

Heat the sugar and water; slice the apricots almost in half, leaving the two halves attached, and pit. Simmer very gently for 5 minutes in the sugar syrup. Remove the fruit with a slotted ladle; add the lemon peel to the syrup and boil to reduce and thicken. Stir the mascarpone well with a wooden spoon, add the sugar syrup a little at a time (discard the lemon peel), and transfer this mixture to a pastry bag with a large tube. Fry the bread slices in the butter; allow to cool a little before piping a wide raised border of the mascarpone inside the edges of each slice; pipe a little mascarpone into each apricot, close the two halves together and place an apricot in the middle of each bread slice so that it looks rather like a fried egg, sunny side up. Serve.

• • •

CINNAMON APPLE SNOW

This light and fluffy dessert takes very little preparation, ideal for a last-minute lunch or dinner party.

Time: 10 minutes
Very easy

6 apples
grated peel and juice of 1 lemon
1½ cups crushed Graham crackers
4 egg whites
½ cup confectioners' sugar
1 tsp cinnamon

DRIED FRUIT

Apricots are among the most flavorsome of dried fruit, followed by dates and figs. Fruit is usually dried in the sun or in special ovens at very low temperatures. All dried fruit is rich in fructose (fruit sugar) and high in nutritional content. Dried fruit preserved (or soaked) in brandy or liqueurs makes a delicious, easy dessert.

Place the peeled, cored, and sliced apples in a food processor with the lemon peel and juice and the crumbled crackers. Process until smooth. Beat the egg whites until firm, beat in the confectioners' sugar. Fold the stiff meringue into the apple mixture and sprinkle with the cinnamon. Transfer to a glass serving bowl and chill.

• • •

CHOCOLATE BREAD PUDDING

If you prefer your pudding to have a golden, crisp crust bake in a slightly cooler oven without the pan of water.

Time: 1 hour
Very easy

7 oz (7 squares) bitter chocolate
1 cup milk
½ lb (approx. 3 cups) slightly stale white bread, broken into small crumbs
3 tbsp butter
½ cup sugar
peel of 1 orange, grated
small pinch salt
4 eggs, separated

Break the chocolate into small pieces and place in a saucepan with the milk. Heat gently, stirring continuously, until the chocolate has completely melted.
Stir in the breadcrumbs, butter, sugar, orange peel, and salt. Draw aside from the heat and stir in the lightly beaten egg yolks one at a time. Leave until completely cold but do not chill. Beat the egg whites stiffly, fold gently into the bread mixture, and transfer to a well-greased charlotte mold or pudding bowl. Cook for 45 minutes, standing in a tray of hot water, at 400° F. Unmold and serve at once.

• • •

239

MIXED FRUIT SOUFFLÉ

The simplest soufflé imaginable, made with just fruit and egg whites. Make sure the fruit purée is very thick and not at all watery.

Time: 1 hour
Very easy
3 apples
3 pears
small piece lemon peel
½ cup sugar
½ lb strawberries
4 egg whites
1 tbsp butter
1½ tbsp vanilla sugar or
   confectioners' sugar

Peel, core, and slice the apples and pears; cook with the lemon peel, half the sugar, and as little water as possible. Sieve. Cook for a little longer, stirring continuously, to thicken the purée further; it must be extremely thick. Wash, dry, and hull the strawberries; push through a nonmetallic sieve and mix with the apple and pear purée. Fold in the stiffly beaten egg whites. Grease a soufflé dish with butter, sprinkle the inside all over with the remaining sugar and fill three-quarters full with the soufflé mixture. Bake at 400° F for 40 minutes or until done. Sprinkle the top of the soufflé with the vanilla sugar or confectioners' sugar and serve immediately.

• • •

CITRON SOUFFLÉ

This is a soufflé made to a more traditional recipe, based on a thick sweet sauce. When done it should be crisp and golden brown on the outside, thick and creamy in the center.

Time: 1 hour
Easy

½ cup seedless white raisins
2¼ cups milk
3 drops vanilla extract
4 whole eggs and 2 eggs,
   separated
½ cup all-purpose flour
½ cup sugar
6 tbsp butter
¼ lb candied citron peel

Soak the seedless white raisins in warm water. Heat the milk and vanilla in a saucepan. Beat 4 of the eggs in a bowl with the flour and sugar. Beat in the hot milk, adding a little at a time. Heat over hot water, stirring continuously, for a few minutes; do not allow to boil. Draw aside from the heat and allow to cool a little. Stir in the melted butter and then the yolks of the 2 remaining eggs, adding one at a time. Drain and dry the sultanas and mix with the citron peel, having first cut the peel into tiny dice; stir into the mixture. Beat the 2 remaining egg whites until stiff and fold in gently. Grease a soufflé dish with butter, turn the mixture into it and bake at 400° F for 30 minutes or until done.

• • •

RAISIN PUDDING

Buy the best raisins you can find for this pudding, ideally dried Malaga Muscatel raisins which are sold still on their stalks. These raisins are more difficult to buy nowadays but are sold in very good food stores as dessert raisins.

Time: 1 hour 30 minutes
Easy

⅔ cup filberts, peeled
½ cup peeled almonds
1 quart milk
pinch salt
1 cup semolina or very fine
   corn meal
½ cup sugar
4 eggs, separated
2 tsp grated lemon peel
½ cup Malaga Muscatel
   raisins or very large
   California raisins, seeds
   removed
1½ tbsp sweet almond oil

If the filberts still have their thin skins on, heat in a hot oven for a minute or two, allow to cool a little, then rub them against a metal sieve to remove the papery skins. Chop them finely, together with the almonds. Do not grind.
Heat the milk and salt to boiling point; sprinkle in the semolina, stirring briskly, so that it does not lump. Add the sugar and cook over low heat, stirring frequently. Remove from the heat. Beat the egg whites until stiff. When the semolina has cooled a little, stir in the egg yolks one at a time, followed by the nuts and lemon peel. Fold in the egg whites and the raisins. Oil the inside of a charlotte or soufflé mold with the almond oil;

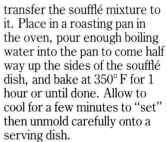

transfer the soufflé mixture to it. Place in a roasting pan in the oven, pour enough boiling water into the pan to come half way up the sides of the soufflé dish, and bake at 350° F for 1 hour or until done. Allow to cool for a few minutes to "set" then unmold carefully onto a serving dish.

• • •

CHOCOLATE AND RUM MOUSSE

*Time: 30 minutes + chilling
  time*
Very easy

7 oz (7 squares) bitter
   chocolate
4 eggs, separated
⅓ cup sugar
1½ tbsp instant coffee
4 tsp rum
1 cup whipping cream

Grate the chocolate and melt over hot water. Draw aside from the heat but leave the bowl over the hot water. Stir in the egg yolks very thoroughly one at a time. Stir in the sugar. Leave to cool further before adding the instant coffee and the rum. Fold in the stiffly beaten egg whites. Spoon into 6 individual glass dishes and chill for several hours before serving. Decorate with the whipped cream or as preferred.

• • •

241

Now that fruit can be transported so rapidly from the grower to far-off markets and consumers, we are no longer so much at the mercy of the seasons. This is particularly good news for those who live in cold climates. Freshly picked fruit, however, which has been left to ripen naturally, has by far the best flavor, aroma, and consistency. Not only is ripe, sound fruit beautiful to behold and delicious to eat, it is also extremely good for us, containing natural fruit sugars (fructose), vitamins, and mineral salts.

PEARS IN WINE WITH GRAPES

If you prefer, use red wine instead of white and add a clove and a generous pinch of cinnamon.

Time: 45 minutes
Very easy

6 pears
1 cup good sweet or medium-
    sweet white wine
1 tbsp lemon juice
½ cup sugar
approx. ¾ lb grapes
½ cup brandy
½ cup grape jelly

Cut the pears lengthwise in half and carefully remove the core. Mix the wine and lemon juice in an ovenproof pan and add the pears, cut side downward. Sprinkle with the sugar and bake for 20 minutes at 350° F.
Cut the grapes in half, remove the seeds, and arrange in a layer on top of the pears. Melt the grape jelly, mix with the brandy, and pour all over the grapes. Serve immediately.

•   •   •

BAKED BANANA AND APPLE MOUSSE

You can adapt this recipe, using a highly-flavored ripe melon instead of the bananas: scoop out the flesh and mix with the apples before returning to the hollowed-out melon to serve.

Time: 30 minutes
Very easy

□ *Fruit in season can be used for the preparation of preserves, desserts, gateaux, and all sorts of other sweet things. There seems to be no end to the number of variations on this theme; all through the summer and into the autumn a succession of ripening fruit tempts the cook to experiment with new recipes (especially when a glut means that there is a big surplus to be turned into preserves, to be frozen or dried, or simply used up in delicious new ways). George Auguste Escoffier must have yielded to much the same temptation when he created the famous Peach Melba for the great Australian soprano, Dame Nellie Melba, in 1893. When cooking fruit, remember that it has a very high water content and must never be overcooked.*

□ *Always choose absolutely sound, ripe (but not overripe) fruit. Try to avoid buying fruit out of season (imported or frozen) as it will have very little flavor and only a fraction of the goodness of sun ripened produce. There are, of course, a few notable exceptions to this rule, such as oranges and most lemons.*

□ *It is usually necessary to peel fruit before use as many skins and peels can be tough and bitter. Use a very sharp stainless steel knife (metal utensils can cause tainting or discoloration). Blanch peaches, apricots, and plums in boiling water for a few seconds and the skin should then come away easily. If your recipe involves using the skin or peel of the fruit, wash it very thoroughly to eliminate any chemical residues from insecticides, fungicides etc. which have been sprayed on it to prevent damage and give it an appearance which the consumer finds appealing.*

2 apples
6 sound, ripe bananas
6 tbsp sugar
½ cup whipping cream
1 egg, separated
1 tbsp butter
1 cup light cream

Peel, core, and slice the apples; cook with a very little water and all the sugar. Sieve or process to a purée and return to the saucepan; cook, stirring continuously, until the purée is very thick. Allow to cool and then chill. Use a very sharp serrated knife to cut the bananas lengthwise in half; without damaging the skins, scoop out the flesh, reserve the skins, and reduce to a purée in a food processor. Mix the two purées together and beat in the stiffly beaten whipping cream. Beat in the egg yolk, followed by the softened butter. Finally fold in the stiffly beaten egg white. Use a pastry bag and large fluted tube to pipe plenty of the mixture into each banana skin. Place carefully in an ovenproof dish and bake for 20 minutes at 350° F. If the skins are damaged during preparation, pipe the mixture into 6 ovenproof ramekin or cocotte dishes instead. Serve immediately, handing round the pouring cream separately.

APPLE AMBER
■ *Pears can be substituted for the apples; choose a good cooking variety which will not release a lot of liquid.*

APPLE AMBER

Time: 45 minutes
Very easy

6 Golden Delicious (or similar) apples
1½ tbsp butter
¾ cup sugar
peel of 1 orange, grated
¼ cup Cointreau
½ cup apricot jam
few drops vanilla extract or 1 vanilla bean
2 egg whites

Peel and core all the apples; cut 4 of them into dice and two into slices. Place the diced apples in a saucepan with the butter, ¼ cup of the sugar, the grated orange peel, and Cointreau. Cook until very tender, remove from the heat and stir in the jam. Leave to cool. Bring ¼ cup water to a boil with the remaining sugar and vanilla, add the sliced apples and cook until only just tender. Grease an ovenproof pan with butter and cover the bottom with the soft apple pulp. Arrange the cooked apple slices in a layer on top. Beat the egg whites until firm, beat in the remaining sugar, and continue beating for a few minutes before spreading this stiff meringue over the top of the apples, drawing it into soft peaks. Bake until lightly browned and set (about 20 minutes at 350° F).

•　•　•

PEARS WITH MACAROONS

Amaretti cookies, made with a mixture of sweet and bitter almonds, are particularly suited to this dish but crisp macaroons or ratafias can also be used.

Time: 30 minutes
Very easy

6 ripe pears
¼ cup (½ stick) butter
6 amaretti cookies
1 tbsp rum
2 egg whites
3 tbsp sugar

Peel and core the pears, using an apple corer to make a neat hole right through the fruit. Sauté the whole pears in the butter for 5 minutes in a fireproof casserole with the lid on, turning carefully once or twice. Draw aside from the heat and remove the lid. Crumble the amaretti,

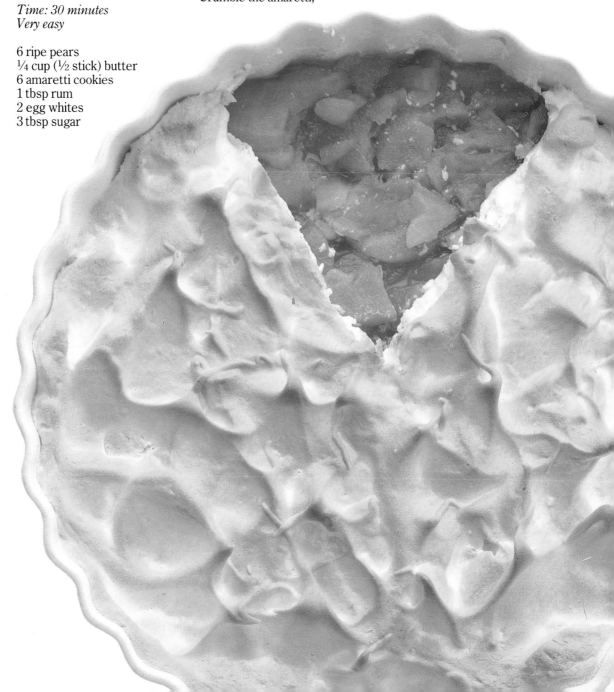

sprinkle with the rum, and use
as a filling to stuff the pears.
Beat the egg whites until firm,
add the sugar, continue
beating until glossy and stiff,
and spoon over each pear.
Bake at 350° F for about 20
minutes or until the meringue
has set and starts to turn
golden brown.

· · ·

BRANDIED
APRICOTS

Time: 30 minutes
Very easy

1¾ lb ripe fresh apricots or
    canned apricot halves
½ cup sugar
2 eggs, separated
small pinch salt
¼ cup butter
3 tbsp brandy
½ cup heavy or whipping
    cream

Cut the apricots in half,
remove the pits, and cook
gently in a little water with
3 tbsp of the sugar (if using
canned apricots do not add this
sugar). Place the egg yolks,
salt, the remaining sugar, and
the butter in the top of a
double boiler over hot water
and cook gently, stirring
continuously, until frothy and
increased in volume (do not
overheat). Remove from the
heat and stir in the brandy.
Allow to become cold before
folding in the stiffly beaten egg
whites followed by the stiffly
beaten cream. Pour this
mixture all over the apricots
and chill briefly before
serving.

· · ·

APRICOTS WITH
RASPBERRY
SAUCE

When apricots are unavailable,
substitute pears or peaches; use
frozen raspberries when fresh
are out of season.

Time: 20 minutes
Very easy

1¾ lb ripe apricots
½ cup sugar
½ cup good white wine
2–3 drops vanilla extract
¾ lb raspberries
small piece lemon peel
3 tbsp kirsch
½ cup whipping cream

Cut the apricots in half,
remove the pits, and boil
gently for 5 minutes with
3 tbsp of the sugar, the wine,
and vanilla. Drain off the liquid
into a saucepan; place the
apricots cut side uppermost in
a shallow serving dish and chill
in the refrigerator. Stir the
rest of the sugar into the
liquid, together with the
raspberries and lemon peel;
boil for 4 minutes, stirring
continuously; discard the
lemon peel and sieve the
raspberries (use a plastic or
other nonmetallic sieve). Mix
the purée with the kirsch and
allow to cool.
Spoon a little of the purée into
each apricot half, topping each
with a piped rosette of stiffly
beaten cream.

· · ·

COMPOTE OF
DRIED FRUIT

Dried apricots and seedless
white raisins go well together
and will keep for many months
if packed loosely in glass jars,

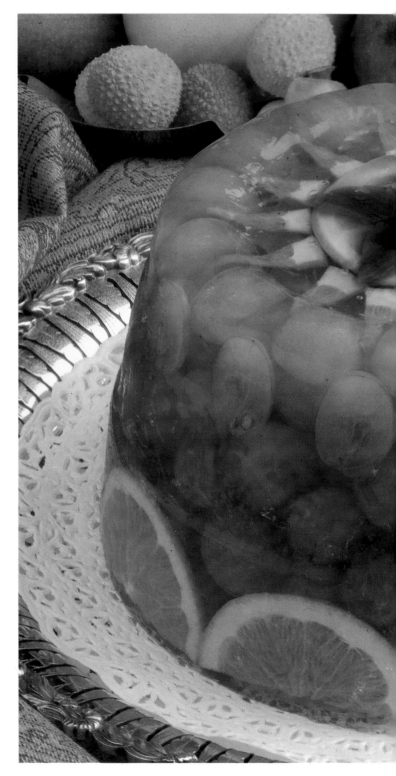

topped up with sweet white wine or brandy and tightly sealed. An excellent end to a meal, served with cookies.

Time: 20 minutes + soaking and chilling time
Very easy

⅓ cup seedless white raisins
2⅓ cups dried apricots
½ bottle Muscat de Beaumes de Venise or California sweet Muscat wine
½ cup sugar
peel of 1 lemon, grated

Soak the seedless white raisins and the apricots overnight in the wine. Transfer the fruit and wine to a saucepan, stir in the sugar and grated lemon peel, bring to a boil, and then simmer for 10 minutes. Drain the fruit, reserving the cooking liquid, and transfer to a serving bowl. Boil the liquid until it has reduced to about 1 cup; pour this over the fruit. Chill thoroughly in the refrigerator before serving.

•   •   •

FRUIT IN LEMON ASPIC

Time: 15 minutes + chilling and setting time
Easy

8 sugar cubes
½ cup granulated sugar
8 juicy lemons
3 tbsp gelatin powder
2 pomegranates
1 melon
1 cup very small or wild strawberries
¾ lb sweet white grapes

Place the empty mold in the freezer before you start. Rub all sides of the sugar lumps hard against the lemons (wash and dry the lemons well before doing this) so that they take up the essential oil contained in the peel. Place these cubes in a saucepan with the ordinary granulated sugar. Juice 7 lemons (reserve 3 tbsp of this juice for later use) and stir into the sugar. Pour 1 cup water into the saucepan and boil until the sugar has completely dissolved. Pour immediately through a sieve into a bowl and sprinkle in the gelatin; stir until completely dissolved. When cool, spoon enough liquid into the ice-cold mold to coat its inside completely and form a layer about ¼ in thick in the bottom (you will need to tip the mold to make the gelatin mixture coat the inside). Return to the freezer until set firm. Scoop out the melon flesh with a melon baller, or dice; extract the fleshy seeds from the pomegranate. Gently mix all the fruit (with the exception of the grapes) with the remaining lemon juice.
Arrange the grapes on the bottom layer and toward the outside of the mold, placing the other fruit in the center, as you fill the mold in layers, adding more lemon gelatin mixture and chilling it until set before adding more fruit and lemon gelatin. Cut the remaining lemon lengthwise in half and slice thinly, positioning these slices against the inside of the mold, near the top (which will become the bottom when unmolded) before you add the last layer of fruit and gelatin.

•   •   •

PINEAPPLE AND RICOTTA DESSERT

Simple, quick and very effective. Use pastry cream instead of ricotta if wished.

Time: 20 minutes + chilling time
Very easy

1 ripe, sound pineapple about 4½ lb in weight
1 cup ricotta
½ cup sugar
¼ cup kirsch

Cut the leafy top off the pineapple taking about 1½ in off the fruit so that you can carefully scoop out all the flesh (use a serrated grapefruit knife). Remove and discard the hard central section and cut the flesh into small pieces; mix these with the kirsch. Sieve the ricotta and stir well with the sugar. Fold in the pineapple and fill the hollowed pineapple skin with this mixture, replacing the top, and chill until it is time to serve.

•   •   •

PINEAPPLE AND BANANA FLOWERS

Time: 20 minutes
Very easy

6 slices pineapple
3 bananas
½ cup grated semisweet chocolate
¼ cup sugar
½ cup milk
6 egg whites

PINEAPPLE AND BANANA
FLOWERS
■ Use fresh pineapple. Peel,
slice and remove the tough,
woody central section with an
apple corer.

Remove the central hard core
from the pineapple slices and
cut out a zig-zag pattern (see
illustration on the right). Lay
flat in an ovenproof pan.
In a blender or food processor
process the bananas to a
purée, add the chocolate,
sugar, and milk and blend
briefly. Use a pastry bag and
wide tube to pipe a mound of
this mixture on top of each
pineapple slice. Beat the egg
whites until stiff, cover the
banana mixture completely
with these, and place in a
preheated oven (400° F) for 10
minutes. Serve immediately.

• • •

BAKED BANANAS WITH COCONUT

*Grate or shred the fresh coconut
flesh onto the bananas or use a
potato peeler to shave off thin
slivers.*

*Time: 30 minutes
Very easy*

1–1½ tbsp butter
1 tsp potato flour or
    cornstarch
1 fresh coconut
⅓ cup sugar
6 bananas

Mix the potato flour or
cornstarch with the liquid
drained off from the fresh
coconut. Stir in the sugar and
then heat while stirring
continually; boil gently for 1–2
minutes, still stirring. Peel the
bananas and cut lengthwise in
half. Grease a wide, shallow
ovenproof pan with butter and
place the bananas in it in a
single layer. Pour the hot
liquid over them. Place tiny
pieces of butter on top of the
bananas and bake for 10

minutes at 400° F. Grate the coconut flesh, sprinkle over the hot bananas, and return to the oven (at the same temperature) for 10 minutes more before serving.

• • •

BANANA AND HONEY WHIP

Use a mild honey such as acacia honey for this recipe. Decorate as liked (e.g. with chopped almonds, sliced banana, grated chocolate, or chopped pineapple).

Time: 10 minutes + chilling time
Very easy

½ cup whole peeled almonds
6 sound, ripe bananas
1 cup ricotta
½ cup honey
2 egg whites
3 tbsp confectioners' sugar

Peel the bananas and blend in a food processor with the ricotta until smooth; leave in the food processor and add the finely chopped almonds and honey. Process very briefly. Transfer to a bowl.
Beat the egg whites until stiff, beat in the confectioners' sugar, and combine this meringue mixture with the banana mixture using a mixing spatula or metal spoon. Spoon into six glass dishes or tall glasses and chill before serving.

BANANA CREAM

Best made with mascarpone but ricotta is also very good and has a much lower fat content. Or use vanilla-flavored homemade custard.

Time: 15 minutes
Very easy

½ cup raspberry jam
6 bananas
juice of ½ a lemon
1 cup mascarpone cream cheese or 1 cup ricotta
¼ cup sugar
¾ cup flaked or slivered almonds

Sieve the raspberry jam. Mash the banana flesh in a bowl with the lemon juice until smooth and creamy. Combine the banana, mascarpone, jam, and sugar thoroughly. Use a pastry bag and tube and pipe into individual serving dishes or tall glasses. Roast the almonds briefly in the oven until pale golden brown; sprinkle over the banana mixture and serve.

• • •

FLAMBÉED BANANAS

An impressive end to a meal. Make sure the rum is really hot (but not boiling) before you attempt to set light to it.

Time: 20 minutes
Very easy

6 bananas
2 tbsp butter
½ cup sugar
1 tsp cinnamon
pinch nutmeg
juice of 2 oranges
1 cup sweet dessert wine
2–3 tbsp rum

Peel the bananas and cut horizontally in half; grease a large, shallow fireproof pan with butter and place the bananas in it, cut side downward.
Mix the sugar with the cinnamon and nutmeg and sprinkle over the bananas. Strain the orange juice, mix with the wine, and pour over the bananas. Cut the butter into very small pieces and distribute over the bananas. Bake at 400° F for 15 minutes, spooning the syrup over the bananas at regular intervals after the first 5 minutes. Remove from the oven, and take to the table; pour the hot rum all over the surface and flame. Serve immediately.

• • •

STRAWBERRY YOGHURT CREAM

A very quick and delicious, fail-safe dessert for the busy or novice cook.

Time: 10 minutes
Very easy

¾ lb very small cultivated, or wild, strawberries
2¼ cups creamy strawberry yoghurt
1 tbsp lemon juice
⅓ cup sugar
1 cup whipping cream

Rinse, dry, and hull the strawberries; reduce half of them to a purée in a blender with the yoghurt, lemon, and sugar. Combine with the stiffly beaten cream, folding in gently but thoroughly. Spoon into individual glass dishes. Top with the reserved whole strawberries and chill until just before serving.

• • •

PERSIMMONS WITH BRANDY

Persimmons are available for a short season in the fall; they must be extremely ripe and squashy. Sharon fruit are virtually the same, cultivated to be sweeter.

Time: 5 minutes + chilling time
Very easy

6 very ripe persimmons
⅓ cup sugar
½ cup brandy

Wash the persimmons, dry them, and pull off the remains of their stalk and calyx. Cut horizontally in half and sprinkle

*APPLES WITH
CARAMELIZED MILK
SAUCE*

■ *Patience is vital for the
long, slow cooking of the
sugar syrup, which must be
stirred constantly until it
caramelizes.*

the cut surfaces with sugar
and brandy. Chill for at least
20 minutes in the refrigerator
before serving.

• • •

APPLES WITH
CARAMELIZED
MILK SAUCE

Time: 2 hours
Very easy

6 apples
1 cup sugar
½ cup good white wine
2¼ cups rich milk
pinch cinnamon or 1 small
    piece cinnamon stick
2–3 drops vanilla extract or ¼
    vanilla bean

Peel, core, and halve the
apples; cook until tender with
3 tbsp of the sugar and the
wine. Drain off the liquid and
transfer the apples to a
serving plate to cool. Pour the
milk into a saucepan (skimmed
milk is not suitable for this

recipe) adding the sugar,
cinnamon, and vanilla. Bring to
a boil, then turn the heat down
very low and continue
cooking, stirring frequently,
for 1½ hours when it should
have thickened and darkened
slightly. Pour the caramelized
milk over the apple halves and
serve when cold.

• • •

CHERRIES IN RED WINE

In winter pears can replace the cherries; use a good, full-bodied wine.

Time: 30 minutes + chilling time
Very easy

1¾ lb cherries
1 pint full-bodied red wine
½ cup sugar
pinch cinnamon or 1 small piece cinnamon stick
1 cup heavy cream

Remove the stalks from the cherries and pit them using a cherry pitter. Place in a saucepan with the wine, sugar, and cinnamon. Bring to a boil, reduce the heat, cover, and simmer very gently for 10 minutes. Drain the cherries and transfer to a glass serving bowl. Boil the cooking liquid fast, uncovered, until it reduces to a thick syrup (this will take some time); remove the piece of cinnamon (if used) and allow to cool before pouring over the cherries. Chill until just before serving, at which time decorate with stiffly beaten cream, piped through a fluted tube.

•   •   •

CARAMELIZED ORANGES

The only watchpoint in this recipe is making sure that the caramel keeps hot enough to remain liquid but does not become dark and bitter. Keep it hot over boiling water, not direct heat.

Time: 15 minutes
Very easy

6 oranges
1½ cups sugar
¼ cup Grand Marnier

Wash and dry the oranges thoroughly. Use a very sharp serrated knife to cut all the skin and peel off the oranges, thin inner skin included. Slice the oranges into fairly thin rounds. Carefully remove all the pith and other remains from inside the peel leaving just the outer, orange part. Cut this into very thin, short strips and reserve. Heat all the sugar in a heavy-bottomed saucepan until it melts and turns golden brown; dip the orange slices one by one and place on a hot serving plate which has been lightly oiled with almond oil. Keep hot. Add the strips of peel last of all to the caramel, stir, and then distribute on top of the orange slices. Heat the Grand Marnier in a small saucepan, set alight and pour quickly all over the oranges. Serve.

•   •   •

GINGER

The root, or rhizome, of a plant which is indigenous to southern Asia, fresh ginger is very widely available. It can also be bought canned in syrup. Its slightly piquant, astringent taste is wonderfully subtle and enhances other flavors; it is popular in both sweet and savory dishes.

FIGS WITH GINGER

If you cannot buy fresh or canned root ginger use a generous pinch of cinnamon instead.

Time: 30 minutes + chilling time
Very easy

2½ cups dried figs
1 lemon
small piece fresh root ginger, peeled
½ cup sugar
1 cup light cream

Rinse the figs in cold water and snip off the hard remains of their stalks. Place in a saucepan and cover with cold water. Wash, dry, and slice the lemon thinly; add to the pan containing the figs, followed by the ginger and sugar; bring to a boil. Simmer for 20 minutes or until tender. Remove the figs with a slotted spoon and place in a serving bowl. Boil the cooking liquid until it has reduced considerably then pour through a sieve onto the figs, discarding the lemon and ginger. Chill for 2 hours before serving, handing round the cream separately.

•   •   •

FIGS WITH LEMON SAUCE

Muscat wine is used for this recipe, but a sweet Marsala or madeira also blends very well.

Time: 15 minutes + chilling time
Very easy

18 ripe figs

1 cup lemon marmalade
½ cup Muscat wine
2 thinly sliced lemons

Peel off the thin outer skin from the figs very carefully and place in a deep dish. Melt the marmalade with the wine in a saucepan. Simmer for a few minutes then pour over the figs. Chill for 2 hours or longer. Decorate with the lemon slices just before serving.

•   •   •

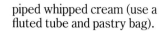

SPICED FIGS

You can vary your choice of spices: anise, cumin, or even a pinch of mild curry powder.

Time: 5 minutes + chilling time
Very easy

18 fresh figs
juice of ½ lemon
pinch ground cloves
1 tsp cinnamon
1 cup light cream

Peel off the figs' thin outer skin with great care; sprinkle them with the lemon juice, with the ground clove, and cinnamon and place in a serving bowl in the refrigerator. Chill the cream as well. Just before serving, pour the cream over the figs.

• • •

FIGS WITH WALNUTS

These figs will become completely caramelized and will keep well for a few days. Substitute dried figs when fresh are unavailable.

Time: 20 minutes
Very easy

18 fresh figs
18 walnut halves
½ cup sugar
½ cup honey

Peel off the thin outer skin of the figs and cut lengthwise almost in half, stopping just short of the bottom so that the halves are still attached. Press a walnut half gently into one cut surface in the center of each fig and press the fig closed again. Spread the honey and the sugar out on 2 separate plates and roll each fig in the honey, then in the sugar, placing them on a sheet of foil spread out on a cookie sheet. Broil, turning them once carefully as soon as the heat has caramelized the sugar and honey. Transfer to a serving plate and serve with piped whipped cream (use a fluted tube and pastry bag).

• • •

APPLES WITH WALNUT SAUCE

This recipe works equally well with pears.

Time: 1 hour
Very easy

6 Golden Delicious apples
⅓ cup brown or white sugar
½ cup seedless white raisins
1 cup walnut pieces
½ cup sugar
1 tbsp potato flour or cornstarch
juice of ½ lemon
1 tbsp butter

Peel and core the apples and place in an ovenproof pan lightly greased with butter. Sprinkle with ⅓ cup water and ⅓ cup sugar. Bake for 30 minutes or until tender at 350° F. Keep hot on a serving plate.
Soak the seedless white raisins in warm water. Chop the walnuts. Place the second quantity of sugar in a fairly small, heavy saucepan and stir with the potato flour or cornstarch (mixing with the sugar prevents it lumping). Gradually stir in 1 cup water and then place over low heat. Continue stirring until the sauce comes to a boil. Add the well-drained raisins, the nuts, lemon juice, and the butter. When the sauce comes back to a boil, remove from the heat and pour over the baked apples. Serve immediately.

• • • •

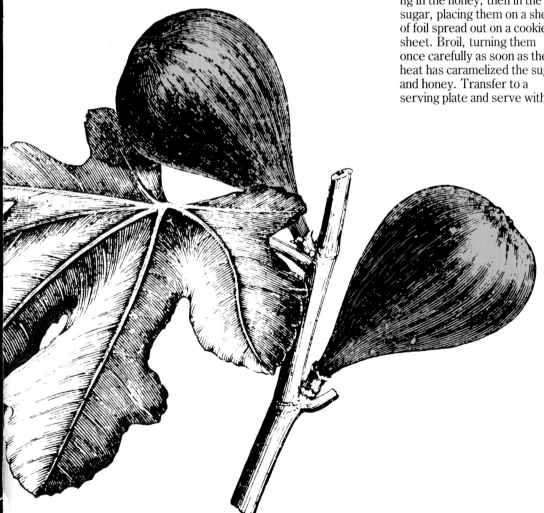

Makes 15 tartlets:

For the sweet egg pastry (pâte sucrée):
1¾ cups all-purpose flour
½ cup sugar
½ tsp salt
½ cup (1 stick) butter
2 egg yolks
1 tsp finely grated lemon peel or a few drops vanilla extract

For the filling:
½ cup best-quality apricot preserve

For the almond and rum pastry cream:
½ cup (1 stick) sweet butter
¾ cup confectioners' sugar
3 egg yolks
3 tbsp rum
1 cup ground almonds

For the topping:
kirsch- or Maraschino-flavored frosting (see page 52)
apricot (or other fruit) preserve
1 cup pastry cream (see page 44)
fresh or canned fruit

Make the pastry following the method given on page 58. Roll out into a rectangular sheet just over ⅛ in thick.

If using tartlet cases or patty pans which are 1½ in in diameter (as illustrated) select a plain round 2½-in pastry cutter.

Fluted tartlets look more attractive; brush the insides with melted butter or margarine. Line each with a disk of pastry, pressing gently into the case; trim off excess.

Spread approx. ½ tbsp apricot (or other fruit) preserve over the base of each tartlet.

Beat the butter with a wooden spoon until very soft and light; add the sugar and continue beating until pale and fluffy; beat in the egg yolks one at a time, followed by the rum, a few drops at a time. Add the ground almonds and mix well.

Fill each tartlet to just below the rim with this almond mixture. Place the tartlet cases on a cookie sheet and cook for 15 minutes in a preheated oven at 350°F.

Cool. When cold spread the kirsch-flavored frosting in a thin layer over the top of each tart. Leave to dry and set. Spread a thin layer of sieved fruit preserve over the frosting before piping a rosette of pastry cream on top of each tartlet.

Soak some fruit in kirsch, drain, and use as decoration.

WATERMELON WITH KIRSCH
■ *Colorful and attractive to look at, this must be served very cold. Once you have stirred in the cream (see recipe) do not keep in the refrigerator for more than 8 hours or the appearance and texture will suffer.*

WATERMELON WITH KIRSCH

Time: 10 minutes + chilling time
Very easy

1 very ripe watermelon weighing approx. 4½ lb
½ cup currants
6 tbsp confectioners' sugar
¼ cup kirsch or other fruit-based liqueur
4 oz (4 squares) semisweet chocolate
1 cup heavy cream
mint leaves (optional)

Cut the top off the watermelon, taking off about one quarter of the fruit. Scoop out all the flesh with a large melon baller or teaspoon and place in a bowl. Pick out all the easily accessible seeds. Mix the watermelon balls with the currants, sugar, kirsch, and coarsely grated or chopped chocolate.
Beat the cream stiffly and combine gently with the watermelon. Fill the empty watermelon skin with this mixture and chill well before serving. Decorate with mint leaves.

• • •

ORANGE RICE SOUFFLÉ

Timing is crucial with this dish: the oranges must be served as soon as they are taken out of the oven.

Time: 1 hour
Very easy

6 tbsp short-grain or pudding rice
2¼ cups milk
1 tbsp butter

pinch salt
1 tbsp finely grated orange peel
6 oranges
½ cup sugar
2 eggs, separated

Place the rice in a sieve and rinse with cold water; transfer to a heavy-bottomed saucepan, adding the milk, butter, salt and orange peel. Cut the oranges neatly in half (use an extra, spare orange for your grated peel so as not to spoil the appearance of this dish). Squeeze out the juice without damaging the skins. Add this juice to the rice, stir, and bring to a boil. Reduce the heat and cook gently until the rice has absorbed all the liquid. Remove from the heat. While the rice is cooking, use a grapefruit knife to cut away all the membranes from inside the orange skin halves. Add the sugar and the egg yolks to

the cooked rice when it has cooled a little.
Beat the egg whites until stiff and fold into the rice. Fill the orange halves with this mixture (not too full, as it will rise as it cooks) and bake at 350° F for 30 minutes or until risen like little soufflés and pale golden brown on top. Serve immediately.

• • •

SPICED PRICKLY PEARS

Time: 10 minutes
Very easy

WATER MELON

This thirst-quenching member of the cucumber family is thought to have originated in Africa but was also grown thousands of years ago in India. Its high water content makes it suitable for the preparation of jellies, and sherbets.

12 prickly pears
½ tsp cinnamon
juice of 1 lemon
⅓ cup sugar

Place the prickly pears in a large bowl full of water and leave to soak for 1 hour or longer. Most if not all the prickles will be released and rise to the surface of the water; skim off with a spoon and dispose of them. Use a

slotted ladle to transfer the prickly pears to a colander and rinse well under running cold water.

Cut off both ends of each pear; make a lengthwise slit in the skin, press the tines of a fork into this slit to secure the fruit, and cut off the skin. Place the peeled prickly pears in a serving bowl, sprinkle with the cinnamon, lemon juice, and sugar; stir and turn once or twice then serve.

• • •

JELLIED APPLE RING MOLD

Time: 30 minutes + chilling time
Very easy

1¾ lb apples
1 cup water
½ cup sugar
3 tbsp gelatin powder
juice of 1 lemon
1 cup quince jelly
½ lb black grapes
½ lb white grapes

Peel and core the apples; slice into fairly thin rings. Place in a saucepan with the quince jelly, sprinkle with the sugar, and cook for 10 minutes, stirring from time to time. Sieve the hot cooked apple and all the liquid into a bowl. Stir in the lemon juice. Heat the water to near boiling point; draw aside from the heat and sprinkle in the gelatin powder (follow the manufacturer's instructions) and when this has completely dissolved, stir into the apple mixture.

Rinse a ring mold with cold water; do not dry. Fill with the apple mixture and, when cool,

place in the refrigerator to set and solidify. This will take 6 hours or longer. Shortly before serving, turn out the mold onto a serving plate and fill the central well with the black and white grapes.

• • •

BAKED APPLES WITH PRUNE STUFFING

Use ready-pitted prunes for this recipe or remove the pits after you have cooked them.

Time: 30 minutes + soaking time for the prunes
Very easy

12 prunes
2¼ cups Muscat wine
½ cup sugar
6 Calville, Rennet or Golden Delicious apples

Soak the prunes in the wine for a few hours or overnight. Cook them in this wine with

1 tbsp sugar for 10 minutes or until tender.

Peel the apples, cut them in half crosswise (not from top to bottom), and remove the cores. Place in a saucepan. Sprinkle with the remaining sugar, add ½ cup water, and cook, covered, for 5 minutes. Transfer the apples to a serving plate using a slotted ladle. Reserve the cooking liquid. Place a prune in the cavity of each half apple and keep hot. Mix the wine left over from soaking the prunes and the apple cooking liquid in a saucepan and boil hard until considerably reduced. Pour this syrupy mixture over the apples and serve.

• • •

APPLE SNOW WITH TOFFEE

To save trouble you can buy almond brittle, nougatine or praline.

Time: 20 minutes + chilling time
Very easy

8 apples
1 tbsp butter
3 tbsp sugar
1 cup whipping cream
½ lb almond brittle or nougatine

Peel, core, and slice the apples; cook them with the butter and 3 tbsp water over low heat. Push through a sieve and return to the saucepan with the sugar, cooking until the mixture has thickened considerably. Leave to become completely cold before folding in the stiffly beaten cream and spoon into a large glass bowl or individual glasses.
Chop the brittle or nougatine; sprinkle over the surface of the apple snow and chill for 2 hours before serving.

• • •

APPLE AND RUM FRENCH TOAST

These must be fried at the last minute and served the minute they are cooked or they will become indigestible. The bread should not be too fresh.

Time: 1 hour
Very easy

6 tbsp seedless white raisins
½ cup rum
6 apples
½ cup (1 stick) butter
½ cup sugar
2 eggs
¼ cup milk
6 fairly thick slices from a medium-sized loaf, crusts removed.

Soak the raisins in the rum for

at least 30 minutes. Peel and core the apples with an apple corer; cut into rings. Cook with 1 tbsp of the butter and 3 tbsp water until just tender, turning carefully. Sprinkle in the drained raisins and half the sugar and cook for a few minutes longer over very low heat.

Beat the eggs and milk together in a shallow plate and dip the bread slices briefly but carefully on both sides. Allow excess egg and milk to drain off and fry in the remaining butter over moderate heat, turning once. Sprinkle these fried slices with the remaining sugar, arrange on a large flat heated serving plate and spoon some apple on top of each slice. Serve immediately.

• • •

APPLE CHIFFON WITH BREADCRUMB TOPPING

This dessert is very popular with young children. Raspberries or blueberries can replace the strawberries.

Time: 45 minutes
Very easy

2¼ lb apples
½ cup sugar
2½ tsp lemon juice
¼ cup (½ stick) butter
2 cups dry breadcrumbs (not toasted or colored)
1 cup whipping cream
¾ cup strawberries

Peel, core, and slice the apples. Cook in a covered saucepan with half the sugar

and ½ cup water until very tender (about 20 minutes). Sieve. Stir in the lemon juice and leave until cold.
Heat the butter in a skillet until it foams; add the breadcrumbs and the remaining sugar. Cook, stirring from time to time, until the breadcrumbs are golden brown. Spoon a layer of the apple purée into a glass bowl, cover with a layer of fried breadcrumbs; follow with another layer of apple, then a layer of breadcrumbs. Beat the cream until stiff and spread over the top as a final layer. Decorate with strawberries and chill before serving.

• • •

APPLE PASTRY SQUARES

You can fill the space left by coring the apples with jam, soaked seedless white raisins or chopped almonds.

Time: 1 hour 30 minutes
Very easy

½ cup sugar
¼ cup water
pinch cinnamon
pinch grated nutmeg
1¾ cups all-purpose flour
pinch salt
2 eggs
6 apples
¼ cup (½ stick) butter + 1 extra tbsp for greasing the cookie sheet and ovenproof pan
2 eggs

Put half the sugar and all the water in a saucepan with the cinnamon and the nutmeg. Bring to a boil, add half the

butter and when this has melted remove from the heat. Sift the flour with the salt in a mound on the pastry slab or work surface; make a well in the center and place the rest of the butter, cut into very small pieces, in it, together with the eggs and the remaining sugar; combine to make a smooth, soft dough. Roll out this pastry with a floured rolling pin to a thin sheet just under ⅛ in thick. Cut this into 6 identical squares.
Peel and core the apples and place each apple in the middle of a pastry square. Bring the corners of the pastry together over the top of the apple, pinching the edges securely together. Use any spare pieces of pastry to cut out leaves to decorate the top of each parcel.
Brush the outside of each pie shell with a little of the spiced sugar and butter mixture. Place on a greased cookie sheet and bake at 350° F for 40 minutes or until done, crisp, and pale golden bown.
Transfer to a wide, shallow ovenproof pan, spoon the remaining syrup evenly over all the pastry and return to the oven for 10 minutes before serving.

• • •

MINTED PEACHES

Time: 10 minutes
Very easy

6 canned or fresh peaches
2½ cups milk
½ tsp vanilla extract
6 egg yolks
⅔ cup sugar
¼ cup all-purpose flour
2 tbsp mint syrup or cordial

Prepare the peaches in a light sugar syrup as instructed in the box on page 24. Bring the milk to a boil, draw aside from the heat, and add the vanilla, followed by the mint syrup. Beat the egg yolks for 5–10 minutes with the sugar until pale and fluffy and beat in the sifted flour. Slowly beat in the hot milk and then cook over very low heat to thicken a little, stirring continuously. Drain the syrup from the peaches thoroughly and place each one in an individual glass dish. Pour some of the hot custard over each one and serve.

• • •

PEACHES IN CHAMPAGNE

A refreshing summer dessert: peaches in champagne or sparkling white wine, slightly sweetened and spiced.

Time: 10 minutes
Very easy

6 ripe peaches
¼ cup sugar
pinch cinnamon
juice of ½ lemon
1 cup sparkling white wine

Put the peaches in a deep bowl and add enough boiling water to completely cover them; leave for a few moments and then drain. Peel, cut in half, remove the pits, and slice. Place the sliced peaches in a bowl, sprinkle them with the sugar, cinnamon, pour the champagne over them and serve.

• • •

BAKED SPICED PEACHES

Cloves have traditionally been a favorite spice in Mediterranean cooking and add interest to this dessert. If amaretti are unavailable, use macaroons or ratafias.

Time: 30 minutes
Very easy

3 peaches
1½–2 tbsp butter
6 small slices white bread
6 crumbled amaretti cookies
6 cloves
6 tbsp sugar

Wash and dry the peaches, cut them in half, and remove the pit. Spread a very small amount of butter very thinly over the slices of bread and place in a hot oven until golden brown. Sprinkle the toasted bread with the cookie crumbs. Push a clove into each peach half. Lightly grease a large, shallow ovenproof pan with butter and place the peach halves in it, cut side downward. Sprinkle with the sugar and bake in a hot oven (400° F) for 10 minutes. Place a peach half on each slice of toasted bread and serve immediately.

• • •

PEACHES IN VERMOUTH

This dessert is very good served cold but can also be served hot. A sweet dessert wine or sherry can be used instead of vermouth.

Time: 30 minutes
Easy

6 peaches
6 tsp raspberry jam
1 cup finely chopped or ground
 almonds
1 cup sweet (red) vermouth
½ cup water
6 tbsp sugar

Plunge the peaches for a few moments in boiling water to make them easier to peel. Cut them in half and remove the pits. Mix the raspberry jam with the almonds and place 2 tsp in the hollow of each peach half. Place the peaches in a deep ovenproof pan. Pour the vermouth, water, and sugar into a saucepan and bring to a boil. Reduce the heat a little and cook for 10 minutes to reduce; pour this sauce over the peaches and leave to cool. Chill before serving.

• • •

PEACHES WITH RICE SOUFFLÉ

For a change, semolina can be substituted for rice. For a lighter dessert, use milk instead of cream.

Time: 1 hour
Very easy

1 cup cream
3 tbsp rice
4 tbsp sugar
2 eggs, separated
⅓ cup seedless white raisins,
 soaked in warm water
pinch cinnamon
3 tbsp confectioners' sugar
6 peaches

Heat the milk to boiling point in a saucepan; sprinkle in the rice and cook slowly until

tender and it has absorbed all the cream. Remove from the heat and stir in the 4 tbsp sugar, followed by the lightly beaten egg yolks, the drained raisins, and the cinnamon. Stir well.
Beat the egg whites until firm, add the confectioners' sugar and continue beating until stiff; fold into the rice mixture. Cut the peaches in half, discarding the pit, place in a single layer, cut side uppermost, in a greased ovenproof pan and heap up the rice mixture on top of each peach. Bake at 350° F for 30 minutes or until the rice has risen a little and set. Serve immediately.

• • •

MELON BASKETS WITH BLACKBERRIES

A dessert for late summer or early fall when both melons and blackberries are ripe.

Time: 15 minutes + chilling time
Very easy

1 ripe melon
½ cup sugar
½ cup Muscat de Beaumes de
 Venise or Californian Sweet
 Muscat wine
3 cups blackberries
juice of ½ lemon

Cut the top off the melon sufficiently low down so that you can scoop out the seeds and filaments easily; discard these, retaining the juice, and scoop the flesh out of the melon. Dice the flesh and mix in a bowl with 3 tbsp of the sugar and the wine.

Rinse and dry the blackberries, place in a bowl, and sprinkle with the remaining sugar. Chill the melon case, flesh, and the berries for 2 hours. Return the melon flesh to the melon, place the blackberries on top and spoon their syrup over them.

• • •

MINTED MELON

Time: 5 minutes
Very easy

1 very ripe, well-chilled melon
approx. 3 cups melon water
 ice (see page 286)
1 sprig fresh mint

Cut the melon horizontally in half, scoop out the seeds and filaments and discard these. Scoop out the flesh (returning empty melon to refrigerator or freezer). Dice and sieve the flesh; transfer to a large capacity blender and add the water ice, processing on the lowest speed setting. When the mixture is smooth, return to the chilled empty melon case. Serve immediately, before the water ice has a chance to soften further; decorate with the sprig of mint.

• • •

MELON WITH BLUEBERRIES

You can soak the blueberries in kirsch instead of gin, or omit the alcohol altogether, and let them stand in the sugar and lemon.

Time: 5 minutes + standing time
Very easy

¾ lb blueberries
¼ cup gin
¼ cup sugar
juice of ½ lemon
3 small melons (Charentais are
 ideal)

Place the washed and dried berries in a bowl, pour the gin over them, sprinkle with the sugar and the lemon juice and leave to stand for 1 hour or longer, stirring and turning gently once or twice.
Cut the melons in half, and discard the seeds and filaments. Spoon the berries and their syrup into the melons and serve.

• • •

MELON WITH GINGER

If you omit the sugar and prepare the melon with just the fresh ginger, adding freshly ground white pepper, you can serve this as an appetizer.

Time: 5 minutes
Very easy

1 ripe melon weighing approx.
 4½ lb
1 tbsp peeled, finely chopped
 root ginger
¼ cup sugar

Cut the melon into sections or wedges, remove the seeds and filaments and cut off the skin. Mix the ginger with the pepper and sugar and sprinkle the melon wedges with this mixture shortly before serving.

• • •

PEAR MERINGUE WITH
SABAYON SAUCE
■ Other types of fresh fruit can
be used for this unusual
dessert, which would be an
ideal choice for a dinner
party. Strawberries would
make a particularly suitable
alternative.

PEAR MERINGUE WITH SABAYON SAUCE

Time: 2 hours
Easy

For the meringue base:
4 eggs, separated
2¾ cups sugar
For the topping:
6 pears
½ cup water
⅔ cup granulated sugar
few drops vanilla extract
small piece lemon peel
4 eggs
½ cup Marsala

Beat the egg whites until firm,
then gradually add the
confectioners' sugar while
continuing to beat until stiff
and glossy. Spoon (in two or
three lots at a time) into a
pastry bag with a wide tube
and pipe onto a greased cookie
sheet, starting in the middle
and spiraling outward to form
a solid circular meringue base.
Bake for 1½ hours at 140° F
or the lowest temperature
available, with the oven door
left very slightly open.
While the meringue base is
cooking, prepare the fruit and
sauce. Peel and core the
pears; cut lengthwise in half
and place in a saucepan with ½
cup water, ¼ cup of the
granulated sugar, a few drops
vanilla extract (or 1 small
piece vanilla bean if preferred)
and the piece of lemon peel.
Cook gently until tender.
Drain. Transfer to a plate and
leave to cool. Boil the cooking
liquid over moderate heat until
it has reduced to only ⅓ cup of
syrup. Pour this over the
pears.
Place the egg yolks in the top
of a double boiler or a

heatproof bowl, stir in the
remaining granulated sugar
and all the Marsala; heat over
very gently simmering water,
beating continuously until the
mixture is pale, fluffy, and has
greatly increased in volume.
Do not overheat or it will
curdle. Leave to cool.
When the meringue base is
completely cold, remove
carefully from the cookie
sheet and place on a flat
serving plate. Arrange the
pears on top as shown in the
illustration, pour the sauce
over them and serve at once.

• • •

MOLDED RASPBERRY MOUSSE

*Use firm, barely ripe, fresh
raspberries, not frozen fruit: if
they are too watery this mousse
will not unmold successfully. If
you want to play safe or have to
use frozen fruit, heat the purée
(do not boil) and dissolve 1 tbsp
gelatin powder in it.*

Time: 20 minutes + chilling
time
Very easy

1¼ lb raspberries
4 egg whites
1 cup confectioners' sugar
1 cup whipping cream
2–3 drops vanilla extract
pinch salt

Reserve a dozen perfect
raspberries for decoration and
push the rest through a plastic
or hair sieve. Place the egg
whites in a large bowl with a
small pinch salt and beat until
they are stiff but not dry;

sprinkle in ½ cup of the sugar through a sieve and fold it gently into the beaten egg whites. Fold in the raspberry purée a little at a time, using a mixing spatula or thin plastic spoon in order to crush as little air out of the whites as possible. Beat in the cream until stiff in a separate bowl; sift in the remaining confectioners' sugar and add the vanilla extract, mix gently but thoroughly, and then fold into the raspberry mixture. Rinse a charlotte mold with cold water; do not dry. Fill with the raspberry mixture and chill for at least 6 hours in the refrigerator. Just before serving, place a serving plate upside down on top of the mold, turn over, and unmold the mousse. (If gelatin is used, dip the mold very briefly in hot water before unmolding.) Decorate with the reserved raspberries.

• • •

STUFFED PEACHES

Canned peaches can be used when fresh are out of season, or if time is short.

Time: 30 minutes
Very easy

6 peaches
12 prunes
½ cup rum
¼ cup sugar
12 amaretti or ratafia cookies or small macaroons
6 candied cherries

Cut the peaches in half and cook briefly in sugar syrup. Arrange cut side uppermost on a serving plate. Place the prunes in the syrup left from cooking the peaches (or left after draining them, if canned) together with the rum and sugar. Cook gently for 20 minutes or until tender, then sieve. Mix the crumbled amaretti with this purée and spoon into the hollows of the peach halves. Decorate with the cherries, cut in half, and chill before serving.

263

CHOCOLATE-COATED PEARS

Time: 45 minutes
Very easy

6 pears
¼ cup (½ stick) butter
¼ cup good white wine
½ cup sugar
9 oz (9 squares) semisweet
    dessert chocolate or bakers'
    chocolate
½ lb strawberries

Peel the pears; use an apple corer to remove the cores, working from the base upward and stop short of the top, leaving the stalks intact. Cook gently in a deep, covered fireproof casserole with the butter. After 5 minutes moisten with half the wine, sprinkle with the sugar, and cook for 5 more minutes before adding the rest of the wine. When they are tender, remove carefully with a slotted ladle and leave to dry. Grate the chocolate and melt it over hot water. Place the cooked pears on a serving dish; dribble the hot chocolate all over them to coat them as completely as possible and chill until ready to serve.

• • •

PEARS WITH BLUEBERRIES

If you use frozen blueberries, put them straight from the freezer in a covered saucepan with the sugar and heat gently. Once they have thawed completely, sieve them.

Time: 10 minutes
Very easy

¾ lb blueberries
⅓ cup raspberry jam
2½ tsp sugar
3 tbsp kirsch
6 pears

Sieve the blueberries and mix with the jam, sugar, and kirsch. Heat this mixture for a few minutes until the sugar has dissolved. Peel, core, and slice the pears into a serving bowl. Pour the hot sauce over them and serve immediately.

• • •

PRUNE MERINGUE DESSERT

Puréed cooked dried apricots or figs can be used instead of prunes; soak these in Marsala (or sherry) also, to soften .

Time: 1 hour + soaking time
Very easy

1 lb pitted prunes
1 cup dry Marsala or sherry
½ cup sugar
3 egg whites
¼ cup sugar

Place the prunes in a bowl and pour the Marsala over them. Leave to soak and soften for 8–12 hours, turning once or twice. Drain off the Marsala and cook the prunes with a little water over low heat for a few minutes.

Drain the prunes; sieve them and spread this purée out in a shallow ovenproof dish. Beat the egg whites until stiff, beat in the confectioners' sugar and use a pastry bag and large fluted tube to pipe meringue all over the prune purée, covering it completely. Place in a moderate oven for the meringue to set and turn a pale golden brown. Serve immediately.

• • •

PRUNE SOUFFLÉ

A simple way for even the inexperienced cook to impress. A purée of other types of dried fruit can replace the prunes.

Time: 1 hour + soaking time
Very easy

1 lb pitted prunes
4 egg whites
½ cup sugar
pinch cinnamon
peel of 1 lemon, grated
1 tbsp butter
1 tbsp all-purpose flour
pinch salt

Soak the prunes in water for 2–4 hours. Drain and push through a plastic or hair sieve. Beat the egg whites and the pinch salt (which will help to produce more volume) until stiff. Fold in the sugar, cinnamon, prune purée and grated lemon rind carefully, using a spatula to avoid crushing the air out of the beaten egg whites. Grease a soufflé dish with butter and dust with sugar, shaking off any excess and transfer the soufflé mixture into it. Place in the oven, preheated to 400° F,

CHOCOLATE-COATED
PEARS
■ An extremely effective,
classic treatment for this fruit
which goes so well with
chocolate. Buy the best-
quality chocolate for this
recipe.

and bake for 30 minutes.
Serve immediately.

• • •

PLUM FOOL

*Use very ripe plums; choose a
variety which does not produce
much juice when cooked.*

Time: 1 hour + chilling time
Very easy

1¾ lb plums
⅔ cup sugar
3 egg yolks and 1 egg white
1½ tsp all-purpose flour
1 cup milk
3 tbsp confectioners' sugar
1 cup amaretti, macaroons, or
   ratafias

Pit the plums and cook with ¼
cup of the sugar for about 20
minutes. Sieve and leave the
purée to cool. Beat the egg
yolks with the remaining sugar
until very pale and greatly

PEARS

There are twenty species of
pear and thousands of
varieties. Use a variety which
stays firm when cooked and
releases little juice even
though these usually have less
flavor.

increased in volume. Beat in
the flour and then the milk,
adding a little at a time. Heat
this custard over hot water
until it reaches boiling point,
stirring continuously.
Combine the custard and the
plum purée; spoon into 6
deep, small glass dishes or tall
glasses and chill for at least 3
hours.

Beat 1 egg white until stiff and
continue beating as you add
the sifted confectioners'
sugar. Put 2 or 3 amaretti on
top of each portion of plum fool
and use a pastry bag and fluted
tube to pipe the meringue
mixture on top.

• • •

YELLOW PLUM
MOLD

Time: 1 hour + setting time
Very easy

2¼ lb ripe yellow plums
1 cup water
2 cups sugar
3 tbsp gelatin powder

Cut the plums in half, pit, and
peel if possible. Cook with
water and sugar for 10
minutes, skimming off any
scum which rises to the top.
Pour the very hot cooking
liquid through a sieve into a
bowl and immediately sprinkle
in the gelatin powder (soften
first if the manufacturer
advises). Make sure the
gelatin has completely
dissolved. Push the cooked
plums through a plastic or hair
sieve into a bowl. Stir in the
liquid containing the gelatin
very thoroughly. Rinse an 8-in
mold with cold water; do not
dry. Pour the plum mixture
into this and chill in the
refrigerator until set (at least 6
hours). When ready to serve
the dessert, dip a cloth in hot
water, wring out, and quickly
wrap round the mold for a
moment or two to loosen.
Turn out onto a serving plate.

• • •

265

COMPOTE OF SPICED DRIED FRUIT

Time: 30 minutes + soaking time
Very easy

2 cups sweet white wine
½ cup seedless white raisins
1 cup pitted prunes
1 cup dried apricots
2 apples
1 tbsp mild curry powder

Soak the seedless white raisins, prunes, and apricots in the wine for at least 12 hours. Drain off a little of the wine and mix with the curry powder. Transfer the fruit and all the liquid (including that mixed with the curry) to a saucepan, cover, and cook until tender, adding a little water if the fruit tends to stick to the pan. If there is too much liquid, reduce by boiling with the lid off.
Peel, core, and dice the apples; mix with the curried fruit and transfer to a serving bowl. Serve.

•   •   •

PRUNES IN WINE

Serve in individual glasses or dishes with rosettes of cream piped on top, using a fluted tube.

Time: 5 minutes + soaking time
Very easy

1 lb pitted prunes
1 tsp cinnamon
¼ cup sugar
2 cups Muscat de Beaumes de Venise or a good sweet California Muscat wine
2 tsp lemon juice

COMPOTE OF SPICED
DRIED FRUIT
■ The inclusion of curry
powder in this dish may seem
incongruous but the flavors
blend very well together. Use
a very mild curry powder.

Place the prunes in a fairly small deep bowl and sprinkle with the cinnamon and the sugar. Add enough wine to cover completely and 2 tsp lemon juice. Leave to soak overnight and then chill in the refrigerator the next day until ready to serve.

• • •

PEAR AND RASPBERRY JELLIED MOLD

The pears are arranged in a deep dish which has been rinsed with cold water; once the jelly has set round the fruit the dish can be turned upside down to release an attractive mold.

Time: 30 minutes + setting time
Very easy

6 pears
½ cup water
⅔ cup sugar
2 drops vanilla extract
1 cup raspberry jelly
1 tbsp brandy

Peel, quarter, and core the pears. Boil the sugar, water, and vanilla until the sugar has completely dissolved. Leave to cool a little before pouring over the pears. Chill for 2 hours.
Melt the raspberry jelly (or sieved raspberry jam) over low heat, stirring with a wooden spoon; add the brandy. Remove from the heat and allow to cool a little. Drain the pears and place them in a serving plate. Glaze with a thin film of the melted jelly. Chill for 2 hours or until the jelly has set again before serving.

• • •

FRUIT JELLY

The contrasting green or orange of the melon and deep pink of the watermelon are very effective set in the jelly.

Time: 1 hour
Very easy

¼ lb sugar cubes
3 oranges, washed and dried
3 lemons, washed and dried
2 egg whites
3 tbsp gelatin powder
1 melon
1 watermelon
½ cup kirsch
½ cup sugar

Rub the sugar cubes against the peel of the oranges and lemons to extract the essential oils. Juice all the oranges and lemons and pour into a bowl adding 2¼ cups water and the sugar cubes. Heat to boiling point, add the lightly beaten egg whites to clarify the mixture and simmer for about 15 minutes. Pour through a fine sieve into a bowl (the egg white and any matter it has collected are discarded) and immediately sprinkle in the gelatin powder. Make sure this dissolves completely. Leave to cool. Rinse a mold with cold water, pour a little of the jelly mixture into it, and tip in various directions so that the inside is coated all over with a thin layer of jelly. Place in the refrigerator. Leave the remaining jelly at room temperature.
Use a melon baller to scoop the flesh out of the melon (having discarded the seeds and filaments) and the watermelon. Place in a bowl and sprinkle with the kirsch and sugar before leaving to stand for 30 minutes. Use a slotted ladle to transfer the

melon balls into the mold; fill with the remaining jelly. Leave to set in the refrigerator for at least 6 hours. Turn out just before serving, dipping the mold in warm water if necessary to loosen and release the jelly before turning out onto a serving plate.

• • •

LEMON CREAM WITH BLUEBERRIES

Time: 1 hour
Very easy

4 eggs, separated
½ cup sugar
¼ cup lemon juice
rind of ½ lemon, grated
1 cup whipping cream
¾ lb fresh blueberries

Place the egg yolks in a bowl with the sugar. Beat thoroughly, adding the sugar a little at a time; when pale and fluffy, beat in the strained lemon juice and the grated lemon peel. Cook over slowly simmering water, stirring constantly until the mixture thickens somewhat, taking great care not to overheat or it will curdle. Draw aside from the heat and leave to cool. Beat the cream and the egg whites in separate bowls until stiff and fold first the cream, then the egg whites gently but thoroughly into the cold lemon mixture. Transfer to a glass serving bowl and chill for 2 hours. Sprinkle the washed and dried berries just before serving.

• • •

Fritter batter can be made with flour, rice, semolina, and other floury substances, mixed with eggs, milk, and other liquids (sometimes beer is added for extra lightness) and this batter is then fried at high heat in various types of oil (which can be low in cholesterol), butter or shortening. By preparing fried foods at the last minute they reach the table when still deliciously crisp, light, and digestible. This is a way of turning very inexpensive ingredients into mouthwatering treats. The batter forms a protective coating when fruit and other foods are dipped in it; the soft, moist center contrasting with the crisp, light surround. The advent of electric deep-fryers, equipped with thermostats and closed while in use, means that deep-frying is now a good deal safer than it used to be, but frying should always be watched carefully (never leave the pan or deep-frying machine unattended) and the fryer turned off or removed from the heat source as soon as you have finished with it.

FRIED BANANAS

Use bananas immediately after slicing them or mix with lemon juice to prevent discoloration.

Time: 1 hour
Easy

6 bananas
1 cup dark (Jamaica) rum
½ cup granulated sugar
½ cup all-purpose flour
oil for deep-frying
1½ tbsp confectioners' sugar

Cut the bananas lengthwise in half. Mix the rum with 1½ tbsp of the granulated sugar and place the bananas in it. Make sure the bananas are moistened all over; leave to soak for 30 minutes, turning once or twice.
Mix the flour with the remaining sugar and coat the bananas all over with this. Fry the bananas in plenty of very hot oil (deep-fry, or shallow-fry turning once). Drain well on kitchen towels. Serve immediately, sprinkled with the sifted confectioners' sugar.

•   •   •

DEEP-FRIED CHERRIES

The only liquid content in this batter is provided by the eggs: it is thick and therefore suitable for coating any other juicy fruits such as strawberries or plums.

Time: 1 hour
Easy

3 eggs
½ cup all-purpose flour
1 tbsp brandy

□ *Sometimes fried foods and fritters fail to achieve the light, airy crispness which makes them so delectable; to avoid this, follow a few guidelines: use best-quality oil which has not been used before for any savory frying or pure lard which gives excellent results. Use suitable, safe utensils, preferably electric deep-fryers, and have the oil or fat at the right temperature. Leave the batter to stand once made.*

□ *In order to know when the oil or fat has reached a suitable temperature a special thermometer is often used but there are other ways of checking. When using olive oil learn to watch for the point just before it begins to smoke and turn paler. Test the temperature by dropping a cube of bread into the oil or fat: when little bubbles form around the bread, the temperature is high enough.*

□ *Always eat fried foods as soon as they are cooked or they will quickly lose their lightness and crispness and become indigestible and soggy. When lard is used, frying at fairly high temperatures helps to prevent too much fat soaking into the fritters; drain these when golden brown on kitchen towels and this will absorb a good deal of the fat.*

□ *Remember always to fry in small batches; if too many items are fried at once the temperature will fall too low. Oils or fats used to fry sugary foods should be disposed of after being used to fry a very large quantity, or several smaller quantities on successive occasions, or they may become toxic. A final safety reminder: never leave a pan of oil unattended for more than a minute or so without first turning off the heat; fat can quickly overheat and present a fire risk if not supervised.*

pinch salt
1½ tbsp olive oil
2¼ lb cherries
oil for deep-frying
1 tbsp vanilla sugar or confectioners' sugar

Break the eggs into a bowl and beat with a fork; gradually beat in the sifted flour, the brandy, salt, olive oil, and just enough cold water to make a very thick coating batter. Leave the batter to stand for 30 minutes.
Wash and dry the cherries; remove their stalks and pit. Thread two or three at a time on a thin wooden skewer (a satay stick is ideal), dip into the batter, and fry in very hot oil. Remove the cherries from the skewer once each batch is fried; place on kitchen towels to drain; serve hot, sprinkled with the sugar.

•   •   •

APPLE FRITTERS
■ *Pears can also be used for fritters following the same recipe. Choose firm cooking pears.*

APPLE FRITTERS

Time: 1 hour 30 minutes
Easy

6 apples
1 cup brandy
3 tbsp sugar
½ cup all-purpose flour
½ cup cold water
1 tbsp olive oil or melted
　butter
1 egg white
oil for deep-frying
1 tbsp confectioners' sugar

Peel and core the apples; slice into fairly thick rings and place in a dish containing the brandy mixed with the sugar (if preferred, dilute the sugar and brandy with ½ cup warm water). Turn frequently to moisten the apples evenly. Prepare the batter by mixing the water and oil (or melted butter) gradually into the flour. Add a pinch salt if wished. When the batter has stood for 1 hour, stir in the stiffly beaten egg white. Heat the oil. Drain the apple slices and dry thoroughly before dipping in the batter. Fry a few at a time in smoking hot oil or lard. They can also be shallow-fried but will not be so crisp or light; turn once. Drain on kitchen towels briefly, sprinkle with the confectioners' sugar, and serve while they are piping hot and crisp.

•　•　•

PINEAPPLE FRITTERS

The moist filling inside these crisp fritters provides a pleasant surprise. Do not overfill the fritters and take care to seal very well.

Time: 1 hour
Easy

1¾ cups all-purpose flour
3 tbsp butter
1 cup sour cream
1½ tbsp clear, runny honey
pinch salt
1 cup finely chopped fresh
　pineapple
3 tbsp shredded coconut
1½ tbsp finely chopped or
　ground almonds
3 tbsp sugar
juice of 1 lemon
oil for deep-frying
1–2 tbsp confectioners' sugar

Mix the flour with the softened butter, sour cream, honey, and salt to make a soft dough. Leave to stand for 20 minutes; roll out into a thin sheet on a floured pastryboard. Cut out into disks with a 3-in cookie cutter. Make the filling: drain off excess juice from the pineapple, and mix with the coconut, almonds, sugar, and lemon juice. Place a little of this filling in the center of half the pastry disks and cover each with another disk, pressing all round the edges to seal thoroughly (moisten the edges with water for a better seal).
Heat the oil until smoking hot. Fry a few fritters at a time until crisp and golden brown. If shallow-fried, turn once. Drain on kitchen towels and sprinkle with the confectioners' sugar. Serve very hot.

271

PINEAPPLE

The prince of tropical fruits, available nearly all the year round. Canned pineapple can be substituted when necessary. Pineapple breaks down gelatin; use agar-agar for setting pineapple-flavored jellos, cheesecakes, and other set desserts.

MARSALA FRITTERS

These are a sweet, crisp version of the more widely known small, savory stuffed pasta shapes. Rum can be used instead of Marsala. Leave out the sugar and these become a good savory fritter, served alone or with meat dishes.

Time: 40 minutes
Easy

3 eggs
3 tbsp olive oil or melted butter
¼ cup Marsala or rum
¼ cup sugar
1 cup all-purpose flour
1 tsp baking powder
oil for frying
1 tbsp confectioners' sugar

Beat the eggs thoroughly with the oil or melted butter, Marsala, sugar; sift together the flour and baking powder and add to the mixture. Heat the oil until smoking hot and add the butter in tablespoonfuls to fry until crisp, puffed up and golden brown. Deep-fry or shallow-fry (turn once if shallow-frying). Drain on kitchen towels. Serve very hot, sprinkled with confectioners' sugar.

• • •

SEMOLINA FRITTERS

The addition of semolina makes these fritters very crisp; they melt in the mouth. Semolina has a lower starch content than flour and is therefore more friable.

Time: 1 hour
Easy

2½ cups water
¾ cup clear, runny honey
1 tbsp lard
pinch salt
2 bay leaves
2¾ cups all-purpose flour
¼ cup semolina
6 egg yolks
oil for deep-frying
3 tbsp sugar

Pour the water into a saucepan, add the honey, lard, salt, and bay leaves and bring to a boil; draw aside from the heat and immediately pour in all the flour and semolina. Stir vigorously with a wooden spoon. Return the pan to low heat and heat, stirring continuously, the very thick mixture as well as you can for a few minutes. Allow to cool a little, remove and discard the bay leaves; beat in the egg yolks very thoroughly one at a time. Shape the dough into rounds and fry, one at a time, in the smoking hot oil. Place on kitchen towels to drain while keeping hot as you finish frying the rings and sprinkle with sugar; serve immediately.

• • •

CHESTNUT AND APRICOT
FRITTERS
■ *You can vary the fruit
preserves used to fill these
delicious fritters.*

FRITTERS AND OTHER FRIED DESSERTS

CHESTNUT FRITTERS

*These are a carnival-time
specialty in their native Italy; a
few pine nuts are often added
and go very well with the
chestnut flavor.*

*Time: 45 minutes
Easy*

2¾ cups chestnut flour (or
    cooked, peeled, and sieved
    sweet chestnuts)
1½ tbsp sugar
½ cup seedless white raisins,
    soaked
1½ tbsp Grand Marnier
1½ tsp baking powder
pinch salt
oil for frying

Sift the chestnut flour into a
large bowl; stir in the sugar,
the drained seedless white
raisins, the liqueur, salt, and
just enough water to make a
fairly thick, creamy batter,
just liquid enough to be called
a pouring batter. Leave to
stand for 15 minutes.
Fry tablespoons of the batter
(deep-fry, or shallow-fry
turning once) and drain on
kitchen towels; serve very hot.

• • •

CHESTNUT AND APRICOT FRITTERS

*Time: 1 hour 20 minutes +
    standing time
Easy*

½ lb dried chestnuts
1½ tsp baking powder
½ cup apricot jam
1½ tbsp liqueur of choice
1¾ cups all-purpose flour
1 egg
2 tbsp butter, melted

½ cup sugar
a little milk
oil for deep-frying
1½ tbsp confectioners' sugar

Soak the chestnuts in cold
water for at least 3 hours.
Drain, place in a saucepan with
fresh water, and boil for 40
minutes or until floury and
tender. Drain and push
through a sieve (or use a
potato ricer) while still hot.
Mix with the apricot jam and
liqueur.
Sift the flour with the baking
powder into a mound on the
work surface, make a well in
the middle and break the egg
into it, add the melted butter
and the sugar and gradually
work the contents of the well
into the chestnut flour, adding
just enough milk to form a soft
dough.
Roll out into a fairly thin sheet;
use a small, round cookie
cutter to cut out as many disks
of pastry as possible. Place a
little jam in the center of each
disk, fold over to enclose the
filling, and press the edges
firmly together. Deep-fry a
few of the fritters at a time in
very hot oil. Drain briefly on
kitchen towels, sprinkle with
the confectioners' sugar, and
serve immediately.

• • •

RUM FRITTERS

*For a more elaborate recipe, do
not cut the disks in half; place
some jam or pastry cream on
each circle, fold in half, sealing
tightly (moisten the edges) to
enclose the filling, and fry.*

*Time: 1 hour + rising time
Easy*

2¾ cups all-purpose flour

RICOTTA FRITTERS
■ Ricotta is a low-fat, very mild cheese, versatile enough to be used for all sorts of desserts and other sweet things. Buy it as fresh as you can.

1 tbsp sugar
1 cake fresh yeast or 1 package (¼ oz) dry yeast
¼ cup warm milk
2 eggs
pinch salt
¼ cup (½ stick) butter
3 tbsp rum
oil for deep-frying

Sift the flour into a bowl, add the sugar, the yeast dissolved in the warm milk, the lightly beaten eggs, salt, melted butter, and the rum and stir well; the dough should be soft and smooth.
Dust the work surface lightly with flour and knead the dough until it is elastic, pulling it away from the work surface and slapping it back down. Shape into a ball, return it to the bowl, and cover with a cloth or towel; leave in a warm place to rise for 3 hours or until doubled in bulk. Pinch down the dough and roll out with a lightly-floured rolling pin to a sheet just over ⅛ in thick. Use a 4-in round cookie cutter or a glass to cut out into disks, cut each circle in half, and deep-fry until crisp and golden. Drain on kitchen towels and serve immediately.

• • •

RICOTTA FRITTERS

Time: 1 hour
Easy

1 boiled floury potato
½ cup ricotta, sieved
1 egg
1½ tbsp sugar
peel of 1 orange, grated
1¾ cups all-purpose flour
1½ tsp baking powder
3 tbsp orange liqueur or orange flower water

pinch salt
oil for deep-frying
1½ tbsp confectioners' sugar

Sieve or rice the potato while still hot and place in bowl with the ricotta. Beat in the egg with a wooden spoon; stir in the sugar, sift in the flour and baking powder together, and add the liqueur and the salt. Continue stirring until the mixture is smooth and evenly blended. Leave to stand for 30 minutes. Break off small pieces of the dough and flatten these between the palms of your floured hands. Shallow-fry a few at a time in very hot oil, turning once, or deep-fry, using a frying basket. Drain on kitchen towels, sprinkle with the confectioners' sugar, and serve immediately.

• • •

BEIGNETS (FRIED CHOUX BALLS)

These will look very professional if the mixture is piped into little heaps on a cookie sheet lightly smeared with almond oil (use a pastry bag and large tube). They can then be deep-fried in batches.

Time: 1 hour
Easy

1 cup water
generous pinch salt
¼ cup (½ stick) butter
¼ cup sugar
1½ cups all-purpose flour
4 eggs
oil for deep-frying

Bring the water to a boil in a saucepan with the salt, butter, and sugar. As soon as boiling point is reached, draw aside from the heat and immediately pour all the flour at once into the pan, stirring quickly and vigorously with a wooden spoon; if you mix quickly and energetically, lumps will not form.
Remove from the heat and beat in the eggs extremely thoroughly one at a time. The choux dough should be smooth, glossy, and dense. Break off small pieces of dough (about 1 rounded tbsp), roll into balls quickly between your palms, and deep-fry a few at a time.

• • •

RICE FRITTERS

The baking powder provides a necessary leavening agent for a mixture which would otherwise be rather heavy when fried: rice has an extremely high starch content.

Time: 1 hour 15 minutes
Easy

1 cup pudding (short-grain) rice
2¼ cups milk
¼ cup sugar
1 egg
2½ tsp baking powder
3 tbsp all-purpose flour
oil for deep-frying
3 tbsp vanilla sugar or confectioners' sugar

Cook the rice gently in the milk until all the liquid has been completely absorbed. Remove from the heat and quickly but thoroughly stir in the sugar, then the lightly beaten egg, the baking powder and enough flour to make the mixture very firm. Leave to stand for 15 minutes before frying firmly packed tablespoonfuls in smoking hot oil. Sprinkle with the vanilla sugar and serve immediately.

• • •

POTATO RINGS

If you like cloves, flavor these fritters with a generous pinch ground cloves or with finely grated lemon peel.

Time: 1 hour 10 minutes + rising time
Easy

½ lb boiled floury potatoes
1 cake compressed fresh yeast or 1 package (¼ oz) dry yeast

½ cup warm water
1¾ cups all-purpose flour
1 tsp salt
1 tsp cinnamon
oil for deep-frying
1½ tbsp confectioners' sugar

Sieve the potatoes while still warm or put through a ricer. Dissolve the yeast in the warm water, mix with the potatoes and the flour; work the dough until smooth and well blended. Add the salt and cinnamon. Roll out pieces of the dough into long sausages of even width (about ¾ in in diameter) and cut off lengths about 6 in long; pinch the ends together to form little rings and leave to rise in a warm place, covered with a cloth or towel until doubled in bulk. Deep-fry a few rings at a time in smoking hot oil; sprinkle with the confectioners' sugar and serve.

• • •

FRITTER BATTER FOR FRUIT

Make sure you dry the fruit to be fried very thoroughly before dipping in this quick and simple batter; sliced fruits can be dusted with confectioners' sugar before dipping.

Time: 10 minutes
Very easy

1¼ cups all-purpose flour
1 tbsp baking powder
1 tbsp sugar
2 egg yolks
pinch salt
½ cup white wine
2 stiffly beaten egg whites

Sift the flour and baking powder together into a bowl; add the sugar, the lightly

beaten egg yolks, and salt. Stir well. Mix in the wine a little at a time. Stir in the stiffly beaten egg whites gently but thoroughly.

• • •

BRANDY BATTER FOR FRUIT FRITTERS

This is an even lighter batter than the previous recipe; Grand Marnier or Cointreau can be substituted for the brandy.

Time: 10 minutes
Easy

1¼ cups all-purpose flour
1 egg yolk
1 tbsp sugar
1½ tbsp brandy
1 tbsp olive oil or melted butter
pinch salt
½ cup water
1 stiffly beaten egg white

Place the flour in a mixing bowl and stir in the egg yolk, the sugar, brandy, oil, salt, and water. Mix in the stiffly beaten egg white. Dip the prepared fruit in this batter and fry immediately.

• • •

CREAM CHEESE FRITTERS

A lighter dough can be made by using sieved ricotta instead of mascarpone.

Time: 1 hour + rising time
Easy

1 tbsp dry yeast
½ cup milk

1¾ cups unbleached all-purpose flour
1 tbsp oil
1 cup mascarpone, ricotta, or other cream cheese
1 tbsp sugar
pinch salt
oil for deep-frying

Scald the milk, cool to the correct temperature, and add the yeast. Have all the other ingredients at warm room temperature. Leave to stand to reactivate the dry yeast until it foams. Place the flour in a mound in a large mixing bowl, make a well in the center, and place the yeast and milk in it together with the oil, mascarpone, sugar, and a pinch of salt. Combine all the ingredients together and then knead until the dough is smooth and elastic. Cover and leave to stand for 1 hour in a warm place. Roll out into a sheet ¼ in thick and cut this into shapes of your choice: rhomboids, diamonds, rectangles, using a fluted cookie cutter. Deep-fry a few at a time in very hot oil until puffed up and golden brown. Drain on kitchen towels.

• • •

CARNIVAL BEIGNETS

Time: 1 hour 30 minutes
Easy

½ cup + 2 tbsp cold water
¼ cup (½ stick) butter
pinch salt
1¼ cups all-purpose flour
3 eggs
¼ cup sugar
peel of 1 lemon, grated
lard or oil for frying
3 tbsp vanilla sugar

Heat the water with the butter and salt. Draw aside from the heat and immediately pour all the sifted flour at once into the pan, stirring fast and very vigorously with a wooden spoon. Return to a low heat and continue mixing until this choux paste leaves the sides of the pan cleanly.

Remove from the heat; beat in the eggs, adding one at a time and mixing very thoroughly before adding the next. Add the sugar and lemon peel. Leave to stand for 10 minutes. Deep-fry 1–1½ tbsp at a time (use a pastry bag and large tube if preferred, cutting off 1½-in lengths into the hot fat. These beignets should be light, airy, and golden brown. Sprinkle with the vanilla sugar or plain confectioners' sugar and serve very hot.

• • •

RAGS AND TATTERS

Time: 1 hour
Easy

2¼ cups all-purpose flour
3½ tbsp butter
1½ tbsp sugar
2 eggs
3 tbsp brandy
pinch salt
oil for frying
1 tbsp confectioners' sugar

Place the flour in a large mixing bowl and rub in the softened butter (or use a pastry blender); stir in the sugar, eggs, brandy, and salt and work into a smooth dough, firm enough to be rolled out easily. Shape into a ball, wrap in a cloth, and leave to stand in a warm place for 30 minutes. Knead the dough again; roll out as thinly as possible. Cut into rhomboids, rectangles, diamonds, wide strips etc. and fry in very hot oil. Drain on kitchen towels and sprinkle with confectioners' sugar.

• • •

NEAPOLITAN FRITTERS

Using lard in pastry in fritter dough gives particularly good results as these featherlight rectangles of pastry prove.

Time: 1 hour 15 minutes
Easy

scant 1 cake fresh yeast (or scant 1 package dry yeast)
2¼ cups all-purpose flour
2 eggs
¼ cup lard, softened
¼ cup sugar
oil for frying
½ cup clear, runny honey
¼ cup alkermes (or other) liqueur

Dissolve the yeast in ¼ cup warm water. Place the flour in a large mixing bowl, make a well in the center, and place the eggs in it together with the dissolved yeast and water, the lard, and sugar. Combine the ingredients thoroughly, and leave to stand in a warm place until the surface becomes wrinkled.

Knead the dough; roll out in a sheet ¼ in thick. Cut into small rectangles; fry these in very hot oil. Drain on kitchen towels. Slightly warm the honey and mix with the liqueur, and drizzle over the fritters.

• • •

SPICED STUFFED FRITTERS

An alternative, lighter filling can be made by mixing chopped candied fruit or peel and spices with 1 egg.

Time: 1 hour 30 minutes
Easy

1¾ cups all-purpose flour
1 tbsp olive oil
½ cup white wine
pinch salt
For the filling:
½ lb sweet chestnuts, boiled, skinned and sieved
1 tsp honey
1 tbsp unsweetened cocoa powder
1 tsp cinnamon
1 tbsp roasted almonds, finely chopped
1 tbsp mixed candied fruit or peel, finely diced
peel of ½ orange, grated
1 tbsp instant coffee powder
1½ tbsp sweet liqueur
oil for frying
1 tbsp confectioners' sugar

Make the pastry, combining the flour, oil, wine, and salt, adjusting the amount of wine according to how dry or soft the pastry is, as it has to be rolled out into a thin sheet. Knead the pastry well before rolling out and cut out disks approx. 2½ in in diameter. Mix all filling ingredients together thoroughly and place 1 heaping tsp of this mixture in the center of half the disks. Moisten round the edges with water. Place another pastry disk on top of each, and press the disks firmly together to seal. Deep-fry a few at a time until crisp and golden brown. Sprinkle with the confectioners' sugar and serve.

Keep each batch of fritters hot while you deep-fry the rest.

6 pears
3 tbsp sugar
1 cup brandy
½ cup all-purpose flour
½ cup water
1 tbsp olive oil
1 egg white
oil for deep-frying
1 tbsp confectioners' sugar

Peel and core the pears (use an apple corer) and cut into rings. Mix the brandy and sugar and soak the pears in this mixture for 1 hour, turning a few times so that they are all evenly moistened and flavored.

Add ½ cup warm water to the brandy and sugar if preferred (for a more delicate flavor and to help dissolve the sugar).

Make the coating batter by mixing the water and oil gradually into the flour. Leave to stand for about 45 minutes or longer, adding the stiffly beaten egg white just before you are going to cook the pear fritters.

Drain the pear rings and pat dry with kitchen paper towels (or drain and coat with extra confectioners' sugar). Dip the rings in the batter a few at a time.

Fry in batches to avoid lowering the temperature of the oil or lard which should be smoking hot.

When the batter coating is crisp and golden brown, remove from the oil with a slotted ladle or spoon and drain on kitchen towels. Sprinkle with confectioners' sugar.

Serve without delay while still very hot.

SWALLOWS' NESTS
■ Use a special long-handled potato nest basket to deep-fry these: the smaller basket sandwiches the pastry between itself and the outer basket, resulting in a very good nest shape.

SWALLOWS' NESTS

Time: 1 hour
Easy

2¼ cups all-purpose flour
2 eggs
oil for frying
¼ cup clear, runny honey
1 cup walnut pieces

Mix the eggs and flour together for the pastry; roll this out on a lightly-floured board to a thin sheet. Dust lightly with flour, roll up as you would a jelly roll and cut into thin strips. (This method helps to ensure an even width for the strips of pastry.)
Use 2 or 3 of these strips to shape spirals in the palm of your hand, pressing the ends of the strips together to join and transfer to a metal tea strainer, pushing the center of the spiral down into the strainer. Lower the strainer very carefully (use tongs if necessary) into the very hot oil and fry until crisp and golden brown. (If you have the special long-handled potato nest basket utensil for frying, use it for ease and safety.)
Drain on kitchen towels.
When all the "nests" have been fried, fill with some of the walnut pieces and some of the honey (see illustration on this page).

• • •

RIBBON FRITTERS

Use the best lard for these fritters and have it at the right temperature, smoking hot, for the crispest, lightest fried pastry.

Time: 1 hour
Easy

2¾ cups all-purpose flour
¼ cup sugar
1 whole egg and 1 extra yolk
2 tbsp butter
3 tbsp white vermouth
pinch salt
lard for frying
1 tbsp vanilla sugar or
    confectioners' sugar

Heap the flour up in a large mixing bowl; make a well in the center and place the sugar, eggs, softened butter, vermouth, and salt in it. Work these ingredients gradually into the flour; the resulting dough should be firm but not stiff or dry. Place between two lightly-floured plates to rest for 5 minutes, then roll out as thinly as possible.
Use a fluted cookie cutter to cut into scalloped ribbons (about ¾ in wide and about 6 in long). Tie each of these into a loose knot in the center, leaving the ends free (see the illustration on pages 268–9) and deep-fry one at a time in very hot lard until crisp and golden brown (if shallow-frying, turn once).
Drain on kitchen towels and sprinkle with the vanilla sugar.

• • •

NEAPOLITAN SWEET GNOCCHI

Lard (made from refined pork fat) keeps well under refrigeration. It is invaluable for successful frying, and gives light results.

Time: 1 hour
Easy

2¾ cups all-purpose flour
2 eggs
¼ cup lard
2 tbsp sugar
2 tsp baking soda
pinch salt
¼ cup brandy
peel of 1 lemon, grated
lard for frying
¾ cup diced candied orange
    and citron peel
2 tbsp grated orange peel
½ cup clear, runny honey

Sift the flour onto the pastryboard or working surface; make a well in the center and in it place the eggs and softened lard, sugar, baking soda, brandy, and lemon peel. Combine all these ingredients together thoroughly; if too stiff or dry, moisten with a little more brandy.

Shape into a ball, knead briefly, and then roll out until ⅜ in thick. Cut into strips ⅜ in wide and then cut these in turn into ⅜-in lengths, resulting in ⅜-in cubes.

Heat the lard until very hot but not smoking (drop a cube of bread in, and if bubbles form around it, the lard is ready) and fry a few cubes at a time. Remove and drain when pale golden brown. A slightly lower temperature than usual is best for these gnocchi, to ensure that they cook inside without burning on the outside.

• • •

MACAROON AND RICOTTA CROQUETTES

Shallow-fry these croquettes in butter; turn so that they color an even golden brown.

Time: 45 minutes
Easy

2 cups crushed amaretti or
  crisp macaroons
2 cups sieved ricotta
3 eggs
1½ tbsp all-purpose flour
¼ cup sugar
1 tsp cinnamon
1 cup dry, uncolored
  breadcrumbs
½ cup (1 stick) butter,
  preferably clarified, for
  frying

Use a food processor to reduce the amaretti to very fine crumbs; place these in a bowl with the ricotta. Stir well, adding 2 of the eggs, one at a time, the flour, sugar, and cinnamon. When well blended, shape into small balls using your floured hands. Dip in the remaining egg, lightly beaten, and then roll in the breadcrumbs.

Heat the butter in a heavy-bottomed skillet and fry the croquettes, turning them carefully. Drain on kitchen towels and serve.

• • •

CARNIVAL FRITTERS

Time: 1 hour
Easy

2¾ cups all-purpose flour
1 tbsp baking powder
2 eggs, separated
1 tbsp olive oil
1½ tbsp rum
¼ cup (½ stick) butter
½ cup sugar
peel of 1 lemon, grated
pinch salt
2¼ cups milk
oil for deep-frying
1 tbsp vanilla sugar

Sift the flour and baking powder together into a large mixing bowl, make a well in the center, and place the egg yolks in it with the oil, rum, the softened butter, sugar, lemon peel, and salt. Mix into the flour, add the stiffly-beaten egg whites to start moistening the mixture, followed by the milk; add just enough milk for a soft, smooth dough. Roll into long sausages ¾ in thick, using the palm of your hand. Cut into ¾-in lengths and press one side of these against the tines of a fork.

Fry a few at a time in hot, but not smoking hot, oil to ensure that they cook through without coloring too darkly. Drain on kitchen towels and sprinkle with the vanilla sugar or plain confectioners' sugar.

• • •

FRIED AMARETTI

These crisp little macaroons are made with a mixture of sweet and bitter almonds and lend themselves to a wide variety of uses.

Time: 45 minutes
Easy

1 egg
1¼ cups all-purpose flour
½ cup water
½ lb amaretti
1 cup rum
oil for frying

Beat the eggs and add the flour a little at a time, beating well. Add just enough water for a thick pouring batter. Dip the amaretti in the rum, then in the batter. Fry in very hot oil; drain on kitchen towels and serve.

• • •

CARNIVAL FRITTERS
■ If wished, these can be given a decorative pattern by pressing the little sausages of dough lightly against the tines of a fork.

CUSTARD FRITTERS

Time: 1 hour 15 minutes
Easy

2 whole eggs and 2 extra yolks
¼ cup all-purpose flour
2¼ cups milk
¼ cup sugar
peel of 1 small lemon, grated
For the coating:
1 cup all-purpose flour
1 egg
1 cup very fine breadcrumbs
oil for frying
1 tbsp vanilla sugar

Beat the 2 whole eggs lightly in a saucepan; mix a little cold milk very thoroughly with the flour, then stir in the remaining milk. Add to the saucepan containing the beaten eggs and heat slowly, stirring continuously; cook for about 10 minutes after the mixture has thickened. Add the sugar and lemon peel, mixing thoroughly. Remove from the heat and continue stirring until the custard has cooled somewhat; stir in the 2 yolks and continue stirring for a little while. Pour this thick custard out onto a marble slab slightly moistened with iced water. Leave to cool and set. Cut into rectangles or rhomboids, dip in the flour, then in the lightly beaten egg, and finally roll in the breadcrumbs.
Fry in very hot oil. Drain and sprinkle with the vanilla sugar or confectioners' sugar while still hot.

• • •

BREADCRUMB STICKS

These are light, delicate, and melt in the mouth; they need careful preparation as they tend to crumble easily. Add 1 egg yolk to the mixture to bind it more securely if wished.

Time: 40 minutes
Fairly easy

3 egg whites
¼ cup sugar
peel of 1 lemon, grated
2 cups breadcrumbs
oil for frying

Beat the egg whites stiffly, add the sugar, lemon peel, and breadcrumbs.
Place 1 tbsp of the mixture at a time between your flattened palms and roll out into little sticks. Deep-fry in very hot oil; drain on kitchen towels.

• • •

281

Legend has it that Nero savored a mixture of snow, honey, and fresh fruit juice as he watched Rome burn; even in those days the great and the fortunate could enjoy early versions of sherbets. These can be served between courses to refresh the palate or at the end of a meal. With all the sophistication of refrigeration, deep-freezing and ice-cream makers at our disposal, it is relatively easy to make these elegant and delicious creations. If you have no ice-cream maker, pour the mixture into a shallow container and freeze until slushy. Beat or process once more, add egg white if the recipe requires it, and return to the freezer. Repeat the operation once more.

GRAPE WATER ICE

For a stronger flavor, boil 2¼ cups grape juice for 5 minutes with 1 cup sugar instead of using a sugar syrup.

Time: 40 minutes
Very easy

1 cup sugar
2¼ cups water
2¼ lb grapes
1 lemon
1 egg white

Heat the sugar and water in a saucepan and boil over moderate heat for 5 minutes. Leave to cool. Wash and dry the grapes, remove their stalks, and crush in a sieve to extract the juice. Pour the juice through a finer sieve; measure out 1 cup and mix with the strained lemon juice. Stir this juice thoroughly into the cold sugar syrup and pour into the ice-cream maker. When the water ice has become thick but not hard, add the stiffly beaten egg white and continue processing until very firm.

□ *The word "sherbet" derives from the Arabic, the Arabs having been the first fully to exploit these thirst-quenching and cooling water ices; citrus fruits were originally used for flavoring.*

□ *Sherbets and water ices play a useful role in refreshing and cleansing the palate after rich food and are often served between courses (lemon sherbet is particularly popular for this purpose). Always serve sherbets in glass, never metal, dishes.*

□ *Special sherbet glasses, parfait glasses or medium-sized wine glasses, preferably crystal, are ideal; small, flattish glass plates or bowls can also be used. The easiest way to make sherbets is in an electric ice-cream maker: this ensures an even freezing temperature and stirs the mixture as it cools to avoid ice crystals forming. If you do not have a machine, freeze your sherbets and water ices in ice cube trays, having first removed the dividers. Stir frequently with a fork to keep the ice crystals as small as possible. Do not increase the sugar quantities given in these recipes; if the sugar solution is too strong, the sugar content may crystallize out, resulting in a rougher consistency. Granitas, making use of the same basic materials, are quicker and even easier to make.*

□ *Sherbets are often a more suitable end to a meal than ice creams as they are lighter. Lemon and mint sherbets and water ices are specifically designed to aid the digestion, either between courses or as a dessert.*

PAWPAW AND MANGO SHERBET

The color of this sherbet will vary, depending on the type of pawpaw used, between a delicate pink and orange. It can be served in a chilled oval dish surrounded by kiwi fruit slices.

Time: 30 minutes
Very easy

1 cup sugar
3 grapefruit
¼ lb kiwi fruit (peeled, stalk end removed)
½ lb pawpaw pulp
½ lb mango pulp

Place the sugar in a saucepan. Strain the juice of 2 grapefruit, add to the sugar, and boil for 5 minutes. Leave to cool. Juice the remaining grapefruit and place in a liquidizer with the flesh of the other fruits. Reduce to a smooth purée and stir this into the syrup, mixing very well, and pour into the ice-cream maker.

•   •   •

WINE SHERBET

Use Muscat de Beaumes de Venise or a fine California Muscat wine. Use the same recipe to make plain orange or grapefruit sherbet, replacing the wine with extra juice.

Time: 30 minutes
Very easy

1½ cups sugar
6 juicy oranges
4 lemons
1 cup sweet dessert wine
1 egg white

Mix the sugar and strained

PAWPAW
■ *A tropical fruit, it contains an enzyme (vegetable pepsin or papain) which makes it very digestible.*

juice of 3 oranges and 2 lemons in a saucepan. Bring to a boil and simmer for 5 minutes. Leave to cool before stirring in the wine and strained juice of the remaining oranges and lemons. Pour into the ice-cream maker and process for the required time. When the sherbet has thickened, add the stiffly beaten egg white; finish processing.

• • •

PASSION FRUIT SHERBET

Slices of this decorative fruit can be sliced and used to decorate the sherbet when it is spooned into glass dishes.

Time: 30 minutes
Very easy

1 cup sugar
4 oranges
1¼ lb fresh ripe passion fruit
1 egg white

Mix the sugar with the strained juice of 3 oranges in a saucepan, bring to a boil, and simmer for 5 minutes. Leave to cool.
Scoop out the passion fruit pulp and sieve. Mix in a bowl with the juice of the remaining orange. Add the orange syrup and stir well. Pour into the ice-cream maker, adding the stiffly beaten egg white when the sherbet has thickened, before the last 5 minutes' processing.

• • •

BANANA SHERBET

Without the swift addition of lemon juice the bananas will discolor once peeled and sliced.

Time: 30 minutes
Very easy

½ lb banana flesh
1 extra banana for decoration (sliced and sprinkled with lemon juice)
juice of 1 lemon
1 cup sugar
2¼ cups water
1 egg white
6 candied cherries

Sieve the banana and stir in the lemon juice. Bring the sugar and water to a boil; simmer for 5 minutes. Leave to cool; mix with the banana purée when cold. Pour into the ice-cream maker and

process in the usual way. When thick but not too firm, add the stiffly-beaten egg white. Process for a final 5 minutes. Serve the sherbet in individual glass dishes or tall glasses decorating each serving with a couple of banana slices and a candied cherry.

• • •

BLACKBERRY WATER ICE

A flavorsome late-summer dessert; decorate with piped whipped cream.

Time: 30 minutes
Very easy

1 cup sugar
2¼ cups water
3 cups blackberries
1 lemon
1 egg white

Place the sugar and water in a saucepan, bring to a boil and simmer for 5 minutes. Leave to cool. Wash and dry the blackberries and sieve into a bowl. Stir in the strained lemon juice. Mix with the cold sugar syrup. Pour into the ice-cream maker; process until thick, add the stiffly beaten egg white, and complete the final 5 minutes' processing.

• • •

CHAMPAGNE WATER ICE

Good sparkling white or rosé wine can be used instead of champagne; add a pinch of cinnamon if wished.

Time: 30 minutes
Very easy

1 cup sugar
2¼ cups water
2¼ cups champagne
4 large juicy lemons
1 egg white

Heat the sugar and water to boiling point; reduce the heat and simmer for 5 minutes. Leave until completely cold. Stir in the champagne and the strained lemon juice. Pour into the ice-cream maker. Stir and freeze until thick; stir in the stiffly beaten egg and process for a final 5 minutes or until very firm.

• • •

MELON WATER ICE

Soak the melon flesh in a little sweet dessert wine for 1 hour.

Time: 30 minutes
Very easy

1 cup sugar
2¼ cups water
2¼ lb ripe melon flesh
1 lemon

Place the sugar and water in a saucepan, bring to a boil and simmer for 5 minutes. Set aside to cool completely. Liquidize the melon flesh with the strained lemon juice. Combine with the cold syrup, stirring thoroughly, and then pour into the ice-cream maker. Process following instructions on your machine.

• • •

KIWI FRUIT WATER ICE

Cut the kiwi fruits in half (crossways, not lengthways) and scoop out the flesh neatly with a teaspoon; this is much quicker than peeling and less wasteful. For a more highly-flavored water ice, omit the sugar syrup and use 2¼ lb liquidized and sieved kiwi fruit; boil this purée with 1 cup sugar.

Time: 40 minutes
Very easy

3¼ lb peeled kiwi fruit
1 cup water
1 cup sugar
juice of 1 lemon
1 egg white

Place 2¼ lb of the kiwi fruit in a saucepan with the water and boil gently for 10 minutes. Strain thoroughly into another saucepan containing the sugar. Bring to a boil; simmer for 5 minutes. Leave this syrup to cool.
Peel the remaining kiwi fruits; liquidize with the strained lemon juice. Stir into the cold kiwi syrup; sieve and then pour into the ice-cream maker.
Process until thick, add the stiffly beaten egg white and complete the last 5 minutes' freezing and stirring.

• • •

MELON

Although honeydew melons are available all the year round they lack the delicious flavor and aroma of Charentais, Cantaloupe, or netted melons.

APRICOT WATER ICE

Time: 30 minutes
Easy

1 lb 6 oz ripe fresh, pitted apricots
juice of 1 lemon
1 cup sugar
2¼ cups water
1 egg white

Peel the apricots, if possible; liquidize to a very smooth purée with the strained lemon juice.
Bring the sugar and water to a boil; simmer for 5 minutes. Remove from heat and cool. When the syrup is cold, mix well with the apricot purée and pour into the ice-cream maker. Add the stiffly beaten egg white in the final stages of freezing and stirring, when the sorbet is thick but still stirrable. Continue processing

LEMON WATER ICE
■ *Traditionally this is served between main dishes (formerly after roasted game and before a casserole) to refresh the palate after a rich course and prepare for the next. Serve after any elaborate meat dish. A small helping will be enough for each guest.*

the 4 oranges; strain this juice into a saucepan, add the sugar and bring to a boil; boil gently for 5 minutes. Leave to cool. Stir in the pineapple purée, pour into the ice-cream maker and process until thick; add the stiffly beaten egg white and complete the last 5 minutes' stirring and freezing. Decorate with neat pieces of the remaining pineapple flesh before serving.

• • •

LEMON WATER ICE

Time: 45 minutes
Easy

12 lemons
1½ cups sugar
1 cup water
1 egg white

Wash the lemons well, dry, and juice them, pouring half

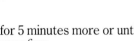

for 5 minutes more or until very firm.

• • •

PINEAPPLE SHERBET

Serve in individual glass dishes or glasses with a topping of stiffly beaten cream, slightly sweetened with confectioners' sugar.

Time: 30 minutes
Easy

1 ripe pineapple
juice of 1 lemon
juice of 4 oranges
1 cup sugar
1 egg white

Peel half the pineapple and cut into slices removing the hard central core. Liquidize with the strained lemon juice. Juice

the juice into a separate bowl. Carefully pare off the yellow part of the peel (with none of the bitter white pith) from 4 lemons. Cut into thin strips or shred, place in a saucepan with half the lemon juice, the sugar, and 1 cup water; bring to a boil then simmer for 5 minutes. Strain and leave to cool. Stir in the strained juice of the other 6 lemons and pour into the ice-cream maker. Process until the mixture thickens, add the stiffly-beaten egg white and complete the last 5 minutes' processing.

• • •

PEACH SHERBET

Chop a few peeled almonds with the kernels extracted from

the remaining peach pits; sprinkle on top of each serving together with a pinch of cinnamon.

Time: 30 minutes
Very easy

3 peach kernels, removed from inside their pits
1 cup sugar
2¼ cups water
6 large ripe, very juicy yellow peaches
juice of 1 lemon

Pound the peach kernels to a paste and place in a saucepan with the sugar and the water. Bring to a boil and boil gently for 5 minutes. Leave to cool before straining.
Liquidize the peach flesh with

the strained lemon juice. Combine the cold syrup and the purée; push through a fine mesh sieve (preferably nonmetallic) and pour into the ice-cream maker. Process as usual, stirring and freezing.

• • •

ORANGE WATER ICE

Time: 30 minutes + standing time
Easy

8 oranges
2 lemons
1½ cups sugar
2½ cups water
1 egg white

Juice the oranges and lemons; strain this juice through a fine mesh plastic or hair sieve. Pare off the peel (with none of the bitter white pith) of 1 orange; cut into strips or shred.
Heat the sugar, water and half the citrus juice in a saucepan to boiling point; simmer for 5 minutes. Draw aside from the heat; add the shredded orange peel immediately; stir and leave to stand for 1 hour before straining.
Mix the rest of the citrus juice with the strained fruit syrup, pour into the ice-cream maker and process until thick; add the stiffly beaten egg white and complete the freezing and stirring, when the water ice should be very firm.

• • •

WATERMELON SHERBET

To add extra flavor to this sherbet, add 1 cup gin; the two flavors complement each other.

Time: 30 minutes
Very easy

2¼ lb peeled watermelon flesh
juice of 1 lemon
1 cup sugar
1 egg white

Remove the seeds from the watermelon flesh and liquidize with the strained lemon juice. Simmer half this purée gently for 10 minutes; strain thoroughly, collecting the juice in a saucepan containing the sugar. Bring to a boil and simmer for 5 minutes. Leave this syrup to cool. When cold add the other half of the watermelon purée, stir well and pour into the ice-cream maker. Add the stiffly beaten egg white when the sherbet is thick, for the last 5 minutes' processing, when its consistency will become very firm.

• • •

STRAWBERRY WATER ICE

For individual servings, reserve a few strawberries; cut these in quarters and arrange to the same general effect as shown for the orange water ice presentation (left).

Time: 30 minutes
Easy

1½ cups sugar
2¼ cups water
juice of 1 orange
juice of 1 lemon
1¾ lb sound, ripe
   strawberries, washed,
   dried and hulled

Bring the sugar and water to a boil in a saucepan, simmer for

RED CURRANT WATER ICE
■ When serving this as a dinner party dessert, decorate with red currants still on the stem and whipped cream, colored with a little cochineal and piped.

5 minutes and leave to cool. Liquidize the strawberries with the strained citrus juice, stir thoroughly into the syrup, strain, and pour into the ice-cream maker. Stir and freeze as usual.

• • •

RASPBERRY AND WILD STRAWBERRY WATER ICE

Serve this sherbet heaped up in a mound in a shallow bowl; buy or gather a few extra strawberries and raspberries: arrange in flower shapes, with a whole raspberry in the center.

Time: 40 minutes
Easy

1 cup sugar
2¼ cups water
1 cup ripe pitted apricots
1⅓ cup raspberries
1½ cup wild strawberries
2 tbsp candied citron peel

Bring the sugar and water to a boil, simmer for 5 minutes and leave to cool. Liquidize the apricots (peel first if wished) with the raspberries and strawberries.
Cut the citron peel into very small dice. Combine the cold syrup, the purée, and the citron peel, stirring well. Pour into the ice-cream maker and process, stirring and freezing until very firm.

• • •

RED CURRANT WATER ICE

Time: 45 minutes
Easy

1 lb red currants
1½ cups black cherries
juice of 1 lemon
1½ cups sugar
2¼ cups water
1 egg white

Wash the fruit, remove the stalks, and dry well. Pit the cherries. Liquidize the fruit with the strained lemon juice and sieve.
Place the sugar and water in a saucepan, bring to a boil and simmer for 5 minutes. Leave to cool. When cold combine with the fruit purée. Stir well and pour into the ice-cream maker. Process until thick, add the stiffly beaten egg white, and continue processing for 5 more minutes or until very firm.

• • •

BLACK AND RED CURRANTS

Black currants are used to make the French drink *cassis* and, being sweeter than red currants, are more suitable for desserts while the very acidic red currants look most attractive but have to be sweetened, even when being used as an accompaniment to roasted meat and game.

TANGERINE SHERBET

This sherbet has a subtle, delicate flavor. Decorate with extra sections of tangerine, either caramelized or just with the thin inner skin removed.

Time: 30 minutes
Easy

12 tangerines
juice of 2 oranges
juice of 1 lemon
1 cup sugar
1 egg white

Juice the tangerines, the oranges, and the lemon and strain. Reserve the peel. Place half this juice in a saucepan with the sugar and bring to a boil; boil gently for 5 minutes. Draw aside from the heat and add the tangerine peel, cut into thin strips or shredded. Leave to stand for 1 hour.
Strain this sweetened juice and mix thoroughly with the other half of the juice; pour into the ice-cream maker and process till thick; add the stiffly beaten egg white and

continue stirring and freezing for 5 more minutes, until very firm.

• • •

CHERRY SHERBET

Cut a few extra cherries in half, remove the pits, and use to decorate individual servings of the sherbet in deep glass dishes or tall glasses.

Time: 45 minutes
Easy

1½ lb very ripe black cherries
2¼ cups water
peel and juice of 1 orange
juice of 1 lemon
1 cup sugar
1 tsp kirsch
1 egg white

Pit the cherries and liquidize. Place the pits in a saucepan with ½ cup of the water, bring to a boil and then simmer very gently for 10 minutes. Strain the orange and lemon juice. Put the sugar in a saucepan with the citrus juice, 1¾ cups of the water, bring to a boil and then simmer for 5 minutes. Add the orange peel (take care not to include any bitter white pith) and leave to cool. Add the water in which the cherry pits were boiled and strain.
Combine with the puréed cherries and kirsch, stirring well, and pour into the ice-cream maker. Process until thick; add the stiffly beaten egg white and continue with the freezing and stirring process until very firm.

• • •

ORANGE GRANITA

Granita, a Neapolitan specialty, is wonderfully refreshing. The ice should be crushed very finely. Decorate individual servings with small strips or dice of candied orange peel or other candied peel.

Time: 15 minutes
Very easy

5 oranges
½ cup sugar
1¼ lb ice cubes

Juice the oranges. Leave the ice cubes in the main part of the refrigerator for about 15 minutes before chopping or crushing (this can be done in a food processor but check that the blade is strong enough or the ice may damage it). When the ice is very finely chopped or crushed and looks like snow, transfer to a bowl, stir in the orange juice and pour into chilled glasses.

• • •

MINT GRANITA

Serve mint granita in tall glasses, garnished with mint leaves.

Time: 10 minutes
Very easy

1¼ lb ice
1¾ cups mint syrup

Chop the ice and crush or process in a liquidizer until very fine and snowy. Stir into the mint syrup. When thoroughly mixed pour into chilled glasses and serve immediately.

• • •

LEMON GRANITA

One of the classic granita recipes, full of flavor, aroma and very refreshing. Add more flavor with a little finely grated lemon peel if wished.

Time: 15 minutes
Very easy

6 lemons
½ cup sugar
1¼ lb ice
12 fresh mint leaves (6 pairs)

Juice the lemons and strain. Stir in the sugar thoroughly until it has dissolved. Crush the ice very finely or reduce to a snowy consistency in a food processor; transfer to a bowl and mix in the lemon juice. Serve in chilled glasses, placing a pair of mint leaves over the lip of the glass or on top of the granita.

• • •

COFFEE GRANITA

One of the best-known Neapolitan granitas. Sprinkle

drinking chocolate powder, or a little cinnamon sugar for a change, over the cream.

Time: 15 minutes
Very easy

½ cup sugar
½ cup very strong black coffee
1¼ lb ice
1 cup whipping cream
1 tbsp drinking chocolate powder

Add the sugar to the hot coffee, stir well, and leave to cool. When the coffee is cold (chill if you wish) chop and process the ice until fine and snowy; stir into the coffee. Serve in chilled glasses or cups with spoonfuls of stiffly beaten cream on top and a sprinkling of chocolate powder.

• • •

COFFEE FRAPPÉ

Time: 10 minutes
Very easy

1½ cups strong black coffee
1½ cups milk
3½ tbsp sugar
10 ice cubes

Process all the ingredients together in a liquidizer or food processor until the ice has dissolved. Pour into tall chilled glasses or tumblers.

• • •

CHOCOLATE FRAPPÉ

Ideal for a children's drink in the middle of a hot morning or afternoon.

Time: 10 minutes
Very easy

2½ cups milk
¾ cup unsweetened cocoa
   powder
10 ice cubes
3½ tbsp sugar

Liquidize all the ingredients thoroughly until the ice has disappeared.
Pour into tall, straight-sided glasses and serve immediately; decorate with a little sweetened whipped cream if wished.

• • •

ICED ORANGE COCKTAIL

A light coupe that can be served at the end of an elaborate meal.

Time: 30 minutes
Easy

3 oranges
3 tbsp seedless white raisins
2 tbsp butter
3 tbsp sugar
1 cup Cointreau
1 lb orange water ice (see
   page 288)
1½ tbsp shelled pistachio nuts

Peel the oranges, divide into sections, and carefully remove the thin inner skin.
Soak the seedless white raisins in warm water until plump, drain, and pat dry with kitchen towels.
Melt the butter in a wide saucepan, add the orange sections carefully, heat for 1 minute before sprinkling with the sugar; pour in the liqueur.
Add the seedless white raisins and cook briskly for a few minutes to reduce the liquid content.

Place 3 small scoops of orange water ice in each of 6 chilled glasses, or small glass dishes; arrange a few orange sections and seedless white raisins on top and around them with a little liquid, sprinkle with the pistachio nuts, and serve immediately.

• • •

TANGERINE SUNDAE

There is almost no end to the combinations of flavors which can be used to make up sundaes, using different sherbets, ice creams, and embellishments.

Time: 20 minutes
Very easy

2 candied tangerines
⅓ cup tangerine syrup
3 tbsp tangerine liqueur
1 cup melon water ice (see
   page 286)
1 cup kiwi fruit water ice (see
   page 286)
1 cup tangerine sherbet (see
   page 289)
1 cup whipping cream

Chop the candied tangerines and soak in a mixture of the tangerine syrup and liqueur.
Place a layer of melon water ice in the bottom of each chilled glass dish, followed by one of kiwi fruit water ice, then of tangerine sherbet.
Pipe the stiffly beaten cream on top, using a fluted tube.
Sprinkle 1 tbsp of the candied tangerine pieces on top; sprinkle with a little of the syrup and liqueur used for soaking these pieces and serve immediately.

• • •

T raditionally a chef was not considered worthy of that title unless he had mastered the art of ice-cream making, and the appearance and taste of old-fashioned ice cream made by an expert is certainly an unforgettable experience. Home ice-cream making is not at all difficult but only the purest, freshest, and finest-quality ingredients must be used. Scrupulous cleanliness is also necessary as the raw materials can easily become contaminated. It is probably wiser not to store homemade ice cream for prolonged periods but to make it only a couple of days before you plan to serve it. Make sure your freezer temperatures are sufficiently low. If you do not have an ice-cream maker, freeze the mixture in shallow freezing trays, and beat 2–3 times during the freezing process.

VANILLA ICE CREAM

Sweet without being cloying, full of natural flavor and creaminess, this ice cream is set off to perfection when served with slightly acid fruit such as strawberries or raspberries.

Time: 1 hour + standing time
Very easy

1 vanilla bean (or 1½ tsp vanilla extract)
1 quart rich milk
8 egg yolks
1 cup sugar

Heat the milk to scalding point, remove from the heat, and place the vanilla bean in it; leave to stand for 1 hour. Reheat to boiling and strain. If using vanilla extract, simply heat the milk once to boiling point.
Beat the egg yolks thoroughly with the sugar (and the vanilla extract if used) until very pale and fluffy (reaching the ribbon stage, i.e. when an unbroken "ribbon" of mixture falls back upon itself when the whisk is lifted high above the surface). Beat in the hot milk, adding it in a thin stream. Continue cooking over hot water, stirring continuously with a wooden spoon, until the custard coats the back of the spoon. Remove from the heat, pour into a large bowl, and stir from time to time until completely cold.
Strain, pour into the ice-cream maker or freezing trays, and freeze.

•   •   •

□ *A rather more sophisticated, elaborate preparation than the sherbet, ice cream in its modern form was invented in the sixteenth century by two Florentines, Buontalenti and Ranieri.*

□ *If you have an electric or other type of ice-cream maker, follow the instruction given by the manufacturer. If you have none, pour the ice cream mixture into the freezing trays usually used for making ice in the ice box of your refrigerator (remove the dividers first) or into a freezerproof bowl. When the ice cream starts to freeze, take it out of the freezer and stir thoroughly; return to the freezer and repeat three or more times as the mixture gradually thickens and then solidifies. In this way your ice cream will be smooth and light, without large ice crystals which would otherwise spoil its texture.*

□ *It is probably wiser to make your ice cream shortly before you need it (earlier the same day or 2–3 days in advance at most). Commercial ice-cream manufacturers have to ensure that their mixtures reach a certain temperature for a set length of time and they are cooled quickly and stored at extremely low temperatures.*

□ *Homemade ice cream is infinitely more delicious and much cheaper than most commercially prepared products. Take ice cream out of the freezer 30 minutes before serving and put it in the refrigerator so that it is not too cold; texture and flavor will both benefit.*

CHOCOLATE ICE CREAM

Buy the best semisweet chocolate you can find for this ice cream. Serve with stiffly beaten cream. Use 1 tsp vanilla extract if you cannot buy beans.

Time: 1 hour
Very easy

1 quart rich milk
1 vanilla bean
5 oz (5 squares) semisweet chocolate
8 egg yolks
½ cup sugar

Place the vanilla bean and milk in a saucepan and bring to a boil. Draw aside from the heat and add the chopped chocolate. Stir until completely melted.
Beat the egg yolks and sugar together (with the vanilla extract if used) until very pale and fluffy (ribbon stage).
Strain the milk and beat a little at a time into the egg and sugar mixture.
Place over hot water and continue cooking, stirring all the time until the mixture thickens enough to coat the back of the spoon.
Leave until completely cold, stirring from time to time as it cools. Strain through a fine sieve and pour into the ice-cream maker or freezing trays.

•   •   •

COFFEE ICE CREAM

Mix a spoonful of coarsely ground roasted coffee beans with a little finely chopped bitter chocolate; sprinkle on top of each serving.

Time: 1 hour
Very easy

1 quart rich milk
⅓ cup instant coffee powder
8 egg yolks
1 cup sugar

Bring the milk to a boil, stir in the coffee thoroughly until dissolved, and remove from the heat.
Beat the egg yolks and sugar together until very pale and fluffy (ribbon stage). Beat the strained milk into the eggs and sugar mixture a little at a time. Place over hot water and continue stirring while cooking until the custard has thickened enough to coat the back of the wooden spoon. Set aside from the heat and cool completely, stirring from time to time. Strain, pour into the ice-cream maker or freezing trays, and freeze.

• • •

EXTRA CREAMY PLAIN ICE CREAM

Time: 1 hour
Very easy

8 egg yolks
1 cup sugar
2¼ cups rich milk
2¼ cups heavy cream

Beat the egg yolks and sugar together until the ribbon stage is reached.
Place the milk and cream in a saucepan and bring to a boil; beat in thin stream into the egg mixture. Cook over hot water, stirring continuously, until the trace of a finger down the coated back of the wooden spoon remains clear. Leave to cool completely, stirring now and then.

Strain and pour into the ice-cream maker or freezing trays; process, freezing and stirring, until very firm; transfer to a cylindrical mold or other suitable container and press down firmly as you fill the mold. Serve on its own or in a variety of bombes.

• • •

FILBERT PRALINE ICE CREAM

Filbert nougatine or brittle can be bought in good confectionery shops or food stores. Decorate this ice cream with tiny meringues, sprinkled with cocoa powder.

Time: 1 hour 15 minutes
Very easy

½ lb filbert nougatine or nut brittle
1 quart rich milk
1 vanilla bean (or 3–4 drops vanilla extract)
8 egg yolks
¾ cup sugar

Reduce the nougatine or nut brittle to a fine, dry paste (praline) by pounding with a pestle and mortar, or use a food processor.
Bring the milk to a boil with the vanilla bean. Beat the egg yolks with the sugar (and the vanilla extract if used) until very pale and fluffy; beat in the strained hot milk a little at a time. Heat over hot water, stirring continuously until the mixture begins to coat the back of the wooden spoon. Stir in the praline and leave to cool completely.
Pour straight into the ice-cream maker or freezing trays without straining again. Freeze until very firm.

PISTACHIO ICE CREAM

This can be molded and turned out onto a serving dish, then surrounded by sliced bananas (sprinkled with lemon juice to prevent discoloration).

Time: 1 hour 15 minutes
Very easy

⅔ cup shelled pistachio nuts
1 quart rich milk
1 vanilla bean (or 2–3 drops vanilla extract)
¼ cup peeled almonds
8 egg yolks
1 cup sugar

Pound the pistachios and the almonds to a fine paste with a pestle and mortar, using 1½ tbsp of the milk to moisten the paste.
Bring the rest of the milk to a boil with the vanilla bean. Stir in the nut paste and set aside in a warm place (or in a very slow oven) for 20 minutes.

PISTACHIO

These delicious nuts have a long tradition in Middle Eastern cooking, in both sweet and savory preparations. Salted pistachio nuts are delicious with drinks. To remove the thin inner, papery skin, plunge in boiling water for a few seconds.

Beat the eggs with the sugar (and vanilla extract if used) over very hot water (the bowl must not touch the water).

Stir in the hot milk and nut mixture gently a little at a time. Place the double boiler over moderate heat and continue stirring with a wooden spoon until the mixture begins to coat the back of the spoon. Set aside to cool completely, stirring from time to time.
Pour into the ice-cream maker or freezing trays when cold and process as usual.

•   •   •

ROSE ICE CREAM

This recipe can be adapted to make jasmine ice cream, using essential oil of jasmine and jasmine water. Select the best-quality natural flavorings.

Time: 1 hour
Very easy

8 egg yolks
3¾ cups rich milk
sugar syrup (made by boiling ½ cup water with ½ cup + 1 tbsp sugar for 5 minutes)
peel of 1 lemon, grated
½ cup rose water
8 drops rose oil

Place the cream, egg yolks, sugar syrup, and lemon peel in a large blender and process at high speed (or beat vigorously in a bowl). Heat over low heat (or over hot water), stirring continuously with a wooden spoon until the mixture coats the back of the spoon. Set aside and leave until completely cold, stirring from time to time as it cools. Mix in the flavorings; pour into the ice-cream maker or freezing trays and freeze.

•   •   •

WALNUT ICE CREAM

Decorate this full-flavored ice cream with walnut halves.

Time: 1 hour 15 minutes
Very easy

½ cup walnut pieces
1 quart rich milk
1 vanilla bean (or 1 tsp vanilla extract)
8 egg yolks
1 cup sugar

Pound the walnuts to a fine paste adding 1½ tbsp water. Bring the milk to a boil with the vanilla bean. Stir in the walnut paste and leave to stand in a warm place for 20 minutes.
Beat the egg yolks and sugar (and the vanilla extract if used) until the ribbon stage is reached and the mixture is very pale and fluffy. Remove the vanilla bean if used and pour the milk a little at a time into the egg mixture while beating vigorously.
Heat over hot water while stirring continuously with a wooden spoon until the custard coats the back of the spoon. Set aside to cool. Stir from time to time. When cold pour into the ice-cream maker or freezing trays. Freeze until firm.

• • •

ALMOND ICE CREAM

Time: 1 hour
Very easy

1 quart rich milk
1 vanilla bean (or 2–3 drops vanilla extract)
⅓ cup peeled almonds
8 egg yolks

Bring the milk to a boil with the vanilla bean. Pound the almonds to a fine paste with 1½ tbsp water; add to the hot milk and leave to stand away from direct heat. Beat the egg yolks with the sugar (and vanilla extract if used) until the mixture forms a ribbon when the whisk is lifted above the bowl and is very pale. Beat in the hot milk and nut mixture a little at a time.
Cook over hot water, stirring continuously with a wooden spoon until the custard starts to coat the back of the spoon. Draw aside from the heat and allow to cool, stirring now and then. Remove the vanilla bean if used and pour into the ice-cream maker or freezing trays when completely cold. Freeze.

• • •

TEA ICE CREAM

This ice cream recipe comes from Japan. Try it with jasmine or Lapsang Souchong tea.

Time: 1 hour 10 minutes
Very easy

1 quart rich milk
1 vanilla bean (or 2–3 drops vanilla extract)
1 tbsp green tea
8 egg yolks
1 cup sugar
⅓ cup brandy

Bring the milk to a boil with the vanilla bean. Sprinkle in the tea leaves; cover and leave to stand away from direct heat for 10 minutes. Strain.
Beat the egg yolks and sugar together until very pale and greatly increased in bulk. Beat in the milk a little at a time.

297

WATERMELONS
■ These have a negligible fat and protein content, and are consequently low in calories. Nineteenth-century engraving.

Cook over hot water, stirring continuously with a wooden spoon until the custard starts to coat the back of the spoon. Draw aside from the heat and leave until cold, stirring at intervals as the mixture cools. Strain, stir in the brandy, and pour into the ice-cream maker or freezing trays.

• • •

CARAMEL ICE CREAM

Trickle a little hot caramel over each serving of this ice cream.

Time: 1 hour 10 minutes
Very easy

1 quart rich milk
1 vanilla bean (or 3–4 drops vanilla extract)
1 cup sugar
lemon juice
8 egg yolks

Bring the milk to a boil with the vanilla bean. Place ¾ cup of the sugar in a small

saucepan with 2 drops lemon juice and cook over medium heat until the sugar melts and turns a pale golden brown. Add the caramel to the boiling hot milk, stir well, and strain. Beat the egg yolks with the rest of the sugar (and the vanilla extract if used) until very pale and fluffy; add the caramel-flavored milk a little at a time while beating continuously.
Cook over hot water, stirring continuously until completely cold. Pour through a fine sieve into the ice-cream maker or freezing trays and freeze until firm.

• • •

WATERMELON ICE CREAM

An example of the ancient tradition of ice-cream making in Sicily where it was traditionally served in a big platter, on a layer of marzipan.

Time: 1 hour
Very easy

1 lb (approx. 4 cups) watermelon flesh
2¼ cups heavy cream
4 egg yolks
1½ cups sugar
2¼ cups rich milk, scalded
4 oz (4 squares) semisweet chocolate
½ cup shelled pistachio nuts
3 tbsp jasmine water (or fresh lime juice)
1 tbsp cinnamon

Blend and liquidize the watermelon pulp with the cream until very smooth. Beat the egg yolks with the sugar until pale; beat in the hot milk a little at a time. Cook over hot water, stirring continuously until the mixture starts to thicken; do not allow to boil. Draw aside from the heat; leave to cook, stirring now and then. When cold, combine with the watermelon and cream purée, the finely chopped chocolate, chopped pistachio nuts, jasmine water (or lime juice), and cinnamon. Stir well and pour into the ice-cream maker or freezing trays. Process as usual.

CHESTNUT ICE CREAM

Serve in individual glass dishes decorated with rosettes of piped whipped cream, sprinkled with unsweetened cocoa powder.

Time: 1 hour 15 minutes
Very easy

1 quart rich milk
1 vanilla bean (or 1 tsp vanilla extract)
8 egg yolks
½ cup sugar
1 cup sweet chestnut preserve or canned sweetened chestnut purée
1½ tbsp rum
½ cup whipping cream

Bring the milk to a boil with the vanilla bean. Beat the egg yolks with the sugar (and vanilla extract if used) until pale and the ribbon stage is reached; beat in the hot milk (remove the vanilla bean if used) a little at a time. Cook over hot water, stirring continuously with a wooden spoon, until the mixture coats the back of the spoon. Draw aside from the heat; stir in the sweet chestnut preserve (or purée) a little at a time, mixing thoroughly. When cold, stir in the rum; lightly beat the cream and stir into the mixture. Pour into the ice-cream maker or freezing trays and freeze until very firm.

• • •

ZABAGLIONE ICE CREAM

Serve in small, deep dishes or glasses, trickling hot chocolate sauce or fresh strawberry sauce generously over the ice cream.

Time: 1 hour
Very easy

2¼ cups rich milk
2¼ cups heavy cream
1 small piece vanilla bean or 2
   drops vanilla extract
small piece lemon peel
8 egg yolks
1 cup sugar
1 cup Marsala

Bring the milk to a boil with half the cream, the vanilla, and lemon peel. Beat the egg yolks with the sugar until very pale; beat in the Marsala and then the hot strained milk in a thin stream. Cook over hot water, stirring continuously, to thicken slightly. Fill a large bowl half-full with iced water and ice cubes; remove the bowl (or the top of the double boiler) from over the hot water and place in the iced water. Leave to cool, beating from time to time to keep plenty of air in the mixture. Stiffly beat the remaining cream; fold into the ice cream mixture, making sure it is evenly blended and pour into the ice-cream maker or freezing trays. Process as usual until very firm.

• • •

YOGHURT ICE CREAM

Use creamy yoghurt for a refreshing taste and good texture.

Time: 1 hour
Very easy

2¼ cups creamy yoghurt (e.g.
   Greek or Bulgarian)
2¼ cups rich milk
8 egg yolks
1½ cups sugar
1 tsp vanilla extract

299

HONEY ICE CREAM
■ If you have difficulty in finding chestnut blossom honey, try orange blossom honey instead, or acacia honey (which gives the ice cream a particularly smooth consistency as it prevents crystallization).

Combine the yoghurt and milk in the saucepan, stirring well, and bring to boiling point. Beat the egg yolks until pale and fluffy with the sugar and vanilla; beat in the hot milk and yoghurt a little at a time. Place over hot water and cook until the mixture thickens somewhat, stirring continuously. Do not allow to boil. Leave until cold, stirring from time to time. Pour into the ice-cream maker or freezing trays and process, freezing and stirring until very firm.

RAISIN AND PORT ICE CREAM

Time: 1 hour 10 minutes
Very easy

1 cup seedless white raisins
6 tbsp port
1 quart rich milk
1 vanilla bean (or 3–4 drops vanilla extract)
8 egg yolks
1 cup sugar

Soak the seedless white raisins in warm water until plump; drain, dry on kitchen towels, and mix gently with the port; leave to soak. Bring the milk to a boil with the vanilla bean. While the milk is heating, beat the egg yolks with the sugar (and vanilla extract if used) until very pale and increased in bulk. Beat the hot, strained milk into the egg mixture (if vanilla extract is used there is no need to strain) adding it a little at a time. Cook over hot water, stirring all the time with a wooden spoon, until the mixture coats the back of the spoon. Remove from the heat and leave until completely cold, stirring now and then as it cools. Strain; stir in the drained seedless white raisins and pour into the ice-cream maker or freezing trays. Freeze and stir as usual.

•　•　•

AMARETTO ICE CREAM

Time: 1 hour
Very easy

1 quart rich milk
1 vanilla bean (or 2–3 drops vanilla extract)
1¼ cups amaretti
6 egg yolks
1 cup sugar

Bring the milk to a boil with the vanilla bean. Pound (or process in the food processor) with the amaretti to a fine powder. Beat the egg yolks with the sugar (and vanilla extract if used) until very pale; add the ground amaretti and beat in the strained hot milk a little at a time. Cook over hot water, stirring continuously with a wooden spoon until the mixture has thickened somewhat. Leave to cool, stirring now and then. When cold pour into the ice-cream maker or freezing trays and begin the freezing and stirring process.

•　•　•

HONEY ICE CREAM

Time: 1 hour
Very easy

1 quart rich milk
¼ cup full-flavored honey (e.g. chestnut blossom)
¾ cup amaretti, ratafias, or crisp macaroons (pounded or processed to a fine powder)
generous pinch cinnamon
8 egg yolks
¾ cup sugar

Bring the milk to a boil with the vanilla bean; turn off the heat and stir in the honey until it has dissolved; add the finely ground amaretti.
　　Beat the egg yolks with the sugar while the milk is heating until the ribbon stage is reached and they are very pale and fluffy. Beat in the hot milk mixture. Cook over hot water, stirring continuously with a wooden spoon until the custard starts to thicken. Leave to become completely cold, stirring occasionally. Pour into the ice-cream maker or freezing trays; freeze and stir as usual.

•　•　•

COCONUT ICE CREAM

Time: 1 hour + standing time
Very easy

1 quart rich milk
2 cups grated fresh coconut or 5 cups shredded coconut
8 egg yolks
1 cup sugar

Mix the milk and coconut in a saucepan and bring to a boil. Remove from the heat and

STRAWBERRY ICE CREAM
■ Reserve some of the best strawberries for decoration; add piped whipped cream if wished.

leave to stand for 2 hours. Strain into a cheesecloth placed in a large sieve; gather up the loose surround of the cloth and twist tightly to force all the moisture out of the coconut. Heat this coconut-flavored milk to boiling point once more. While it is heating, beat the egg yolks with the sugar until pale; beat in the hot milk a little at a time. Place over hot water and cook, stirring continuously with a wooden spoon, until the custard coats the back of the spoon. Leave to cool, stirring at intervals to prevent a skin forming. Transfer to the ice-cream maker or freezing trays and process as usual.

• • •

STRAWBERRY ICE CREAM

Time: 1 hour 15 minutes
Very easy

2¼ cups rich milk
peel of 1 lemon, grated
1 lb ripe strawberries
2¼ cups heavy cream
4 egg yolks
1½ cups sugar

Bring the milk and lemon peel to a boil. Wipe the strawberries with a damp cloth or kitchen towels, and hull; liquidize in a blender, then sieve. Leave to stand for a few minutes before beating into the stiffly beaten cream. Beat the egg yolks thoroughly with the sugar; when they are very pale and greatly increased in bulk, beat in the hot milk a little at a time. Place over hot water and stir until slightly thickened; do not allow to boil. Pour into a bowl and leave to cool, stirring occasionally to prevent a skin

BOMBE NEW YORK

Serves 8–10
For the outer almond ice cream:
(see method on p. 297)
⅓ cup peeled almonds
1¾ cups rich milk
¾ cup heavy cream
3 egg yolks
½ cup sugar
½ cup sugar
1½ tsp kirsch
For the chestnut filling:
¼ lb (generous ½ cup) canned marron
   (sweet chestnut) purée
½ cup sugar
5 egg yolks
1 tsp vanilla extract
3 tbsp orange Curaçao
1½ cups whipping cream
¾ lb (approx. 2½ cups) fresh
   raspberries
1½ tbsp maraschino or kirsch
2 tbsp sugar

Make the almond ice cream a few
hours in advance. Place a bombe mold
or deep bowl (approx. 2-quart
capacity) in the freezer for 10
minutes; remove and place in a bowl
of ice cubes. Line the inside with the
almond ice cream and reserve a little;
place this and the bombe in the
freezer, covering the bombe mold
with a tight-fitting lid or waxed paper
and foil.

Stir the sugar, egg yolks, and vanilla
into the marron purée.

Place the bowl over very gently
simmering water and stir continuously
until the mixture thickens. Do not
overheat.

Place this bowl in the bowl containing
the ice cubes and beat until the
mixture is completely cold. Take the
small bowl out of the larger bowl and
stir in the Curaçao. Combine gently
with the stiffly beaten cream. Freeze
and stir as usual.

Mix the raspberries with the sugar
and maraschino or kirsch and leave to
stand for 15 minutes.

Take the lined bombe mold and the
spare almond ice cream out of the
freezer; return the bombe to the large
bowl with fresh ice cubes; half fill the
center with raspberries; spoon in the
chestnut ice cream, leaving enough
room for another, thinner layer of
raspberries. Top with the remaining
almond ice cream; level the surface,
cover with waxed paper and snap the
lid in place (or cover tightly with foil).
Freeze for about 4 hours.

Shortly before serving the bombe, dip
briefly in hot water, and unmold onto a
chilled plate. Decorate with
raspberries.

forming. When cold combine with the strawberry and cream mixture. Pour into the ice-cream maker or freezing trays and process as usual until very firm.

• • •

MIXED FRUIT ICE CREAM

Decorate with mint leaves, red currants, and wild strawberries.

Time: 1 hour + standing time
Very easy

4 egg yolks
1 lb sugar
2¼ cups rich milk
1 lb mixed, ripe fresh fruit, cleaned and prepared
juice of 1 lemon
2¼ cups heavy cream

Beat the egg yolks with the sugar until the ribbon stage is reached and they are very pale and frothy. Beat in the scalded milk a little at a time and heat this mixture over hot water, stirring continuously until it thickens slightly; do not allow to boil. Liquidize the fruit pulp in a blender, pour in a large mixing bowl, stir in the custard, and leave to stand and cool for 1 hour. Add the lemon juice and the cream; beat for 10 minutes with a hand-held electric beater or for a little longer with the wire whisk. Pour this light mixture into the ice-cream maker or freezing trays and process until very firm.

• • •

NOUGAT ICE CREAM

Chop a little extra nougat into small pieces and sprinkle over each serving.

Time: 1 hour 20 minutes
Very easy

1 quart rich milk
1 vanilla bean (or 1 tsp vanilla extract)
8 egg yolks
1 cup sugar
¾ lb nougat

Pour the milk into a saucepan, add the vanilla bean and bring to a boil. Turn off the heat and leave to stand for 20 minutes. Strain. (If vanilla extract is used, simply heat the milk and do not strain.) Beat the egg yolks with the sugar (and vanilla extract if used) until greatly increased in volume and very pale. Add the warm milk, beating well. Cook over hot water while stirring continuously with a wooden spoon. Set aside and leave to cool completely, stirring at intervals. Chop the nougat very finely and stir into the ice cream mixture. Pour into the ice-cream maker or freezing trays.

• • •

PEACH ICE CREAM

Serve in individual small, deep glass dishes with a little stiffly beaten cream and a sprinkling of cinnamon on top.

Time: 1 hour 10 minutes
Very easy

1 lb very ripe yellow peach pulp
2¼ cups heavy cream
2¼ cups rich milk
juice of 1 lemon
4 egg yolks
1½ cups sugar

Blend the peach pulp with the cream in a food processor until very smooth. Bring the milk to a boil. Beat the egg yolks and sugar until very pale and fluffy; gradually beat in the hot milk. Cook over hot water, stirring continuously, to thicken (until it coats the back of the wooden spoon). Leave in a cool place, stirring occasionally, until completely cold. Combine thoroughly with the peach and cream purée and transfer to the ice-cream maker or freezing trays. Freeze and stir until very firm.

• • •

COFFEE BOMBE

Decorate the unmolded bombe with little meringues and chocolate coffee beans.

Time: 20 minutes + freezing time
Easy

1 lb Coffee Ice Cream (see page 294)
approx. 1¼ cups Extra Creamy Plain Ice Cream (see page 295)
approx. 1¼ cups Chocolate Ice Cream (see page 294)
12 chocolate coffee beans

Place a 6-in diameter bombe mold with hermetically sealing lid (or a pudding bowl with lid or a deep rounded mixing

CHOCOLATE BOMBE
■ Marron glacé (candied
sweet chestnut) or zabaglione
ice cream can be teamed
with the chocolate ice cream
in place of the pistachio
flavor; if you keep to the
original recipe, sprinkle the
bombe with chopped
pistachio nuts.

bowl) in the freezer 10
minutes before commencing
preparation. Line the inside of
this icy cold mold with the
coffee ice cream. Return to
the freezer for 5–10 minutes.
Fill with alternating layers (4–
6) of the extra creamy plain
ice cream and the chocolate
ice cream. Snap the lid on (or
cover tightly with waxed
paper and foil) and return to
the freezer for 2–3 hours. Just
before serving, lower the
mold briefly into a bowl of hot
water, turn out onto a chilled
plate, decorate, and serve.

• • •

FRUIT BOMBE

*Line the cold bombe mold (or
bowl) with slices of banana,
pineapple, kiwi fruit etc. before
proceeding with the ice cream
lining; when turned out the
bombe will look most attractive.*

*Time: 30 minutes + standing
    and freezing time*
Easy

½ cup canned Morello
    cherries
⅓ cup canned pineapple
    pieces
½ cup canned peaches
1 cup whipping cream
1½ tbsp confectioners' sugar
1 lb Strawberry Ice Cream
    (see page 301)

Drain the fruit very
thoroughly; pat with kitchen
towels to remove excess
moisture. Cut into very small
dice and leave to drain in 3
separate sieves for a few
hours. Place a 6–7 in diameter
bombe mold with hermetic
seal (or similar-sized pudding
bowl) in the freezer. Beat the
cream with confectioners'
sugar until very stiff; fold in

the diced fruit. Take the mold out of the freezer and line the inside with a thick layer of strawberry ice cream. Return to the freezer for 10 minutes. fill the mold with the cream and fruit mixture. Seal tightly with the lid or cover tightly with waxed paper and foil. Return to the freezer for 4–5 hours. Lower the mold into hot water for a second or two to make it easier to unmold onto a chilled serving plate.

•   •   •

CHOCOLATE BOMBE

Do not try to work with hard ice cream straight from the freezer; allow to soften slightly in the refrigerator before using for these bombes.

Time: 30 minutes + freezing time
Easy

3 oz (3 squares) unsweetened chocolate
1 cup heavy cream
1½ tbsp confectioners' sugar
1 lb Chocolate Ice Cream (see page 294)
1¼ cups Pistachio Ice Cream (see page 296)

Place a 6-in diameter bombe mold with hermetically sealing lid (or pudding bowl) in the freezer at least 10 minutes before you start making the bombe. Chop the chocolate very finely; beat the cream with the confectioners' sugar until very stiff and fold in the chocolate. Line the cold bombe mold with this mixture. Return to the freezer for 15 minutes. Place a layer of pistachio ice cream against the

lining, as an interlining. Return to the freezer for 10 minutes and then fill with the chocolate ice cream. Press the airtight lid in place (or cover tightly with waxed paper and foil) and freeze for 3 hours. Dip the mold into hot water for a second or two to loosen the bombe very slightly; turn out onto a chilled serving plate.

•   •   •

VANILLA BOMBE

Drizzle melted bitter chocolate all over the surface of this bombe when unmolded (use a pastry bag and very small tube if wished).

Time: 20 minutes + freezing time
Easy

1¾ cups whipping cream
1½ tbsp confectioners' sugar
5 oz meringues
1 lb Vanilla Ice Cream (see page 294)

Place a 6–7-in diameter bombe mold with lid (or pudding bowl) in the freezer at least 10 minutes before preparing the bombe. Beat the cream stiffly, sweetening with the confectioners' sugar. Crumble the meringue into small pieces and fold gently into the cream. Line the freezing cold mold with a very thick, even layer of the vanilla ice cream; fill the mold with the cream and meringue mixture and return to the freezer for at least 3 hours. Dip very briefly in hot water prior to unmolding the bombe onto a chilled plate.

•   •   •

COFFEE PARFAIT

Time: 1 hour 10 minutes + freezing time
Easy

1 cup sugar
½ cup water
¾ cup ground roasted coffee beans
6 egg yolks
2¼ cups whipping cream
3 tbsp confectioners' sugar

Heat the sugar and water until the large thread stage is reached. Draw aside from the heat and add the coffee. Leave to stand until cold; strain through a piece of cheesecloth placed in a sieve. Heat slowly again (if the syrup becomes a little thicker this will not matter). Beat the egg yolks vigorously with 1–2 tsp water; beat fast, adding the hot sugar syrup a little at a time. Continue beating until cold. Beat the cream stiffly with the confectioners' sugar and fold into the egg mixture. Transfer to the parfait or timbale mold

(with a central tube, so that the unmolded ice cream has a well or hollow in the center) cover the top with a tightly sealing lid or layers of waxed paper and foil, and freeze for 5–6 hours. Dip the mold briefly into room-temperature water to loosen before turning out onto a chilled plate.

•   •   •

FILBERT PARFAIT

Time: 1 hour + freezing time
Easy

1⅓ cups filberts, shelled, skinned and lightly roasted in the oven
1 cup sugar
½ cup water
6 egg yolks
2¼ cups whipping cream

Pound or process the filberts to a fine paste. Make a thick sugar syrup by heating the sugar and water together until the large thread stage is reached (place a drop of syrup

on your thumb pad, press your index finger down onto it, and when you pull your fingers apart a thread should link them).

Beat the egg yolks well with 1–2 tsp water, beat in the hot sugar syrup, adding it in a very thin trickle and continue beating until the mixture is cold. Beat the cream until stiff and fold into the egg mixture. Transfer to a parfait mold (see previous recipe) and freeze for 5–6 hours.

Dip the mold into a bowl of water which is at room temperature for a few seconds to make it easier to unmold onto a chilled plate.

• • •

APRICOT PARFAIT

If wished, arrange kiwi slices so that they overlap in circles in the central well of the parfait.

Time: 1 hour + freezing time
Easy

1 cup sugar
½ cup water
6 egg yolks
9 oz canned apricots
2¾ cups whipping cream

Boil the sugar and water together until the large thread stage is reached (see previous recipe). Beat the egg yolks thoroughly with 1–2 tsp water and continue beating while adding the hot sugar syrup in a thin stream. Continue beating without interruption until the mixture is cooled. Drain the apricots and liquidize to a smooth purée, combine with the egg mixture, and fold in the stiffly beaten cream. Transfer to a parfait mold or timbale, seal with the airtight lid (or cover tightly with

waxed paper and foil) and freeze for 5–6 hours.
When it is time to serve the parfait, lower carefully into a bowl of water which is at room temperature and turn out onto a well chilled plate.

• • •

KIWI PARFAIT

Time: 1 hour + freezing time
Easy

½ lb kiwi fruit
1 cup Marsala
1 cup sugar
½ cup water
6 egg yolks
2½ cups whipping cream

Peel the kiwi fruit, slice, and soak in the Marsala.
Make a syrup by boiling the sugar and water together until the large thread stage is reached (i.e. when a drop of syrup is pressed lightly between thumb and forefinger and these are then drawn apart, a long thread is formed). Beat the egg yolks well with 1–2 tsp water; gradually beat in the hot sugar syrup, adding a little at a time, and continue beating until the mixture has cooled. Add the drained, liquidized (or puréed) kiwi fruit; stir well. Beat the cream until stiff and gently but thoroughly fold into the egg, syrup, and fruit mixture; transfer to a parfait or timbale mold, seal (or cover tightly with waxed paper and foil) and freeze for 5–6 hours. Lower the mold carefully into a bowl of water which is at room temperature for a few seconds; unmold onto a chilled plate and serve at once.

• • •

CHOCOLATE PARFAIT

Cover the parfait with chocolate curls or shavings and rosettes of piped whipped cream.

Time: 1 hour + freezing time
Easy

1 cup sugar
½ cup water
4½ oz (4½ squares) bitter chocolate
8 egg yolks
2¼ cups whipping cream

Make a syrup by boiling the sugar and water until the large thread stage is reached (i.e. when a drop of syrup is pressed lightly between

thumb and forefinger and these are then pulled apart, a long thread is formed). Remove from the heat, add the chopped chocolate and stir until this has totally melted and the mixture is smooth and well blended. Return the syrup to low heat. Beat the egg yolks well with 1–2 tsp water; continue beating vigorously while adding the hot sugar syrup, trickling it in slowly. Continue beating until

KIWI PARFAIT
■ This could be decorated
with wild strawberries and a
sprinkling of finely chopped
bitter chocolate.

the mixture has cooled. Beat
the cream until stiff and fold
into the chocolate mixture
gently but thoroughly;
transfer to a parfait or timbale
mold, seal or cover tightly
with waxed paper and foil and
freeze for 5–6 hours. Lower
the mold carefully into a bowl
of water which is at room
temperature for a few seconds
to loosen; turn out onto a
chilled plate and serve.

• • •

WALNUT PARFAIT

*If you are fond of cinnamon,
sprinkle the unmolded bombe
with it; decorate with candied
violets.*

Time: 1 hour + freezing time
Easy

1¾ cups walnut pieces
1 cup sugar
½ cup water
6 egg yolks
2¼ cups whipping cream

Pound or process the walnuts
very finely. Boil the sugar and
water together until the syrup
reaches the large thread stage
(see Apricot Parfait method,
opposite).
Beat the egg yolks with 1–
2 tsp water; beat in the hot
syrup a little at a time and
continue beating until the
mixture is cold. Fold in the
walnuts and the stiffly beaten
cream gently but thoroughly.
Transfer to a parfait mold or
timbale mold and freeze for 5–
6 hours.
When ready to serve the
parfait dip the mold briefly into
a bowl of water at room
temperature before turning
out onto a chilled plate.

• • •

ICED RASPBERRY CHARLOTTE

*This charlotte can also be made
with strawberries, blackberries,
red currants, blueberries, or
ripe gooseberries*

*Time: 40 minutes + freezing
    time*
Easy

30 ladyfingers
1 cup Marsala
1½ lb Extra Creamy Plain Ice
    Cream (see page 295)
3 cups raspberries
juice of ½ lemon
⅔ cup sugar

Rinse the inside of a charlotte
with cold water. Dip the
ladyfingers briefly in the
Marsala as you use them to
line the base and sides of the
mold. Fill with the slightly
softened (but not at all melted)
ice cream, pressing down

well, and cover neatly with the
remaining sponge fingers.
Press down well; cover with
lid or with foil or saran wrap
and place a freezerproof
weight on top. Freeze for 3–4
hours.
When it is nearly time to serve
the charlotte, liquidize the
raspberries with the lemon
juice, sugar, and 3 tbsp of the
Marsala in which the
ladyfingers were dipped. (If
none remains, use some fresh
Marsala.) Unmold the
charlotte onto a chilled serving
platter (lower into hot water
for a second or two to make it
easier to turn out) and serve
the raspberry sauce
separately in a jug.

• • •

ICED FRUIT CHARLOTTE

*Decorate this fruit charlotte
with whipped cream and mint
leaves.*

*Time: 30 minutes + freezing
    time*
Easy

⅔ cup sugar
1 cup water
2½ tsp Cointreau
16 ladyfingers
1 cup whipping cream
¼ cup confectioners' sugar
1–1¼ cups small strawberries
1⅓ cups blackberries

Boil the sugar and water for 5
minutes; leave to cool a little
before adding the Cointreau.
Cut the ladyfingers
horizontally in half and dip
briefly in the warm syrup. Use
to line a 1-quart charlotte
mold. Beat the chilled cream
with the confectioners' sugar

ICED COFFEE CHARLOTTE
■ Sprinkle the top of the dessert with cocoa powder (not sweet drinking chocolate powder) and finish with piped cream and coffee beans (or chocolate replicas).

until very stiff.
Fill the lined charlotte mold in layers: first some of the whipped cream, then some strawberries, followed by more ladyfingers dipped in the syrup, half the blackberries, then more cream and so on, ending with a layer of ladyfingers dipped in the syrup. Cover with a freezerproof plate and weight; freeze for about 3 hours. Lower the mold into hot water for a few seconds to facilitate unmolding onto a chilled plate.

• • •

ICED COFFEE CHARLOTTE

Time: 30 minutes + freezing time
Easy

2¼ cups whipping cream

½ cup sugar
1¼ cups very strong black coffee
30 ladyfingers
few chocolate coffee beans

Beat the cream with ½ cup of the sugar until stiff; continue beating as you add 3 tbsp of the coffee a little at a time. Transfer to a metal or plastic container, seal tightly, and freeze until firm.
Use the remaining sugar to sweeten the rest of the coffee. Dip the ladyfingers briefly in the coffee and use most of them to line the base and sides of a charlotte mold; fill the lined mold with the frozen cream and coffee mixture,

pressing down well. Cover with the remaining ladyfingers, dipping them in the rest of the coffee. Place a piece of waxed paper on top of the charlotte mold, then a plate with a weight on top. Place in the freezer for 2 hours.
Lower the mold into hot water for a few seconds to make it easier to turn out the frozen charlotte. Decorate with the chocolate coffee beans.

• • •

ICED CHOCOLATE MOUSSE

Time: 40 minutes + freezing time
Easy

1 rectangular Classic Sponge Cake weighing about ¾ lb (see page 146)
3 tbsp coffee liqueur (e.g. Tia Maria, Káhlua)
5 oz nougatine or nut brittle
1½ cups whipping cream

308

1½ tbsp confectioners' sugar
1 lb Chocolate Ice Cream (see
    page 294)

Cut the sponge cake into thin
slices (cut downward working
from one end of the rectangle
to the other) and line the base
and sides of a loaf pan or deep
rectangular mold. Sprinkle the
sponge with the liqueur.
Pound or process the
nougatine in a food processor,
reducing it to a fine powder or
paste (praline).
Beat the cream with the
confectioners' sugar until stiff,
stir in the praline and fill the
lined mold half-full with this
mixture. Cover the surface of
this filling neatly with a piece
of waxed paper cut to size and
foil; place in the freezer for 3
hours. Remove from the
freezer, remove the foil and
paper, and fill with the
chocolate ice cream. Place a
layer of sponge slices on top;
return to the freezer for 3
hours more.
Twenty minutes before
serving, take out of the
freezer, unmold onto a chilled
plate, and leave at room
temperature (this variety of
ice cream should not be eaten
less cold and firm than other
varieties).

• • •

ICED PINEAPPLE
MOUSSE

*Time: 1 hour 10 minutes +
    freezing time*
Easy

10 canned pineapple rings
½ lb ladyfingers
1 cup port
6 egg yolks
¾ cup sugar

2½ cups mascarpone (or
    similar low-fat, fresh
    cheese)
3 egg whites

Drain the pineapple well,
reserving ½ cup of the syrup,
and chop into very small
pieces.
Mix ½ cup of the port with the
pineapple syrup; dip the
ladyfingers briefly in this and
use to line the base and sides
of a charlotte mold.
Beat the egg yolks and sugar
until very pale and increased in
volume; beat in the
mascarpone 1 tbsp at a time.
Stir in the pineapple with a
wooden spoon. Fold in the
very stiffly beaten egg whites
with a wooden or plastic
spatula. Fill the lined mold
with this mixture; dip the
remaining ladyfingers in the
port and syrup mixture, and
use to cover the mold. Freeze
for at least 4 hours.
Unmold the charlotte 30
minutes before serving and
leave at room temperature.

• • •

ICED VANILLA
MOUSSE

*For a very impressive finishing
touch, pour plenty of very hot
melted bitter chocolate all over
the unmolded charlotte.*

*Time: 50 minutes + freezing
    time*
Easy

1 rectangular Classic Sponge
    Cake weighing about ¾ lb
    (see page 146)
1 cup sweet dessert wine
    (e.g. Muscat de Beaumes
    de Venise or California
    sweet muscat wine)
½ cup finely-diced mixed

candied fruit or peel
¼ lb sugared almonds or
    nougatine or almond brittle
⅓ cup shelled pistachio nuts
2 oz (2 squares) bitter
    chocolate
2¼ cups whipping cream
3 tbsp confectioners' sugar
1 lb (approx. 1 pint) Vanilla Ice
    Cream (see page 294)

Slice the sponge cake fairly
thinly; sprinkle each of these
with little of the wine as you
use them to line the base and
sides of a deep rectangular pan
or mold. Chop or pound the
almonds and the pistachios
into tiny pieces (do not grind).
Chop the chocolate finely or
grate coarsely. Beat the
cream until stiff with the
confectioners' sugar; fold in
the nuts, fruit, and chocolate.
Use half the vanilla ice cream
as the first layer on top of the
sponge lining, pressing down
gently; use the cream mixture
as the next layer. Press a
piece of waxed paper cut to
size on top of the cream and
place in the freezer for 3
hours. Remove the paper;
place the rest of the vanilla ice
cream in the mold, pressing
down gently. Cover with a
layer of sponge cake slices
sprinkled with the rest of the
wine. Return to the freezer
for 3 hours. Unmold this
sponge-encased iced mousse
20 minutes before serving and
leave at room temperature.

• • •

LITTLE
CHOCOLATE ICES

*A very simple, quick treat
which children adore.*

*Time: 15 minutes + freezing
    time*
Very easy

4 oz (4 squares) bitter
    chocolate
½ cup hot water
2¼ cups heavy cream
½ cup sugar
2–3 drops vanilla extract

Break the chocolate into small
pieces and melt in the hot
water; stir well. Stir into the
cream; add the sugar and
vanilla, and mix well. Pour into
small lindividual molds and
freeze.

• • •

EXTRACTS

Always buy pure extract.
These flavorings are invaluable
and a few drops are usually
enough to impart the delicious
flavor and scent of vanilla,
orange, lemon, almond to the
simplest cake or dessert.

ICED STRAWBERRY MOUSSE

Time: 20 minutes + freezing time
Easy

1¾ lb strawberries
½ cup whipping cream
¼ lb mascarpone (or similar low-fat, fresh cheese)
2¼ cups confectioners' sugar

Wash, dry, and hull the strawberries; lightly crush 1 lb of them with a fork, stir in the lightly beaten cream, the mascarpone, and the sugar. Beat this mixture with an electric beater or balloon whisk until it is light and airy. Line a rectangular mold or loaf pan with waxed paper, fill with the strawberry mixture, and place in the freezer for 4 hours. If the ice cream will not unmold easily, dip the mold in hot water for a second or two, turn out, and remove the paper.

• • •

ICED CHOCOLATE, NOUGAT, AND NUT MOUSSE

Time: 30 minutes + freezing time
Easy

5 egg yolks
½ cup sugar
2¼ cups whipping cream
2 oz nougat
2 oz (2 squares) bitter or unsweetened chocolate
⅔ cup amaretti

Beat the egg yolks and sugar until the ribbon stage is reached and they are very pale and increased in bulk. Beat the cream stiffly and fold into the egg and sugar mixture. Break the nougat into very small pieces, coarsely grate the chocolate, and crumble the amaretti very coarsely. Stir all these gently into the egg and cream mixture. Line a rectangular mold or loaf pan with waxed paper; fill with the mousse mixture and freeze for at least 4 hours before serving. If necessary, dip the bottom half of the mold in hot water very briefly to loosen the iced mousse. Unmold onto a chilled plate, and decorate with piped whipped cream and chocolate cream (see illustration on the right and whole amaretti. Press crushed amaretti round the sides of the mousse.

• • •

ICED CHOCOLATE, NOUGAT, AND NUT MOUSSE
■ *Press crushed amaretti cookies or macaroons into the sides of the mousse once unmolded and finish by piping plain and chocolate cream through a fluted tube.*

PEACH AND ALMOND SUNDAE

Time: 30 minutes
Very easy

3 ripe fresh peaches
1 cup sweet dessert wine (e.g. Muscat de Beaumes de Venise or sweet California Muscat wine)
½ cup sugar
approx. 2½ cups Extra Creamy Plain Ice Cream (see page 295)
1¾ cups slivered almonds, lightly roasted in the oven

Peel the peaches neatly (plunge briefly in boiling water if necessary) and cut in half; discard the pit. Boil the wine and the sugar gently for 5 minutes; add the peach halves and cook gently, turning carefully after 5–8 minutes (do not overcook). Leave to cool completely in the syrup. Place scoops of the ice cream in chilled individual deep glass dishes; place a drained peach half on top. Sprinkle with the almonds and serve at once.

• • •

STRAWBERRY FRUIT SUNDAE

Time: 20 minutes + chilling time
Very easy

2¼ cups good-quality white wine
1 cup sugar
1 lb ripe fresh fruit of choice
3 tbsp rum
approx. 2½ cups Strawberry Ice Cream (see page 301)

Boil the wine and sugar together until reduced to half the original volume. Leave to cool before pouring an equal amount into each of 6 large wine glasses. Cut the fruit into small dice, and spoon equal quantities into the syrup. Chill in the refrigerator for 2 hours. Just before serving add a little rum to each portion and 3–4 scoops of strawberry ice cream.

• • •

GRAND MARNIER SUNDAE

Time: 30 minutes + chilling time
Very easy

approx. 2½ cups Mixed Fruit Ice Cream (see page 303)
1 cup Grand Marnier
2 cups fresh orange sections, thin skins removed
1 cup whipping cream

Place scoops of the ice cream into chilled, freezerproof dishes or large wine glasses (also freezerproof). Pour an equal amount of Grand Marnier over each serving, arrange the orange sections decoratively on top, and place in the freezer for 2 hours. About 15 minutes before serving, remove, and pipe whipped cream on top.

• • •

CHOCOLATE AND RUM SUNDAE

Time: 30 minutes
Very easy

¾ lb Classic Sponge Cake (see page 146)

311

1 cup rum
approx. 2½ cups Extra
    Creamy Plain Ice Cream
    (see page 295)
½ lb mixed canned peaches
    and apricots
1 cup Chocolate Sauce (see
    page 50)

Cut the sponge cake into small
rectangular slices. Dilute the
rum with a little cold water.
Dip the sponge slices briefly
into the rum and place in the
bottom of 6 deep glass dishes.
Place 2–3 small scoops of the
ice cream on top of each and
some of the well-drained fruit,
cut into dice. Make sure the
chocolate sauce is very hot
before pouring over each
serving.

•   •   •

MERINGUE
SUNDAE

*Time: 15 minutes + freezing
    time*
Very easy

1 lb plum cake or very light
    fruit cake (see page 182)
1 lb Vanilla Ice Cream (see
    page 294)
1 cup whipping cream
6 small meringues
¾ cup chopped almonds

Slice the plum cake fairly
thinly; arrange the cake and
ice cream in alternate layers
(starting with the cake) in 6
individual freezerproof glass
dishes; place in the freezer for
3 hours. Shortly before
serving, remove from the
freezer and pipe the stiffly
beaten cream on top of each
portion, place a meringue on
top of each, and sprinkle
generously with the almonds.

312

ICED APRICOT
CHARLOTTE
■ The same recipe can also
be made with peaches or
pineapple (in which case
omit the candied fruit and
seedless white raisins given in
our list of ingredients).

ICED APRICOT CHARLOTTE

Time: 40 minutes + freezing time
Easy

1½–1¾ lb ripe apricots
1¾ cups sugar
juice of ½ lemon
1 cup whipping cream
½ cup mixed candied fruit or peel
½ cup seedless white raisins
1 cup rum
30 ladyfingers

Wash, dry, and pit the apricots; reduce to a smooth purée in a liquidizer; add 1½ cups of the sugar to the purée and the lemon juice and blend well. Beat the cream stiffly and fold into the purée. Mix the candied fruit and the seedless white raisins with ½ cup of the rum. Heat the water with the remaining sugar and rum briefly, pour into a shallow dish and when cool dip each ladyfinger quickly in it before using to line the base and sides of an 8–9-in charlotte mold neatly, leaving no gaps. Spoon part of the apricot mixture into the mold and smooth level; sprinkle with some of the candied fruit and sultanas and cover with a layer of dipped ladyfingers. Continue layering in this way (making the layers fairly thick) until you have used up all the ingredients with the exception of a final layer of dipped ladyfingers for the top layer. Freeze for 4 hours or longer; transfer to the refrigerator 2–3 hours before serving so that the charlotte will not be too hard. Unmold onto a chilled serving plate.

PINEAPPLE SPLIT

Time: 30 minutes + freezing time
Very easy

1 large pineapple
1 cup kirsch
approx. 2 cups Pistachio Ice Cream (see page 296)
1 cup mixed seedless white raisins, pine nuts, and candied citron peel
1 cup Vanilla Sauce (see page 49)

Peel and slice the pineapple; remove and discard the hard central core; chop into small pieces and mix in a bowl with the kirsch. Leave for 30 minutes. Place 2–3 small scoops of the ice cream in 6 individual deep freezerproof glass dishes; place a couple of spoonfuls of the pineapple on top; sprinkle with some of the mixed fruit and nuts, place another layer of pineapple on top and sprinkle with more nuts; end with a pineapple layer. Pour a layer of vanilla sauce on top of each serving; place in the freezer for about 20–30 minutes and serve.

• • •

CHAMPAGNE SURPRISE

Time: 30 minutes + standing and chilling time
Very easy

2 kiwi fruit
1 banana
juice of ½ lemon
1 pink grapefruit
12 fresh lychees (peeled and pitted)
approx. ½ cup wild strawberries
3 tbsp unrefined cane sugar
2¼ cups chilled champagne or sparkling wine
1 cup Coconut Ice Cream (see page 300)
1 cup Watermelon Ice Cream (see page 298)
1 cup Mixed Fruit Ice Cream (see page 303)

Prepare all the fruit. Leave the pitted lychees whole; cut the kiwi fruit and banana into small pieces, and mix with the lemon juice. Remove the thin skin from the grapefruit sections. Wash and dry the

CLOVES

The flower buds of *Eugenia cariophyllata*, an evergreen tree native to the "Spice Islands" of Southeast Asia are dried and put to several uses; in patisserie they should be used sparingly as their flavor and aroma are very strong. Commercially prepared ground cloves lack the powerful aroma of freshly crumbled cloves.

wild strawberries. Mix all the fruit with the sugar in a large bowl and chill for 1 hour in the refrigerator.
Place an equal amount of fruit salad in each of 6 deep glass dishes or bowls. Pour some champagne over each portion. Place 3 scoops of ice cream on top (one of each flavor); pour a little more champagne on top and serve immediately.

• • •

ORANGE AND WALNUT SUNDAE

Time: 40 minutes + chilling time
Very easy

6 oranges
scant ¾ cup sugar
1½ tbsp orange Curaçao
24 walnut halves
1 cup whipping cream
approx. 1 cup Strawberry Ice Cream (see page 301)

Remove the peel of 2 oranges (take care no bitter white pith is attached) in very thin strips; peel the oranges with a very sharp knife, removing the pith and thin inner skin as you do so and keeping them whole. Cut into thick round slices and place these in a bowl with ½ cup of the sugar and the Curaçao. Mix well and chill in the refrigerator.
Reserve 12 walnut halves and chop the rest finely. Heat the remaining sugar in a small saucepan until melted and then stir in the shredded peel thoroughly with wooden spoon. Set aside.
Just before serving, place a layer of strawberry ice cream in the bottom of 6 large glasses, cover with half the orange slices, cover these in turn with half the stiffly beaten cream; sprinkle with the walnuts and orange strips. Top with a spoonful of the remaining cream, surround this with orange slices (cut in half, arrange curved side uppermost) and place 2 walnut halves in the center of the cream.

•   •   •

COFFEE WALNUT SUNDAE

Time: 35 minutes
Easy

2 cups walnut pieces, lightly roasted in the oven
½ cup mascarpone (or similar fresh cream cheese)
2 eggs
½ cup sugar
3 tbsp brandy
2½ cups Coffee Ice Cream (see page 303)
6 walnut halves

Pound or process the walnut pieces to a fine paste, adding 1½ tbsp of the mascarpone to bind the paste a little. Beat the 2 egg yolks with ¼ cup of the sugar until very pale and frothy; combine the paste with this, stir in the rest of the mascarpone, the stiffly beaten egg whites, the remaining sugar, and the brandy. Spoon this mixture into 6 deep glass dishes or large wine glasses; place 2–3 small scoops of coffee ice cream on top and decorate with the walnut halves.

•   •   •

YOGHURT PISTACHIO SUNDAE

Time: 30 minutes
Very easy

1 lb mixed fresh fruit (e.g. peaches, bananas, strawberries)
2¼ cups creamy natural yoghurt
1½ cups whipping cream
approx. 1½ cups Pistachio Ice Cream (see page 296)

Prepare all the fruit: wash, dry, peel, and cut into dice (sprinkle the banana with a little lemon juice, if wished, to delay discoloration). Place in a large nonmetallic mixing bowl. Pour in the yoghurt and mix well. Beat the cream stiffly, sweeten with the sugar and fold into the fruit and yoghurt mixture. Place equal quantities in 6 glass dishes and add a scoop of pistachio ice cream to each. Serve at once.

•   •   •

SUNSET SUNDAE

Time: 30 minutes
Very easy

6 ripe peaches
¾ cup sugar
4 cloves (optional)
1 vanilla bean or 2–3 drops vanilla extract
1½ cups Extra Creamy Plain Ice Cream (see page 295)
1 cup whipping cream
1 cup fresh raspberries

Peel the peaches neatly, cut in half, pit, and arrange cut side down in a wide saucepan; add the sugar, cloves (if used) vanilla, and a little water. Cover and simmer very gently for 15 minutes. Leave to cool. When it is time to assemble the sundaes place a large scoop of ice cream in each deep glass dish and arrange 2 drained peach halves on top (cut sides down). Pipe stiffly beaten whipped cream on top, using a fluted tube. Top with the raspberries and serve.

•   •   •

MARRON GLACÉ COUPE

For an even lower fat content, substitute very thick yoghurt for the cheese lightly sweetened with sugar or honey.

Time: 30 minutes + freezing time
Very easy

3 egg yolks
½ cup sugar
1½ cups mascarpone (or similar fresh cream cheese)
peel of 1 orange, grated
2 egg whites
2 oz (2 squares) bitter chocolate
6 marrons glacés (candied chestnuts)
1 cup whipping cream

Beat the egg yolks with the sugar until the ribbon stage is reached and they are very pale and fluffy; beat in the mascarpone and orange peel. Fold in the stiffly beaten egg white.
Spoon equal amounts of this mixture into 6 deep glass

6 large scoops Mixed Fruit Ice
   Cream (see page 303)
6 maraschino cherries

Use a melon baller to scoop
out the watermelon flesh in
small balls, removing as many
seeds as possible. Place in a
large nonmetallic mixing bowl.
Repeat the operation with the
melon and add to the
watermelon balls.
Slice the peaches, add to the
bowl, followed by all the other
fruit, the wine, and the sugar.
Chill in the refrigerator for 2–
3 hours.
Divide the fruit salad equally
between 6 deep glass dishes;
place a scoop of fruit ice cream
in each. Top each serving with
a maraschino cherry.

• • •

CHOCOLATE COUPE

*For a change, use coffee or
zabaglione ice cream.*

Time: 25 minutes
Very easy

1 cup chopped almonds
2½ cups Extra Creamy Plain
   Ice Cream (see page 295)
4 oz (4 squares) bitter or
   semisweet chocolate
1½ tbsp milk

Place 3–4 small scoops of ice
cream in each of 6 chilled small
glass dishes or large wine
glasses; sprinkle with the
almonds. Melt the chocolate
with the milk over hot water;
stir, and pour over the ice
cream as you serve it.

• • •

---

dishes and place in the freezer
for 1–1½ hours.
(Alternatively chill in the
refrigerator for at least 3
hours.)
Serve with grated chocolate
sprinkled over the top, and
decorate with rosettes of
piped stiffly beaten cream and
the marrons glacés.

• • •

BANANA COUPE

*Sprinkle a pinch of cinnamon
on top of each assembled coupe
and scatter a few chopped
almonds in the center.*

*Time: 30 minutes+ chilling
   time*
Very easy

6 bananas
1 cup rich milk
¼ cup sugar
juice of 1 lemon

1 cup whipping cream
4 oz (4 squares) bitter
   chocolate
Graham crackers
¼ cup ground almonds
¼ cup rum
⅓ cup seedless white raisins
stiffly beaten cream, slightly
   sweetened (optional)

Liquidize the bananas with the
milk, sugar, and lemon juice
until smooth. Fold in the stiffly
beaten cream.
Grate the chocolate, crumble
the Graham crackers, and mix
with the ground almonds. Mix
the seedless white raisins with
the rum.
Spoon an equal amount of
banana cream into each of 6
deep glass dishes; place a
layer of the chocolate and nut
mixture over this. Top with
the well-drained seedless
white raisins.
Pipe more whipped cream on
top if wished, and chill in

the refrigerator until just
before serving.

• • •

COUPE ROYALE

*For an even lighter and more
refreshing version of this
dessert, use lemon sherbet
instead of the fruit ice cream.*

*Time: 30 minutes + chilling
   time*
Very easy

1 small (or ½ large)
   watermelon
1 ripe melon
3 peaches
¼ lb black grapes
¼ lb white grapes
½ cup ripe blueberries
½ cup blackberries
1½ cups sweet dessert wine
   (e.g. Muscat de Beaumes
   de Venise or sweet
   California Muscat wine)
⅓ cup sugar

315

Homemade cookies are usually far more tempting and delectable than the commercial variety; they are easy to make and keep well in airtight tins or containers. Also included in this chapter is a selection of elegant petits fours, exquisite little morsels that may be served at the end of a formal meal, a finger buffet, or with tea or coffee.

CHOCOLATE FINGERS

For more flavor and sweetness, substitute seedless white raisins and 3 tbsp sweet dessert wine for the peanuts.

Time: 40 minutes + chilling time
Very easy

3½ cups finely crushed plain cookies
½ cup peanuts
½ cup peeled almonds
11 oz (11 squares) bitter or semisweet baking chocolate
½ cup mascarpone (or similar fresh cream cheese)
1 cup sugar
pinch salt
For decoration:
½ cup sugar

Crush or process the cookies very finely; chop the peanuts and almonds finely. Melt the chocolate over hot water. Mix all the ingredients listed above except for the chopped almonds and the sugar reserved for decoration. Use a wooden spoon and combine very thoroughly; the mixture should be firm. Shape into fingers 2 in long and roll these in the chopped almonds. Place on a serving plate, sprinkled with the sugar, and chill in the refrigerator until served.

• • •

□ *While cookies are still firm favorites for home-baking enthusiasts and have never lost their popularity, petits fours have tended to be reserved for grand occasions: served at the end of a banquet, grand dinner party or at smart receptions. This is a pity as they are an extremely enjoyable (and original) way to round off a good meal, with coffee or liqueurs, often after a simple dessert of fresh fruit salad or insubstantial mousse, providing that taste of sweetness which so many people crave.*

□ *Petits fours can be turned into miniature works of art. A box of your own homemade selection would also make an unusual and welcome present for your hostess when you are a guest at a dinner party instead of the more prosaic box of chocolates.*

BRUTTI MA BUONI

Unprepossessing to look at but delicious to eat, these are made to a very old recipe from northern Italy. ("Brutti ma buoni" means "ugly but good.")

Time: 40 minutes
Very easy

3 cups all-purpose flour
1 cup (2 sticks) butter, softened
1 cup sugar
2 eggs, separated

pinch salt
1 cup peeled almonds
1 tsp vanilla extract
1 tsp cinnamon

Sift the flour into a large mixing bowl; make a well in the center, and place the butter in it (softened at room temperature) with ¼ cup of the sugar and the 2 egg yolks beaten with the vanilla and salt. Work into the flour until well blended. Roast the almonds briefly in the oven until pale golden brown; chop finely.
Beat the egg whites stiffly; beat in the remaining sugar and the cinnamon; fold the egg

whites and the almonds into the contents of the bowl. Place heaping teaspoonfuls or dessertspoonfuls of this mixture onto a greased cookie sheet, making no attempt to make them look tidy. Bake in the oven at 350°F until pale golden brown.

• • •

LEMON COOKIES

Time: 45 minutes
Very easy

½ cup (1 stick) + 2 tbsp
    butter, softened
½ cup sugar
grated peel and juice of 1
    lemon
generous pinch cinnamon
2 egg yolks
pinch salt
2¼ cups all-purpose flour
¼ cup cane sugar

Beat the softened butter with the first quantity of sugar until very pale and creamy; add the lemon peel and juice, the cinnamon, 1 egg yolk, and salt. Add the sifted flour and stir thoroughly or knead. Shape the mixture into a sausage, wrap in foil, and chill in the refrigerator for 2 hours. Beat the remaining egg yolk, unwrap the sausage of cookie mixture, and brush the yolk all over its surface. Roll in the cane sugar, covering the surface of the roll evenly. Cut the sausage into slices just under ¼ in thick and place on one or more greased cookie sheets. Place in a preheated oven at 400°F and bake for 15 minutes.

• • •

CATS' TONGUES

Add ¼ cup sifted unsweetened cocoa powder and a generous pinch cinnamon to this mixture for chocolate cats' tongues.

Time: 1 hour
Easy

1 cup (2 sticks) butter
1¾ cups confectioners' sugar
pinch salt
6 egg whites
1¾ cups all-purpose flour
3 tbsp olive oil
5 oz (5 squares) bitter or
    semisweet baking chocolate

Beat the softened butter with the sugar and salt, using a wooden spoon, until it is very pale and soft. Stir in the stiffly beaten egg whites and the flour.
Use a pastry bag and medium plain tube to pipe the mixture onto a greased and floured cookie sheet, in 4-in long strips, well spaced out from one another. Leave to stand for 10 minutes.
Place in a preheated oven at 485°F and bake for 4 or 5 minutes.
Lightly oil a rolling pin; while the cookies are still warm, place lengthwise along the rolling pin (underside of the cookie against the rolling pin) and press so that they are slightly curved (optional). Melt the chocolate over hot water, dip a pastry brush into the chocolate, and brush a little inside the curved side of the cookies (optional).

• • •

SWEET WINE COOKIE RINGS

Delicious as they are or with the addition of a little cinnamon: brush the top of the uncooked rings with egg white and sprinkle with the cinnamon before baking.

Time: 1 hour
Very easy

2¼ cups all-purpose flour
½ cup sugar
¼ cup baking powder
½ cup (1 stick) butter
1 egg
pinch salt
1½ tbsp sweet dessert wine
1 cup confectioners' sugar

Sift the flour onto the work surface, make a well in the center, and in it place ½ cup sugar, baking powder, softened butter cut into small pieces, the egg, salt, and wine. Work gradually into the flour and knead lightly until the mixture is evenly blended and smooth.
Break off pieces of the dough, roll between your palms into long, thin cylinders and join the ends of each one so that they form rings.
Sprinkle these with the confectioners' sugar and bake on greased and floured cookie sheet at 320°F for 20 minutes or until done.

• • •

AMARETTI

Time: 45 minutes
Very easy

1½ cups sweet almonds
2 egg whites
1½ tbsp all-purpose flour
2 tbsp vanilla sugar
1 tsp cinnamon
peel of 1 lemon, grated
1 cup sugar
pinch salt

Try to use almonds with their brown inner skins on, otherwise use peeled almonds. Pound them to a very fine paste, leaving the skins on (or grind in a food processor). Beat the egg whites stiffly. Mix the almonds, flour, vanilla sugar, cinnamon, grated lemon peel, sugar, and salt and fold into the egg whites. When thoroughly (but gently) stirred, break off small pieces, roll these lightly into balls between your palms (they should be about 1–1¼ in in diameter) flatten them slightly, and space out on a greased cookie sheet; bake at 350°F for about 25 minutes, making sure they do not brown too much.

• • •

FILBERT MACAROONS

Time: 45 minutes
Very easy

1¼ cups filberts
1 cup sugar
3 egg whites
pinch salt
1 tbsp butter
1½ tbsp all-purpose flour

Roast the filberts lightly in the oven, chop finely, mix with the sugar, then fold into the egg whites, stiffly beaten with the salt.
When gently but thoroughly mixed, spoon into a pastry bag with a plain tube. Pipe small mounds of mixture, well spaced out, on a greased and floured cookie sheet. Bake at 350°F for about 30 minutes.

• • •

HALF MOON COOKIES

These cookies can be half dipped in melted chocolate to add more flavor and visual appeal.

Time: 1 hour
Easy

2 cups all-purpose flour
¼ cup (½ stick) butter
¼ cup sugar
pinch salt
2 eggs
peel of 1 lemon, grated
1½ tbsp baking powder

Mix the flour, softened (not melted) butter, sugar, salt, 1 whole egg and 1 yolk (the spare white will be used later),

NUTMEG

The seed of a tree (*Myristica fragrans*) that is native to the Molucca Islands of Indonesia which, when freshly grated, imparts a lovely flavor and fragrance to sweet and savory foods.

grated lemon peel, and baking powder. Work thoroughly until the mixture binds well; roll out fairly thinly and cut out into disks about 2½–3 in in diameter. Cut these in half. Beat the egg white stiffly and spread a little on top of each half moon. Place on a greased cookie sheet. Place in a preheated oven at 350°F for 10 minutes, checking that they only brown slightly.

• • •

HONEY COOKIES

The taste of honey is unmistakable in these cookies. The stronger the flavor of honey you use (such as chestnut blossom) the more pronounced the taste.

Time: 40 minutes
Very easy

½ cup (1 stick) butter
¼ cup clear, runny honey
1 egg
2¾ cups all-purpose flour
1½ tbsp baking powder
pinch cinnamon
pinch salt

Have the butter softened at room temperature and beat until very pale and creamy; gradually beat in the honey, adding a little at a time and continue beating, gradually adding the lightly beaten egg and the flour, baking powder, cinnamon, and salt all sifted together.
Shape the mixture into a firm ball and leave to stand for 20 minutes. Roll out fairly thinly; use variously shaped cookie cutters to cut out a selection of shapes. Bake at 375°F for 20 minutes or until done.

• • •

APPLE AND KIRSCH CROSTINI

Time: 20 minutes
Very easy

½ cup (1 stick) butter
12 small slices white bread
1 lb apples
1 cup kirsch
½ cup sugar
3 tbsp cinnamon

Fry the pieces of toast gently in the butter in batches (use more butter if necessary). Place on a serving plate and keep hot. Peel, core, and slice the apples neatly and cook in the kirsch for 10 minutes. Drain and place the apple slices on the fried bread; mix the sugar and cinnamon together and sprinkle over the apples. Serve the crostini immediately.

• • •

RASPBERRY CREAM MERINGUES

Time: 1 hour + cooking time
for the meringues
Fairly easy

3 egg whites
pinch salt
3½ cups confectioners' sugar
¾ lb raspberries
½ cup whipping cream

Beat the egg whites with the salt until very stiff; fold in 2¾ cups of the sugar.
Cover one or more greased cookie sheets with foil. Use a pastry bag and medium-sized tube to pipe the meringue into flattish oval shapes, well spaced apart, on the foil. Bake

RED CURRANTS
■ Engraving taken from an illustrated nineteenth-century botanical treatise.

in a very slow oven (about 200°F) with the door left very slightly open; the object is to set and dry out the meringues; they should not color at all. Check to see if they are ready by removing one meringue: if it is dry all the way through it is done. Reserve a few raspberries for decoration; crush the others with a fork and fold into the very stiffly beaten, sweetened cream. Chill this in the refrigerator until 10 minutes before serving. Sandwich spoonfuls of the fruit cream between the flat sides of pairs of meringues and top each with a whole raspberry.

• • •

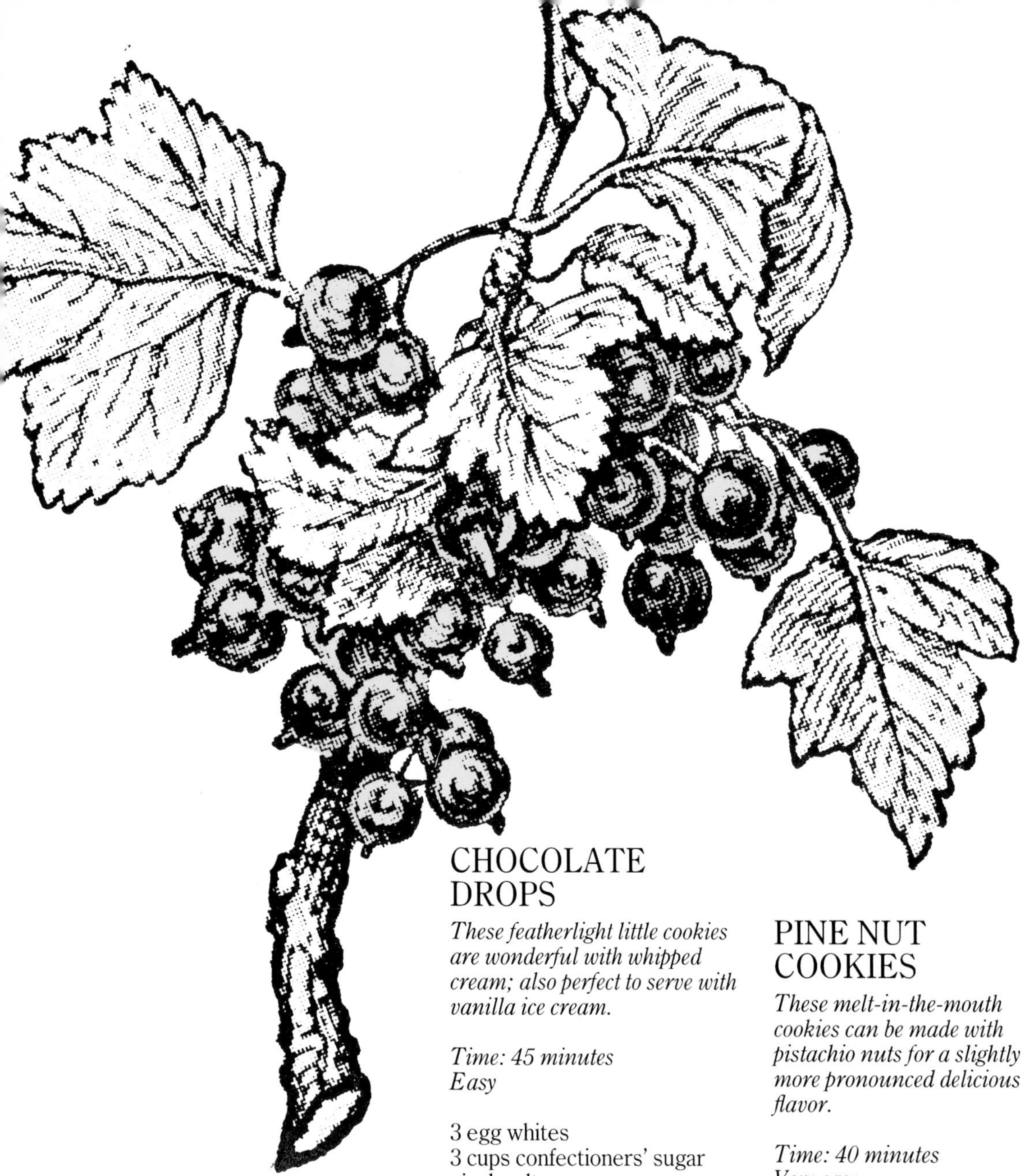

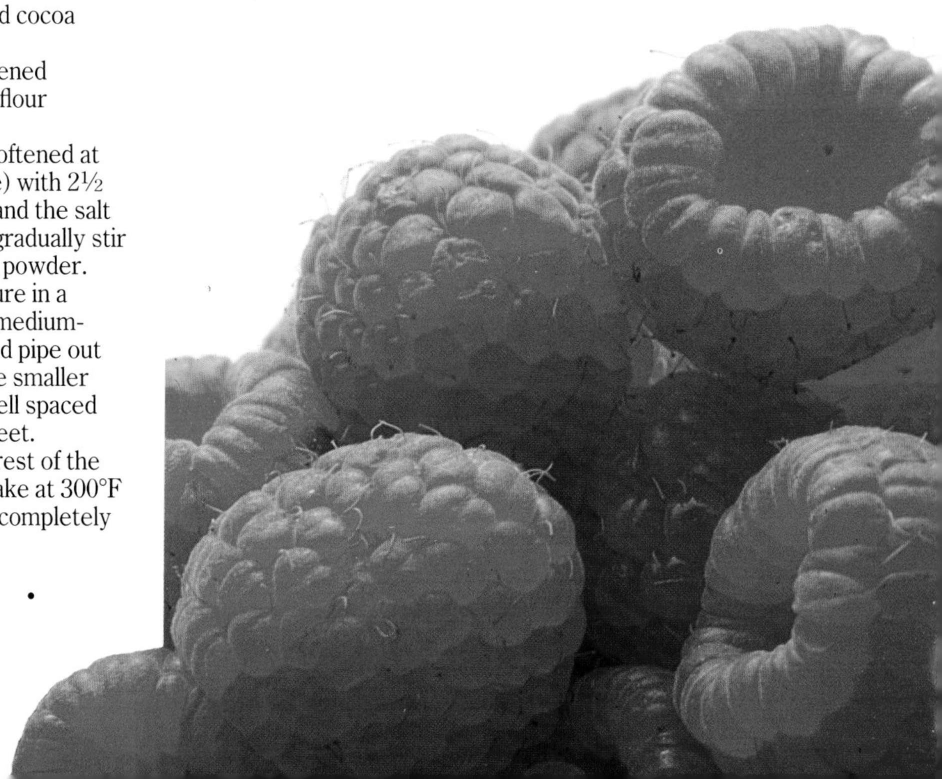

CHOCOLATE DROPS

These featherlight little cookies are wonderful with whipped cream; also perfect to serve with vanilla ice cream.

Time: 45 minutes
Easy

3 egg whites
3 cups confectioners' sugar
pinch salt
1 cup unsweetened cocoa powder
1 tbsp butter, softened
1 tbsp all-purpose flour

Beat the butter (softened at room temperature) with 2½ cups of the sugar and the salt very thoroughly; gradually stir in the sifted cocoa powder. Put this firm mixture in a pastry bag with a medium-sized plain tube and pipe out into mounds a little smaller than an apricot, well spaced out on a cookie sheet. Sprinkle with the rest of the sifted sugar and bake at 300°F for 1 hour or until completely dry.

• • •

PINE NUT COOKIES

These melt-in-the-mouth cookies can be made with pistachio nuts for a slightly more pronounced delicious flavor.

Time: 40 minutes
Very easy

2 egg whites
1 cup sugar
1½ cups pine nuts
3 tbsp all-purpose flour
pinch salt

Beat the egg whites until fairly firm and fold in the sugar, coarsely chopped pine nuts, flour, and salt. The mixture should be thick but soft. Spread the mixture out on a marble slab, lightly oiled with sweet almond oil, using a spatula. The mixture should be just under ¼ in thick. Cut out into rectangles or rhomboids and use a spatula to transfer these onto a greased cookie sheet.
Bake at 350°F until pale golden brown.

• • •

SEMOLINA COOKIES

A generous pinch of salt is vital to bring out the taste of these simple biscuits. Ideal with coffee.

Time: 1 hour
Very easy

scant 1 cake fresh yeast or 1 package dry yeast
1½ tbsp clear honey
1 cup fine semolina or wheat farina
1 cup fine yellow maize flour
½ cup (1 stick) + 2 tbsp butter
½ cup sugar
2 eggs
1 tbsp cinnamon
generous pinch salt

Stir the yeast gently into the honey; if dry yeast is used, dissolve in 3 tbsp warm water and add the honey. Mix with the semolina or wheat farina (do not use quick breakfast farina) and place the resulting dough ball, or ferment, in a bowl in a warm place, covered with a towel, until doubled in bulk.
Mix all the other ingredients together and combine with the risen ferment, adding a little warm water when necessary. Break off pieces equivalent to 3 tbsp from this soft dough, shape into balls and place at least 4 in apart on greased cookie sheets. Dip the base of a glass in cold water and press down on the dough balls to flatten to a thickness of about ⅜ in. Cover with a towel and leave in a warm place to prove for about 1 hour.
Bake at 375°F for about 20 minutes.

• • •

LADY'S KISSES

Do not overcook or these cookies will be dry and lose their soft texture. These keep well in an airtight tin.

Time: 1 hour 20 minutes
Easy

½ cup peeled almonds
1¾ cups all-purpose flour
pinch salt
1 cup sugar
½ cup (1 stick) butter
1 cup brandy
2 oz (2 squares) good bitter or semisweet chocolate

Roast the almonds briefly in the oven until they are pale golden brown. Pound to a fine powder with a pestle and mortar or process in the food processor.
Sift the flour into a large mixing bowl. Make a well in the center, place the almonds, salt, sugar, ½ cup of the softened butter cut into small pieces and the brandy in it. Mix quickly and thoroughly into the flour. Break off walnut-sized pieces, place these on a cookie sheet generously greased with the remaining butter.
Bake at 400°F for 20 minutes. Leave to cool. Break the chocolate into small pieces and melt over hot water (if you are using ordinary block chocolate 2–3 tbsp warm water can be added if the chocolate is too thick).
Dip the flat bases of the cookies in the chocolate and immediately join together in pairs before the chocolate sets.

• • •

ROASTED ALMOND CAKES

These are very light and can be frosted using the recipe on page 51.

Time: 45 minutes
Fairly easy

½ cup peeled almonds
½ cup sugar
pinch salt
10 egg whites
¾ cup confectioners' sugar
3 tbsp butter for greasing

Roast the almonds briefly in the oven until very pale golden brown. Pound or process to a fine powder with the sugar and salt.
Beat the egg whites until very stiff; fold in the almond mixture gently but thoroughly, using a mixing spatula to avoid crushing too much air out of the whites.
Spread a lightly-greased sheet of foil over one or more cookie sheets; arrange little mounds of the mixture about the size of an apricot on this, well spaced out. Bake at 350°F for about 30 minutes; do not open the oven door until absolutely necessary. Serve warm.

• • •

COCONUT FANCIES

These bite-sized cookies would be suitable for a finger buffet.

Time: 40 minutes + chilling time
Very easy

½ cup (1 stick) butter, softened
7 oz (7 squares) bitter or

323

semisweet chocolate
1 cup confectioners' sugar
few drops vanilla extract
2½ tsp rum
2 egg yolks
pinch salt
1 cup shredded coconut

The butter should be softened at room temperature; melt the chocolate very gently over hot water, remove from the heat, and mix in the butter, sugar, vanilla, rum, followed by the egg yolks one at a time and the salt, using a wooden spoon. The mixture should be smooth and creamy.
Chill in the refrigerator until hard enough to shape. Rinse your hands in cold water and roll cherry-sized pieces between your palms into balls (or use a melon baller); roll these in the shredded coconut to coat well.
Place in tiny paper confectionery cups and chill until time to serve.

•   •   •

ALMOND KISSES

Time: 1 hour + chilling time
Very easy

1 cup peeled almonds
1¼ cups all-purpose flour
¼ cup (½ stick) butter
¼ cup sugar
1 egg yolk
1½ tbsp Marsala or sherry
pinch salt
⅓ cup chopped candied fruit
   or peel

Chop the almonds finely. Sift the flour into a large mixing bowl, make a well in the center, and place the softened butter (cut into small pieces) in it, with the sugar, egg yolk, Marsala, and salt. Mix quickly into the flour; work in the chopped almonds and candied fruit or peel.
Wrap in foil and chill for 2 hours in the refrigerator. Break off pieces a little larger than a cherry, roll into balls between your palms, then flatten slightly. Place on a greased cookie sheet and bake in a preheated oven (400°F) for about 20 minutes.

•   •   •

324

DRIED FRUIT COOKIES

Orange flower water gives these cookies a delicious flavor.

Time: 1 hour
Very easy

2¼ cups all-purpose flour
½ cup + 2 tbsp butter, softened
3 tbsp orange flower water
1½ tbsp sugar
pinch cinnamon
pinch salt
½ cup chopped, pitted dates
¼ cup peeled almonds
⅓ cup filberts
⅓ cup pistachio nuts

Sift the flour into a large mixing bowl; make a well in the center and in it place ½ cup of the butter (softened at room temperature and cut into small pieces) and the orange flower water. Use a pastry blender to cut the butter into the flour if wished, then work and knead the dough until firm, gradually working in the sugar, cinnamon, and salt. Place the dough between two floured plates and leave to stand. Chop the dates finely with the almonds, filberts, and pistachio nuts; add the rest of the softened butter, working it in with a wooden spoon. Rinse your hands in cold water and break off small pieces of dough about the size of an apricot, shape into balls, press your thumb down into each, making a hole in which a small amount of the fruit and butter mixture is placed. Place on a cookie sheet which has been lightly greased with butter and bake at 350°F for 30 minutes or until done.

• • •

BLUEBERRY BOATS

You will need barquette (boat-shaped) molds for these delicious little tarts; other acid fresh fruits such as black currants, raspberries, or blackberries can be used, or preserves.

Time: 1 hour 10 minutes
Very easy

1¾ cups all-purpose flour
1 tbsp baking powder
½ cup sugar
½ cup (1 stick) butter
few drops vanilla extract
pinch salt
1½ cups blueberries
½ cup whipping cream

Sift the flour and baking powder together; mix well with 6 tbsp of the sugar, the softened butter, vanilla, and salt. Roll out with a rolling pin until just under ¼ in thick. Use to line small barquette molds, place these on a cookie sheet and cook at 350°F for 30 minutes or until done. Leave to cool; fold the blueberries into the cream (stiffly beaten and sweetened with the remaining sugar) and fill the barquettes with this. Chill until serving (fairly soon after filling).

• • •

CINNAMON COOKIES

These have a very pronounced cinnamon flavor; if cinnamon is not to your taste, use grated lemon peel instead.

BLUEBERRIES

In season in summer and fall, blueberries also freeze well. Cranberries, brighter red but similar in appearance, are extremely sour and are therefore chiefly used as an accompaniment to poultry (especially turkey) and feathered game.

Time: 1 hour
Very easy

2¼ cups all-purpose flour
1 tbsp baking powder
½ cup melted butter
¼ cup sugar
1 whole egg and 1 extra egg white
few drops vanilla extract
1 tsp cinnamon
1½ tbsp light cream
pinch salt
⅓ cup pine nuts, chopped

Sift the flour into a mixing bowl with the baking powder and mix with the butter, sugar, whole egg, vanilla, cinnamon, cream, and salt. Work the mixture until smooth and firm; roll out with a rolling pin to a sheet just under ¼ in thick. Use a cookie cutter (preferably star-shaped) to cut out cookies and place on a greased cookie sheet. Beat the egg white stiffly, fold in the chopped nuts, and spread a little over the center of each star.
Bake at 350°F for 20 minutes or until done.

• • •

325

*SWEET EGG PASTRY
COOKIES*
■ *Perfect for children, half a
candied cherry could add
even more appeal to the star-
shaped cookies.*

SWEET EGG
PASTRY COOKIES

Time: 1 hour 30 minutes
Easy

½ cup (1 stick) butter,
    softened
½ cup sugar
1 egg yolk
peel of 1 lemon, grated
pinch salt
2¼ cups all-purpose flour

The butter should be softened
at room temperature. Beat,
together with all but 1½ tbsp
of the sugar, using a wooden
spoon, until very pale and
light; beat in the egg, lemon
peel, and lastly the salt.
Sift the flour into a large
mixing bowl and mix in the
butter mixture quickly; do not
overwork the mixture. Leave
to stand for 1 hour in a cool
place. Roll out into a sheet just
under ¼ in thick and cut out
into stars, triangles, diamonds
etc. Place these shapes on a
greased cookie sheet.
Bake at 400°F for 20 minutes
or until done. Remove from
the oven and while still very
hot, brush their surfaces with
a little water, and sprinkle
with the remaining sugar.

•   •   •

SEEDLESS WHITE
RAISIN CAKES

*These keep very well if stored in
an airtight tin. Excellent with
coffee.*

Time: 1 hour
Very easy

1 cup seedless white raisins
½ cup (1 stick) butter
½ cup sugar
few drops vanilla extract

■ *Sandwich a vanilla cream or chocolate filling between two round sweet egg pastry cookies.*

2 eggs
1½ tbsp rum
pinch salt
1¾ cups all-purpose flour
1½ tbsp baking powder

Soak the seedless white raisins in warm water until plump. Drain, dry, and shake with a little flour to coat. Beat the butter (softened at room temperature) with the sugar and vanilla until very pale; beat in the eggs one at a time, then add the rum, salt, the flour sifted with the baking powder, and the seedless white raisins.
Take heaping tablespoonfuls of the mixture and shape into balls; place on a greased cookie sheet, well spaced out. Bake at 350°F for 20 minutes or until done.

• • •

LADYFINGERS

The secret of successful ladyfingers lies mainly in prolonged, vigorous beating of the sugar and egg yolks until they are pale and creamy and form a ribbon when the whisk is lifted above the bowl.

Time: 1 hour 15 minutes
Easy

1¼ cups confectioners' sugar
6 eggs, separated
1 tsp vanilla extract
1¼ cups cake flour or all-purpose flour
few drops lemon juice or pinch cream of tartar
extra confectioners' sugar for glaze

Have 2 or more cookie sheets ready greased with butter and coated with flour.
Beat the sifted sugar with the egg yolks and vanilla essence until very pale indeed and foamy (this can take up to 30 minutes if using a balloon whisk). Sift in the flour a little at a time, folding it into the mixture gently but thoroughly and alternating with additions of the very stiffly beaten egg whites (beat these with a few drops of lemon juice or a pinch of cream of tartar to help them keep their aeration if wished). Spoon batches of the batter into a pastry bag with a plain ¾-in tube and pipe strips of mixture 4 in long and well spaced out. Lift up the tube tip in a swift stroke against the direction of piping at the end of each ladyfinger to avoid a long tail.

Sprinkle confectioners' sugar generously over the ladyfingers; leave to stand for 5 minutes, then sprinkle again with more sugar. If you are feeling brave, turn the filled sheet upside down and tap gently twice with the handle of a knife on the bottom to dislodge the excess sugar (the sponge mixture should not fall off if it is the correct consistency).
Bake in a preheated oven at 350°F, leaving the door slightly open, for about 15 minutes. They should be set, dry, and pale golden beige in color.

• • •

327

ALMOND HALF MOON COOKIES

These may look simple and homely but their taste is out of this world!

1 cup peeled almonds
½ cup (1 stick) butter
½ cup confectioners' sugar
3 tbsp Marsala
1¾ cups all-purpose flour

Have the butter ready softened by leaving to stand at warm room temperature for at least 45 minutes before you start work. Chop the almonds coarsely and roast briefly in the oven, taking care not to let them color darker than pale golden brown. Beat the softened butter with the sugar until very pale and fluffy.

Gradually beat in the Marsala, adding a very little at a time.

Add the flour and the almonds a little at a time, stirring thoroughly.

Shape into a rectangular "loaf" and leave to stand for 30 minutes. Cut into 4 equal portions. Shape these firmly into 4 long sections and cut these in turn into small pieces.

Roll the pieces into small sausages, thicker in the middle than at their ends, using the palms of your hands (rinse in cold water beforehand) and pull round the ends so that they curve in a moon shape.

Arrange on a greased cookie sheet. Place in the oven, preheated to 325°F and bake for 15–20 minutes or until done. They should not color too darkly.

MARRON GLACÉ
BONBONS
■ These very rich sweetmeats
may be served instead of
chocolates after dinner.

ALMOND MERINGUES

*Ideal as an accompaniment
when classic custard (vanilla
or chocolate), pastry cream or
zabaglione are served hot in
little custard cups or glasses.*

*Time: 1 hour 15 minutes
Easy*

½ cup peeled almonds
3 egg whites
1¾ cups confectioners' sugar

Roast the almonds briefly in
the oven until pale golden
brown; chop finely.
Beat the egg whites very
stiffly with half the sugar,
continue beating while very
gradually adding the rest of
the sugar by which time the
mixture should be extremely
firm. Beat in the chopped
almonds.
Place heaping teaspoonfuls of
the mixture in tiny fluted
paper candy cups and cook in a
cool oven (approx. 200°F)
with the door fractionally open
for about 30 minutes–1 hour
or until set and dry.

• • •

MARRON GLACÉ BONBONS

*Time: 40 minutes
Very easy*

¾ lb marron glacé pieces (sold
　　as débris de marrons
　　glacés)
1 tbsp butter
3 tbsp rum
½ cup nibbed sugar
4 oz (4 squares) bitter
　　chocolate, finely grated
⅔ cup finely chopped filberts
⅔ cup finely chopped almonds

329

Push the broken marron glacé pieces through a sieve; mix them very thoroughly with the softened butter, rum, and nibbed sugar.

Rinse your hands in cold water and break off cherry-sized pieces of the mixture, rolling these into balls between your palms. Roll one third of the balls in the grated chocolate, one third in the chopped filberts and one third in the chopped almonds.

Place in fluted paper confectionery cups and arrange in a checkerboard effect on a big plate.

• • •

COFFEE CREAM TARTLETS

Other fillings can be used for these tartlets: pastry cream flavored with orange flower water; zabaglione or chocolate custard.

Time: 1 hour
Easy

1¾ cups all-purpose flour
½ cup (1 stick) butter
2 egg yolks
¼ cup sugar
pinch salt
For the filling:
1 cup very strong black coffee
½ cup sugar
4 egg yolks
2⅓ cups ground almonds

Make the pastry: rub the butter (softened at room temperature and cut into small pieces) into the flour (or use a pastry blender) then stir in the 2 egg yolks, sugar, and salt. Grease small, deep tartlet pans lightly with butter; roll out the pastry fairly thinly

and line the pans with it. Fill the uncooked tartlets two-thirds full with the following filling: boil the coffee with the sugar for 5 minutes; remove from the heat and allow to cool a little before beating in the egg yolks vigorously one at a time and stirring in the ground almonds.

Bake at 350°F until golden brown; remove the tartlets from their pans while still hot; leave to cool.

• • •

CHOCOLATE COOKIES

For coffee cookies, simply substitute 3 tbsp instant coffee powder dissolved in 3 tbsp water for the cocoa powder.

Time: 45 minutes
Very easy

2¼ cups all-purpose flour
¼ cup butter, softened and cut into small pieces
6 tbsp sugar
1 egg
1 tbsp baking powder
½ cup milk
pinch salt
½ cup unsweetened cocoa powder

Sift the flour into a large mixing bowl, make a well in the center, and place all the ingredients except for the cocoa in it. Combine very thoroughly with the flour, mixing until very smooth. Divide into 3 equal portions and work the cocoa powder into one portion.

Roll out each portion into as thin a sheet as possible without it breaking; place

JAM-FILLED PASTRIES
■ *Instead of using preserves for the filling, you could chop mixed dried fruit, moisten with lemon juice, and sweeten with a sprinkling of sugar. If you are in a hurry use puff pastry; cut out circles with a cutter and fold in half to enclose a spoonful of preserve.*

the sheets one on top of the other so that you have a sandwich with the chocolate layer in the middle. Roll together lightly.
Cut into rectangles about ¾ in × 2 in and place on a greased and floured cookie sheet.
Bake at 350°F until done.

• • •

JAM-FILLED PASTRIES

Time: 1 hour 15 minutes
Easy

1 cake fresh yeast or 1
   package (¼ oz) dry yeast
2½ tsp clear honey
2¾ cups unbleached all-
   purpose flour
¼ cup sugar
2 eggs
¼ cup (½ stick) butter
peel of 1 lemon, grated
pinch salt
1 cup jam or preserve of
   choice

Mix the yeast, honey, and ½ cup warm water gently until completely dissolved (if using dry yeast leave to stand in the warm water for 5–10 minutes, then stir in the honey).
Sift the flour into a large mixing bowl, make a well in the center, and place the activated yeast and honey in it. Gradually mix into the flour, adding a little more warm water if necessary to form a firm dough.
Shape into a ball and leave to stand in a warm place, covered by a cloth or towel, for 15 minutes. Work in the eggs, softened butter, lemon peel, and salt, pinching down the dough as you do so. Roll out with a rolling pin into a sheet about ⅜ in thick; cut out

into rectangles about 2½ × 5 in and place 1½ tbsp of jam in the center of each. Fold into triangles, folding the spare borders of pastry left when the rectangles are folded, above and below the triangles and pinching along the edges to prevent the jam oozing out.

PRESERVES

Always use the very best preserves and jam for desserts, cakes, and pastry cooking as it will be immediately apparent if an inferior-quality product has been used. Good homemade preserves and jam are probably best of all.

Place on a greased cookie sheet, cover with a kitchen towel, and leave to prove until well risen.
Bake at 350° F until done and pale golden brown.

• • •

RICOTTA SURPRISES

These will be even lighter if finely chopped chocolate is used instead of the candied fruit.

Time: 20 minutes
Very easy

2 cups ricotta
½ cup sugar
½ cup candied fruit or mixed
   peel
1½ cups finely crushed
   amaretti or macaroons

WALNUT COOKIES
■ Add ½ cup chopped dried figs to the mixture before cooking instead of the candied orange peel, if you prefer.

Beat the ricotta and sugar with a wooden spoon; stir in the finely diced candied fruit (or peel) and shape into very small oval pieces, looking like little eggs. Roll these in the powdered amaretti and arrange on a serving plate. Chill for at least 2 hours before serving.

CRESCENT COOKIES

These can be made with 3 tsp vanilla extract instead of the cocoa powder.

Time: 50 minutes
Very easy

2¼ cups all-purpose flour

1 cup fine yellow maize flour
⅔ cup sugar
2 tbsp unsweetened cocoa powder
pinch salt
2 whole eggs and 2 extra yolks
2 tbsp clear honey
1 cup (2 sticks) butter, softened

Mix the two types of flour

together thoroughly with the sugar, cocoa, and salt in a large mixing bowl. Make a well in the center and place in it the 2 eggs and 2 extra yolks, the honey, and the butter (softened at room temperature and cut into very small pieces). Combine all these ingredients together well and leave to stand,

covered, for 1 hour.
Use a pastry bag and large-gauge fluted tube to pipe the mixture out onto a greased cookie sheet, making the shapes slightly curved and about 3 in long.
Bake in a preheated oven at 400°F for 20 minutes or until done. Leave to cool before serving.

•   •   •

WALNUT COOKIES

Time: 1 hour
Very easy

2¾ cups all-purpose flour
pinch salt
⅓ cup candied orange peel
½–1 tsp anise seeds (to taste)
1 cup walnut pieces
½–1 tbsp cinnamon (to taste)
½ cup water
1½ cups sugar

Place the flour in a mixing bowl with the salt, finely chopped orange peel, crushed anise seeds, and pounded or ground walnuts. Mix well and add the cinnamon. Heat the sugar and water, boiling gently until the syrup thickens but does not color at all; stir very well into the contents of the bowl. Turn this firm paste out onto a floured pastryboard and knead by hand until smooth. Roll out with a rolling pin to a thickness of ¾ in and cut into various shapes using small fancy cookie cutters.
Place on a greased and floured cookie sheet and bake at 350°F for 30 minutes or until done; the cookies should be firm and dry but should not color.

•   •   •

LITTLE RUM COOKIES

Sprinkle these cookies with sifted cocoa powder the minute they come out of the oven and leave to cool before serving.

Time: 1 hour
Very easy

½ cup seedless white raisins
½ cup (1 stick) butter, softened
½ cup sugar
2 eggs
3 tbsp rum
1¾ cups all-purpose flour
pinch salt
⅓ cup pine nuts
½ cup potato flour or cornstarch
1 tbsp baking powder

Soak the seedless white raisins in a little water until plump; drain, dry, and shake with a little flour to coat. Have the butter softened at room temperature and beat it until pale and creamy; add the sugar and beat well. Stir in the eggs one at a time, the rum, flour, salt, seedless white raisins, finely chopped pine nuts, and the potato flour or cornstarch sifted with the baking powder. Grease a cookie sheet with butter and dust with flour. Break off cherry-sized pieces of the mixture, roll between your palms, and then flatten. Arrange these on the sheet, well spaced out, and bake at 350°F for 20 minutes or until done.

•   •   •

RICE CAKES

Time: 1 hour 15 minutes
Very easy

1½ cups short-grain (pudding) rice
1 quart rich milk
⅔ cup sugar
¼ cup (½ stick) butter
⅓ cup candied citron peel
pinch salt
⅓ cup rum
4 eggs

Mix the rice and the hot milk in the top of a double boiler and cook, stirring from time to time. Add the sugar when the rice is half cooked, with the butter, finely chopped peel, and the salt. When the rice is extremely soft and has absorbed all the milk, turn into a bowl, leave to cool and stir in the rum, the egg yolks and finally the stiffly beaten egg whites, using a wooden spatula.
Grease individual dariole molds, small, deep cake pans or muffin molds with butter and fill with the rice mixture; bake at 350°F for 40 minutes standing in a roasting pan containing hot water.

•   •   •

CRUNCHY HONEY COOKIES

Time: 40 minutes
Very easy

1⅔ cups thick, set honey
3 egg yolks
pinch baking soda
½ cup peeled almonds
½ cup all-purpose flour
1 tbsp butter

Place the honey in a bowl; add the egg yolks and the baking soda and stir well with a wooden spoon. Chop the almonds finely and add to the honey; add the flour. Mix well to form a soft dough.
Roll portions of the dough beneath your floured palms on a floured pastryboard; the object is to have slightly flattened, long cylinders about 2 in wide. Place on a greased cookie sheet and bake at 350°F until golden brown. Remove from the oven, allow to cool, and cut into slices about ⅜ in thick.

•   •   •

CREAM PUFFS

These can be filled with pastry cream, chocolate or coffee confectioners' custard, or Sabayon sauce. Sprinkle with sifted confectioners' sugar, or frost (see recipe on p. 51).

Time: 1 hour 15 minutes
Easy

1 cup water
pinch salt
¼ cup (½ stick) butter
1¾ cups all-purpose flour
6 whole eggs and 2 extra yolks
¼ cup sugar
3 tbsp all-purpose flour
small piece lemon peel (no pith)
1 pint milk
1½ tbsp confectioners' sugar

Bring the water to a boil with the salt; add the butter and once it has melted, draw aside from the heat and immediately dump in all the sifted flour, starting to mix vigorously with a wooden spoon the minute you have done so. Return to a low heat while stirring hard,

333

until the mixture leaves the sides of the pan cleanly. Draw aside from the heat and continue stirring for a few minutes. Add the lightly beaten eggs one at a time, stirring extremely well before adding the next one. Leave to stand for 10 minutes. Place tablespoonfuls of the choux paste in small heaps on a cookie sheet covered with greased nonstick paper (or use a pastry bag and medium-sized plain tube). Bake in a preheated oven at 425°F for 15 minutes without once opening the oven door. Slit each bun partially in half horizontally and leave to cool. Make the pastry cream following the recipe given for Apricot Tartlets on page 336. When the pastry cream is cold, transfer to a pastry bag, and pipe a little into each slit choux bun. Sprinkle with confectioners' sugar and serve.

• • •

COCONUT COOKIES

Time: 1 hour
Easy

4 cups all-purpose flour
1½ cups sugar
pinch salt
1½ cups (3 sticks) butter
peel of 1 lemon, grated
4 egg yolks
2⅓ cups shredded coconut

Mix the flour, sugar, and salt in a mixing bowl. Make a well in the center and pour in the butter, melted over hot water, the grated lemon peel, the egg yolks, and coconut. Mix lightly but thoroughly.
Roll out into a sheet about

APPLE

■ *Engraving taken from a nineteenth-century botanical treatise. Apples form a very valuable item in a healthy diet, as well as featuring prominently in cake and dessert cookery.*

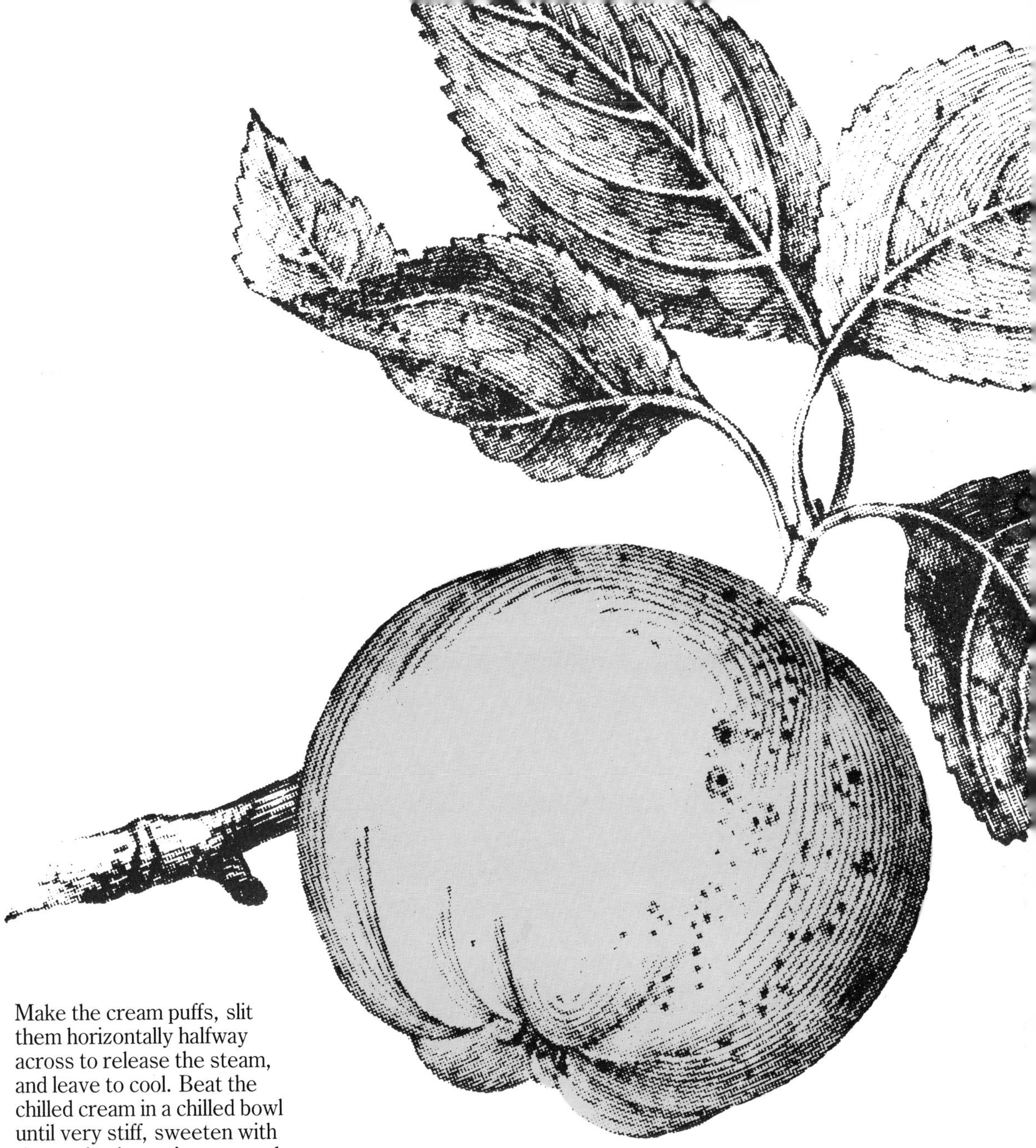

½ in thick and cut out disks with a round cookie cutter. Grease a cookie sheet with butter and arrange the cookies on it, leaving plenty of space between each one; bake at 350°F for 30 minutes or until done.

• • •

PROFITEROLES

These are lighter than those filled with pastry cream. Instead of topping them with caramelized sugar, a little melted chocolate can be used.

Time: 1 hour 15 minutes
Easy

1 quantity cream puffs (see page 334)
1 cup whipping cream
3 tbsp confectioners' sugar
½ cup sugar
1½ tbsp lemon juice

Make the cream puffs, slit them horizontally halfway across to release the steam, and leave to cool. Beat the chilled cream in a chilled bowl until very stiff, sweeten with the confectioners' sugar, and place in a pastry bag which will enable you to fill the choux buns neatly. Arrange in a pyramid as you fill them. Heat the sugar with the lemon juice and cook until a pale golden brown; immediately drizzle all over the mound of cream puffs.

• • •

JAM TARTLETS

These tiny jam tartlets look most effective. Good with tea or coffee.

Time: 1 hour
Very easy

2¾ cups all-purpose flour
1 cup + 2 tbsp (1¼ sticks) butter
½ cup sugar
1½ tbsp orange flower water
1 egg yolk
1 cup good-quality strawberry jam

Follow the pastry method given for Apricot Tartlets on page 336; leave to rest in a cool place and then roll out into a sheet ⅜ in thick.
Use three quarters of the pastry dough to line very small greased round tartlet pans.
Melt the jam gently; stir in the orange flower water and spread a little in the bottom of each little pie shell. Cut the remaining pastry into very narrow strips and arrange these in lattice coverings over the tartlets.
Bake at 350°F until pale golden brown.

• • •

CROISSANTS

Time: 1 hour 15 minutes
Fairly easy

3½ cups unbleached all-
    purpose flour
1 tsp salt
2 tbsp sugar
1 cake fresh yeast or 1
    package (¼ oz) dry yeast
2½ tsp clear honey
1 whole egg and 1 extra yolk
½ cup (1 stick) butter
½ cup milk
1½ tbsp nibbed sugar

Sift the flour into a mound on the pastryboard; add the salt and sugar. Make a well in the center.
Mix the yeast gently with the honey in a small bowl (if dry yeast is used, dissolve in 2 tbsp warm water, and leave to stand for 5–10 minutes until it starts to foam, then stir in the honey) and add to the flour. Add the egg, the extra egg yolk, 2 tbsp softened butter cut into small pieces, and the milk. Mix with your finger tips, gradually incorporating all the flour. Knead vigorously until firm and elastic. Shape into a ball. Place in a floured bowl, cover with the towel, and leave to rise in a warm place until doubled in bulk.
Roll out on a lightly floured board with a lightly floured rolling pin. Place the remaining softened butter in the center of this rather thick sheet. Fold the four corners into the center so that they overlap like an envelope. Wrap in foil or saran wrap and chill for 20 minutes in the refrigerator. Roll out again and repeat the folding exercise. Chill. Repeat the rolling and folding exercise. Chill for the

last time, then roll out into a thin sheet ⅛ in thick. Cut into 18 identical squares; cut these in half into 2 triangles; roll these up, starting at the base and rolling toward the point. Curve the ends round and place on a greased cookie sheet.
Sprinkle with the nibbed sugar and bake at 400°F for 20 minutes or until done.
Serve immediately, straight from the oven, or reheat briefly before serving.

• • •

APRICOT TARTLETS

Delicate and delicious, these can be served with a sweet dessert wine at the end of a dinner party.

Time: 1 hour 30 minutes
Easy

2¼ cups all-purpose flour
½ cup sugar
½ cup (1 stick) butter
peel of 1 lemon, grated
2 egg yolks
pinch salt
For the filling:
2 egg yolks
3 tbsp sugar
1½ tbsp all-purpose flour
1 pint milk
1 lb very ripe fresh apricots
¼ cup sugar
3 tbsp rum
1 cup amaretti, ratafias, or
    macaroons
1 cup apricot jam

Sift the flour and salt into a large mixing bowl; make a well in the center and pour the melted butter into it; add the lemon peel, egg yolks, and salt. Mix the pastry briefly,

CROISSANTS
■ Eaten just as they are (warm them for a few minutes unless they have just been baked) or with a filling of peach, apricot, raspberry, or cherry preserves they are the classic accompaniment to breakfast coffee.

working it as little as possible before rolling it out into a thin sheet. Use small plain cookie cutter to cut out disks to line tiny tartlet molds, lightly greased with butter. Weight the pastry lining down with small pieces of waxed paper with some of the beans on top. Bake at 350°F for about 15 minutes.

Make the filling: beat the egg yolks with the sugar until pale, gradually beat in the flour a little at a time, followed by ½ cup of the cold milk. Heat the remaining milk to a boil and then beat into the custard mixture a little at a time. Cook over low heat, stirring continuously until the mixture nears boiling point. Remove from the heat and leave to cool.

Remove the beans and paper from the cooked and cooled tartlets, remove from the molds and half fill each with some of the filling. Peel (if wished) and pit the apricots and place an apricot half on top of the filling, cut side uppermost.

Heat the sugar and rum until the sugar has completely dissolved; stir in the finely crushed amaretti. Fill the hollows of the apricots with this.

Barely melt the sieved apricot jam with 3 tbsp hot water and glaze the contents of the tartlets generously with this, using a pastry brush.

•　•　•

CHOCOLATE CLOUDS

Useful for decorating sundaes and coupes made with ice cream and whipped cream. Also good just on their own.

Time: 45 minutes
Very easy

6 eggs
1½ oz (1½ squares) chocolate
1 cup sugar
¾ cup all-purpose flour

Beat the egg yolks with the sugar until very pale and fluffy; add the finely-grated chocolate and the stiffly beaten egg whites. Fold in the sifted flour; place spoonfuls of this mixture in little paper baking cases and bake at 375°F until done.

•　•　•

CARAWAY SEED RINGS

If you do not like caraway seed (which has a strong taste) use poppy seeds instead.

Time: 40 minutes
Very easy

2 tsp baking powder
½ cup milk
2¾ cups all-purpose flour
¼ cup lard or shortening
½ tsp salt
1 tbsp butter
⅓ cup oil
5 tbsp sugar
2 tsp caraway seeds

Dissolve the baking powder in the milk. Place the flour in a bowl, make a well in the center, and place the milk and all the ingredients in it. Mix briefly, just long enough to combine the ingredients thoroughly.

Divide the mixture into 3 equal portions, roll each one with your palms on a pastryboard to form a long cylinder about ¾ in thick. Cut into 8½-in lengths and join the ends of each piece to form a ring. Place these on a greased and floured cookie sheet and bake at 350°F for 15–20 minutes. These rings will still seem soft when they come out of the oven; they will become crisp as they cool.

•　•　•

SUGAR PUFFS

These are light and airy, rather like meringues. Pipe into rosettes or fingers.

Time: 40 minutes
Very easy

1 cup all-purpose flour
pinch salt
3 eggs, separated
1½ cups sugar
1 tbsp butter

Sift the flour and salt into a bowl. Beat the yolks until pale and frothy. Beat the egg whites stiffly with half the sugar. Mix the flour with the remaining sugar and stir, a little at a time, into the egg yolks. Fold in the egg whites and use a pastry bag with large tube to pipe out in 1¼-in long fingers on a greased cookie sheet and bake at 350°F for 15 minutes. Leave to cool, before removing with a spatula.

•　•　•

SICILIAN CANNOLI

Time: 2 hours
Fairly easy

For the pastry:
4¼ cups all-purpose flour
1 egg yolk
pinch cinnamon
¼ cup sugar
¼ cup lard or shortening
1½ tbsp coffee
1½ tsp cocoa powder
juice of ½ lemon
oil for frying
For the filling:
2 cups ricotta, sieved
⅔ cup sugar
5 oz (5 squares) bitter or
    semisweet chocolate
⅓ cup mixed candied fruit or
    peel
peel of 1 lemon, grated

Combine all the ingredients to make the pastry, kneading it well; shape into an oval log and leave to rest in a cool place (or wrap and chill in the refrigerator) for a few hours. Roll small pieces of the pastry out into oval shapes; these must then be wrapped round heatproof metal *cannoli* tubes and fried in the very hot oil until golden brown and crisp. Leave to drain on kitchen paper. Beat the ricotta with the sugar, stir in the finely-chopped chocolate, the finely-chopped candied fruit, and the grated lemon peel.
Slide the cannoli shapes off the tubes when cold and fill with the ricotta mixture just before serving: the contrast between the rich yet fresh tasting filling and the crisp pastry is irresistible.

• • •

CHOCOLATE BRAIDS

This same dough can be rolled into a sheet and cut into all sorts of shapes: hearts, stars, diamonds etc.

Time: 40 minutes
Very easy

1 cup (2¼ sticks) butter
⅔ cup sugar
7 oz (7 squares) bitter or
    semisweet chocolate
pinch salt
1 egg
4¼ cups all-purpose flour

Beat all but 1 tbsp of the butter (softened at room temperature) with the sugar to a pale, fluffy cream. Break the chocolate into small pieces and melt over hot water; stir into the butter and sugar mixture, adding the salt at the same time. Stir in the lightly beaten egg and the sifted flour a little at a time; mix thoroughly.
Roll into thin cylinders about 4 in long and braid these together in threes (like plaits), pinching the ends together. Place on a greased cookie sheet and bake at 350°F for 20 minutes.

• • •

PECAN COOKIES

Time: 45 minutes
Very easy

6 eggs, separated
½ cup sugar
½ cup all-purpose flour
pinch salt
1¾ cups chopped pecans
1 tbsp butter
½ cup peeled almonds

Beat the egg yolks with the sugar until almost white; stir in the sifted flour and salt. Beat the egg whites stiffly and fold into the batter. Chop the walnut pieces very finely and fold in also. Place rounded tablespoonfuls of this onto a greased cookie sheet.
Bake at 350°F for 20 minutes; place a peeled almond on top of each cookie, press down very lightly, and return to the oven for the last few minutes' cooking.

• • •

CRUNCHY CHOCOLATE COOKIES

This mixture is hard and crunchy when cooked and cooled and must therefore be cut into squares while still warm. Use a sharp knife dipped in cold water.

Time: 45 minutes
Very easy

½ cup (1 stick) butter
5 oz (5 squares) bitter
    chocolate
2 eggs
1 cup sugar
½ cup shelled unroasted
    peanuts
1 cup all-purpose flour
pinch salt

Melt all but 1 tbsp of the butter over hot water with the chocolate, broken into small pieces. Leave to cool a little before beating in the eggs one at a time; stir in the sugar. Chop the peanuts finely and add to the chocolate mixture. Sift the flour with the salt and stir in a little at a time.

Grease a cookie sheet with the reserved butter; spread the mixture out in it to a thickness of ¼ in and bake in a moderate oven (350°F) for 30 minutes.
Leave to stand for a few minutes; cut into rectangles while still warm.

• • •

PRUNE CUPS

To save time, buy no-soak prunes or use fresh fruit, such as large strawberries, for the filling.

Time: 45 minutes
Very easy

approx. ¾ lb sweet egg pastry
    (see page 56)
2 tbsp butter
20 large prunes
⅓ cup sugar
2 cloves (optional)
1 cup marmalade

Roll out the pastry into a fairly thin sheet and use to line 20 small round tart pans (just large enough to accommodate the prunes) greased lightly with the butter. Prick the bottom of the pastry shells with a fork and fill with the beans. Bake at 350°F for 20 minutes or until done; leave to cool.
Cook the prunes in a little water with the sugar and cloves if used. When very tender, drain well, and leave to cool.
Carefully take the pie shells out of the molds and place on a serving dish; place a prune in each.

• • •

338

SICILIAN CANNOLI
■ These Sicilian cream-horn pastries must only be filled with the ricotta mixture at the very last minute or the pastry will soften; the contrast between the soft, delicate cheese and the crisp "shell" is irresistible. They should be deep-fried wrapped around special aluminum cannoli cornets (see recipe).

FIG BOATS

When well soaked, then cooked with cream and sugar, the figs make a delicate, flavorsome filling which can also be used for a larger tart.

Time: 1 hour
Very easy

2 cups dried figs
1¾ cups all-purpose flour
2 egg yolks
1 cup sugar
½ cup (1 stick) butter
1 tsp grated lemon peel
½ cup whipping cream

Soak the figs in warm water for several hours until softened. Sift the flour into a mixing bowl, make a well in the center, and place the yolks in it with half the sugar, all but 1 tbsp of the softened butter (cut into small pieces), and the lemon peel. Combine these ingredients, shape the pastry into a ball, cover, and leave to rest in a cool place for about 30 minutes.
Use the reserved butter to grease little barquette molds, roll out the pastry fairly thinly, and line them, pricking the pastry with a fork. Fill with dried beans and bake at 350°F until the pastry is pale golden brown.
Empty out the beans and leave the pie shells to cool before carefully removing them from their molds. Place on a serving dish.
Drain the figs; cook gently in a saucepan with the remaining sugar and the cream for 10 minutes after the cream has come to a boil.
Sieve the figs and cream and when cold fill the barquettes with this purée.

BLACK CURRANT BOATS

Strawberries, bananas, blackberries or raspberries can also be used to fill these pie shells.

Time: 1 hour
Easy

2¾ cups all-purpose flour
½ cup sugar
¾ cup (1½ sticks) butter
2 egg yolks
pinch salt
2 cups black currants
½ cup sieved raspberry jam or red currant jelly

Mix the flour and sugar with the melted butter, egg yolks, and salt. Roll out in a sheet ¾ in thick.
Line greased barquette molds with this pastry; place a small piece of waxed paper in each, weighted down with dried beans or rice, and bake "blind" at 350°F. Do not allow the pastry to color.
Remove the beans and paper; take the little pie shells out of their molds and fill with black currants; glaze with the sieved jam or the jelly.

• • •

COCONUT RICOTTA BALLS

A slightly lighter alternative to chocolates which can be served at the end of a dinner party.

Time: 20 minutes
Very easy

½ cup (1 stick) butter
1½ cups ricotta, sieved
1¾ cups drinking chocolate powder
2 cups finely-grated fresh coconut or 2 cups shredded coconut
½ cup sugar

Beat the butter, softened at room temperature, until pale and very light. Beat in the ricotta and then the chocolate, adding a little at a time.
Add half the coconut and stir well, followed by the sugar. Shape into cherry-sized balls. Roll the balls in the remaining coconut to coat well and chill until served.

• • •

340

MINIATURE MONT BLANCS

Sweet chestnuts are in season in the fall and early winter; at other times you can use canned sweetened chestnut purée, imported from France.

Time: 1 hour
Very easy

about ¾ lb Classic Sponge
   Cake (see page 146)
1 lb sweet chestnuts or ¾ lb
   sweetened chestnut purée
2¼ cups milk
1 tsp vanilla extract
½ cup sugar
½ cup whipping cream

Cut the sponge cake horizontally into thin layers and use a small cookie cutter (the size of the inside base of the paper cases) to cut out little disks of sponge cake. Place one of these in each case.
Remove the chestnuts' outer tough brown skin; bring to a boil in plenty of water and cook for 15 minutes. Drain and remove their thin inner skin (do not worry if they break up). Cook them gently with the milk and vanilla, crushing them with a fork, until quite a thick purée is formed. Stir in the sugar. Push through a fine sieve.
Pipe a little of this purée onto each disk of sponge cake. Beat the cream stiffly and pipe a rosette on top of the chestnut mixture. Chill before serving. If canned sweetened purée is used, simply pipe this straight onto the sponge cake and omit the milk, vanilla, and sugar.

• • •

MARRON GLACÉ PUFF PASTRY TARTLETS

These elegant and tempting morsels are very small, ideal to serve at a formal reception or as part of an after-dinner petit four selection.

Time: 2 hours
Easy

approx. ¾ lb puff pastry (see
   page 86)
1 tbsp butter
20 marrons glacés (candied
   sweet chestnuts)
1 cup whipping cream
1 cup confectioners' sugar
1½ tbsp drinking chocolate
   powder

Make the puff pastry as directed and roll out on a lightly floured pastryboard. Cut out into oval or round shapes to line lightly greased, very small barquette molds or tiny round tartlet pans (just large enough to hold one whole marron glacé each). Place a few beans in each uncooked shell. Bake at 350°F for 15 minutes or until done. Remove the beans. Take the pie shells out of the molds when cold; place a marron glacé each. Beat the cream stiffly with the sugar and use a pastry bag with fluted tube to pipe the cream decoratively around the chestnuts.
Dust with the chocolate, using a small sieve. Arrange on a serving dish and serve.

• • •

DESSERT WINES

· · ·

The vexed question of whether to have wine with a dessert and if so, which one, remains a very personal choice only to be answered, perhaps, by extensive (and extremely agreeable) experimentation.

When the most suitable wine is chosen it will complement the pudding, pastry, gateau or other sweet food, enhancing the flavor. At worst, it will either drown the taste or make for a sickly combination which will detract from the enjoyment of something on which the cook has spent a good deal of time and trouble. It is often quite difficult to choose the right wine for some desserts: a fruit sorbet is acid and will need a wine which can "correct" this acidity on the palate or attenuate it. Gourmets and sommeliers the world over have debated endlessly on the subject without, fortunately, ever coming to an unequivocal decision. The most sensible (and prosaic) general guideline is to select fuller, "bigger" wines for highly flavored sweet preparations, reserving the lighter wines for the simpler ones. Or there is always pure, cold water which will refresh your mouth if the sweetness becomes a little cloying; then a glass of superb dessert wine can be savored all on its own, as a glorious ending to the meal.

One can follow general practice and serve sparkling or *pétillant* white wines with tarts, flans, and other pastries; light, soft red or rosé wines with fruit-based desserts, while aged white wines made with semidried grapes, and fine fortified wines are traditional with various types of cookies and very light desserts (such as mousses, some soufflés etc.).

Champagne

One of the most famous wines in the world and probably France's most widely known export. Many other countries produce very good champagne type wines, the USA (California), Italy, and Australia among them, following the correct Champenoise method of production but, although often excellent, they have so far not managed to achieve the consistently outstanding quality of the original, the only wine with a right to call itself champagne. Synonymous with celebration and luxury the world over, this wine can be made with white or black grapes. Vintage champagne, made with the wine from one outstanding year, is the best and most expensive and the *cuvée spéciale* even more so, made from specially selected grapes. All champagne is blended. The variations in "dryness" are indicated by the descriptions of brut (the driest); sec; demi-sec, and doux (the sweetest). Champagne should be served chilled but not iced, and is often served too cold. The driest (brut) champagne goes well with a very wide variety of food, and is particularly suited to the prevailing fashion for lighter, fresh-tasting food. Champagne is recommended for drinking with tarts, pastries, soufflés, and cream-based desserts. It is perfect with most ice creams.

Vin Santo

A superb white dessert wine from Tuscany, limited quantities of which are exported. The aromatic white wine is made with semidried grapes (Trebbiano and Malvasia grapes), picked when very ripe which are then spread out on straw mats or hung from the rafters in airy lofts to dry. Types of *vin santo* range from the very sweet to dry and in their native region they are drunk with little crisp almond biscuits which are dipped into the wine.

The name *vin santo* (holy wine) may have originated in one of three ways: this wine was used as communion wine during an outbreak of plague in 1384 and is said to have cured several sufferers; another relates that Cosimo de' Medici gave some to Cardinal Bessarione, Archbishop of Nicea who in return presented him with wine from Xantos or it may have originated from the fact that the wine was often bottled just before Christmas.

DESSERT WINES

• • •

Madeira

Although no longer as fashionable as it used to be, a good-quality madeira is deliciously mellow, rather like the climate of the island whence it takes its name. The best madeira, Malmsey, is aged in the wood for at least twenty years before being bottled and sold: made from Malvasia grapes and with a slightly smokey aroma, this is the sweetest of the madeiras and goes very well with rich desserts. The wine is amber-colored, warm-toned, and you may have to order it specially from your wine merchant as production is limited, especially of the well-aged wines. Other, less outstanding madeira wines are the dry Sercial, Verdhelo, clean tasting and paler in color, while the very sweet, full-bodied, dark-toned Bual is best drunk with cookies.

Sherry

Takes its name from the city of Xerez de la Frontera, center of the sherry industry in Spain. Only the ripest grapes are gathered for its manufacture and spread out to dry on special beaten earth platforms under the hot Spanish sun, with special protective coverings drawn over them at night to protect them from the dew. Sherry undergoes prolonged ageing in wood and is the classic, original example of the *solera* method of making fortified wines. Dry sherry (Fino) makes a very good apéritif, marvelously stimulating to the appetite, and it should be served chilled. The long-standing English love affair with medium-dry or Amontillado sherry has helped to popularize this all over the world. Cream sherries are quite sweet and although they can be pale in color themselves, fall under the larger description of *Oloroso*, dark, heavier sherries which have a slightly nutty flavor; these last two are ideal as dessert wines, adding a warming note to puddings made with stewed dried or fresh fruit and enhancing other desserts with their well-defined flavor.

Muscat (Moscato)

Just as champagne is France's most famous sparkling wine, so Moscato, especially when used for Piedmont's sparkling sweet *Moscato d'Asti spumante*, is Italy's proud boast. This dessert wine (usually, but not always sweet) has plenty of bouquet, and a natural sweetness coming from the high natural fruit sugar (fructose) content of the Muscat grapes. Asti spumante sparkling white wine goes well with all sorts of desserts and puddings. Still Muscat wines are produced in other regions of Italy but made in a totally different way, the grapes being spread out on wickerwork shelves for partial drying. Usually this wine is golden with an amber tinge, with a very pronounced bouquet, ideal for drinking with cassata, cannoli or desserts made with cooked fruit. The superb French *Muscat de Beaumes de Venise* can be drunk with the same foods.

Marsala

In 1773 an Englishman who had realized that conditions in northwestern Sicily favored production of the raw materials for a fortified wine, started making Marsala. Being a full-bodied, aromatic wine as befits a grape which ripens under the hot Sicilian sun, it can hold its own with very rich desserts, even with chocolate, and is indispensable when making Zabaglione. Marsala Vergine is the finest and will have been aged in the wood for at least five years. The winemaking method involves very concentrated cooked must being added in precise quantities to the fermented must, giving the wine a warm color and a smooth taste, with a very aromatic and decided bouquet. The wine was already popular in England by the time of the Napoleonic wars and when Lord Nelson ordered a very large quantity in 1798 while the British Fleet was anchored off Sicily, thus setting his seal of approval on the wine, it began to rival madeira. Outside Italy and Britain it has hitherto been less well known as a dessert wine and the inferior-quality Marsala has been used to create sauces for escalopes of veal and other meat. Dry Marsala makes a good apéritif, served cool (50° F), while sweet Marsala should be served at room temperature (65° F).

Port

Port is a fortified wine, having a minimum alcoholic strength of 18° and usually 20°; brandy is added to the partially fermented red wine or must to halt the fermentation process. It is then aged in oak casks for about 2–4 years (depending on the quality of that particular year) before being bottled. An exceptionally good year's vintage port may be aged in the bottle for as long as 50 years and Portugal is justly famous for this product. Historically, Britain has been the biggest importer of vintage port and fine old ports are highly prized as the essential conclusion to a good dinner. There are many types: ruby, the least expensive and blended; tawny, a fine quality blend, and others, the best being vintage.

Sauternes

A fine white dessert wine, at its best perhaps the greatest of all dessert wines. Produced in the Bordeaux region of France, this wine is straw-colored with a full bouquet and well-balanced taste. Sometimes described as the wine of kings and the king of wines, Sauternes should be reserved for the most delicate, elegant desserts such as soufflés; small, delicate pastries, featherlight tarts or flans. Sauternes is made with very ripe grapes, left on the vine until the so called *pourriture noble* ("noble rot") shrivels them; they give this wine its unmistakable subtlety and aroma. The harvest lasts two whole months, the grapes being harvested one by one, not in bunches, selected by experienced grape pickers who know exactly when they are ready.

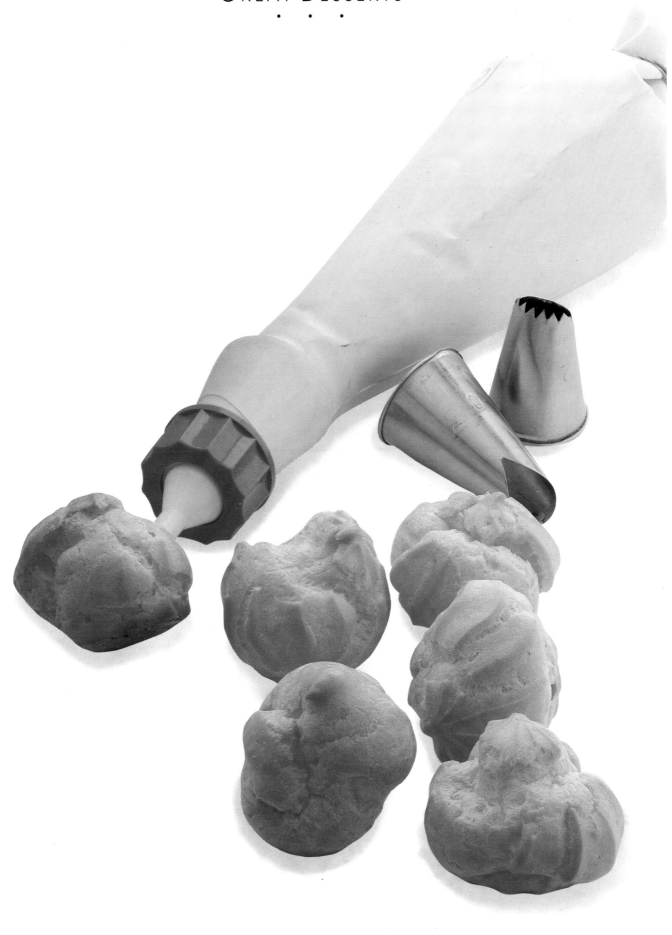

GLOSSARY

. . .

Almonds

These can be sweet or bitter, depending upon the variety of tree (Prunus amygdalus) from whence they come. The fruit resembles the apricot although the flesh of the almond is green, tough and inedible. Probably native to the eastern Mediterranean, they are the most useful nuts of all for the purposes of patisserie and have been used in cooking since ancient times. The almond is the earliest flowering orchard tree, the blossom often appearing as early as January, which makes it vulnerable to frost. The greater part of the world's production of sweet almonds now comes from Spain, Italy, and California but they are widely grown elsewhere. Bitter almonds are grown mainly in southern France, North Africa, Sicily, and Sardinia. When ground or mixed with water they produce a poison, hydrocyanic (prussic) acid and must on no account ever be eaten raw (this also applies to peach kernels). Roasting these bitter nuts until golden brown destroys the poison. Peach leaves are sometimes used to mimic their flavor but here again, after soaking these in the liquid to be flavored, this liquid must be boiled to be safe. For these reasons, commercial sale of bitter almonds is banned in the United States. We recommend using only sweet almonds even if you are able to find the bitter ones, for safety reasons. When roasting almonds, blanch and peel then spread out on cookie sheets and cook in a moderate oven until pale golden brown. Take care not to overroast them, as they burn very easily. Caramelize almonds by mixing with melted and caramelized sugar (in the proportion of ½ cup peeled almonds to 1 cup + 2 tbsp sugar. When finely ground they can be substituted for flour and used in a particularly delicate and delicious pastry often used for fruit tartlets. Also used for marzipan.

Bain Marie

Method used for cooking foods which run the risk of spoiling if cooked over direct, or too fierce, heat. A double boiler can be used, or a heatproof bowl placed over a saucepan of barely simmering water (the container holding the liquid to be cooked should not touch the hot water). Can also be used when cooking in the oven. Do not fill the roasting pan too full of hot water: it should not come more than halfway up the side of the dish containing the food which is being cooked. Invaluable not only when cooking but also for melting, liquefying, or heating.

Beaters or whisks

You may choose to use a balloon whisk or a hand-turned rotary beater, hand-held electric beater or the beating attachment and bowl of your food processor. Electric beaters take a great deal of the hard work out of whisking and are very effective, although most professional cooks maintain that egg whites are best beaten in copper semispherical bowls using a balloon whisk (no food must be left to stand in a copper bowl for longer than say, 30 minutes as they could become toxic; the bowls must be kept scrupulously clean and free of verdigris) since a harmless reaction takes place with the copper over a brief period which makes it easier and quicker to beat the eggs and incorporate a great deal of air. Remember that cream beats most successfully when the cream itself, the bowl, and the whisk are well chilled in the refrigerator for at least 30 minutes beforehand.

Always wash your beater attachments and whisks very carefully: food can easily become trapped between the moving parts or pieces of wire.

Boiling

When boiling sugar syrups they must be watched all the time as the temperature will rise very quickly after a certain point. If syrups and sauces (especially fruit sauces) need reducing they can be simmered very gently, boiling only just enough for some of the water content to be given off in the form of steam; they will gradually thicken.

Butter

A mixture of fats, lactose, with a small quantity of protein and mineral salts which forms when rich milk is churned. Butter plays a vital role in patisserie and cannot be successfully replaced by other shortenings: flavor, texture, and appearance may suffer. Always buy the best, freshest butter you can as it is usually a mistake to try to economize on cost or quantity (substituting another shortening for part of the butter weight) simply because it is to be used for cooking. For most of the recipes in this book sweet butter is preferable.

Leave butter which you are going to beat at room temperature for an hour or more before you start. It will then be easier to work and become pale soft and light far more quickly.

Cake markers, stencils

Marking rings are very useful when decorating cakes to help you divide the surface evenly and achieve a symmetrical design; these are often included as part of domestic frosting sets and vary in sophistication. Stencils are used for cakes which only need a liberal dusting of sifted confectioners' sugar over the surface to complete their decoration. You can use plastic or paper stencils, buying them or designing and cutting out your own versions of the paper ones.

Cake pans

These are so many and varied that it would be impossible to describe them here. Buy the best you can afford. When choosing which pan to use, remember that the batter should fill the pan by no more than two thirds. Rich, dense cake and bread batters and doughs are best baked in pans made of strong heavy-gauge steel. Light cakes, sponge cakes, and pastry need quicker cooking and do better in lighter, thinner pans so that the heat can penetrate faster. Nonstick pans are very practical but in time the lining will wear off, so you may prefer to use traditional pans. Springform or spring-clip pans are very useful when baking fragile cakes or pastries as the side opens to release the contents with little or no disturbance.

Caramelize

When sugar is heated either on its own or in solution with water it will eventually color and turn into varying degrees of caramel. Dark caramel, called black jack or *brulé* with its slightly bitter, burnt odor, is used to color sauces, syrups, and liqueurs, fortified wines etc. To coat the inside of a mold with caramel, heat the mold in the oven; heat ½ cup sugar with 1 tbsp water in a saucepan over low heat; when the syrup turns golden brown remove from the heat immediately, pour into the hot mold, and tilt the mold carefully in all directions so that the caramel coats the inside.

Many cooks caramelize the sugar in the mold to be coated: this needs care, good protection for the hands, and is only really feasible when cooking with gas as a heat source.

Chocolate

A mixture of sugar, cocoa, cocoa butter, and powdered milk. The basic substance is the cocoa bean, fruit of a tree native to the Amazon but now cultivated throughout tropical zones of the Americas, the Philippines, the Islands of Sri Lanka and Java, and West Africa. These beans are scooped out of the pods with the adhering pulp, fermented, dried, and roasted, then ground. This last process turns them into a paste; they are then processed into a powder which, after the addition of several ingredients, results in such products as bitter chocolate, *couverture*, bakers' chocolate, unsweetened, milk chocolate, and all the variations which are marketed for the confectionery trade. For successful chocolate frosting it is best to use proper good-quality bakers' chocolate or *couverture* as these have a very high cocoa butter (fat) content; failing this use the best eating chocolate available. Again, it is a false economy to buy cheaper so-called "cooking chocolate"; these cakes of chocolate are often difficult to work with and will lead to a deterioration in the taste and texture of the finished cake, candy, ice cream, or dessert. Break the chocolate into pieces and melt very slowly over hot water (in a bowl or bain marie) stirring with a wooden spoon. Care must be taken if using *couverture* chocolate not to let any moisture come in contact with it either during or after melting (while you are still working with it) as it will then become impossible to handle.

Cinnamon

The aromatic, golden-brown dried bark of the *cynamomum zeylanicum* tree which belongs to the laurel family. Although it is available in little curled sticks, it is more widely sold ground. Buy the freshest you can and do not keep for too long. Used in very small quantities, it confers a warm spicy touch on puddings, pastries, syrups, and liqueurs.

Cloves

The sun-dried unopened flower buds of *Eugenia Cariofillata*, a tree which is native to the Moluccas. Cloves have medicinal properties and also act as a preservative of meat and meat products. When used in pastry cooking and desserts care has to be taken that their heady flavor and aroma does not overwhelm the other ingredients as they are not to everyone's taste.

Coffee

Just as there are "chocaholics" so there are coffee addicts: the taste of good coffee is wonderful on its own or as a flavoring for delicious frostings, fillings, custards, and mousses, ice creams etc. Use very strong, good-quality instant coffee for your flavoring. If using freshly ground coffee, Costa Rican and Colombian coffee have the fullest taste and aroma. Or use a fine coffee extract.

Coloring

This can play an important part in enhancing the appeal of all types of sweet things. Use in very small quantities, sticking to natural, vegetable colorings and avoiding synthetic products. If you cannot buy yellow coloring, dissolve some saffron in a little hot water; use dark caramelized sugar for brown (or coffee or chocolate if the flavor is right); cochineal is nearly always available and so is sap green but if the latter is not, you could make your own coloring by preparing a strong infusion of fresh mint.

Coriander

Herb belonging to the *Umbelliferae* family, native to southern Europe and the Middle East, now widely grown in Mediterranean type climates all over the world. The seeds are used whole or ground to give a warm, intense (but not overpowering) flavor and aroma to savory dishes, marinades, and to cakes, cookies and other pastries as well as to certain liqueurs (such as Chartreuse). The green parsley-like leaves of this herb are also used in savory dishes.

Cream

The fatty part of milk, being less dense, collects on the surface of the milk if left to stand. The thick, pale yellow cream which can be bought in specialist dairy shops and from some farm creameries is usually produced by this simple method of standing the milk and then skimming off the cream, but your supermarket cream will most probably have been produced by separator (the milk is spun and the cream concentrated by centrifugal force). Always use the freshest cream you can buy. For some of the ice cream recipes in this book, half-and-half can be substituted for the milk and heavy or whipping cream but the ice cream may not be so light. Chill cream thoroughly, together with the utensils you are going to use, before beating it, as it will then thicken far more quickly.

Eggs

Always use the freshest eggs possible; store them in the refrigerator away from highly-scented foods, raw meats etc. (Eggshells are porous and smells and microorganisms can penetrate them. Always wash off any dirt, etc. from the eggs for this reason before storing them.) Eggs cannot be frozen in the shell: crack them, either separating the yolks and whites and freezing separately or beat the whole eggs lightly before freezing. Mix, preferably, with either salt or sugar depending on their intended use when thawed, allowing approx. 1 tsp salt or sugar per dozen eggs; freeze as usual in freezerproof containers. You can tell whether eggs are fresh or stale by placing the egg in a bowl full of cold water (slightly salted or fresh); eggs which lie flat on the bottom of the bowl are absolutely fresh; if the egg floats partially, standing vertically in the water, the rounded end peeping out of the surface of the water, it is stale. There is an in-between stage when the egg tips up in the water, the angle veering increasingly toward the vertical the older the egg becomes.

When egg yolks are beaten for cake making and patisserie purposes (e.g. for confectioners' custard, pastry cream etc.) they should usually be beaten until very pale and frothy, especially when beaten with sugar; they will increase considerably in bulk, reaching the "ribbon stage" when the mixture falls back into the bowl from a lifted whisk in an unbroken, flattish ribbon, folding on itself as it touches the mixture left in the bowl. The addition of cream of tartar or lemon juice is very small quantities to egg whites when they are being beaten helps to stabilize the protein and leads to quickly beaten and very firm, snowy egg whites.

Flame

Alcohol is warmed (never boiled, as this would destroy the alcohol content and prevent it from igniting) then set alight. This technique is particularly effective with Christmas puddings, fruit, charlottes, and pancakes. Use good-quality liquor for this purpose. Much used by some restaurants when dishes are finished in front of the customers to provide them with an impressive spectacle.

Flour

Can be made from many different types of cereals and vegetables. Wheat flour is most frequently used in patisserie but flours made from rice, potato, barley, corn, and rye also play an important part. The wheat grain is composed of three parts: the embryo (or germ), the endosperm, and the husk or bran. The germ is rich in nitrogenous material and fatty substances. The purified endosperm pieces (semolina), when the wheat has undergone the initial milling processes, have a high starch content; they also contain calcium, phosphorous, and other mineral salts and vitamins. Further processing produces white flour of varying fineness, the flour being removed from the sifters at various stages throughout the milling. Bread flour (unbleached all-purpose flour) has a high protein content, strong gluten, and has a high moisture-holding capacity, whereas cake and cookie flours (soft flours) have a lower protein content and weak glutens.
Cornstarch and potato flour, particularly high in starch, lend softness and lightness to cakes but are usually mixed with wheat flour.

Grease

Greasing ensures that your cakes and pastries do not stick to the pans in which they are cooked; unless otherwise indicated, butter is used for this purpose. You can use butter wrappers to spread the softened butter but it is better to melt the butter gently over hot water and use a pastry brush; this will ensure that the butter penetrates every nook and cranny of the pans (particularly when using springform cake pans). It is often a good idea to dust the greased pans with flour also; this is indicated in the recipes where advisable.

Honey

The oldest sweetening agent known to man. Honey made by bees which collect their nectar from certain flowers granulates or crystallizes less quickly than honeys made from other flower nectar: acacia and heather honeys do not granulate easily. Granulation will be encouraged if honey is stirred. If your honey has started to crystallize, keep at a temperature of approx. 150°F for about 30 minutes (over hot water in a double boiler, for instance). Much used in making nougat, toffees, and candy. Except where otherwise stated clear, runny (sieved or strained) honey is called for in these recipes.

Ice-cream makers

There are two types of ice-cream maker: one (also called a sorbetière) consists of a wooden pail with a container in the center and a handle which turns the paddles inside the container. Ice and coarse salt (which lowers the temperature of the ice) is packed around the container to freeze the ice cream or sherbet as it is stirred. The only drawbacks to this type of ice-cream maker are 1) care must be taken that none of the salt and ice mixture is inadvertently allowed to get into the ice cream container and 2) as the ice cream grows firmer and then harder you will need a certain amount of muscle power to turn the handle working the paddle. The second type of ice-cream maker is, of course, electrically powered. There are various makes and sizes sold and there is often little to choose between them as regards efficient freezing and stirring of the ice cream. These machines mean that you can decide to serve ice cream an hour or less before the meal and make it there and then, serving it straight from the ice-cream maker. You will have to decide whether you need a large capacity ice-cream maker or whether a smaller model will answer your purpose. Check that the machine you are thinking of buying has an ice-cream container which is easy to remove and wash, as scrupulous cleanliness is vital when making ice cream. If you do not have an ice-cream maker, you can still make delicious ice creams and sherbets; simply pour your ice cream or sherbet mixture into freezing trays or a bowl and place in the icebox of your refrigerator or in the freezer. Check the mixture frequently as it starts to freeze and stir very thoroughly with a fork or whisk as soon as it starts to thicken. Repeat this several times during the freezing process, until it is too hard to stir. In this way you will avoid the formation of large ice crystals which can spoil the smooth, creamy texture of ice creams.

Knead

One of the most ancient culinary processes known to man, presumably practiced since bread was first made. Kneading not only mixes the ingredients thoroughly but also develops the elasticity of the gluten in the flour, to give a well-textured loaf. If done energetically, it is not usually necessary to knead dough for more than 10 minutes and often less; with practice you will come to recognize the point at which it has reached the ideal consistency.

Margarine

This is widely used instead of all or part of the butter content in commercial bakeries (a special type of margarine which behaves well when used in pastry etc.) but it is usually a mistake to use it for home baking as flavor and texture will probably suffer.

Milk

Cows' milk is always used in ice cream making and patisserie. A very complete food in liquid form, containing emulsified fats, proteins, lactose, minerals (mainly calcium), and vitamins and, of course, a large amount of water. Rich milk (or half-and-half, see Cream entry) is used for ice-cream making and this is also best for the other recipes in this book, but semiskimmed milk can also be used in some cases. Long-life milk, powdered milk, and canned milk are not recommended for these recipes. Make sure the milk you use is very fresh and unscented, this is particularly important for such foods as ice cream (store in the refrigerator away from highly scented foods or it will become tainted).

Oven

Perhaps the most important advice to any cook who enjoys home baking is "get to know your own oven." Ovens seem to have their little idiosyncrasies and with practice these can be allowed for. The hottest part of a conventional gas, electric, or solid-fuel oven will be at the top of the oven, the coolest at the bottom. Always allow plenty of room for air circulation or your baked goods will not cook evenly; very large cookie sheets or roasting pans (used when cooking by the bain marie method) should not be too tight a fit or they may impede the circulation of air. Fan-assisted ovens have an even cooking temperature throughout the oven and cooking times are usually a little shorter than in conventional ovens; temperature settings also need to be a little lower (the instruction manual provided with your fan-assisted oven will give equivalent temperatures to guide you). One of the added advantages of this type of oven is that two cakes or two batches of baked goods can be cooked on separate shelves, one above the other. In a conventional oven this usually leads to one item or batch cooking more quickly than the other. If you suspect that your oven is overheating or underheating and that the thermostat control is faulty, you can always check the temperature for yourself by means of an oven thermometer; these are not very expensive and you will then know whether your oven needs attention from a qualified electrician or mechanic from the manufacturers' maintenance service network. If you have a conventional oven, preheat the oven at the correct setting before baking. Fan-assisted ovens need less time to heat to the correct temperature. Remember to level the surface of your cakes gently before placing in the oven, as not all cake batters level out during the baking process. A well-lit oven with a glass door is a decided advantage when baking: there will be less temptation to open the oven door to see how things are getting on.

Papers

Some of the most useful types of paper for use in patisserie are: parchment, waxed paper and non-stick, silicone-coated paper. You will also find brown paper and wafer paper useful. Waxed paper, as the name suggests, has film of wax on one or both sides and is useful when you wish to cover surfaces closely without the paper sticking. Brown paper makes a good insulator for wrapping round cake pans if you do not want the contents to cook too fast. Paper bags can be used for coating seedless white raisins and other dried fruits lightly with flour (put a little flour in the bag, add the drained and dried raisins, and shake. Holding the bag firmly closed).

Pastry brush

The humble pastry brush can be made with hog's bristles, goose feathers, or nylon filaments. A bristle brush is the best all-purpose type but a goose-feather brush is extremely useful for delicate tasks, such as glazing a cooked fruit flan or delicate pastries and cakes. Wash gently but thoroughly by hand with mild, soapy detergent and see that the bristles do not become distorted.

Pine Nuts

These have been used in cooking since ancient Roman times and have an excellent taste; they are soft in texture and develop more flavor when lightly roasted (they burn extremely easily). Gathered from the Mediterranean Stone pine, these kernels are nowadays extracted from the nuts by machinery; the cones are gathered through the winter, stored until the summer when they are spread out in the hot sun to open, and then shaken to release the nuts.

Pastry bags

These are invaluable, making many tasks quicker, neater and easier. Buy a selection of tubes, plain and fluted, so you have a suitable one for each purpose. The bags are made of canvas (old-fashioned and difficult to wash quickly) nylon or plastic and the tubes are usually metal or plastic. If you already have a cake-decorating syringe, this may do duty instead of a pastry bag. You can make your own bag with heavy-duty parchment.

Reduce

When a recipe calls for a liquid to be thickened without the addition of any thickening agent, or when the flavor of a mixture has to be concentrated, the liquid is boiled in an uncovered pan until its volume has considerably reduced, giving off water in the form of steam. Obviously the wider your pan, the quicker this process will be.

Refrigerator

Never put hot or warm foods in the refrigerator; cool foods as quickly as possible and then refrigerate. When storing such foods as cream, milk, butter, and eggs remember that these should be stored away from highly scented foods to avoid tainting and away from raw meat and poultry etc. to avoid any danger of cross-contamination. Eggs are permeable to odors and will pick up the scent of onions, spices, and other pronounced flavors and aromas if they are stored in close proximity. Likewise milk and cream can pick up other smells very quickly. Make sure your refrigerator is on the correct setting, adjust the thermostat when the weather changes if the temperature of your kitchen is affected. If your refrigerator is not a self-defrosting model, defrost it very regularly or it will not chill food efficiently. Try to avoid opening and shutting the door of the refrigerator too often if you have highly perishable food stored in it. Remember that although cold air falls (and for this very reason) the icebox is always at the top of the refrigerator, so the top of the refrigerator (so long as you place food just below the icebox) is in practice cooler than the bottom.

Rolling pin

Every pastrycook has his or her favorite type of rolling pin: this may be made of wood (often of beech-wood) with or without handles (most professionals prefer pins without handles). "Cool" rolling pins are often used for pastry making; made of china, marble or glass; some (including plastic pins) are hollow and meant to be filled with ice or cold water. These "cool" pins have no real advantage over the good wooden pins.

Scales

In pastrycooking, cake making and confectionery, ingredients should be weighed as accurately as possible for a successful outcome. The weight of a cupful of flour can vary greatly depending on prevailing humidity and other factors. A cup of all-purpose flour is calculated to weigh 4 oz for the purposes of these recipes; cake flour is slightly lighter and 1 cup + 2 tablespoons normally weighs 4 oz. Use the displacement method for measuring cups and half-cupfuls of butter or calculate how much of a stick of butter will give you the correct weight, if you do not have any good kitchen scales.

Sieve

When sieving fruit, especially acid fruit, always use a nonmetallic sieve as the fruit will react with metal. A hair sieve or plastic sieve is suitable. You will need sieves of varying fineness, and sizes; experience will show you which are the most useful and suitable. Always wash and dry sieves extremely thoroughly after each use.

Slake

To mix a substance with a liquid, often to avoid lumps forming when a thickening agent (such as flour, potato flour, cornstarch, arrowroot etc.) is added to a larger quantity of hot or cold liquid. Usually cold water or milk is used to slake the thickening agent but it can be done with fruit juice, wine etc. when suitable. This cold mixture is then stirred into the bowl or pan containing the mixture to be thickened.

Spatula

Indispensable for patisserie. The most useful spatulas are made of flexible rubber attached to a plastic handle; perfect for folding beaten egg whites, cream etc. into other ingredients without crushing out the air you have taken so much trouble to beat in. Also useful for scraping batters cleanly out of bowls. Never wash in a dishwasher, always by hand with soapy washing up liquid. Wooden spatulas are also useful for these and other purposes. Long metal spatulas are used for leveling and smoothing batters (dip in cold water first if necessary) and frostings (when they are often dipped in hot water).

Liquor and liqueurs

Liquor, wines, and liqueurs or cordials used in patisserie are usually sweet. Among the most widely used liqueurs or cordials are kirsch, maraschino, Grand Marnier, Curaçao, alkermes, and Amaretto but many others play their part. When a recipe calls for rum, dark Jamaica rum is usually the most suitable. Choose a good brandy; use good-quality dessert wines for your cakes and desserts and they will greatly enhance the taste.

Sugar

Without sugar (or sucrose) patisserie would hardly exist. Before the introduction of sugar made from

sugar beet, sugar cane was the only source of sugar and before that honey was man's only sweetening agent. Cane sugar has a definite, pleasing taste to it, but less sweetening power; sugar from sugar beet is just sweetness and no taste. Cane sugar originated in tropical Asia; it is said to have been known in ancient times to the Polynesians and was certainly known to the Indians as our name for it, "sugar" is derived from a very old Sanskrit word. The ancient Persians (as early as 510 B.C.) and the ancient Greeks knew of sugar but in appearance it was nothing like the sugar we know today. In the Middle Ages sugar was only for the rich; toward the end of the fifteenth century cane sugar plantations were planted in the Canary Islands and in the following century in Brazil. It was only toward the very end of the eighteenth century that sugar became widely available and much less expensive.

In 1747 a German chemist discovered that sugar could be extracted from what we now call the sugar beet. From 1811 onward his discovery was exploited by the French, desperate to find an alternative source of sugar since their imports of cane sugar had been stopped by the Royal Navy as part of Britain's blockade of Napoleonic France.

Much has been said in recent years about the desirability of having a diet low in refined sugar: like most things in life, moderation is probably the best policy. If you are eating a well-balanced diet of fresh cooked, home-prepared food (and not a lot of commercially prepared, mass-produced foods, many of which have a very high – and hidden – salt and sugar content) there is no reason to suppose that enjoying cakes, cookies, and desserts, ice creams and confectionery which you have prepared yourself will do you anything but good. It is a case of not overdoing it. Eating the results of these recipes will certainly give you, your friends, and family an enormous amount of enjoyment.

Vanilla

The fruits (pods and seeds) of a climbing plant which is native to Mexico and which has the most wonderful scent and flavor when harvested barely ripe, plunged into boiling water and dried (or covered and warmed in the sun). The vanillin crystals which form after this treatment are what gives the vanilla bean its unmistakable smell and taste. Used as beans, or in vanilla extract, as vanilla sugar (which you can make yourself by burying two or three beans in a large, tightly-sealed jar of sugar usually superfine or confectioners') for a week or more. Very widely used in cake making, desserts, and generally in all forms of patisserie and confectionery. Synthetic vanilla flavoring is no substitute for the real thing.

Yeast

A microscopic fungus that multiplies at a considerable rate when given suitable conditions: warmth and moisture. The yeast reacts with the sugar and starch in the dough to which it is added and produces carbon dioxide which causes the dough to rise. For baking purposes, fresh yeast or dried yeast can be used. Fresh yeast should be stored in the refrigerator and used as quickly as possible. Dried yeast needs to be left for a little longer than fresh yeast when mixed with warm water, to give it time to reactivate (it will start bubbling and frothing) and less is needed to produce the same effect as fresh yeast. Most bakers prefer fresh yeast. Yeast is a good source of Vitamin B.

INDEX

· · ·

INDEX

• • •

Picture sources

The photographs in this book belong to the following agencies and
photographers:
Adriano Brusaferri (studio Adna), Milan
Riccardo Marcialis, Milan
Franco Pizzochero, Milan
Prima Press, Milan
Luigi Volpe Mad. Figaro, Milan
page 161: Hisashi Kudo, Tokyo

Step-by-step photographs by Sonia Fedrizzi, Milan except for
those on pages 72, 118, 132, 150, 160, 186, 192, 196, 224, 232,
254, 328 which belong to Shogakukan, Tokyo.

Antique prints supplied by Ketto Cattaneo, Bergamo.

The photographs at the beginning of each chapter are by Franco
Pizzochero. The paintings reproduced within these photographic
spreads are as follows:
pps 6–7: Vincenzo Campi, *La cucina*, Pinacoteca di Brera, Milan
(Scala)
pps 22–23: Patricia Barton, *La venditrice di canditi*, Pro Arte
Lugano (Ricciarini)
pps 36–7: detail from the *Feast offered to Emperor Charles IV*,
Bibliothèque Nationale, Paris
pps 54–55: Pieter Claesz, *Still Life with Pie and Glass of Wine*,
National Museum of Fine Arts, Budapest
pps 84–5: Jan Davidszoon I de Heem, *Still Life*, Musée de Louvre,
Paris (Ricciarini)
pps 112–13: Jean-Baptiste-Siméon Chardin, *Nature morte au
gâteau* Musée du Louvre, Paris (Ricciarini)
pps 144–5: Pietro Fabris, *Colazione sulla spiaggia*, Biblioteca
Nazionale, Naples (Scala)
pps 176–77: Edmund Tarbell, *My Family*, Hirschl and Adler
Galleries, New York
pps 210–11 Jean-Baptiste-Siméon Chardin, *Les debris d'un
déjeuner* Musée du Louvre, Paris (Ricciarini)
pps 242–3 Vincenzo Campi, *La venditrice di frutta*, Pinacoteca di
Brera, Milan
pps 268–9: M. De Vito, *Venditore di pasticciotti*, Museo Nazionale
di San Martino, Naples (Ricciarini)
pps 282–3: Olga Costa, *The Fruit Seller*, Museum of Modern Art,
Mexico City
pps 292–3: Matteo Pelliccia, *Il gelataio*, Museo Nazionale di San
Martino, Naples (Ricciarini)
pps 316–17: eighteenth-century oil panel, Museo Poldi Pezzoli,
Milan (Ricciarini)

Acknowledgements

The Publishers wish to extend their thanks to the following for
having kindly supplied materials for the photographs:
Argenteria Christofle
Bernardaud, Limoges
Cristalleria artistica La Piana
Croff, Milan
Daum Cristal
Koivu, Milan
La Galerie, Milan
La Rinascente, Milan
Pisapia Fiore, Milan